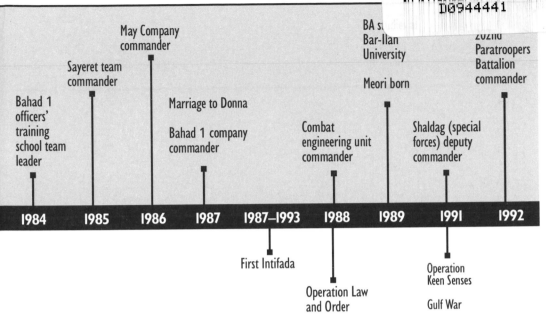

| 1984 | 1985 | 1986 | 1987 | 1987–1993 | 1988 | 1989 | 1991 | 1992 |

Bahad 1 officers' training school team leader

Sayeret team commander

May Company commander

Marriage to Donna

Bahad 1 company commander

Combat engineering unit commander

BA st... Bar-Ilan University

Meori born

Shaldag (special forces) deputy commander

202nd Paratroopers Battalion commander

First Intifada

Operation Law and Order

Operation Keen Senses

Gulf War

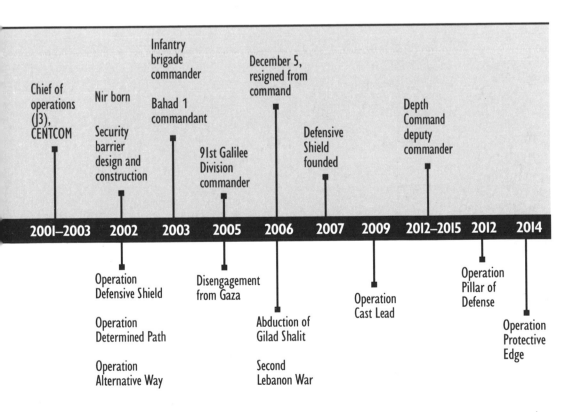

| 2001–2003 | 2002 | 2003 | 2005 | 2006 | 2007 | 2009 | 2012–2015 | 2012 | 2014 |

Chief of operations (J3), CENTCOM

Nir born

Security barrier design and construction

Infantry brigade commander

Bahad 1 commandant

91st Galilee Division commander

December 5, resigned from command

Defensive Shield founded

Depth Command deputy commander

Operation Defensive Shield

Operation Determined Path

Operation Alternative Way

Disengagement from Gaza

Abduction of Gilad Shalit

Second Lebanon War

Operation Cast Lead

Operation Pillar of Defense

Operation Protective Edge

DEFENSIVE SHIELD
An Israeli Special Forces Commander
on the Front Line of Counterterrorism

DEFENSIVE
SHIELD

AN ISRAELI SPECIAL FORCES COMMANDER
ON THE FRONT LINE OF COUNTERTERRORISM

THE INSPIRATIONAL STORY OF
BRIGADIER GENERAL
GAL HIRSCH

Translated and adapted from the Hebrew
by Reuven Ben-Shalom

gefen
publishing house בית הוצאה לאור
JERUSALEM ◆ NEW YORK Est. 1981

Scripture quotations are modified from *The Holy Scriptures According to the
Masoretic Text*, published by the Jewish Publication Society in 1917.

Photograph of helicopter on cover: Ziv Koren
Photograph of Gal Hirsch on cover: Haim Azoulai
Cover Design: Dragan Bilic – Pixel Droid Design Studio
Typesetting: Raphaël Freeman, Renana Typesetting

ISBN: 978-965-229-865-2

1 3 5 7 9 8 6 4 2

Gefen Publishing House Ltd.
6 Hatzvi Street
Jerusalem 94386, Israel
972-2-538-0247
orders@gefenpublishing.com

Gefen Books
11 Edison Place
Springfield, NJ 07081
516-593-1234
orders@gefenpublishing.com

www.gefenpublishing.com

Printed in Israel

*   *   *

Library of Congress Cataloging-in-Publication Data

Names: Hirsch, Gal, 1964– author. | Ben-Shalom, Reuven, translator.
Title: Defensive Shield : an Israeli special forces commander on the front
line of counterterrorism : the inspirational story of Brigadier General
Gal Hirsch / Gal Hirsch ; translated and adapted from the Hebrew by Reuven
Ben-Shalom.
Other titles: Sipur milhamah sipur ahavah. English
Description: Springfield, NJ : Gefen, [2016] | 2016 | Includes index. |
Original work carries the English title, "War story love story".
Identifiers: LCCN 2015051253 | ISBN 9789652298652
Subjects: LCSH: Hirsch, Gal, 1964- | Soldiers--Israel--Biography. | Israel.
Tseva haganah le-Yisrael--Personal narratives. | Lebanon War,
2006--Personal narratives, Israeli.
Classification: LCC CT1919.P38 H5713 2016 | DDC 956.9204/52092-
-dc23 LC record available at http://lccn.loc.gov/2015051253

To Donna

Contents

Part 3: Love Story

Preface

The original Hebrew edition of this book was titled *Sippur milchamah sippur ahavah*, "War story, love story." Some may ask if having the word *love* in the title is appropriate for the memoir of a general who has dedicated his life to war. To this I answer that war and love are indeed two inseparable themes in my personal history, and one cannot be understood without the other. The story of war is obvious, and I describe it in detail. But more important are the reasons for going to war – and they are the love for my country and the love for my family. There is also a theme that is paramount for any leader and has been a constant element throughout my career, and that is love for my soldiers: the men and women in uniform who serve Israel and enable its existence and freedom.

It took me two years to write the first edition of this book, in Hebrew, beginning with a conversation I had with my wife, Donna, shortly after my retirement in 2006. It was exhausting work, reliving the events of each chapter. I wrote day and night, in many beloved places in Israel – the shores of the Dead Sea, Tel Aviv, Eilat, Jerusalem, and Rosh Ha'ayin. As these were the first days of my civilian business activity, many chapters were also written in airport lounges, during long flights, and in hotel rooms across the four corners of the earth.

I strictly followed operational security regulations, and after submitting the full manuscript to the authorities, I fully complied with the corrections and omissions and carefully recompiled as directed. Naturally, not all of my experiences could be, or ever will be, revealed, but those described are true and accurate. Some details may have been altered, and for personal and professional reasons, some names have been replaced with pseudonyms.

This is not a history book, but a personal account of my journey, which has taken me through the most significant milestones in Israel's defense in the past thirty years. I make no pretense that this memoir constitutes a full and accurate documentation, only an honest description of events as seen through my own eyes. It is my story.

There are many people whom I wish to thank. First, I would like to express my gratitude and appreciation to my teachers and educators throughout the years, including my commanders in the IDF. I also learned much from my subordinates. Leadership entails the empowerment of others, but also much self-growth and development through listening and absorbing. I hope I have left valued lessons for students and subordinates.

As I carry with me the scars of my wounds, I am reminded daily of the huge debt I owe to the many medical teams who treated me with devotion, brought me back to life, and rehabilitated me.

The biggest asset I possess is the long list of acquaintances and friends accumulated over the years. I have learned that beyond the inner circle of close family is a close circle of friends – an invaluable treasure. Some are mentioned here, and many others are treasured in my heart as prize jewels. A special thank-you is due to my close friends, members of my "crisis team," who stood by me day and night and are still there for me until today.

I wish to express my utmost appreciation and esteem to the men and women serving in the IDF, especially those who chose the IDF as a career. I thank the servicemen and women of Israel Police, Border Police, Mossad, Israel Security Agency (ISA), and all those who fight for Israel's independence and defense, with and without uniform, in the open and clandestinely.

I always carry with me the memory of my brothers-in-arms who made the ultimate sacrifice: the seamen, airmen, soldiers, agents, and operators who are no longer with us, and to whom we owe an unimaginable debt. I share the pain of their families. All are sealed in my heart, especially those who fell under my command, in the Second Lebanon War and throughout my career.

I would like to acknowledge and strengthen our wounded and disabled warriors. As a permanently disabled veteran, I share their daily struggle and pain, and the mental burden, incomprehensible to others.

I owe special thanks to the residents and leaders of communities along Israel's borders and areas of conflict. My deep thanks and appreciation go to the communities in northern Israel, in Judea, the Jordan Valley, Samaria, and Gaza, for their strong support and the deep experience of togetherness we shared during long days of fighting terror and strengthening Jewish settlement of our homeland. I am grateful to my friends in the Negev Desert, Jews and Bedouins, for living together and promoting the region, realizing the vision of the first prime minister of Israel, David Ben-Gurion.

Thank you to the many Israeli citizens who showed their support through letters, by stopping me in the street, waving at traffic lights, or approaching me in airplane terminals and on planes.

I owe a special thank-you to my parents, Yitzhak of blessed memory and Rachel, as well as Donna's parents, Shlomo of blessed memory and Zehava. Thank you to my brother Moshik and sister Didi, and Donna's brothers Nati and Itzik. I thank my entire family and regret the pain they experienced following the war. During the tumultuous days we passed together, my extended family was at its best, both supportive and protective. They were a fountain of strength and love, and I am glad that they also remember days of pride, values, and a sense of belonging, throughout my military service.

I thank my business friends and partners for their patience and comradeship as we pave roads in this new chapter of my journey.

Four years after publishing the first edition of this book in Hebrew, after much convincing and pressure from colleagues and friends, I felt it was time to publish the book in English. Dr. Alice Butler-Smith was inspirational and instrumental in initiating this project, and I thank her for her friendship and guidance.

I asked my friend and comrade LTC (Ret.) Reuven Ben-Shalom to translate and edit the English edition, knowing that he would be able to both capture the operational aspects as well as master the task of bridging the language and cultural gaps. I first met Reuven when he flew me in his CH-53 helicopter during Operation Had Hushim, and our paths have crossed numerous times over the years, including during many of the missions and operations described in the book. We delved into the material with a mutual passion, discussing and debating each sentence to ensure the book would be both comprehensible and beneficial to the English-speaking reader. The result is by no means merely a translation of the Hebrew version. Written some years after the first edition and having a completely different target audience, it differs in scope, perspective, and presentation. Where necessary, appropriate background information has been added, and on the other hand, minor Israeli anecdotes have been omitted. Additional chapters have been added, describing the continuation of my career and my continued involvement in Israel's defense.

The appendices at the end of the book are intended to bridge gaps pertaining to various characteristics of Israel and the IDF, such as organizational structure and culture, as well as military terms and acronyms. It may be useful to review these first.

I would like to extend my sincere appreciation and gratitude to Ilan Greenfield and his superb team at Gefen Publishing House, for their dedication, professionalism, and friendship.

Lastly, and most importantly, I wish to thank Donna, my wife and friend, and daughters Meori, Ofri, and Nir. This book is, after all, about love. At the end of the day a man comes home to his true castle – his family, which he created, and from which he is recreated every day. Many years of friendship with Donna have withstood every challenge. The story of this partnership is described throughout the book, as well as our girls' story, and even Shoko, our faithful Labrador, is mentioned with love.

GAL HIRSCH
Rosh Ha'ayin
May 2016

Part 1

Foundations

Chapter 1
The Beginning

Amnon Passes the Baton

My Uncle Tzion and I were returning home from the small shopping center in my hometown of Arad. Dad had asked us to get soda for my bar mitzvah party. It was 1977.

Before dawn that day, still in the dark, my classmates and I had all ascended to the top of Masada. We stood there in prayer, wearing tefillin for the first time, and swore: "Masada shall not fall again." The ceremony was impressive and very touching.

Now the relatives were gathering at my home for my bar mitzvah dinner party. As we approached the house, we saw my Aunt Levana, Tzion's wife, clasping her hands. "There has been a terrible accident," she cried. "Amnon was killed."

My cousin Amnon, an Israel Air Force (IAF) Bell 212 Anafa helicopter pilot, had participated in an exercise with the Paratroopers Brigade in the Jordan Valley. The Sikorsky CH-53 Yasur in which he was a passenger had crashed, killing all fifty-four soldiers and pilots on board.

Inside the house, it was total bedlam, with sounds of crying and shouting, and frantic attempts at making arrangements. Leaving the tables laden with food, the family all ran to the cars to join the mourners in the city of Petah Tikva and prepare for the funeral. Since I still had to attend my official bar mitzvah ceremony, I stayed behind alone, stunned and hurting.

That evening my classmates and I went up onstage to receive Bibles and certificates. They were singing, but I was choked up. "Amnon was killed," I told myself over and over, "Amnon was killed."

During the days of mourning, I decided that my plans were changing: I would not attend the "Science-Oriented Youth" program at the Negev

University (later to become Ben-Gurion University). Instead, I would go to the military academy at the Herzliya Gymnasium. This is where Amnon began, and as if the baton had been passed in a relay race – this was now my mission!

When I began my military journey, I was not accustomed to military matters or the requirements of military units. These were all strange to me. But the values of Zionism and defense were always a part of me. Both my grandfathers, Aaron and Marco, became members of the Haganah after a long voyage from Turkey to the land of Israel, and they had inspired me with the spirit of pioneering Zionism. This journey of theirs, of making aliyah – of "going up" to the homeland – lived within me as if I myself had experienced it.

In the yard near our shack was a "slick" – a cache used by the Jewish underground organization to hide weapons during the British Mandate in Palestine, and in nearby streets lived the families of fighters from our neighborhood who were hung by the British. My grandfather had once barely escaped from their hands, having been accused of being a terrorist and marked for deportation to Eritrea. As a child, I was told of missions in a quiet and trembling whisper, as if the British troops were still searching and making arrests.

Zionism, pioneering, and love of country were the bedrock on which I was raised.

My pioneering family had been one of the first to settle in Arad, the newest town in the Negev. I grew up in the first shacks and then later in the first patio houses built there. My father, Yitzhak, supported the family working long shifts, day and night, constructing the Dead Sea embankment. My mother, Rachel, imbued me with a passion for reading from a very young age. Life was very simple – there were no luxuries.

Holidays were rich with tradition. Our synagogue was where I absorbed a deep connection to Jewish heritage and tradition. I returned to this place more than once later in life, to say Birkat Hagomel – the blessing thanking G-d for deliverance.

I remember, as a child, hearing sirens wailing during the Six-Day War in 1967. In my mind's eye I can still see the sight from our window of a barrage of Katyusha rockets in a terror attack on Petah Tikva. I cannot forget the fright the first time I heard the shriek of a rocket and the huge explosions as it hit not far from me. I remember the sudden and turbulent outbreak of the Yom Kippur War in 1973, running to the bomb shelter, and my father being drafted to service.

The Tryouts

On the holiday of Purim 1978, I reported to the Israel Defense Forces (IDF) recruiting office in the southern town of Beersheba and began the screening process for acceptance to the military academy in Tel Aviv. I was fourteen years old. I passed the medical examination and psychiatric evaluation and was able to continue on in the selection process. From there, I was sent to a three-day military exercise in Tel Aviv and the nearby IDF training center at Glilot that was extremely difficult for me. I was mentally tough but not strong enough physically.

Military academies in Israel are boarding schools serving as high-school level preparatory programs for the IDF. The military curriculum is additional to regular high school studies and focuses on military studies, discipline, and leadership. Unlike in other countries, graduates of Israeli military academies are not commissioned as officers, but recruited as enlisted soldiers. They are then expected to serve in key fighting units, move on to officer training, and assume leadership positions. Indeed, many graduates have served in key positions in the IDF throughout the years. Not surprisingly, military academy graduates comprise a significant percentage of Israel's fallen soldiers.

The standard of the education was high, and it was not with ease that I met the academic requirements. The exams involved immense mental strain, and the physical tests – such as carrying wooden logs, obstacle courses, and swimming – were new to me and difficult. I had never before encountered such challenges.

I was used to different challenges. With a backpack, a few thick pieces of bread, and a water canteen, I would head out on long treks into the desert, testing my abilities, feeling the ground, following animals, learning nature. I would wander for long days and nights in the Negev Desert, learning to navigate by the starry skies, and could manage even when it was dark, cloudy, rainy, and very cold. I exchanged warm greetings with Bedouins, followed shepherds' trails, read animal tracks, breathed the desert air, read books in rock crevices, and reflected deeply while observing the wild and rugged scenery.

As a boy, I was perceived by my peer group as unusual.

One Yom Kippur, the high holiday of atonement and fasting, my cousin Ofer and I headed out into the desert. It was a very hot day, yet we decided to observe the fast and didn't use the emergency rations of food and water we carried in our backpacks. We walked all day, taking a roundabout route, and reached Arad toward dusk, in time for the traditional meal breaking the fast. We held out.

Now I had to practice a different sort of endurance: patience. I had no way of knowing how I had done in the evaluation exercise for the military academy. I returned home after completing it, doubtful, and then the waiting began.

One evening I saw a big white envelope protruding out of our mailbox. My fingers trembled as I opened it. I had been accepted!

A month later I began the preparation phase at the military academy. I was wearing the IDF uniform.

Nachshon Company

In the summer of 1978, the initial preparation phase at the military academy included rigorous daily studies in order to bring all students up to similar levels, especially in math and English. Our commanders also began to expose us to other subjects such as military procedure and discipline, and physical and combat fitness. I can still recall the first lesson on wearing a uniform, the first hike with combat gear, and the first time at the firing range. And after exhausting days of mental and physical work, we would begin guard duty. My classmates and I were fourteen years old.

The physical training was particularly strict and demanding, and we were able to reach a high level of performance through intense swimming, training at the largest facility in the area – a nearby country club. Our group of eighty students was divided into platoons and a certain competitive group dynamic began to develop, for each of us knew that 60–70 percent would probably not make it to graduation.

The high school study phase began, and for the next four years, we would all live a military routine, including early morning wakeup call after night guard duty, morning formation, and breakfast, followed by the ceremonial flag raising. Then we would board the buses and head out to an intellectually challenging day at Herzliya Gymnasium, where we joined the regular high school curriculum and "civilian" kids.

I was the "country mouse" who came from a peripheral town to the big city, and a new reality opened up before me, that of a northern Tel Aviv experience and northern Tel Aviv girls.

After school, the "civilians" would go to their homes, and we would head back to base. We would have lunch and then study and do homework in our dorms. Then later in the afternoon, and until 10 o'clock at night, we engaged in military studies and training. We were left with an hour until lights out.

Subjects that were part of military studies included military history, tactics, topography and navigation, judo, and a uniquely Israeli form of hand-to-hand combat called Krav Maga. These were always accompanied by professional discussions at the platoon and company levels.

Every Tuesday after duty, we had a night off. While my friends partied and saw movies in Tel Aviv, I used to go home to help Moshik and Didi, my brother and sister, with their homework, check up on family matters, and take a drive around town with them.

Every other weekend we all stayed on base. After the Friday night Sabbath meal, we engaged in social bonding activities, and on the Sabbath day we attended lectures on various issues. Many of them were very good, and I especially remember our discussion with the late Yitzhak Rabin on Israel's foreign policy. I appreciated the variety of ideas and perspectives. This was a period during which I carefully absorbed all that I was hearing, experiencing, and learning, and spent the limited free time I had left reading books.

Vacations were partially "confiscated" by the military academy for training. We spent many weeks doing combat maneuvers in various tactical scenarios, such as open and urban terrain, and raiding fortified positions. We conducted day and night navigation, traversed obstacle courses, and performed parachute jumps.

When I was only seventeen years old, we were also exposed to routine security operations, which culminated in a deep reconnaissance (recon) mission into Lebanon with the Golani Brigade. We searched for terrorists in caves south of Tyre, and spent nights in outposts and patrolling the border.

These experiences proved to be vital in preparing me for service in the IDF as a soldier and a commander. A key principle that I learned and adopted was that no virtual replication or simulation can ever match the benefits of real-world experiences.

The curriculum included long tours and hikes. By walking throughout the length and breadth of the land of Israel, I became attached to its geography, its history, and its profound place in our national identity. When you are exposed to your land in such a way, you better understand what you are fighting for!

I was always fascinated with the Bible, and felt humbled and blessed that my generation was entrusted with resurrecting the land of the Bible as the homeland of the Jewish people. I read it not only as a religious and cultural manuscript, but literally walked the land with an open Bible as a practical guide to our history and heritage.

In the very competitive environment of the military academy, my strengths were persistence, stubbornness, and a steady approach. I did not allow myself any slack and insisted on maintaining my serious dedication throughout the program.

Throughout the course, students had heated debates, even arguments, and our own inside jokes pertaining to various aspects of our course. We coined phrases that became our own unique language to describe those who took everything seriously and worked hard, and those who did not. I was one of the "serious" ones – probably too much so.

We argued on many topics – from smoking to shirking duty and refusing orders – probably the natural dynamics of any group, but especially among those in uniform.

On the wall above my bed in the dorm, I hung a quote from a letter that had been written by LTC Yonatan (Yoni) Netanyahu: "Death . . . I do not fear it, because I do not attach much importance to life itself without a purpose. And if I should have to sacrifice my life to attain its goal, I'll do so willingly."* He was a role model for me and had a significant influence on who I wanted to become – as a person and commander.

An inspirational focal point for all of us was the memorial room within the academy library, where we read about the lives – and deaths – of the academy's graduates. I found this fascinating and inspirational. My cousin Amnon Hager looked down at me from the memorial wall for four years, and his name engraved on the entrance wall was, and still is, an important personal landmark.

During the last two years in the academy, the eleventh and twelfth grades, I was a dominant figure in the Nachshon Company, the name of our school unit. I was a member of various student committees, and, during my senior year, I was unanimously elected by my peers to serve in the prestigious position of chairman of the student council. I was very physically fit and kept a rigorous routine of training. Almost every morning I would head down to the beach

---

* *The Letters of Jonathan Netanyahu: The Commander of the Entebbe Rescue Force* (Jerusalem: Gefen Publishing House, 2001), 13.

before dawn, run along the coastline waist-high in the water, then run up the sandstone cliffs and back to the dorm to another morning formation and a long day of studies. It was a daily personal struggle not to quit running.

Since I wanted to serve in an elite unit, I worked very hard to prepare myself both physically and mentally. I was a voracious reader and, even then, viewed this as an important part of a holistic forging of body and soul.

Before bestowing on me the rank of corporal on graduation day, my commander informed me that I had been chosen as the outstanding cadet in our company. I am still very proud of that honor and value it because it was a decision made by my peers – the graduates – and it reflected four long years of diligence and hard work, alongside friends, and under the careful evaluation of experienced commanders.

The Paratroopers' Sayeret

The First Lebanon War began on June 6, 1982, as Operation Peace for Galilee, but it developed into a prolonged campaign. After fulfilling the objective of ousting the PLO and successfully confronting Syrian forces, the IDF eventually designated a security zone in southern Lebanon, to defend northern Israel from attacks. From there it conducted security operations to counter terror attacks on Israeli civilians and guerrilla warfare perpetrated by the terror organization Hezbollah, which had emerged to fill the vacuum after the decline of the Palestinian organizations. Israel withdrew to the international border in 2000, after eighteen years of presence in southern Lebanon.

The Paratroopers' Sayeret is an elite commando reconnaissance unit within the Paratroopers Brigade, which spearheads the brigade's operational efforts. Its missions include recon, intel (intelligence) collecting, ambushes, raids, and special operations. The unit has participated in all of Israel's wars and is famous for its professionalism, originality, and valor. To be accepted to the Sayeret, soldiers must pass a special tryout, in addition to the standard tryouts for admittance to the Paratroopers Brigade.

I volunteered for the Paratroopers Brigade and was sent to a tryout, designed to push potential recruits to the limits of their physical and mental stamina. On the physical side, we carried wooden beams, stretchers, and jerry cans of water, and passed various obstacle courses. Our ability to function under extreme pressure, and our decision-making, teamwork, and leadership skills were observed and reviewed as a test of our mental skills.

The tryout was extremely difficult, but I felt quite confident that I had performed well and would be accepted.

I was in top shape, partly because I had spent the days before recruitment as a construction worker for my Uncle Dror, himself a former paratrooper. Every day, at daybreak, I would run ten kilometers (six miles) to the construction site and work until sundown, carrying sacks of cement to high floors instead of using the elevator.

In IDF elite units, peer review, in which soldiers evaluate each other, is considered a valuable evaluation tool, and the analyzed results carry much weight in promotion and assignment considerations. My results showed that I was highly regarded by my peers, who viewed me as very suitable, as did the officers who tested us.

After the tryout, we got twenty-four hours' leave. Since my parents lived abroad at the time, I headed to Aunt Rina and Uncle Moishe's house in Ramat Gan, which was like a second home for me. I removed my shoes and found that my feet were a mass of blood and raw flesh as a result of the rigorous tryout. I limped over to a nearby military clinic, where a doctor bandaged my feet and prescribed a few sick days, but I threw the document away and went to sleep to gain strength for the next phase of tryouts.

I returned to the recruitment base the next morning, all geared up and eager to succeed in the tryouts for the famous Sayeret, the commando recon unit. By nightfall I was in the paratroopers' base in Sanur, a mountainous area in northern Samaria. The next three days were extremely difficult, and my abilities were tested to their limits. By the end of the tryouts, we were just a small group of soldiers who survived, and from them, only a handful were chosen. I was in!

Shortly after the commencement of the long training course for the Sayeret, we were sent to Lebanon, not far from Beirut, on our first operational assignment. Those days, during the First Lebanon War in 1982, became my first intensive fighting experience, and came with much sweat, blood, and even tears. We operated in Beirut, the Shuf Mountains, Jabel Baruch, Damur, and many other places.

My first experiences in the Sayeret were fundamental in the process of molding me into a commander in the IDF. I adopted a spartan approach: "When in doubt, choose the hard way." I learned professionalism, determination, boundless toughness, the understanding that there is no mission that I could not accomplish, and that the outcome depended mostly on my actions.

When the long course ended and I was qualified as an operational soldier, I was selected to attend the officers' training school at the training base Bahad 1. Our training at the Sayeret had been so intense and challenging that I felt confident and well prepared.

I found the officers' training program to be highly professional and value oriented. We were instructed by fine officers, who set the stage for my learning and growth process. During the course, I developed my fundamental concepts of command and leadership that would serve me throughout my career.

But the most dramatic event during the course happened just before the final exercises. I was assigned to lead one of the drills as a commander in training and rushed to the clinic to see why our medic had failed to show up at the range. At the entrance to the clinic I met a soldier from the Air Force. Her name was Donna – and she became the love of my life.

I graduated with honors, in a touching ceremony, where the insignia of second lieutenant (2LT) was pinned on by the chief of the general staff (CGS), LTG Moshe Levi, also known as "Moshe and a half." I was overwhelmed with a sense of fulfillment and eager to take on the great challenge of becoming a team leader in the Sayeret.

Chapter 2

First Command Posts

___

Instructor at Bahad 1

To my dismay, I discovered on graduation night that I was not returning to the Sayeret as I had planned. The commandant of the officers' training school, COL Shaul Mofaz, had an intense exchange with the Paratroopers Brigade commander, and demanded that I stay as an instructor at Bahad 1. He also promised that I would return to my unit after my tenure at the school. He claimed – correctly from his perspective – that those who graduate at the top of their classes should stay on to instruct and only then return to their units.

I fought him with all my might. I brazenly showed up at the home of the chief of personnel branch, MG Amos Yaron. To my surprise, he let me into his kitchen and listened as I presented my case – mainly that it was customary for outstanding graduates to choose their first assignments – but to no avail. Mofaz was persistent and he won.

The new staff of the officers' training school gathered for the opening briefing. COL Mofaz described a mission of the Paratroopers' Sayeret, sent on a special commando operation deep into Syria during the Yom Kippur War. To my surprise, he turned to me and said: "Second Lieutenant Gal Hirsch, don't look so gloomy. Soon you will be a team leader in the Paratroopers' Recon Sayeret."

After the session, he summoned me to his office. My mind was still set on returning directly to the Sayeret, and I stood there with tears in my eyes, but Mofaz insisted that I teach a new generation of officers as team leader, and only then return to my unit.

A few days later, I was called to meet the Paratroopers Brigade commander, Colonel Menachem Zotorski, who told me that in his view Mofaz was right:

those who excel should instruct officers. He asked me not to worry; they were waiting for me.

They were both right. From that point on, I would view training officers as a valuable mission, and would return time and time again – as a company commander and then later as the commandant of the school. Of course I too then insisted on having the best officers stay as instructors.

Return to the Sayeret

After a meaningful and enjoyable term as a team leader at Bahad 1, I was assigned to command a team at the Sayeret, but arrived a few months before the change of command, so I was tasked in the meantime as the unit's counterterror officer, responsible for preparing the unit for various scenarios, mainly hostage rescue.

I assumed command of a team, replacing an experienced and talented officer, who gave me a thorough rundown on every soldier. But one of his pronouncements I could not accept: "Do not believe your soldiers. They do not deserve your trust unless proven otherwise." I viewed this as the complete antithesis of my own approach.

I considered all the team members excellent unless proven otherwise. I believed that the correct approach was to create a leadership development environment, seeing it as an accomplishment if the team fulfilled its missions while at the same time preparing many of them to be officers in the Paratroopers Brigade. I was extremely proud of every officer who grew under my charge.

I based my developing leadership skills on ancient Jewish concepts as well as modern IDF values and tradition. Gideon led his troops on the same soil we now defended, and I followed the description of his deeds in the book of Judges (7:17): "Watch me and follow my lead...do exactly as I do."

In the modern era, Israeli commanders display humility and asceticism. It is obvious to us that a commander must lead his troops first into battle, but stand last in line to eat or shower.

I perceived myself as primus inter pares – first among equals. I knew that I bore more responsibilities than privileges and was constantly obligated to set a positive personal example.

During most of my tenure as team leader, we were engaged in operations, mostly in Lebanon, but also in Judea and Samaria (J&S), countering Palestinian terror. My team was the first to carry out covert missions in disguise, both as Arabs to infiltrate Palestinian territory, and as Jewish settlers, as "bait" to draw out terrorists.

After a series of successful operations performed by my team, MG Ehud Barak, commander of Central Command (CENTCOM), decided to establish a new special unit called Duvdevan, which would specialize in disguised operations. I was asked to construct the unit and serve as its first commander, but COL Nehemiah Tamari, our newly appointed brigade commander, objected, explaining that while the new unit was important, I would serve the IDF better by continuing on the track to become a company commander and battalion commander. I respected his view.

From Nablus to Hebron, along the Jordan Valley, the Golan Heights, and then to the Beaufort fortress in Lebanon, we carried out missions nonstop, around the clock. We conducted detention operations, ambushes, patrols, intel operations, counterterror missions, and training. It was 1985, and the IDF was defining the security belt in southern Lebanon, after our withdrawal from the Awali region. As expected, terrorists positioned themselves around the newly defined lines.

In the first such secret operation beyond the newly established Red Line – the northern border of the security belt – my team penetrated to the area of the hostile villages Yater and Kafra, for observation and intelligence collection. On our first mission, we spent all night quietly climbing the extremely steep Salhani Cliff and reached our target zone on schedule. Late that morning we were discovered by the enemy – I don't know how. We spent that whole day fending off their attacks, assisted by Air Force Cobra attack helicopters. Their cannon fire was so close, it even passed between my men. The enemy kept advancing, and when we began enduring close impacts of mortar shells, we disengaged and changed position. At night we made our way back to Israel.

We learned many lessons and had many opportunities to implement them, for in those days my team practically lived beyond the border, conducting dangerous and complex missions.

"Push Your Way In"

After a few months, my team was on counterterror alert in the Golan Heights. Due to intel on possible infiltration of terrorists into a village, we were on constant alert, even while training, ready to respond in case of a hostage situation or pursuit.

One evening, we could see from our vantage point on the Golan that the sky west of the Hula Valley, along the Lebanese border, was illuminated with flares. The command frequency was filled with fast and confused reports. Something big was going on. I ran to the brigade's operations tent at Waset Junction and tuned in to the Galilee Division's frequency.

"There may have been an infiltration of a terror cell in the 91st Division's area," explained MAJ Eyal Ragunis, the Paratroopers Brigade's intel officer. Eyal was a brilliant officer, a true leader and venerable professional.

I listened to the communications and made out the location of the events on a coded map. I updated Eldad, my team's sergeant, and asked him to roust the soldiers and prepare the team in case we were activated.

"*Nu!*" (Hebrew slang for "so?" or "come on!"), urged Eyal Ragunis.

"What?" I wondered.

"Push your way in," he said. "Call the division commander on the radio and tell him that you're here and you want to help."

"But who will be on alert in the Golan? There is an alert in this region," I argued.

"That doesn't matter now, there's an incident close to you, so push your way in and show involvement," Eyal coached me.

I got on the radio and called 91st Division Commander BG Ilan Biran, who immediately recognized my call sign as the paratroopers' counterterror team. He directed me to join Regional Brigade 300: "Get right down there. Good to have you."

We dashed toward the Lebanese border, although it was neither within my nor the division commander's authority to relieve my team from the Syrian border in the Golan Heights. I knowingly took a risk and assumed responsibility, and crossed the Hula Valley with our two specially equipped counterterror trucks. Twenty minutes later I was ordered to stand down and double back to the Golan. False alarm.

Back at the operations table, I found Eyal waiting for me, sourly.

"What now?" I asked.

"Did you call the division commander?"

"No. Why?"

"Call him and tell him that you're angry that he didn't think to call you immediately. Ask him not to forget that you're in the north, and that from now on, he should scramble you to any incident in his area."

Amazed at Eyal's assertiveness, I called the division commander and conveyed my message. "You did very well," he answered, "that's the way to do it." He then promised not to forget me next time...

Sadly, Eyal passed away a few years later, after retiring from an important and meaningful service in the IDF.

Test of Values

We operated all around the country, along the borders and beyond them, day and night, with very little sleep, and rarely got home. When I finished my assignment as team leader, I applied to become the next unit's deputy commander, but events unfolded very differently from my plans.

One evening, all the soldiers were working on their gear and preparing the counterterror vehicles in the parking lot. Just another hectic day of assuming on-call status.

Suddenly, I heard a loud bang, a gunshot. I was on the top floor, and it sounded like it came from the first. I dashed downstairs and found two officers giggling and looking embarrassed.

"What happened?" I asked.

"Nothing."

"Don't tell me 'nothing.' I heard a gunshot or other explosion. What happened?"

"Relax, Hirsch, I just threw a dummy grenade," said one of the officers, who was also trying to become the deputy commander.

"Inside the building? A dummy grenade? Are you crazy?!"

"OK, don't be so tough..."

I went back to my room and found Amir and Dror, soldiers in my team, looking very pale.

"Someone shot at the counterterror truck. The bullet passed right over me when I happened to duck," said Amir.

It all became clear. "Show me the truck."

In the operator's compartment at the back of the truck, I saw the shattered window and the point where the bullet had struck. This was no dummy grenade, but a 9-millimeter bullet from a pistol!

We were very lucky. The two soldiers in the truck were unharmed. If the bullet had hit one of the many ammunition boxes, our base would have looked like the scene of a truck bomb detonation.

The rumor traveled fast, and everybody was talking about the incident. I asked the officer who had so irresponsibly shot his handgun to report the incident to the unit commander, but the next day I found that my request had not been fulfilled.

At the weekly commanders' meeting, the tension was high. A few officers demanded that the officer report the incident before the meeting started. He didn't, and the session "exploded" soon after it began. One of the officers brought it up, and I was asked to describe what I had heard from my men and what I saw in the truck.

After a few days, in another meeting, I confronted the unit commander and insisted that such a serious incident should be reported, as regulations dictated, and appropriate measures should be taken.

No one submitted written investigative results, and with the officer guilty of negligent discharge, it was business as usual. I understood that the intention was to cover it up.

I viewed this as a serious violation. I believed that every commander has a constant mission to foster a safe training environment in general, and specifically to fight against negligent discharges. In my opinion, when an officer accidently fires his weapon, it should be seen as a very serious matter and he should be punished – certainly if it is the intention of his superiors to keep him in a commanding capacity. When I was commander of the combat engineering platoon of the paratroopers, one of the team leaders accidently discharged his weapon near his soldiers and was sentenced to a week in prison. Upon return, he was able to demand from his soldiers the utmost responsibility, discipline, safety, and accountability for their mistakes. His personal example, by paying the price for his own mistake, morally enabled his continued functioning as commander. This is especially appropriate when there are no casualties.

My experience in investigating mishaps has shown me that, many times, we could have identified early signs that were "writing on the wall" but went unheeded, leading to disaster. We must search for and identify these early signs and deal with them as they occur.

Most safety failures stem from the unit's atmosphere, "safety culture," and accepted standards in all activities, from training to operations.

Few accidents are the result of mechanical failure, and most human errors could have been mitigated by careful examination of the plans for military action and analysis of the potential scenarios that might unfold. After identification, it is easier to create a "prevention plan" to lead to the desired outcome.

I learned with experience and developed this approach for many years. I assimilated its principles in all the units I commanded. Safety and professionalism are closely intertwined, and in military units this determines the quality of the operational outcome.

Unbiased and honest investigative debriefing and reporting are critical to fighting accidents.

To my disappointment, the unit commander in this incident chose to act differently. In the next weekly meeting, he claimed that my demands to investigate, learn lessons, and report the incident were aimed at bettering my chances at succeeding his deputy. I told him what I thought of this observation and accusation, and the argument became quite confrontational. I notified him that in light of the values he demonstrated, I would refuse to serve as his deputy and would leave the unit when I concluded my current position. I assumed that with this I was bringing my career in the IDF to an end, but I was confident in my decision, and knew that the ultimate decision on my career would be made by the Paratroopers Brigade commander, Colonel Nehemiah Tamari, not the unit commander.

Nehemiah called me to a personal meeting. He opened by expressing his appreciation of my performance as combat team leader, and appointed me, right then and there, as company commander, although I hadn't even served as a deputy commander yet.

I exited his office dazed and happy. It was obvious that the brigade commander had heard about the incident, and I understood his decision to be a clear vote of confidence and support for my conduct. The Sayeret commander ended his position within a few months and was not promoted.

Nehemiah was honest and straightforward. He was a man of values. Tragically, MG Tamari was killed in January 1994, while commander of CENTCOM, in a helicopter crash at his headquarters in Jerusalem.

May Company

In the summer of 1986 I was immersed in the task of recruiting the new young company, where all paratroopers' recon, combat engineering, and antitank units undergo basic training.

One night the phone rang at the apartment Donna and I were renting in

Ramat Gan. On the line was Yoav, commander of the brigade training base. May Company – so named because its soldiers were recruited in the month of May – was in a serious situation. Their commander had been dismissed after beating a soldier, who was wounded and hospitalized. I was to replace him immediately.

I was surprised and disappointed. "What about my company?"

"A replacement will be found. You need to hurry to Hamam el-Maliach [the company's training facility in northern Samaria]. The situation isn't good."

"Where is the company now?" I asked.

"Don't know," answered Yoav honestly, "they ran away..."

In fact, the soldiers, shaken by the serious injury inflicted on their friend Patrick, had decided to take retaliatory action. They marched by night to the nearby village of Tyasir, awakened a Palestinian truck driver, and forced him to drive at gunpoint. After pointless and aimless driving around the Jordan Valley, they were finally located at the archeological site of Beit Shean and taken back to base, where I met them after a short meeting with Dedi, the platoon commander. The soldiers sat in front of me, in a semicircle on the cement floor of the tent.

"I'm Gal," I introduced myself simply.

Dozens of pairs of eyes were staring up at me, and I was moved. I loved them from that very first moment. I knew that I must take them out immediately and divert their energies in positive directions after the negative experience they had just had, and the terrible thing they had done.

"I came here from the Sayeret," I continued, "and now we will go out on a combat march together. In ten minutes I want you ready with all your gear."

All through that night, I led the company at a fast pace, along the ancient Roman route in Samaria. It was a very difficult march, and I made it even harder when I ordered that stretchers be opened and "wounded" soldiers placed on them. The march ended with a sprint and shouting. I saw smiles in the tired red faces. I realized that I could achieve anything with these men, but I knew it wouldn't be easy.

After a month of rigorous training, we achieved high operational qualification. The company went up to hold the line at Mount Manor, near Zar'it, on the Lebanese border. We patrolled along the border, set up ambushes, and conducted recon missions deep into Lebanon, and here, too, it wasn't easy. I continued to face disciplinary problems, and I wanted to solve them without breaking my men. It would have been easy to throw out the troublemakers, but I wanted to keep them. Some of them came from poor, hard-working families, and I related to each and every one of them personally, and saw them as my own mission and challenge.

I understood that I risked paying a personal price if holding on to the weaker links meant a reduction in my unit's operational performance, but I believed that I served a national cause by making the IDF a "people's army." After their mandatory service in a combat unit, these soldiers would become better citizens of the State of Israel.

I did everything I could to keep them all. They were mine, and I loved them.

Many times I found the balance and was flexible up to a point, but I set strict boundaries.

My insistence on discipline and order was not always supported by my three platoon commanders. They regularly gave in to the soldiers, so much so that I sometimes couldn't differentiate between them and the soldiers. I could not tolerate such behavior by the officers in my company, and I even threatened them with expulsion. This friction reached the battalion commander, LTC Elazar Stern, who summoned me to his home one evening and scolded me for my toughness and the friction with the officers under my command. I was deeply offended and viewed his actions as flawed leadership and a failure to support a subordinate. I swallowed my pride, drove back to my company, ground my teeth, and carried on with the mission.

A few days later, our battalion received an unexpected mission change, which assigned our company to a mission inside the security belt in Lebanon. One platoon was stationed in a position near Taibe, and the company headquarters with two other platoons in Hasbaya, a remote Druze town. At the time we were positioned the farthest north of any IDF force in Lebanon.

The weather was harsh: snow, ice, pouring rain, and fog, and in these conditions, we set out night after night to position ambushes, accompanied at times by Centurion tanks. I sent 2LT Nisim's platoon to Taibe. I instructed him and clarified my expectations from him as a paratroopers platoon commander, alone in a multiservice outpost. I understood the immense responsibility, after commanding a team alone in Lebanon, and the significance of this independence, for better or worse.

One morning, a report reached me that Nisim had decided to exercise his platoon with a sudden wake-up call at dawn. This was a good thing, I would say – only he did so by throwing hand grenades around the compound! I was struck with a sense of disappointment and disgrace at his lack of responsibility.

I was hugely frustrated because I could not get there myself. I was isolated in a distant and hostile region, burdened with operational duties. We had few convoys heading south, and a phone line was a rare commodity. So I debriefed Nisim over the radio, and asked him tough questions. He didn't have good answers for me and he acknowledged his mistake.

I asked Stern to relieve Nisim from his command immediately. He had demonstrated a lack of responsibility, risked lives, and violated safety regulations. My arguments and reasoning were to no avail. Stern refused. I was extremely frustrated and made up my mind to continue dealing with the matter when we returned to Israel from our mission. A few days later I was called to the Operations Center. "Your battalion commander wants you," I was told.

"Yes, Stern," I said.

"Shalom, Gal, it's Jerry. I'm the new battalion commander."

"Shalom, Jerry."

"I hope I can come up there soon to visit. You're all doing a great job."

"Thank you, thank you, sir."

"It's Jerry," he corrected me, "and one more thing – I gave an order to relieve Nisim from his position today. I think you are 100 percent right. He acted irresponsibly and cannot be a platoon commander in our battalion."

I was so surprised, I was silent.

"Do you hear, Gal?"

"I…hear and…thank you. I truly appreciate this backing."

"Good luck, Gal. See you soon."

Hamarmar Actual

For a large brigade exercise, I was assigned the call sign "Hamarmar," and it stuck. The brigade prepared for its attack after parachuting in Sanur Valley and flying by helicopter to the Jordan Valley, near the village of Bardale. A malfunction in our C-130 Hercules caused a late jump, so while the entire brigade was preparing for attack at H-hour, my company was racing to gather the jumpers and run to the helicopters, only to discover after landing that we had been dropped off at the wrong landing zone (LZ). After getting my bearings, I led my troops in a crazed navigational dash, in order to join the brigade in time for the attack. Over the radio I heard Jerry and COL Mofaz, who was now commander of the Paratroopers Brigade, debating: "Will he make it?" "Do you think he'll arrive on time?"

All the brigade's battalions were in position, waiting for us. I tried to identify the exact location from which I was to launch our attack. Minutes away from H-hour, and only hundreds of meters away from the gathering point, I decided not to waste time and requested the battalion commander's forward command post to assist me with the exact location in order to prevent unnecessary mistakes.

"Hagai, give us a marker," requested Walter, my radio operator. LT Hagai Mordechai, the battalion operations officer, answered immediately: "Do you have a visual on the marker?" "Got it," I answered, and then ordered: "Machine gunners to me." I took two minutes for us to catch our breath and took out my compass. "Prepare ammunition boxes and drum magazines. Platoon commanders approach me."

We took out binoculars, useful even on a moonless night, and night-vision goggles for a quick commanders' observation of the target.

"That one's yours," I instructed Dedi, 1st Platoon's commander. "And you take the knife-shaped ridge," I said, pointing out the 3rd Platoon commander's target. "Second Platoon stays with me for cover and fence breaching."

"Coming or not?" I heard Mofaz over the battalion frequency.

"He's here," Jerry reported merrily," and we are commencing attack."

"Way to go, 'Hamarmar,'" called out Mofaz.

"Open fire."

"Bangalore detonated." This meant that a Bangalore torpedo had been exploded to blow open the fence and clear any mines.

"Follow me!"

During the brigade debriefing, Mofaz concluded by referencing May Company – Hamarmar. "It is not obvious," he said. "A malfunction in the C-130, a late jump, wrong LZ, fast night navigation stretching for many kilometers with heavy gear on their backs and then entering the battle on time and in place and going on for a few days of fighting. This is exactly what I expect from every company and company commander. He must cope, improvise, and persistently stick to the mission. He should be like Hamarmar."

Following this performance, our company was deployed to the hottest region in Lebanon at the time – Shomria. I perceived this as a wonderful reward, for I wanted to serve in the most dangerous location. My company's morale was high, and I was happy.

On the eve of our deployment, during a Saturday on alert at Qalqilya fire station, I asked Morris Azulay, an operator and amateur barber, to give me a short haircut. He fulfilled this assignment with particular devoutness, and within minutes I was bald. "I said short!" I protested, patting my shining scalp. I'm getting married in a month – how am I supposed to show up looking like this?"

"Well?" smiled Morris calmly, "you said short and you got it."

A few hours later, as an act of solidarity and sympathy, everyone became commander look-alikes. We were a company of bald and battle-ready warriors.

On the banks of the Litani River, the company exposed an improvised explosive device (IED) arena, which had been laid by Hezbollah, before it detonated and caused any damage. We also located weapons caches of the enemy, functioned well under mortar fire, and, during an encounter with enemy fighters in the Saluki River, we carried out deep recon and ambush missions.

End of training period. The company moved on to the paratroopers' corporal course.

My own next assignment was widely debated. Mofaz, the brigade commander, wanted me to attend the senior intel officers' course and serve as the brigade's intel officer before assignment as commander of the Sayeret. His unusual and creative plan was supported by the CGS, LTG Moshe Levi, and commander of CENTCOM MG Ehud Barak, but was strongly opposed by the chief of Infantry and Paratroopers Corps, BG Shmulik Arad, who felt I should continue in a command position rather than sidetracking.

I asked Mofaz what had been decided. "There's a problem with decision-making on this matter," he answered. "I myself am not sure yet," I told him. "Doubts are important," he said, "but next week you're off to Bahad 1, to be a company commander. You will train new officers for us and then return to command one of our elite units."

"What?" After all the discussion about my next assignment, I was stunned by this new twist, which had not been on the table at all.

"Good place, Bahad 1, don't you think?" smiled Mofaz. "We met there. Good luck."

Mofaz was a guest at my wedding later that month. Donna and I were married under the canopy of a parachute, and even the brigade's red beret was incorporated in a traditional Jewish ritual. Mofaz was the first guest to arrive, declaring: "I always arrive at the H-hour!" followed by a cheerful group of company commanders, officers from the battalion headquarter, Jerry the battalion commander, and many more fellow fighters.

After the wedding it was back to business as a company commander at Bahad 1. But it would be anything but routine: the First Intifada was about to break out. It started explosively. Friday night dinner at Bahad 1 began as usual. After blessing the wine and breaking bread, I delivered the commander's address to my company's cadets, and then we all sang songs typical of IDF fighting units. Suddenly the operations sergeant came dashing in.

"Scrambled! Hurry up! SOUTHCOM is deploying your company."

"Where to?"

"Unclear. They said you should mobilize and they'll fill you in on the move."

We quickly left the laden tables and ran outside to the trucks. After a short inspection of the gear, we were on our way. I received instructions over the radio to head toward Gaza, because "everything is ablaze there. Heavy fighting." Later on I pressed to be issued a specific mission and was told to "hurry to Khan Yunis because the situation is out of control."

When we reached Khan Yunis I realized that the Gaza Strip was, in fact, ablaze. A deadly car accident had served as the spark that ignited an already tense situation, and events developed into a popular uprising leading to what we now call the First Intifada.

From December 1987 we were engaged, as an infantry company, in complicated missions involving civilian population, terrorists, and violent demonstrations. I distinctly remember the confusion, the lack of terminology necessary to describe reality in military terms, the shortage of nonlethal weapons, and the need to improvise, cope, block, and defend. Nothing was as it had been before the outbreak of the First Intifada. Although the effectiveness of the IDF and other security agencies was constantly improving, the result of this crisis was eventually the political initiative leading to the Oslo Accords in the beginning of the 1990s.

During the next half year of continued officer training, my company also took part in the fighting, demonstrating excellent infantry capabilities.

Chapter 3

Law and Order

Striving to Engage

It was 1988, one day around noontime, during the final phase of the infantry officer training course. We were at the legendary Egoz training compound all cadets in officer training have conquered.

The Bahad 1 commandant, COL Zeev Zacharin, and the battalion commander, LTC David Zarchin, stood observing the landscape before the beginning of the final practical exercise, discussing various attack alternatives, the fire support plan, and targets for the Air Force. I made notes, learned, and occasionally expressed my opinion.

"Well?" Zeev turned to me. "Where are you headed?"

"I have a meeting with Mofaz tomorrow night at Beit Lid. He wants me to command Orev [an elite antitank unit that operated the TOW missile], or the combat engineering unit." I was about to conclude my tenure as company commander at the officers' school. I loved it there, but was eager to return to the Paratroopers Brigade – my home.

"Forget Orev," said Zeev. "We aren't the kind of fighters who fire from afar. We strive to engage. You go to engineering." "I'll remember that," I answered with a smile. "That's my personal preference."

"You did a great job here. Good luck." Zeev smiled and shook my hand. Zarchin slapped me on the back of my neck. "See you, Gal."

I was touched by the positive feedback. "Thank you," I told them, as I slid down the rocky slope to join the company of cadets, my cadets, soon to be infantry officers and platoon leaders in the IDF.

The following night, at Beit Lid, I stood in the small waiting room outside the brigade commander's office, occasionally meeting and hugging comrades, while surrounded by much affection, support, and brotherhood.

Beside me was Aviv Kochavi, a very talented officer and excellent company commander, who was also there to receive one of two assignments. He had already received a message that Mofaz intended to nominate him for the combat engineering unit, and I understood that the idea was that I receive the antitank company. We entered the office and were welcomed cheerfully and affectionately.

Inside the brigade commander's room, the tables turned. Aviv and I each wanted the job intended for the other. I wanted combat engineering, and Aviv the antitank company. Mofaz laughed: "OK, so be it, and good luck to both of you."

I headed down south toward Mitzpe Ramon and stopped at home on the way, to update Donna (this was before cell phones). I savored a few precious moments of home, then continued south to my company, to undertake preparations for the final phases of the course and the graduation ceremony. After that, I would take a short vacation before transitioning to the new job.

"Decide how you want to begin your tenure," said Roni Alsheich, whom I was about to replace. "Either in a grand ceremony following a thorough review of the unit, or during a full-scale exercise, where you set the tone and future standards."

The unit was widely deployed between the Golan Heights and Adorayim, in the Judean mountains. We visited all the teams, spoke to soldiers and commanders, and utilized driving time to discuss fitness and competence of the unit as a whole, as well as that of individual soldiers and commanders.

Neither one of us was aware at the time that a third option was materializing – in fact I would enter the unit by fighting a bloody battle together with its soldiers. Around midday Friday, I was preparing for a jump – fastening the straps, attaching the reserve chute to my chest, and concealing the duffle bag I would later use to collect the gear.

Out of the corner of my eye, I saw the brigade commander, Mofaz, being called from the jumpers' shed to a vehicle that pulled up alongside the runway. He spoke to someone for a while, hunched over a map they had spread on the hood of the car. "Something's up," I murmured to myself, as I proceeded to the harness check and jumpers' brief, delivered skillfully by a senior parachuting instructor.

Mofaz returned and passed between the jumpers. "Well, did you fit in a vacation before the new job?" he asked with a smile. He knew that Donna and

I could not take a long vacation as we had planned, because I was asked to take command earlier than anticipated, in order to relieve Roni, who in turn was required in his new position as deputy battalion commander.

How did Donna feel about this? She understood and accepted the personal sacrifices common to all military families. I was hoping to at least get to see her that following weekend.

All of the officers hobbled over to the jumpers' shed, with our parachutes strapped on, where we were briefed on developments in the north. The terrorist organization Hezbollah had taken over another village in southern Lebanon, expelled its citizens, and created another stronghold. This brought it within closer range of Israeli villages and enabled it to strike the South Lebanese Army (SLA) and IDF forces with mortars and rockets, as well as to inflict terror on Israeli civilians.

As soon as this jump was completed, our brigade was to assemble in the north and commence a battle procedure, augmented by armor, engineering, artillery, intel, and the Air Force assets.

The parachuting instructor attached the yellow static line to the overhead anchor line cable, and we were soon airborne, after "assisting" liftoff of the C-130 Hercules with our rhythmic calls of "hey-hop, hey-hop," following a decades-old paratroopers' tradition. We chanted "check equipment," I examined the gear of the jumper in front of me and he checked mine. "One OK," "Two OK," I notified the instructor, and proceeded toward the open door, beside which a red light was illuminated.

The light turned green, and the first group of jumpers was out. I was first in the second group. I was focused on the jump and naturally anxious, but I was also contemplating the operational challenges awaiting us in the north. I reached the door and felt the strong gusts of wind, as well as the two instructors who held me so I wouldn't jump prematurely. The light was red again, and I could see the Mediterranean Ocean and the red roofs of the houses in Palmachim Air Force Base. The green light came on, and the instructor yelled "Jump!" as he gave me a strong pat on my back. I kicked hard with my left leg as I exited the aircraft, head low, hands clasping the reserve chute – just as we had learned and practiced many times. I felt the jet wash from the turbo-prop engines and counted as I free-fell: "21, 22, 23 . . ." expecting that with the number "3" would come the relieving sensation of the sudden tug as the line yanked my parachute. It opened above me.

"I didn't exit the door as well as I should have," I reprimanded myself. Looking up, I could see a few twists in the lines, so I kicked and twisted to release them. I was happy to see a full, round, and flawless parachute, without cords cutting across it, giving it the bra-shape – thank God. I then released one side of the reserve chute and looked around. I could see some of my friends on the ground, collecting their gear, and used the short time left to enjoy the scenery and the flow of air.

"Prepare for landing," I said to myself, joining feet and bending knees. The ground was coming at me fast and my body tensed. I hate the impact of landing. Thud, side roll, and I quickly folded the parachute in the "8" pattern and stuffed it into the duffle bag. Above, I could hear the planes coming back for another pass.

Mission Planning

In the Golan Heights, things were quite tumultuous. At the orders group (OG1) session (the initial planning phase), the brigade was divided into two main forces. LTC Amos, the brigade deputy commander, took the 890th Battalion and elements from the 50th Battalion, accompanied by an armored force. Their mission was to comb the "Fatahland" (an Israeli-coined term describing an area in southeast Lebanon once controlled by the Palestinian organization Fatah) and clear it of terrorists. They were also supposed to determine whether Hezbollah had situated itself there too, and to deter it from doing so.

A smaller force, led by the brigade commander, consisting of some two hundred soldiers, included two companies from the 202nd Battalion, engineering, recon, and antitank companies, a Merkava tank company, an artillery battalion, Air Force helicopters, and intel assets. Its mission was to strike a terrorist compound in the village of Maydun, in an extremely mountainous and thicketed area near Qaraoun Lake in the Beqaa Valley. The terrorists had ousted the inhabitants and fortified the place with bunkers, trenches, antiaircraft positions, and ammunition warehouses.

Intel estimated that twelve terrorists permanently occupied the place, but they might have been easily reinforced by others from the nearby villages of Mashara and Ein Atina.

"Don't let these big arrows fool you," Jerry, the 202nd Battalion commander, comforted his deputy Rami, as they examined the tactical map.

"There may be a lot of them drawn all over Amos's area in Fatahland. But here," he said pointing at a little arrow near the village of Maydun, "here there will be war."

We began careful study and planning for the mission. The engineering company was to be split into two forces. One would join the 202nd Battalion and the Sayeret and move on foot to quietly surround the village and seize high ground, then, at dawn, attack terrorists standing guard.

The second element of the brigade, joined by the second half of the engineering company, was to move on wheels and tracks, bringing more tanks, medical and rescue forces, and bulldozers and other heavy equipment, to join the infantrymen for an attack at daybreak.

Roni and I split the unit between us. I was supposed to assume command during the following week, and he was the outgoing commander. Roni was assigned two teams, and I commanded the remaining teams. The plan was to rendezvous and conquer the western segment of the target, nicknamed "the command post," and the large bunker that overlooked and controlled the village.

Roni used his call sign, while I used the last one assigned to me as a company commander at the 202nd Battalion – "Hamarmar."

I assembled the team leaders for a mission brief combined with a short introduction, for we did not know each other that well yet. I designed the force structure and then, in order to save time and ensure the clarity of my orders, we carefully planned the mission together, crouched over a map that provided aerial imagery.

I was called out of the tent to receive an interesting message from brigade headquarters. My force was assigned a new kind of armored personnel carrier (APC), based on the hull of the Centurion tank. It was nicknamed "Nagmashot," a combination of the words *nagmash* (APC) and *Shot* (the Centurion's Hebrew name). They were already in use at the time by engineering forces, but we were not familiar with them, had not trained in them, and lacked operational proficiency.

"The Nagmashot offers better protection," the brigade's operations officer told me. "And believe me, you're going to need them. They will be essential for rescue and evacuation."

"How will we drive them?" I asked.

"You will receive drivers from the engineering battalion."

The first vehicles arrived, and we began familiarizing ourselves with their operation. I insisted on full simulation of combat scenarios, including movement, recovery, loading casualties, and offloading soldiers.

"Jump, climb aboard."

The soldiers, tired and sweaty, expressed their dissatisfaction with the strenuous preparations, but I felt it was imperative. Intimate familiarity with the new APCs, and how they would be incorporated into our operations, could prove vital in fulfilling the mission and reducing casualties.

On Sunday at noon, my force was organized and briefed, after satisfactory training and weapons test firing. All teams were convened for a parade before action, and I walked from soldier to soldier, trying to get to know them, shaking hands, and resolutely making final personal gear adjustments.

One of the drivers, a nice soldier named Heni, joined us with two serious pieces of equipment – his Nagmashot and a huge tape recorder, emitting loud music.

"Will you have room for it, Heni?" I asked him. "Don't worry, it'll fit," he smiled back. "Just make sure to give it to my mother if I get killed, OK?"

Move Out

On Monday, May 2, 1988, Operation Law, led by the deputy battalion commander, was underway in Fatahland, while our half, Operation Order, was awaiting approval. That evening, I visited the brigade headquarters at Waset Junction, in the Golan Heights, where I learned more about the operation and read intel reports. Mofaz spoke with me briefly about the mission and my force, then departed, saying, "See you later, 'Hamarmar.'"

I called home but there was no answer, so I left a message for Donna with our neighbors, Doron and Liat, using our private code: "Looks like I won't be coming home for a while. And remember," I added, "I love you."

That night we conducted a final full-scale exercise, with an emphasis on coordination between the various forces, using a mockup of the target, at the deserted village of Za'urah in the northern slopes of the Golan Heights. I also used this opportunity to once again practice movement with the heavy Nagmashots and to demonstrate the swift transition from a motionless, passive paratrooper to an alert and active warrior, on the ground. This is a tricky transition to master, and it takes mental preparedness and training. It is a unique and challenging experience when moving from a helicopter to the ground, from a ship to the shore, and from the protection of an APC to the inferno outside.

The following morning, we began our final day of preparation, including loading the Nagmashots on the tank carriers. We were to attack that night. At dawn, a helicopter flew the commanders to Astra, a remote IDF outpost on Mount Hermon, from which there was a direct line of sight to our target area. Although the village of Maydun looked like a speck, it was very useful to grasp the magnitude of the extremely rugged terrain.

We approached the border aligned in our preplanned order of movement. First came the trucks with the infantry soldiers, which crossed the gate and moved through the security belt in southern Lebanon, toward the dismounting point, near the village of Huna. From there, the forces were to infiltrate on foot and take control of the outskirts of the target.

The heavy armored convoy, with my force within it, was commanded by LTC Avi Rothstein, former commander of the 202nd Battalion, who was recalled from his university studies for the mission.

Near the gate, I shuddered at the sight of an overturned command car. Out of it climbed Omri, our tank company commander, wounded in the face. He was bandaged and quickly joined his tanks, being offloaded at the Egel Gate, near Metula. I would meet Omri again eighteen years later, during the Second Lebanon War, when he served as a reserve Merkava battalion commander. He was to lead the first reserve tank battalion into Lebanon.

After final arrangements, and one last briefing, darkness was falling, and the order was heard: "Move out."

I listened over the radio and followed the progress of the other forces, while moving carefully behind two tanks leading my force into Lebanon. I could feel the ground shake beneath my feet. Our procession was interrupted once in a while, due to concerns that Hezbollah might detect our heavy force and reveal and disrupt our deception of taking over the outskirts of the target with the other force.

Again and again, we stopped, evaluated the situation, and continued.

A full moon rose over the horizon, and it crossed my mind that the holiday of Lag Ba'omer was coming up in two days. Until this day, the traditional Lag Ba'omer bonfires are to me as memorial torches to my brothers who fell in this battle, and the date is a permanent landmark in my schedule, attending memorial services.

"What a bad night for an operation," I pondered. The silvery full moon illuminated the night, and I was concerned it would assist the enemy to detect us. We pushed forward. The soldiers huddled in the compartments and I stood in the turret, listening to the radio and pulling up the lapels of my shirt, fighting off the extreme cold. My eyes occasionally drooped, only to shoot open.

Near the village of Huna, in an area I was very familiar with, we crossed the Red Line – the northern boundary of the security belt, and continued toward the target, aiming to link up with the other force moving on foot.

All forces made their way toward their predetermined positions, coded Tzefa (Viper) 1–13. Each hilltop was designated by name and number.

Captain Tzion Mizrachi's support company prepared the Dragon medium-range antitank missile in a reverse slope, facing uphill under the ridge line, concealed from the enemy. His plan was to strike an enemy position the moment we went "hot."

Hezroni's recon team began reporting directly to commanders, as did the teams led by Benda and Amir, the Orev company deputy commander. They both infiltrated quietly to dominating areas, from which, using binoculars and night-vision equipment, they could direct forces and deliver early warning as threats emerged.

Suddenly, all hell broke loose.

There were jumbled calls over the radio, and I could hear sounds of explosions and gunfire as helicopters passed overhead.

"Gal, we have casualties! We need you now! Do you understand?" someone cried frantically over the radio.

"Got it."

Omri picked up speed, and my Nagmashots accelerated to a wild dash in order to keep up.

"Hurry up, Gal."

We were driving on a narrow ledge, when Heni slammed on the brakes just in time to save us from plummeting off a cliff. The hull was partly in the air, and we needed to back up a bit and correct course.

"Why did you stop?" Avi asked furiously.

"Wait, Avi. Proceeding, not stopping."

I did my best to piece together bits of information coming in over the radio, and figure out who was engaged and where the casualties were, while conducting complicated driving and navigation.

"Prepare to dismount. Prepare for battle." I shot out brief orders. I knew it would be difficult to snap into action after being crammed in the vehicles all night.

"Get the gear ready. Update the soldiers on what's going on." But what was going on? There was great confusion and immense pressure.

"General picture: Engaged. Casualties. Pushing forward to linkup. Expect changes. Prepare the men," I tried to sum it up for my team leaders as best as I could.

"I'm going as fast as I can," Omri reported, as if he had been reading my mind.

My attention now focused on a tank barrier made of huge concrete blocks, which Hezbollah had placed in the middle of the road. We had planned to follow the drill and clear it in order to proceed, assuming it was aligned with IEDs. I was to stop, dismount, and lead an explosive ordnance disposal (EOD) team to inspect and neutralize any devices found, then have our accompanying bulldozer clear the concrete blocks.

Reading my mind again, and demonstrating improvisation and valor, Omri rammed the barrier. To my relief, no detonation occurred, and after a few more heaves, the barrier was pushed aside and we continued toward the smoke ahead, indicating the location of our forces, engaged in combat.

"Hamarmar Actual will evacuate the casualties." I recognized the voice of MAJ Meir Klifi, the brigade's chief of operations (G3).

"But how? He will get hit – he needs protected vehicles," Mofaz said.

"Hamarmar has the new vehicles we supplied him," reminded Klifi.

"OK."

"Yehuf Actual was hit," I heard an unidentified voice report. I had no idea who "Yehuf" was, because a new signal operating instructions (SOI) sheet had been issued the night before the operation. I was the only one who had maintained his old call sign; the rest were all new and therefore unrecognizable to me.

I pulled the SOI out of my pocket and handed it to Shlomo.

"Check out who 'Yehuf' is."

I directed Heni toward the smoking hills, into the fire, followed by the rest of my company and Omri's tanks.

An inferno of explosions, smoke, and bloodcurdling whizzing of bullets. We were spotted and heavily shelled, as were the soldiers who infiltrated here by night and encountered this bedlam at daybreak. I could see them all around me on the ground, laying low. We had brought their ballistic vests for them, to lighten their load as they hiked in.

"Give them out," I ordered.

I was trying to locate the casualties and made my way to what seemed to be the focal point of the battle.

"Hamarmar, don't go so high, you'll get hit!" Mofaz cried out over the radio.

"Got it," I answered, "where's Yehuf Actual?"

"On Tzefa 1. Get there and extract him, but don't expose yourself! You'll get hit."

I positioned a tank for cover, while the others remained in the rear. Avi began coordination for aerial medical evacuation (medevac). We threw a few smoke grenades and then, while delivering a mass burst of fire, managed to get out one stretcher, then another.

One soldier was laid under my Nagmashot and I could see that he was critically wounded; a bullet had pierced his chest through a pair of binoculars and exited his back. Doctors and medics were all over him, as he tried to sit up but was pushed back down. Suddenly I recognized him. It was my friend and brother, Tzion, commander of supporting company 202. We'd known each other since we were soldiers, and served together for many years, meeting time and time again, during training, in Lebanon, at officers' training school, and at my wedding.

"He's in critical condition, we need a helicopter!" Dr. Liav yelled.

We were targeted from multiple directions by mortars and machine guns. The whole area was literally on fire from the frightening impact of phosphorus shells which ignited the fields around us.

Demonstrating extreme courage, pilots of a Bell 212 Anafa helicopter landed near us, under fire, while mortar shells kept exploding all around. We ran toward the helicopter and thrust Tzion's stretcher inward, as the operators from the 669 Air Force rescue and evacuation unit pulled him from our hands. The helicopter sprang into the air, swerved around, and flew away at a very low altitude, then abruptly pulled upward and climbed out of sight, on the way to Rambam Hospital in Haifa.

"He'll be OK," I said to myself, "he has to be."

Another stretcher arrived, covered with a sleeping bag. The doctor indicated with a hand signal that he was dead. Golden curls of hair were protruding from under the sleeping bag. Marco Bernstein, a soldier in the supporting company, had sustained a direct hit in the neck and was killed instantaneously.

I pulled the stretcher up onto the Nagmashot and dashed toward the battalion casualty collection point (BCCP), deployed a few hundred meters back. We left Marco's body and returned to the ridge line overlooking the village.

The plan had been disrupted. We would not attack at dawn, and entry to the village would be delayed.

A bullet passed by my head and ricocheted off the ground. A soldier near me, named Yoav, saw it too, and turned pale. I also blanched, but forced myself to smile and wink at him.

I could spot the line of fire, the ridgeline, a few hundred meters up ahead, and instructed Heni to take us there again.

"Hamarmar stations – Hamarmar Actual is going up to observation point."

It was important, at this time of pressure, to use tactical discipline, common and familiar terminology, and basic drills.

Resembling a forest of antennas, Mofaz's forward command group (FCG) was seen passing south of my force, crossing the road and climbing another ridge. I was impressed by the courage he demonstrated, leading from the front, so exposed.

Rescue Mission

"Gal, you're wanted on the radio," my radio operator called out, yanking my pants.

"Hamarmar here, go ahead."

"This is Mofaz. Jerry has problems – weakening eastern flank and running low on ammunition. Change of mission – you're to reinforce him on Tzefa 9."

"Wilco!"

"Hamarmar stations," I began briefing over the radio, "change of plan, we are..."

A huge explosion shook us, as a barrage of shells impacted. I was thrown backwards amidst choking smoke and the splatter of shrapnel off the hood of my Nagmashot.

Out of the corner of my eye, I spotted two tanks trying to backtrack, while a tank near me sustained a direct hit on its top deck.

I pulled myself back up to the turret. Realizing we were exposed and could no longer proceed on the Nagmashots, I resumed my radio brief.

"Hamarmar stations, change of plan. Moving on foot to reinforce eastern flank, linking up with 202nd Battalion commander. Prepare for disembarkation and follow me."

I turned sharply and maneuvered the Nagmashot to a depression in the ridge, hoping it would supply some protection and require the enemy to readjust and re-aim during the sensitive phase of disembarkation.

"Prepare for daytime fighting," I reminded the force, regretting that I had not done so at daybreak. I assumed that they had transitioned independently, as we had learned and practiced – change to day sights, roll up sleeves, prepare for exposure to the enemy, wear knee pads. I glanced at them and was happy to see they had done so.

"Disembark!" I gave the order.

A Merkava tank was positioned ineffectively in a reverse slope, and I needed all the cover I could get. Despite our position in the depression, enemy fire was crawling toward us again and we were sustaining heavy fire. I could hear machine gun bursts and occasionally identified the sound of sniper fire.

All through the battle, Cobra and Defender attack helicopters were passing overhead, occasionally firing a TOW missile at enemy positions, as directed by our ground teams.

Why was the tank positioned this way? I needed its cover. I jumped down, my team following.

"Heni, you're staying here with your leader, is that clear, buddy?" I said.

"Sure, sure," Heni answered, sounding exhausted.

The teams all jumped off their Nagmashots and having emerged from the crowded compartments, the soldiers stood close to each other, getting their bearings and gearing up for movement. I did not like the sight of it.

"Come with me," I called out to my radio operator, as I ran toward the tank.

"Shlomo," I called over the radio, "get everyone ready to move, bullets in the chamber, ready for battle. We are linking up with Jerry. I'm bringing the tank up to give us cover."

I found the tank motionless, engine off and hatches closed. I thought it might have been hit. I moved around it, close to its tracks, and found the back phone.

"Tank, can you hear me?"

"Hear you." What a relief.

"Why aren't you in position? Why is your engine off? I need you to cover us!"

"OK," answered the tank crewman, "I'm coming up."

I was astounded. They had not been issued an order and did not initiate. Later, at the debriefing, we would learn that as in training, they had turned off the engine to save engine-hours.

Now the engine sprang to life, black smoke pouring out of the exhaust.

Boom! An impact and explosion hurled my body backwards, slamming me against the tank, as shrapnel peppered the metal. Through a cloud of dust, I saw my radio operator had been tossed to the ground beside me and I could see others who were hit. A direct hit on my force. I was stunned for a moment and felt my body for injuries. I was OK, except for ringing in my ears.

"Let's go," I sprang back into action and pulled the men after me, "we must get out of here."

"Maintain gaps, maintain gaps!" I shouted. I was navigating toward the ridge I knew Jerry was on, and I knew he needed help.

"I'm on my way, Jerry."

"Got it," a voice answered. It wasn't Jerry. I would have recognized his voice anytime. Maybe his radio operator?

"Gaps!" I begged my men, but they remained close to each other. Probably fear coupled with lack of proficiency. During training we had learned and memorized this principle, and here we were sustaining fire for two hours and still it didn't sink in. I was afraid that one shell would teach us the hard way.

"Gaps!" I panted. I had not drunk water before disembarkation and my throat was dry. It was hot, smoke covered the ridge, and repeated exploding sounds rang out. We continued uphill, dropping off a squad for cover. In order to reach Jerry, we needed to cross an inferior area, exposed to the enemy.

"Two machine gunners and assistant gunners forward." We continued the climb, after waiting for the covering force to assume their position on the right. The tank on the left was firing, and I spoke briefly with the artillery coordination officer, requesting that he launch mass barrages at the time we would cross the exposed area, and possibly also a smoke screen, although I knew these were always scarce.

All I was lacking now to give me peace of mind was an attack helicopter, but I didn't have high hopes. Who was going to allocate helicopters to me now? Everyone was fighting. Omri's tanks were firing, Jerry was fighting in the eastern flank and Gadi in the northern. To the west, machine gunners and snipers with Rami, the deputy battalion commander, were engaged, and forward observers were directing fires on artillery positions near Qaraoun Lake that were targeting us.

I heard a shrieking sound, then another, and the ground shook – another barrage of artillery shells was coming down on us. Everything was covered with smoke, and I couldn't see a thing. Dry thorny bushes burned from phosphorus rounds, and I could hear people yelling. Another directly aimed salvo impacted. I rolled over and felt for injuries, finding that I was covered with dirt but still in one piece. I rose and ran, passing between the teams.

"Hamarmar stations – report status. Disengage. Change position."

Cover force, tank, and artillery were all firing, as we took another hit, only not so close this time. We had five casualties, and the medical team was running between them. Dr. Liav was crouched over a critically wounded soldier who was spurting blood, feverishly fighting for his life.

"Bring the wounded, and let's get out of the artillery target!" We had to change position and buy time until we were identified and targeted again. We climbed about twenty-five meters sideways and lay our wounded there.

I leapfrogged from one to another. One of the soldiers, Yoav, was rolling on the ground bleeding. I kneeled over him and tore his pants, revealing a large piece of shrapnel stuck in his thigh. I did not spot arterial bleeding.

"Not too bad," I said.

"No, not too bad." Yoav did his best to overcome the pain, but then he rolled over again, letting out a moan. A medic appeared and treated his wound.

"Pull him to the rear door of the Merkava," I ordered.

Major Yehuda Ofri, the battalion intel officer who was assigned to me, was critically wounded.

"Come here, take care of them. Evacuate them to the rear with a tank, but not with the one covering us." I gave a few short orders to one of the team leaders. "Take a Nagmashot and you can also carry stretchers on foot to the BCCP."

"Wilco."

I was balancing between the need to care for the wounded and the mission. It is imperative to assign someone to command the evacuation efforts, and leave the treatment to the medical teams. Still – the mission is above all.

"Everyone follow me! Move out. No stopping, is that clear?"

The battle was still raging. Snipers from the engineering company, under Roni's command, were succeeding in delivering direct hits on terrorists in a protected trench.

Lieutenant Adam replaced Tzion and led his soldiers up to shooting positions.

"Take good aim," he coached his men, "and hit your targets." He called two soldiers to him and instructed them to open their bipods. "Be ready, the terrorists are going to come out from that side." Two terrorists were hit by the sharpshooters of the support company.

"We took out three of them," Adam reported over the radio.

"Prepare to attack," he instructed his men, instilling them with fighting spirit. He was answered with internal jokes, understood only by the initiated.

On Jabel Rachayet, Orev company deputy commander Amir Nadan was hard at work directing fires from helicopter formations and artillery batteries. His team surrounded him, guarding their rocky position, but Amir alone was doing the coordination.

Using a map, a pair of binoculars, a compass, an SOI sheet, and a radio, Amir was doing remarkable work neutralizing the artillery batteries that were firing at us. He also set up smoke screens to conceal our position, coordinated effective artillery fire, integrated three helicopter formations, and served as a forward observer by directing force movement and alerting us on developments in the battlefield, such as enemy movement near our forces.

From his excellent vantage point, he commanded a view of the battlefield and utilized his skills and capabilities as an infantry officer to effectively assist the entire brigade.

Years later, at the officer school, I would tell my cadets of Amir's actions that day, emphasizing the importance of professionalism and the profound impact one individual can have on the overall outcome.

Sayeret forces circled the enemy compound from the north. Despite the ongoing battle, the disruption to the plan, and the casualties, Gadi was sticking to his mission and isolating the village. Benda was positioned on a ridge west of the village, awaiting possible enemy reinforcements or attempts to escape. Both scenarios would soon materialize, and thirteen terrorists and vehicles were hit.

On the brigade channel, I heard a conversation between Northern

Command (NORTHCOM) commander MG Yossi Peled and Mofaz. After a status report, MG Peled signed off, saying, "Operate slowly, methodically. I trust you guys."

"Attention, Hamarmar stations: linking with 202. Careful with friendly fire."

"Hamarmar, this is Mofaz."

"This is Hamarmar, go ahead."

"Abort mission. Repeat – abort mission." I froze and listened, breathing hard. "Jerry is OK on his own. Return to your Nagmashots and prepare to enter the village and take control of your section, in coordination with Roni."

"Wilco."

"Attention, Hamarmar stations, fall back to the vehicles with mutual cover, force after force. Prepare to enter village, conducting originally planned mission."

"Efi here, got it."

"Shlomo, got it."

"This is Arik, I'm still dealing with the casualties. I'll link up with you later."

"Danny, roger."

"Attention: expect constant fire, big gaps – and move fast!"

"Shlomo, bring the Nagmashots closer to us."

"Gal." It was Avi, the convoy commander. He sounded strange, concerned. "There are many casualties at Jerry's. Mission change. You're the evacuating force. Go."

"Run to the vehicles," I ordered, already running myself. I climbed on my Nagmashot, tossed my backpack aside, and dived toward the turret.

"Liav, come here." I was taking this extremely talented doctor with me.

"Everyone stay here. Shlomo, you come with me. Let's go, Heni." I was going to carry out this rescue mission alone, with only my Nagmashot.

We lunged forward to the destruction area, where my men were previously hit, and crossed it fast, heading toward the ridge being heavily targeted.

"Stop, Heni." I wanted to wait for a short break between the shells. "Now, when I tell you, we drive as fast as we can toward that hill, twenty meters ahead, to the right of those trenches. See?"

"Yes."

The break came. "Go, Heni, fast!"

The Nagmashot raced forward, maneuvering between shells. We lay low in the turrets and fighter compartment, waiting for an impact. "Sharp right, Heni, that's it, now straight. Jerry, I'm coming."

"Got it."

I saw a red flag up ahead and then a trench with the casualties.

"Swing around with the rear toward the casualties," I told Heni, who carried it out like a stunt driver. We jumped off the vehicle and began loading casualties, most of whom seemed to be wounded from shrapnel.

"There are more!" someone shouted from the trench, but we were full and could take no more.

"I'll be right back," I promised.

"Drive, Heni!" We hurried downhill to the BCCP.

"Avi, get helicopters, we have casualties."

"The BCCP is waiting for you. I'm taking care of the helicopters."

We let off the casualties and headed back toward the smoking ridge, making another two trips alone. Twenty casualties were evacuated this way, including three fatalities. One of them was Captain Boaz Ravid, an intel officer temporarily assigned to the 202nd, who sustained a direct hit and was killed immediately.

It was already 10:30 AM. The sun was beating down and there was still heavy fire.

"They can fight, the bastards!" someone said.

The Attack

"Attention, all brigade stations, we're commencing the attack as planned," Mofaz ordered, then briefly clarified what he expected from each force commander.

"Hamarmar, this is Roni. Where are you?" Roni Alsheich sounded angry. Apparently he had called me several times, but I was too busy fighting. "I'm right here, to your right," I answered, signaling him.

We coordinated the attack on the western flank, from the outskirts of the village to a fortified position we nicknamed "the large bunker."

Roni was to attack a cluster of houses called "the headquarters," while I was to clear structures and their connecting trenches east of him, all the way to "the large bunker." The idea was that we work in close cooperation, covering each other while proceeding cautiously with tanks.

Upon entering the village, soldiers from the 202nd Battalion conducted face-to-face combat with Hezbollah fighters defending the village outskirts, who fired RPGs (rocket-propelled grenades) and hurled hand grenades from close range.

Adam was leading the support company. "Follow me!" he called out, joined by the battle cries of his men as they rose and ran toward the buildings to be cleared. They had sustained casualties, including Tzion, but they pressed on without losing momentum or heart.

"Cover to the right, Efi. Shlomo – cover the flank. Run to that house. Of course if you see 'innocents' – don't shoot, but we know that there are no civilians present," I told my team leaders. "Fight aggressively, not selectively. Use grenades and charges. We're going in hard!"

I signaled to the tank on my right and pointed to a nearby house. Two shells tore a big opening in the side of it, making it easier to clear. A grenade was tossed in, and we entered.

"Give me numbers," urged Omri, referring to the numbered houses on the aerial footage of the area. The tanks were moving alongside the houses and stopping at peeking positions, from which they would strike buildings before the soldiers moved in.

The forward team assumed their position at the outskirts of my target, and I was close behind with my FCG after dropping off Efi's team again as a right flank cover.

There was a sickening shriek followed by a horrific explosion, and Efi disappeared in a cloud of dust. A direct hit.

"My God," I heard myself mumble, and then witnessed His intervention. In a surreal scene, as if from a movie, Efi rose, followed by his men, and they stood there, brushing the dust from their uniforms.

Up ahead I heard a few short bursts of gunfire, so I dashed forward. A pile of corrugated galvanized iron had aroused the soldiers' suspicion, so they fired toward it, driving out a frightened and wounded Hezbollah fighter, who cried, "Doctor, doctor!"

"Hold your fire!" I ordered. "Medic – treat him. Try to interrogate him and find out the location of the mortars that are firing on us."

An Arabic-speaking soldier interrogated the fighter as he was being treated. He claimed the mortars were firing from within the village.

Clearing structures and fortified positions in an urban environment was extremely challenging. We were constantly being targeted with mortar shells, occasionally resulting in casualties, and every few minutes we would dive for cover as a chilling shriek was heard. This made our progress very slow.

My forward teams reached the main intersection of the village as enemy fire kept coming down on us. Before crossing, Jerry asked MAJ Fuchs, commander of brigade fire support, to coordinate a smoke screen on the intersection, along with high explosive shells. He complied, and the ground shook as a well-aimed salvo was delivered by the artillery battalion. Under this cover, all forces proceeded through the intersection, which was a key area.

Near one of the buildings at the intersection, I happened to find Jerry lying beside me.

"Hey, Gal, we'd better not be so close, so we don't both 'get it.'"

I crawled around to another corner of the building.

"Mass fire," I ordered my forces, and coordinated mutual cover with Roni. We sprang across the intersection, a burst of bullets passing between me and one of my men. We dived into a connecting trench and went on to clear it.

This was where Benda's blocking force killed thirteen enemy fighters, as he would later describe during the debriefing: "They began running toward the intersection from the direction of Gal and Roni's engineering forces, as our force approached it. Snipers and machine gunners took them out one by one."

The large bunker's entrances came into sight, as Hezbollah fighters were seen running into it. I lifted my weapon, aimed, and fired. While I gave cover, Roni proceeded above the hatches and threw in smoke grenades and then explosive charges. The bunker roof collapsed on its inhabitants in a thunderous blast.

My force continued to the hilltop, clearing all the way to the end points of the connecting trenches, while covering each other, and in close coordination with Roni. There we linked up with the Sayeret, approaching from the right. It seemed that we had control of the compound.

"Prepare the houses for demolition." I ordered the next phase.

"Extract now," Klifi ordered. "The force that came on foot will link up with the trucks after Palmeria route, and the other force will drive out using the same road."

"Count everybody."

Someone opened a canteen. My lips were parched. I replaced a magazine in my weapon.

"Get me a list of our casualties," I asked Shlomo.

We exited to the outskirts of the village, maintaining large gaps. Smoke was seen billowing over houses, trenches, and bunkers.

We passed by the bodies of dead Hezbollah fighters, who seemed well outfitted and equipped.

"They were also determined," I thought to myself. Hezbollah fighters confronted us with a willingness to sacrifice.

Linking up with the Nagmashots brought a sense of relief.

I gave a few short orders over the radio.

"Go, Omri." We followed his tank, the same way we came.

The way back to the border took a long time. We were tired, red-eyed, and our uniforms were sweaty and stained with blood.

At Egel Gate border crossing near Metula, I jumped off my Nagmashot. Our staff was waiting with tables laden with food, but more importantly, I was happy to see telephones.

I dialed the Carlton Hotel in Tel Aviv, where Donna was working the night shift.

"May I speak to Donna, please?"

"Gal?!" a woman shouted. "Sure, hold."

I heard the sound of running feet. "Donna, it's Gal! He's on the line."

"Gali!"

"Donna…"

There was a moment of silence.

"I heard what happened. I know that Tzion was killed. Oh, Gal, I'm so sorry…"

Killed? I felt faint and collapsed, tears filling my eyes.

"But I evacuated him, I tried to save him, we did everything we could, a helicopter landed under fire, he was alive!" I choked up.

Oh, my God – Tzion had been killed. I did not think he could die. I learned that he had arrived in critical condition at Rambam Hospital and died on the operating table.

A blood connection was established between me, my family, and all those who fought this battle – and Tzion's parents, Eliyahu and Malka, his brother Kiko, and his sister Betty. An exemplary family of farmers from the village of Megadim, representing hard work and values, as Tzion Mizrachi himself did.

It was a very difficult day in Haifa. I was one of six company commanders and close friends of Tzion carrying his casket. Eulogies were said by family and commanders with broken voices and hearts. Mofaz attended and helped us cover the grave. I then stood aside, tired, hurting, wiping my eyes with a sleeve, and looking out over the sea of red berets surrounding the fresh grave.

The Student Life

My tenure as engineering company commander was spent mostly in combat missions in Lebanon. During the short training phases we had, I made a point of combining the need to construct an elite engineering company for the Paratroopers Brigade and the duty of becoming the best commando company. I was happy to have the opportunity to learn firsthand the profession of combat engineering. I would later discover that an engineering force is a significant and sometimes central operational tool in the hands of the combat commander. Combat engineering forces are many times the bottleneck resource, and are irreplaceable.

I began to study at Bar-Ilan University for my bachelor's degree, where I combined Middle East and Land of Israel studies. Every week we would go on field trips, studying various topics such as botany, zoology, archeology, and history, all in my favorite format: learning through your feet.

Academic degrees are integrated into the career development in the IDF, but even while at school, operational status is maintained through periodic training, and students may be called for duty at a moment's notice.

Our Middle East studies commenced with Arabic language courses at the Hebrew University in Jerusalem. I was familiar with the language, but it was a good preparation for the upcoming studies.

Donna and I felt that this study period was a much-needed pause in order to invest in ourselves, as a couple and soon-to-be young parents. Our firstborn girl, Meori ("my light" in Hebrew), was born during the holiday of Hanukkah, December 1989.

Our peaceful break did not last long.

During the First Gulf War in 1991, Iraq launched thirty-nine Scud ballistic missiles toward Israel, in an attempt to push Israel to respond – a move that most likely would have fractured the American-led coalition. But Israeli prime minister Yitzhak Shamir adhered to US pressure and chose restraint. Threats by Iraq's dictator, Saddam Hussein, coupled with his use of chemical weapons in the Iran-Iraq war, led to wide preparations in Israel for coping with chemical weapons, but all warheads proved to be conventional.

At home, we followed the guidance from Home Front Command and prepared a sealed room. Every siren had us putting on our gas masks and fighting Meori's resistance to be put into the infant gas mask hood. But after a Scud missile disintegrated over our house, destroying our neighbor's roof, we were convinced that it was worth persisting.

There was a sense of great helplessness. We felt exposed, and quite frankly humiliated. I hoped for an Israeli operation in Iraq, and of course wished to take part in it. I wanted to fight back.

I was thrilled to receive a phone call from the new Paratroopers Brigade commander, COL Moshe "Bogie" Ya'alon, telling me that I had been chosen to serve as the operations officer of an ad hoc planning team for possible retaliation in Iraq. Although we were not activated, it was a fascinating exposure to the vast capabilities of special forces, intel, and the Air Force. The special operations community now considered me one of their own, and toward the end of my studies, I was appointed to serve as deputy commander of the Air Force commando unit, Shaldag.

We moved to on-base housing at Palmachim Air Force Base, and a fascinating and important phase in my life began.

Chapter 4
Shaldag, the 202nd, and Back

Operation Had Hushim

At the time, the IDF had not yet established the Depth Command (created in 2012), and each service operated its own elite special unit, which mostly promoted the unique missions of the service, but also participated in General Staff–directed operations, such as hostage rescue. There were and still are three such units in the IDF, but today they are also coordinated via the Depth Command.

Shaldag is the Air Force commando unit. It carries out a variety of covert missions, ranging from recon and intel gathering to deep infiltration and kinetic strikes. Almost all of the unit's missions are classified and never published.

I was received with some reservations at the unit, but slowly established my position. I was considered the outsider "green" paratrooper, new to the world of hush-hush operations. I decided to dedicate myself to thorough learning of doctrine, methods, and technologies employed by the unit, and immerse myself in the new codes, folklore, and unique language, as in a tribe. I trained myself for the unique professionalism of special operations forces (SOF).

Shaldag utilizes highly advanced technological means to fulfill their missions, and I made a point of going out to train with the various departments and teams as a common operator. I was not always successful and brought on myself many jokes at my expense, but I took it with good spirit and knew that with time and persistence, my leadership would strike roots and my abilities as an experienced combat officer would be valued.

I learned to appreciate the unique quality of the designated professional soldiers and understand their operational envelope of equipment and assignments. I was fascinated by the seriousness, efficiency, and focus of the Israeli

Air Force, and especially marveled at the unique integration of an SOF unit with airpower capabilities and qualities. The Air Force perceives Shaldag as an integral capability – an operational building block, as any jet fighter formation or weapon system.

With time, I was integrated into the unit and began commanding special operations.

One evening, I was asked to come to the Air Force headquarters in Tel Aviv, together with Eyal, our unit commander. There had been another incident in Lebanon, and we had casualties.

In an underground facility, a planning session was convened in order to answer NORTHCOM's request for a deep penetration retaliatory response, aimed at strongly affecting the enemy's perception, so they would know that we could reach their doorstep.

The chosen course of action was Operation Had Hushim (keen senses), an abduction operation, focused on interrogation and intel gathering.

"We also do not have enough intel," explained NORTHCOM's representative. "Whoever you apprehend will be able to shed light on what is going on in the villages, who lives where, and infrastructure data that we also lack."

Back at the unit, the senior staff planning team was seated around a table.

"Short battle procedure, no more than two or three weeks." Eyal began outlining the work cut out for us. "It'll be a small team, but this operation is complicated. We need to get close to the village of Jibshit, in the heart of Hezbollah territory, and in proximity to a Lebanese Armed Forces (LAF) camp. Our challenge is to stop cars and bring their occupants back to Israel."

So far, two challenges had been presented. For a regular military unit, two weeks might seem like a long time, but special operations sometimes take months to plan. Secondly, stopping speeding cars without harming the people in them was a technique we would have to invent.

"This is deep covert infiltration into enemy territory," continued Eyal. "And the area is filled with enemy scouts, ambushes, and alert citizens. This is some mission!

"One more thing," Eyal said, turning to me, "you are the mission commander. Choose your team, show me preliminary plans and ramifications tonight, and tomorrow show me something more developed and begin preparing your operators."

I was thrilled! There is always a concern that the deputy will be left behind to deal with peripheral issues, such as training and logistics, but that was not Eyal's way. He himself would control the operation FCG.

On the way back, over the radio, I began summoning various people who would make up my team. Tzur, Mickey, and Assaf were asked to meet me in my office. I would have no one as the team's doctor other than Dr. Gillis – a special and trustworthy person, who was called from his home. I also requested the assistance of designated personnel from our technical shop, for we would surely need to be original if we intended to extract people from cars safely. At this point, I had no clue how we were going to pull this off. I also knew I could depend on Adi, an extremely talented team leader, and of course, I would need one of our Arabists, for it would be crucial to decide in real time who to take and who to leave behind.

"OK," said Michal, who was with me on the radio and jotting down all my requests. "Anything else?"

"Yes, have the transportation department prepare a few cars of various makes, and...a donkey."

"A donkey?"

"Yes. The kind that brays."

"OK," she answered, still in doubt.

The small office was filled with the joyous sounds of excitement before an operation. "Keep it down," I requested. I had a lot on my mind and sat down to make notes. Qualified operators needed to begin their preparation of personal gear and weapons. We needed a hangar where we could prepare and store everything needed for the operation.

I would need to balance between the tendency to supply full protective gear for my operators and the need to move lightly. It was a distant target, and even if we flew by helicopter, we would still need to walk a substantial distance.

"Have the intel department pull out the most recent aerial footage," I instructed. "Begin terrain analysis and request another sortie to get us up-to-date material."

I ordered the designation of a compartmentalized planning room in the intel shop, scheduled a meeting in three hours' time, and continued basic planning and preparing. Later I would designate team structure and commanders.

It was going to be Lebanon again, where most of my service had been carried out, and where I had lost many friends. I had strong conflicting feelings toward this country. On the one hand, vast, exquisite, and breathtaking scenery, but on the other hand, cruelty, war, instability, and lack of law and order.

Years after serving in Lebanon, I still suffered from a powerful dissonance when it came to beautiful scenery. Even in distant places around the world, I would say to myself: "What does nice scenery matter? Lebanon had nice scenery, too." I learned that scenery begins with people – the human landscape.

In the intel shop, we understood the picture better, now that it was all laid out on maps and imagery. I chose a curve in the road, in the outskirts of Jibshit, assuming this would be a place drivers would naturally tend to slow down. Another upside to this point was a nearby hill, overlooking the ambush site. But there were also two downsides: first, a nearby LAF base a few hundred meters away, occupied by a few dozen soldiers equipped with machine guns and APCs; second was the proximity of the houses of the village, introducing the complexity of warfare involving civilian population.

It was an extremely dangerous operation, leading right into the lion's den, and there were complex time and space constraints.

"We could be outnumbered three to one within minutes," Tzur said. "On the other hand," said someone else, "no one will suspect we're there, because no one is crazy enough to do such a thing. This would be a utilization of the principle of surprise and a demonstration of the daring approach of the unit."

We began constructing the stratagem and derived operational concept, and I assigned personnel. "Tzur, you are responsible for isolating the LAF. I don't want you to engage them unless they move and try to interfere."

"How many operators do I take?"

"How many do you need?"

"As few as possible."

I liked his answer. Fewer soldiers meant fewer problems – so the reality of special ops had taught me.

"Mickey, you deal with the focal point of the mission – stopping the vehicles and apprehending the people."

"Understood."

Mickey Edelstein was a talented company commander whom I trusted, and we would serve together in various capacities for many years.

"How many operators will you need?"

"It depends on the method we use."

"Take fifteen for now, begin training, and choose from them."

The next allocation was for the task of observing and blocking movement from the town, a very dangerous mission that carried heavy responsibility. I had excellent officers, but also extraordinary sergeants.

"Assaf."

"Assaf?" one of the officers wondered, "a sergeant?" I could see the officers exchanging looks and I understood their reservations, but I trusted my operators and certainly Assaf, who was an officer at heart.

"A commander is needed there, and it will be Assaf. He will command team one, and Adi will command the second."

There was still the need to assign eight more operators to my personal command team, a nearby backup and observation team, and two snipers.

"Do we have an Arabist?"

"There's Doron."

"Gal, they want us to perform other missions while we're there," our operations officer read from the printed Air Force orders.

"We will learn them, but now I want you to focus on planning our route. I would rather use the element of surprise and avoid using a helicopter, except maybe for extraction. Examine two options – one on foot and one mounted. It must be a quiet penetration and infiltration."

We had multiple task forces working simultaneously, in order to meet our timeline and produce an outstanding operational capability. I gave special attention to defining the mission, constructing the operational concept – the heart of the scheme we would use – and approving the plan with my commanding officer (CO). Additionally, I determined the basic outline of the methods we would use to penetrate enemy territory, carry out the mission, and return safely to Israel.

The first planning phase concluded with the presentation of a detailed schedule for the battle procedure and mission execution. From this point on, I would supervise the various components working in tandem.

All operators prepared the arsenal of weapons at our disposal. Our navigators divided the route among them and began detailed analysis and study, using all available sources. Our air coordinator began collaborative planning with the various helicopter crews scheduled to participate, from attack to rescue, and aligning it all into the various scenarios and contingencies. Our medical planning was underway, and a detailed physical training program was devised to make sure we were in top shape.

"Ahron's hangar," our main meeting point, was covered with blankets, on which we laid out night-vision instruments, personal radios, a variety of weapons, and other equipment, protecting them from dust. There was much work to be done – preparing, oiling, calibrating, and fastening and securing items with strong cords. Everything was checked and rechecked.

Once in a while, an operator would walk over to an industrial scale and carefully weigh various pieces of equipment. We were under strict weight restraints and needed to make sure we did not exceed the limits set for each operator. In the intel department, the light was on throughout the night.

Mickey began addressing the main task and challenged his operators to come up with original ideas on how to stop vehicles and extract their occupants. He was flooded with brilliant ideas and began experimentation, which resulted in complaints by drivers on the base who encountered strange experiences.

The Air Force supplied us with everything we needed, demonstrating their flexibility and responsiveness, even if it meant purchasing far from standard equipment or sending a cargo plane abroad to bring us a specific article we needed.

How do you stop cars traveling at such a speed? We found that the mission could be carried out noisily or quietly. Naturally, we preferred the quiet option, so as to attract minimum peripheral attention.

The donkey I had requested was contributed by Kibbutz Givat Brenner. The idea was to bring it with us and lay it in the middle of the road, creating an innocent-looking obstacle, forcing drivers to stop. We would then detain the people in the car, and after a short interrogation, disappear into the darkness taking with us only those who we felt could contribute information.

A minor problem we encountered was that our donkey was a shiny white.

"We'll color it," the operators suggested, "don't worry."

"What if the donkey decides to walk off the road?"

"We'll shoot it. It won't move after that – guaranteed."

"No way!" I was feeling less and less enthusiastic about the donkey tactic, but my operators continued to insist on its importance. Only during a night model did I fully understand why – the donkey was carrying half of the equipment the operators were to carry. But our donkey was behaving more like a mule, and stubbornly refused to walk the mountainous trails at night. Ronen, who was officially designated as the donkey driver, fought and pulled it all night long, calling out, "This is no good!" as we all doubled up with laughter.

Two operators promised me that they would solve our donkey problem, and the following night I was led to the hangar to see their proposal. At first I shuddered to see our donkey lying motionless on the floor, but then understood, amid sounds of laughter, that it was a replica of a donkey, built from rubber, sponge, and fiberglass rods by our artistic operators, and complete with ears stuck into its head and a folding tail.

"You wanted a donkey – you got one."

I still wasn't fully satisfied. "What if the driver runs over it or simply drives around it? We need something more massive."

"OK," the operators grumbled, "we'll come up with something." During the following model they demonstrated a simple, clever, and creative solution, which would withstand attempts to pass it with a jeep.

"You got it," I declared, "that's how we'll stop the cars."

The mission was presented and approved by the CGS, and we were on our way.

The trucks climbed up at night toward the Beaufort post near the ancient crusader fortress. A wave of memories came over me, as this was where I had served as a young team leader in the Sayeret.

After final preparations, positioning observation teams and final communication check, the advance team set out, and soon afterwards the main force as well. We quietly infiltrated between villages and crossed the first road undetected.

The second road took up precious time, as an enemy patrol was stubbornly passing back and forth. I sent the teams, one by one, every time the patrol went by, until we were all on the other side.

"We need to speed up. Time. Time," I thought to myself. We still had much to accomplish that night, and our window was shortening. We climbed a steep mountain, felt the bite of bitter cold, and strained under our heavy load. It was a deep penetration, and it took much effort.

"There it is!"

We located the curve in the road. It was extremely close to the houses of Jibshit, practically under the nose of Hezbollah. I gave out short instructions, sending each commander to his mission. Tzur deployed quietly above the LAF base, while Assaf and Adi prepared their blocking points on both flanks.

Mickey descended discreetly to the road and began preparing the blocking equipment. I positioned my command team where I could easily see and control all elements and assist with direct sniper fire, if necessary.

"Ready," I reported to Eyal at the headquarters. Lights appeared, and I examined the vehicle through binoculars and then night-vision goggles. "Medium-sized car," the observer reported.

"Take it, Mickey."

A screeching of brakes was heard, the car came to a full stop, and it was immediately surrounded by operators. "Out!" I could hear Doron's voice call out in Arabic. "There are five of them," Mickey reported. "All men, one of them elderly."

In the distance, the lights of another car were seen.

"Take him too, Mickey."

The first car was quickly hidden from view. The same procedure was repeated, only this time the report was different.

"They don't want to come out," Mickey said, out of breath.

"Extract using force. Breach the doors."

A stressful minute passed.

"We got them," Mickey reported.

"Good job. Prepare to disengage."

The second car was also hidden, to avoid suspicion.

"There's a 'Shlonski' here," Mickey reported. "Lots of material to carry back." By using the name of a known Israeli journalist, Mickey was implying that they were holding a journalist with an abundance of raw footage. This was good news, for it could be used to extract valuable intel.

"We have eight people," he continued, sounding somewhat concerned.

"We will choose three," I decided. "I'll speak to Doron. Bring them all here and I'll decide who to take. Make sure to leave the road without a trace of our presence." Another car was already approaching.

Mickey's team climbed up to my position, leading a column of Lebanese men. The valuable journalistic material was loaded into the operators' backpacks while Doron briefed me shortly on the results of his field interrogation, adding his recommendation on who to take back. I approved it.

What was to be done with the remaining five people? I knew that releasing them would mean that they would alert Hezbollah and we would be chased all the way home.

"Let's tie them up," someone said. "They'll be found in the morning." I looked at them – frightened and stunned civilians. I felt a hand on my shoulder and turned. It was Dr. Gillis.

"Yes, doctor?"

"We can't do that. They will freeze. They are our responsibility. They are human beings," he insisted.

I agreed and was so thankful for his remarks, I felt like hugging him. Still, we needed to figure out what to do. Just then, Eyal's voice from the command post was heard: "Gal, the helicopter is heading your way in a few minutes. It'll be in landing zone 33." The force was ready to move, including our three abductees.

I reached a decision.

"Doron, tell them to sit on the ground facing away from us, and explain that we positioned an ambush nearby for those who will come looking for them. Warn them that observers are watching them and they'd better not test us, for we will shoot anyone who moves."

"And we'll just leave them sitting there?"

"Exactly."

"Remove their leg shackles, but leave their handcuffs and blindfolds on. I want them to be able to move around. It's below freezing temperature tonight."

Doron went over to threaten the five Lebanese. "Thank you," Dr. Gillis said to me, his face radiating.

"No, thank you," I answered, knowing I had made the right decision, but still concerned.

Dr. Gillis, a dear man with a pure soul, was murdered in 2001 by terrorists, on his way home from Hadassah Hospital, where he had become a renowned physician, teacher, and researcher. I will always remember him as a wonderful person, doctor, officer, and colleague.

Mickey and I discussed alternatives for the route back.

"OK, let's head out."

We navigated to the LZ. I told Sagi, my radio operator, to prepare to communicate with the pilots, and I gave instructions to prepare the signals used to mark the LZ for them. I could feel the vibration of the helicopter already.

"Come on, everybody, get ready."

The massive Yasur came in low and fast, touching down near us. We quickly boarded with our extra passengers, the ramp closed, and I gave the thumbs-up to indicate that we were all aboard and good to go.

As the powerful helicopter took off, I felt a strong hand on my shoulder. I turned as Sagi leaned and yelled into my ear, "Gal, I dropped one of my radios!"

I grappled at the cord and pressed the PTT (push-to-talk).

"Benny," I said to the pilot, "turn around and head back to the LZ."

"What? Why?"

"We lost a radio. We have to find it."

"Got it," Benny replied, immediately turned, and updated the command post on the developments. As we approached the LZ again, we were approved to land, but requested to make it as short as possible.

"I'm going out with Sagi. If you get shot at, take off and we'll make it back on our own."

We leaped out and searched the area in vain. A strong hand grasped me – it was the airborne mechanic, ordered to drag me back to the helicopter. I tried to resist and persist but he couldn't hear me over the loud noise of the helicopter.

We reentered the helicopter and were airborne instantly.

"How did this happen?" I yelled into Sagi's ear.

"I untied the radio."

"But you're not allowed to untie cords behind enemy lines," I said, furious.

"I know. I made a mistake."

While airborne, I made up my mind that Sagi would not join us on the next mission. The following day, however, I decided to back him up – true, he made a poor judgment that led to a bad outcome, but things like this happen. The important lesson, both privately and collectively as a unit, would never be forgotten.

Camouflage Face Paint

One evening, I received a phone call from Major Zeev Bernstein, my dear friend from the military academy and teammate in the Sayeret, who was now the operations officer of the Paratroopers Brigade. Sounding worried and sad, he told me that during an exercise, the engineering unit of the paratroopers "attacked" the 202nd Battalion's bunker in the Golan Heights, but the guard had not been briefed, and thinking it was a real attack, opened fire and killed 2LT Yiftach Ottolenghi.

"It looks like they're out to get Rami," Zeev said, referring to my friend LTC Rami Zur, whom I was scheduled to replace as the 202nd Paratroopers Battalion commander in eight months' time.

"Be prepared," he went on, "because if he's out, you'll be sent there immediately."

The next day, the commander of CENTCOM, MG Danny Yatom, decided to dismiss Rami, and I was called to his office in Jerusalem, where he asked me what would be the ramifications if I were to be called to replace Rami immediately. He later consulted the Air Force commander, who fully cooperated, and sent me back from air force blue to ground forces green.

I was assigned as the 202nd Battalion commander at the age of twenty-seven.

I met Rami at his house in Kiryat Tivon and found him bitter and hurt. I couldn't blame him for feeling this way, for I believed that they had hurried to serve the commander's head on a platter, as an easy scapegoat for what was referred to as "overall responsibility," relating only to the result and not the process.

Rami gave me a detailed review on the unit he was passing on to me, patiently explaining and teaching me all I needed to know.

The following day, as I entered the 202nd Battalion encampment, near Waset Junction in the Golan Heights, I encountered a strange-looking guy wearing a bathrobe and slippers, holding a huge toiletries bag, and calling out hot-tempered remarks toward the support company's tents. He disappeared into a tent and I followed him in. The interior looked more like a hotel room than a military tent. There was a furnace, a TV set, a rug covering the basalt surface of the Golan, and other articles of indulgence. In the middle of it all sat a grinning man who introduced himself as MAJ Yaniv Adam, my new deputy in the battalion, and later on in Shaldag, and a partner and friend for life.

We began a brief rundown of the tasks ahead, beginning with a serious challenge – the upcoming battalion exercise in two days. I had not been part of the preparation process, and had not even met my brigade commander or my subordinate officers yet.

"What are we going to do about it?" Adam asked.

"You'll help me and we'll manage," I assured him.

My main concern was connecting with the battalion and raising their morale after the traumatic training accident and the resulting change of command.

Near the Petroleum Road in the Golan Heights, I addressed my battalion for the first time. I had ordered special camouflage face paint, considered scarce and only used by special forces back in those days. I asked that everyone paint his face, and did so myself, while hundreds of soldiers and officers cheerfully painted each other in black, green, and brown.

Then I introduced myself and told them that Tzefa was a unique battalion, that I had served there as a company commander a few years back, and that I had just come from Shaldag, so from now on we would be a commando battalion.

"Commando is a state of mind," I told them, explaining my philosophy. "It's a matter of attitude and nothing else." I went on telling them that in my opinion, a commando unit is characterized by strict selection, superb weaponry and equipment, excellent combat fitness, and a tradition of relentless learning. I have no doubt that even an armored battalion can function as a commando unit, a special force. It is up to its commander, a spirit of daringness, and mainly a decision to be so.

This is what I demanded from the 202nd Battalion on the eve of our big exercise, and the camouflage face paint symbolized it.

The effect on the battalion was immediate, and officers and soldiers alike set out high-spirited, with smiles on their faces. During the exercise I constantly encouraged my officers and complimented them after every report they gave. I made it a point to be heard often over the battalion channel, but spoke quietly, using a deep voice and a touch of humor.

During one of the exercise scenarios, while inspecting a breach we had made in the fence, I met COL Mati Harari, the brigade commander and my new commanding officer (CO).

"Only in the IDF would you meet your CO for the first time like this," he said, smiling. All through that night he followed the implementation of my plan, inspected the battalion's performance, the implementation of my plan, activation of tanks and helicopters, and mainly the utilization of the battalion's capabilities and the synergy between its elements.

"Very good, Gal," he told me at daybreak, not concealing his satisfaction.

I especially appreciated the positive feedback from my company commanders and my deputy Adam, for at the outset, I was deeply concerned and not sure if I could successfully lead such an exercise. During those three intense days of fighting, I sensed my own improvement and even shed some of the fear inherent to leading soldiers, at least during an exercise. I felt the battalion was on the right track.

Before the battalion was deployed to hold the line on the Lebanese border, Adam left to attend a course in the United States Marine Corps, leaving me to manage alone without a deputy.

I faced challenges on the home front too. Having left the Air Force, we were asked to vacate our apartment at Palmachim Base. I hadn't the time to find another place and deal with the hardships of moving, so CENTCOM came to our assistance, by asking Kibbutz Ma'ale Hahamisha to accept us, which they did wholeheartedly. Donna taught new immigrants Hebrew at the ulpan and Meori was integrated in the kindergarten. The kibbutz has a warm place in our hearts until today.

Those were days of intense operational activity, and I rarely visited home, so when possible, I would send a vehicle to bring Donna and Meori to me. My devoted family joined me during weekends, whether it was in a dusty tent, the headquarters in the casbah of a Palestinian town, or a position on the border.

The battalion carried out operations confronting Hezbollah, then trained for a few months before switching gears and deploying to the city of Nablus to fight the Hamas terror organization.

I decided to radically change many customary patterns and operate the battalion as a recon unit or special force. We worked in close collaboration with the ISA – Israel Security Agency ("Shin Bet") and used Duvdevan forces and methods of disguised penetrations. We operated in a flexible, random mode, spending days concealed in hostile environments and conducting unexpected raids on terrorist infrastructure and in Palestinian villages.

This was an unfamiliar mode of operations for Hamas terrorists and civilian rioters who were throwing stones and hurling Molotov cocktails. Soon our efforts began to pay off.

One of the ambushes that we set up apprehended a car loaded with weapons, and a quick follow-up interrogation by ISA led to the apprehension of a terror cell in Jerusalem. In another case, a truckload of stone throwers were arrested, after a paratroopers company led by Captain Dror Mar Haim surprised them. Senior Hamas commander Zaher Jabarin was apprehended in a combined operation with ISA and Duvdevan.

Captain Eitan Belhassen, who was my subordinate at engineering company, was a company commander by now, and he led his young company in a way that completely negated the enemy's ability to recognize a pattern as a weak point to attack. He was an extremely thorough, independent, and dedicated commander.

We would lose him years later, fighting terrorists in the mountains of Lebanon, as the commander of the Sayeret. I became very close to Eitan's family, Claude and Tsiona Belhassen, who built their home in the Galilee and raised an exemplary family of farmers, dreamers, and fighters.

Our unorthodox pattern-breaking did not suit every area of operations. It took me much time and effort to explain this operational rationale to some commanders.

During a visit of the National Defense College, comprised of senior students from all security and governmental agencies, we stood on Mount Gerizim, overlooking Nablus, and I presented an operation we had conducted with Duvdevan, where I drove my jeep into the casbah serving as bait, while soldiers in disguise surprised the terrorists who came to attack me.

"Wait a minute," a student asked, "who did you say was in the jeep?"

"Why, me, of course," I answered.

There was a murmur of disapproval and someone voiced it clearly: "That is irresponsible. A battalion commander is a battalion commander."

"I do not agree with you," I argued.

One of the students, Ehud Yatom from the ISA, who would later become a Member of Knesset, came to my assistance. "Excuse me," he said, butting in to the heightened debate, "but I would be happy if my son served in your battalion!"

With time, our recon teams were being required to participate in operations in other areas. It added an extra burden on our already high operational tempo, but it attested to the value of the concepts I introduced.

We did not only enjoy success, but suffered bitter failure too. A force from Captain Eitan Belhassen's company was deployed outside the battalion's area of operations, where they set up surprise ambushes on route 5 – the Trans-Samaria Highway. Thinking they were facing a terrorist breaching their roadblock, the force shot and killed police officer Eitan Mesika.

A force from our spearhead company, commanded by Captain Guy Tzlil, was operating covertly in a different regional brigade area, near the city of Jenin, when they encountered an undercover border police force. Due to faulty coordination, they both believed they were confronting terrorists, and by the time the mistake was figured out, a gunfight resulted in two wounded soldiers, one from each force.

We dealt intensively with learning lessons from every incident. I knew that an inherent part of an operational unit's routine was to make mistakes, but the idea is to learn from each failure and get better.

In 1992 my battalion sustained another operational failure. S SGT Samuel Tiahu, a wonderful soldier from a family of immigrants from Ethiopia, was killed by terrorists in the stairwell of a building in Nablus, as he attempted to resupply an observation point on the roof.

We suffered a heavy blow, after a long period of successes, and I perceived this as an awful and painful failure.

I spoke to Dotan, the company commander, who was very upset, and told him I assumed full responsibility as the battalion commander.

"And I'm the company commander!" Dotan cried out, tears in his eyes, "and I have failed."

"We failed," I insisted. "We have also known successes, don't forget that. It is a bitter enemy we face, not cardboard targets. I will assume responsibility."

After a series of debriefings and inquiries, I reported to BG Moshe (Bogie) Ya'alon, the commander of Judea and Samaria Division (J&S).

"Gal, this was a grave incident," he said softly, "but you have an excellent battalion, which has delivered a series of operational and even strategic successes. The effect of your activities is felt throughout the region." He shook my hand.

Bogie would later repeat his words of praise and encouragement, addressing the entire brigade staff at a final debriefing of the battalion's operational tour. It was an important lesson in backing.

I stood before the CENTCOM commander, MG Nehemiah Tamari, in Tel Aviv.

"I have failed, sir," I said. "I don't know how I overlooked this vulnerability. I have had multiple forces deployed in and around Nablus, and such a thing has never happened. I feel responsible for this failure and accept whatever you decide to do."

At the time, I was a candidate to become the next commander of Shaldag, and I had heard that the CGS, LTG Ehud Barak, had postponed the decision until the ramifications of the Nablus incident on my career were clear. Terror had succeeded, and I knew I might pay a heavy personal price, but my promotion was nothing compared to the pain of losing Samuel.

Nehemiah sat behind his desk and looked up at me. "I will write an administrative remark in your personal file," he said.

"Please don't touch Dotan," I requested. "He's an excellent fighter and good company commander, and the responsibility is mine."

"I know what you're doing out there. Dotan will continue in his position." He stood up and shook my hand. I saluted and walked out. A few days later, Nehemiah insisted on appointing me as commander of Shaldag commando unit.

Outside I met Dotan, excited and red-eyed. We hugged and I said, "Let's get back to the battalion." But Bogie's aide ran up to us. "Minister of Defense Yitzhak Rabin wants to speak to you. He'll be coming to your battalion tomorrow, and he wants to see exactly what happened."

My heart was pounding. "Should I bring him to the battalion encampment?"

"Yes, but first he wants to see the exact location, near the Clock Square."

Rabin arrived the next day, under heavy security, and was led to the building where the incident had taken place, near the Clock Square.

I had made careful preparations, including closing off all floors leading to the location and drills to answer for various developments. I escorted Rabin up the stairs to the blood stains where Samuel was killed. I explained what had happened and introduced Raz, the soldier who was injured during the incident. Then an ISA agent filled in a few background details. Rabin listened carefully and occasionally asked sharp, practical questions.

"I assume that you learned all that can be learned," he said, in his deep, measured voice. I nodded and said no more.

"I understand," he concluded, and headed down the stairs. When we reached the vehicles, MG Danny Rothschild told me that Rabin wanted to sit and talk with me in my tent.

"I would like to bring company commanders with me, if that's OK," I asked.

"Sure, bring them. You know him, he would like that."

Inside my tent, situated near the western entrance to Nablus, the typical military-style Turkish "mud" coffee was poured into blue cups, and a lively discussion was underway between Yitzhak Rabin and my company commanders. I watched how, with his solemn and confident leadership, and a modest, shy smile, Rabin was reconstructing the battalion, strengthening and balancing us after the blow we had suffered, and instilling trust and loyalty.

On the way out, there was another issue on Rabin's mind: "I heard that terrorists shot at your tent."

"True," I confirmed, somewhat embarrassed.

"Show me where the shots came from."

I led him to the center of the tent, with the whole procession following us, then pointed to the hill from which terrorists had opened fire on my headquarters. I described how we responded with a burst of retaliatory fire and then took over the hill. I also pointed out the house in which we had caught Zaher Jabarin.

The battalion concluded its operational tour in Nablus, conducted a term of training, and was once again deployed to the Lebanese border, in the area of Zar'it.

At this point I departed from the battalion and moved on to what would become a peak in my military career – commander of Shaldag.

Walking a Tightrope

"… This operation will cost the lives of dozens of this nation's finest sons, all because of ambitions of a commander who is uncontrollable by his superiors. Therefore, I have decided to resign my position as mission leader and retire from active service in the IDF."

It was a year into my tenure as commander of Shaldag. My heart was pounding violently as I read the letter, written by one of my reserve officers, who was serving a period of time in active service in order to lead a mission. Was this a single point of view, or did he represent a group? Was this considered mutiny? What was going on here? What would the Air Force commander think? What would the CGS say?

Bad timing. I was traveling overseas that day and had stopped at the office first. Now, as I made my way to Ben-Gurion Airport, I called Donna to update her, beginning, as always with "Everything's OK, but you should know that…" She was overwhelmed, angry, and full of questions.

"If you decide to stay," Dr. Yossi (Yoli) Liran said, leaning close to me as if it were a secret, "and if you decide to deal with the unit, you are in for a rough period, during which you will be acquiring a valuable asset. You will be creating the ability to withstand hardships and achieve your goals while working with different people, even those who oppose you."

Yoli knew me intimately, serving as my organizational advisor from back when I was an engineering company commander. I had asked him to continue on with me, and here he was again, coaching me during this crisis, over a cup of tea in a gas station near the airport.

"Opposition is a positive thing," he went on, "and you have always allowed it. You've got guts and you've got patience, but you must continue in your own style, leading while coping with the objections. In a few years people will understand what you have accomplished here. Right now people can't grasp the magnitude of the changes you're making in the unit."

An investigative commission assigned by the commander of the Air Force was at work in the unit, interviewing officers in an attempt to understand the "mutinous" reservists, claiming that I was "ruining the unit, endangering its people, and creating a 'black box' with no way of knowing what happens inside it."

I was very hurt and was not sure if I would be able to continue commanding the unit with these rebellious reservists and some of the regular service officers complaining to the Air Force commander and the CGS.

There was still so much to be done. We had operations, training, and exercises to attend to, new equipment to develop, and buildings to construct. I was redefining rules and regulations, setting new goals and directions, introducing more structure and discipline, and raising the bar of daring operations and more involvement in counterterror operations in Lebanon and J&S.

My actions were aimed at changing and adapting, in order to prepare the unit for future challenges, using the year 2020 as reference. But with the extreme objections to those changes by those who felt I was ruining the unit, I was not sure whether to stay and fight or get up and leave.

Creativity but Not Foolishness

"It's over," I announced, facing the entire unit in the mess hall, approximately a month after assuming command of the unit, "no more going wild." I then began spelling out what I meant.

"No more wearing civilian clothes. Everyone will wear uniforms, according to their phase of training and location. We will have discipline here. Not everyone can carry a pistol, and you can't drive a vehicle that you are not qualified to drive. Discipline."

I knew how important it was to foster a spirit of creativity and openness in the unit, but I also thought it must be accompanied by strong discipline and rules – special rules, but still rules.

I implemented my announcement about uniform and decided that soldiers in initial training would wear full uniform, while those who completed the course and became qualified operators would wear black T-shirts with the unit's logo, but only inside the unit compound. All were expected to wear full class A dress uniforms outside the base, and class B work uniforms for training.

We were returning one night from an operational exercise where we had fielded a new vehicle that we were planning to use for the mission. The Air Force had acquired special vehicles at my request, and our combat vehicle team had reinforced them, installed infrared headlights and navigation systems, and mounted strong and lightweight equipment bins.

I insisted on having the best operators with me in order to ensure the best performance in every field, and my finest vehicle expert was Major R., an extremely talented professional and great fighter, who was also fun to be with and talk to. I needed his professionalism, but was also concerned about his lightheartedness, an attribute shared by quite a few operators in the unit. A whole generation had been raised on the myth that in special units it was OK to disregard regulations and rules. Those who believed in this demonstrated tough resistance to the new path I had set for the unit.

I believe in the need for special forces to step out of frameworks, but one cannot do so without first establishing what the framework is.

As we landed at an Air Force base after the mission rehearsal, I was flabbergasted to see R. drive his vehicle swiftly and skillfully up onto the vehicle transporter, without guidance as required by safety regulations. He demonstrated impressive driving, but also reckless behavior and unnecessary risk to himself and others.

That evening, I dismissed him from the operation, despite his pleading with me to reconsider. I simply could not accept such an attitude. My decision had a huge perceptional impact on the unit, as every operator's ultimate goal was to participate in operations behind enemy lines.

I had acted the same way with another company commander, an excellent officer who did not adhere to numerous remarks about safety. When he was about to leave the base, driving a new prototype vehicle that was still in R&D and not yet cleared for off-base driving, loaded with operators from the unit, I notified him that he would be removed from his position, for a recurring violation is no longer merely a mistake, but negligence, and demonstrates a lack of discipline.

I do not hastily dismiss people, and believe that a leader must allow room for error and learning. Willingness to absorb a certain level of error is key in developing commanders and soldiers, but not when negligent acts are repeated over and over.

I tried to eliminate this negative spirit from the unit. I liked occasional mischievous behavior and promoted creativity, but not foolishness. The thin line between controlled mischief and chaos is very hard to delineate, and must be stubbornly and persistently maintained until the commander's intent is clear and a new standard is set.

I gave special emphasis to educating the commanders, for they were the ones to instill these values and influence change within the unit.

I dealt with a company commander who refused to admit the findings of an internal inspection which had revealed that his senior sergeants were harassing younger soldiers, for no reason other than upholding the "tradition," doing to others what was once done to them. I was especially horrified to hear that they would place cucumbers in the mouths of tired and hungry soldiers standing in formation, and then inspect for bite marks to see who fell asleep. The unfortunate soldiers whose cucumbers gave them away were sent on another round of harassment drills.

I had brought this platoon leader from the Paratroopers Brigade, after he successfully passed a screening process, and I did not want to end his career or even expel him from the unit. I decided to assign him to temporary duty at the Air Force headquarters, in order to convey a message, but this act was not looked upon favorably by some, who thought I was undermining the tradition of the unit.

I had early signs of this dissatisfaction when my deputy reported to me that a group of officers had met with the base sociologist. I did not see a problem with the idea of conducting such a meeting, but felt that the sociologist should have informed me. I was so furious that day that I went home and spoke to Donna about it, and she recommended, "Go speak to the base commander."

Shaldag is under the command of the Air Force special operations headquarters, and is only hosted on this Air Force base, but I made a point of integrating as much as possible with the base routine and unique organizational culture and atmosphere.

"Blending a special operations unit into an Air Force base is like mixing sugar and honey," I used to say. "The outcome is always sweet."

My relations with the base commander were good. He was known to be a highly professional pilot, and I had heard about his daring actions during the First Lebanon War. I had also heard criticism of his management skills, but I found that with his pleasant demeanor, professionally oriented leadership style, and especially his steadfast support and backing of his subordinates, he managed to overcome many obstacles.

We had occasional clashes, but they were settled one morning, when he invited me to his office and asked that we make up. He told me in rare candidness: "I don't feel comfortable going on like this, especially when I run into Donna." He knew that with families living on base, every tension reached the minimarket and the kindergarten. This was a lesson in leadership – there is no point in dragging on with inherent tensions, and they should be addressed and dealt with directly and practically with one's subordinates, regardless of their rank.

There was an unforgettable experience we shared. We were attending an exercise debriefing together and heard the base siren. We all ran outside to see what it was about, and I drove toward the base headquarters. When I saw flashing lights in the sand dunes west of the helicopter squadron, I assumed that that was the reason for the siren, so I headed that way, finding an awful sight. The mangled hull of a Bell 212 Anafa helicopter was lying on its side in the sand, and not far from it, the body of the airborne mechanic. One critically wounded pilot was quickly extracted and taken to the hospital, and the body of the second pilot was found, crushed under the wreckage.

I quickly entered the wreckage, and found Yossi, the squadron commander, an experienced pilot who had performed brave rescue missions, including during the battle of Maydun, when I was a company commander. His hand was resting on the pilot's skull, and he took out a handkerchief and covered it. Jet fuel was dripping all around us, and to my astonishment, a team from the Air Force rescue unit 669 approached us and began preparing welding equipment. I was afraid the sparks would ignite the fuel so I stopped them and instead asked my unit's combat vehicle team to bring their rescue equipment, including high-pressure lifting cushions, which we used to lift the helicopter enough to retrieve the pilot's body.

Near the covered body of the mechanic, I found the base commander, who told me about the men who were killed, for he knew them personally. Then he sighed and looked at me in silence, as if waiting for me to say something, but I just stood there in silence beside him.

I will never forget the base commander's face that evening, and the open eyes of the dead pilot we pulled out of the crashed helicopter. I still see them today.

Dismiss Whomever You See Fit

"Your base sociologist was wrong," I told the base commander, after explaining the recent events. Like other Air Force commanders, he placed a lot of trust in sociologists and their recommendations, including the "peer evaluation," or sociometry test, which had always been a source of strength in the organization.

"I'll speak with her," promised the base commander. "I don't know why she didn't talk to you. But you should be aware that there are accusations circulating, claiming that you don't know enough about commando operations and that you don't compromise. I know how much pressure the unit exerted to have you as their commander, and I also appreciate your professionalism, but there is a murky wave going around. I will look into it and we will speak again."

As always, I spoke with Yoli. His main task was to assist me in reorganizing the unit and preparing it for the year 2020 (selected by the air force as a reference point for future planning), but because I trusted him, I also consulted with him regarding the stormy atmosphere and undercurrents.

There was no doubt that a deep organizational change had to be made. This was apparent to every professional eye, and I received many recommendations to make it, including from the Air Force commander. During my second week in the unit, COL Nahum Lev, the commander of the Air Force special operations headquarters, told me: "The unit must change, it can't go on like this."

"You're probably the most unsafe unit in the world," BG Moti Regev, the previous base commander, had told me one day, "but no one knows this because you dodge external inspection using the good old 'operational security' excuse. Everything is too secret to show to outsiders, so you can go on doing whatever you want, including driving unmarked cars and carrying special badges making you immune to military police. This is unacceptable."

When he spoke of avoiding MPs, I thought of Omri and Ronen, operators who were fed up with police ambushes on the road leading to the base and carried out a commando raid, using a chainsaw to hack down all the bushes that were concealing the speed radar.

I was very concerned with safety and discipline, but more utterly dissatisfied with fundamental operational issues. I believed that we should be more operationally involved and carry out more daring missions. I did not accept our disassociation from the bloody battles in Lebanon and J&S, and completely rejected an arrogant pronouncement I heard from our operations officer: "Our general is the commander of the Air Force, not the NORTH-COM commander."

I believed that a wide-scale confrontation was just a matter of time in J&S, and thought we should be activated and utilized. I expressed this to MG Gabi Ofir, commander of the J&S Division, and during our meeting we analyzed various options of integrating Shaldag, perceived up until then as a hush-hush special ops unit. I thought that the IDF should benefit from the implementation of our special capabilities during routine security activity, on and beyond Israel's borders.

These ideas were strongly opposed by senior operators in the unit. They did not want the new direction I was leading and preferred secretive special operations behind enemy lines instead of routine security missions in the West Bank.

Tension in the unit peaked with the appointment of the investigative commission, but began to dissipate when the conclusions were presented and fully accepted by BG Dan Halutz, head of Air Operations. My ideas and actions were fully supported by the commission, and the recommendation was to back me up.

I was summoned to meet the commander of the Air Force, who looked me in the eye, expressed full support, and explained why it had been necessary to assign the investigative commission.

"Dismiss whomever you see fit," he said, and went on to praise my course of action. Herzl always gave his people full backing, unless they failed ethically, just as expected from a senior leader. I received his support to continue the processes I had begun.

I was faced with a delicate leadership dilemma, but after much consideration I decided not to dismiss anyone, following my philosophy that it is wise not to use a hammer unless it's utterly necessary. It is easy to break things, but much harder to reconstruct them, and I believed that with time I would be able to lead even my opposition. I was determined to carve a new path through this stubborn bedrock and eventually change the natural flow of the stream.

So, I temporarily suspended a few reservists in order to avoid their direct interference with the changes I was leading, but they were eventually accepted back, during Operation Grapes of Wrath in 1996.

The tension began to dissipate during the preparations for a special operation in Lebanon. At the time, the IDF was conducting a bitter campaign against Hezbollah, in the security belt in southern Lebanon and to the north of it.

Chapter 5
Special Missions

Across the Border

"I want you to know," Herzl Bodinger said emotionally, "that if you fall into enemy hands or if anything goes wrong, the State of Israel will do all in its power to bring you back home!"

The shadows were getting longer near the underground aircraft shelter at the Air Force base where we were conducting the final brief before taking off on a special operation in Lebanon. It was the culmination of a long preparation process, and we were now isolated in a designated compound on an Air Force base, detached from the outside world. All were engaged in thorough final checks and preparations, from the CH-53 mechanics to the operators themselves. Special sleeping quarters were assigned to us to allow for some rest before the long night ahead.

We wore special clothing and boots, and made final inspections of the fighting gear. I wired up with a tiny earpiece, microphone, and push-to-talk micro-switch fastened between my thumb and index finger with adhesive tape. I made sure the wires ran comfortably under my uniform.

My weapon of choice was augmented with a silencer and various devices, and I rechecked that all the necessary equipment was fastened to my fighting vest and comfortably stowed – flashlight, night-vision goggles, commando knife, survival gear. Sensitive secret equipment was secured with double cords. Fighting gear was carefully inspected and sealed in a duffle bag, not to be opened until we were airborne.

After the final briefing, which included intel and weather updates, we all attended the traditional "last meal." Our cook, Itach, always did his best to supply us with delicious dishes, although the unit doctor had the final word on the exact composition of our diet. We were always warned by doctors that inadequate nutrition could lead to operational hazards and the unwanted result of leaving bodily by-products in enemy territory. So we ate "stable food" – huge schnitzels with lots of ketchup and various carbohydrates. Before takeoff the unit bathrooms were crowded.

"When fear comes," one of the operators told me knowledgeably, "it smells a whole lot worse."

Not only nutrition was monitored and regulated. I had my operators inspected by the Air Force Aerial Medical Unit to ensure they were all in top shape. To preserve the force, I also set clear rules on what physical activities were allowed, forbidding free-time motorcycling and excluding all ball games and Krav Maga lessons, where we regularly suffered injuries.

"If you want to play, play chess," I answered those who complained.

It was getting dark. We opened the duffle bags and took out the equipment, painted our faces, and cross-checked that everything was secure and ready. The CH-53 Yasur helicopters lowered their ramps. We boarded the aircrafts, arranged the gear, and checked communication with the pilots.

While we were preparing for takeoff, other elements and forces were preparing different aspects of the mission, from command and control headquarters to fighter jets and attack helicopters. All were aligned and attuned to support our small force and assist us with carrying out the mission.

The helicopters lunged forward, gained speed, and then heavily lifted off the runway and headed north.

"I'm so afraid – my heart is in my stomach," the copilot was heard saying over the intercom. "Don't worry," the captain answered, "it's not that bad."

I exchanged smiles with one of the operators, pressed the PTT and said, "What's there to worry about when you're with us?" After the operation, the captain would tell me, "I wanted to kill him. What was he thinking, saying something like that on open mic?"

I stood at the door on the right side of the helicopter and gazed out using night-vision goggles, the green scenery whisking by as we flew fast and low. Boaz, commander of the unit's operations company, stood at the left window, and two operators sat on the back ramp, all manning outward-pointing machine guns. I noticed the operators making quick adjustments to their helmets and gear.

I could see the silhouette of the other helicopter in close formation, and imagined Eylon and his team inside, making final preparations.

Two distinct buzzes indicated we were crossing the border into enemy territory.

"We crossed the border." Itay, the captain, added a verbal notification.

"I saw," I answered, having recognized the place after seeing it many times, from the air and the ground.

My hand gripped the handle of my weapon. Safety checked. Extremely stressful. Heart pounding.

"They are great warriors," I reminded myself. It's good to head out to a mission with such a sense of trust.

The helicopters were flying fast and low. Coded reports were transmitted back to the headquarters. The operators used the time to rest, except those positioned at the windows to assist with navigation and identifying threats.

As we whisked over villages, ridges, and wadis (an Arabic term meaning valley or riverbed), I recognized key navigational points, identifying them by nicknames that we had given them for common language, during cooperative learning of our teams with the helicopter pilots.

"There's the cucumber!" We all heard the joyous cries from the cockpit, as the LZ came into sight. The name was given by the lead navigator due to a distinct long shape of the landing strip. "There it is!" my navigator chimed in, as he recognized the familiar shape from the left window.

"Five minutes," Itay announced. "Roger, five minutes," I confirmed, signaling to my men, who could not hear the communication with pilots. They saw my open hand in the darkness and signaled back.

"We're taking fire from nine o'clock and five o'clock," the copilot reported.

"Gunners – hold your fire," I said. The LAF probably heard the helicopters and were firing in the general direction, so opening fire would only help them pinpoint our location and aim better.

"Two minutes. Still fire from the right," Itay said. I could see the long streaks of bullets from my position at the door.

"I don't think we were spotted," I answered, as I signaled my men with two fingers. "Proceed as planned."

The pilots were calling out navigational names more frequently now, and their high-pitched voices indicated the tension they were in, to put the bird down on the exact designated LZ. I did not bother Itay at this point, as he multitasked, coordinating with the air traffic controller, his wingman, his copilot, and the accompanying Apache attack helicopter formation.

I recognized the Apache lead pilot's relaxed and confident voice. It was Noam, the squadron commander, who was also my former neighbor on the base. I considered him a prudent and courageous pilot. The result of being embedded within the Air Force and carrying out many missions and exercises together was a unique bond, with deep understanding and appreciation between commando Shaldag operators and the pilots.

"One minute." I raised one finger and got the confirming response, then saw my men quickly unfasten the tie-down ropes securing our gear. The helicopter jolted violently and pitched upward as the pilots reduced speed for landing.

"That's close," I thought to myself, seeing heavy fire.

"After you let us off, make a 180-degree turn and take the same route back, keeping low," I suggested.

"You're right, we'll do just that," Itay answered. Planning the return route was no less important than the way to the target, as the enemy was now alert and eager to shoot down an Israeli helicopter.

I could hear the teamwork going on in the cockpit as we descended: "fifty feet, twenty-five feet," "I have visual," "ten feet, five feet, touchdown."

"Good luck, Gal."

"See you before dawn," I answered, then took off the headset, unlocked the gun's safety, and was the first to exit the aircraft.

Would the mission be successful? Would we experience major deviations from our plan? I knew there was no such thing as a "smooth" execution. A leader must find good solutions to bridge the gap between plans and the unfolding reality, caused by the inherent "friction" in the battlefield, as military theorist Carl von Clausewitz called it. This is true in special operations, and certainly during war.

We grouped outside the helicopter, my first priority being its safe and fast departure.

"Itay, go!" I said into the mic, and then felt the turbulent downwash as both helicopters leaped into the air, spun around a few feet above the ground, then accelerated and disappeared, leaving us in a cloud of dust.

Suddenly, the newly established quiet was disturbed by a loud burst of gunfire.

"That was close, Gal!" Boaz said, concerned.

"They can go to hell for all I care," I answered with confidence. "Let's get going."

I rarely use strong language, but in this specific situation, my authentic and confident encouragement seemed to have a positive effect on my men, and they hurried to their positions and prepared to move out.

We were carrying very heavy backpacks, consisting of explosive charges, medical equipment, radios, food and water, various fighting gear, and ammunition. We headed out toward our target in tactical formation. I headed the column, with Boaz at my side. My radio operator was close behind, using code names to report our position to the FCG.

I was coordinating with three small Shaldag teams, who had been pre-positioned in key locations a few days earlier in order to assist us with continuous intel coverage before the execution and peripheral security during the mission. Tzur, Dror, and Doron reported that all was calm and expressed their anticipation to see us and receive the resupply of food, water, and other equipment that we carried, which would allow them to sustain themselves longer in enemy territory.

We made our way to the rendezvous point, where we would meet soldiers from Doron's team. They had discreetly left their concealed position and were navigating to meet us at the resupply point, where they would give us empty backpacks and receive new ones. They would later link up with the other teams and resupply them too.

I was very appreciative of Doron's performance in the preceding days. When the mission was postponed for two days due to weather conditions, his team was left without supplies and there were serious debates whether to abort the mission.

"Don't worry," he told me over the radio, "we will manage."

And manage they did. Doron and his three men moved around discreetly, found and purified water, ate emergency candy, used minimum energy, and carried out the mission superbly, reporting back quality information. Their performance was highly appreciated at the highest levels in the IDF.

"One minute to rendezvous," my navigator whispered. I recognized the preplanned signal from Doron's operators through my night-vision goggles and returned the expected response signal. I sent a small team led by Boaz forward to the resupply point and stayed back with the main force.

"I have visual," Boaz reported. "Fifty meters, twenty meters, contact." Soldiers embraced each other in excitement. It should have now been a quick exchange of backpacks and each team would be on its way.

"They're still hugging out here," said Boaz.

Outsiders would never understand this, I thought to myself. *This is the camaraderie of soldiers.* But time was of the essence.

"Enough hugging, Eylon. Let's get going."

I was very concerned about keeping up with the schedule, for we had a long night ahead of us – a long march to the target area, a complicated climb up a cliff, penetration of the compound, and placement of the charges. Then we planned to disengage and board the helicopters in a different location from the drop-off point. At daybreak, when we were safely home, the charges would detonate and wreak havoc on the Hezbollah camp. Only then would the three teams led by Dror, Doron, and Tzur make their way back to Israel.

"Come on, there's no time." The two forces departed, and I could see the silhouettes of Doron's operators, walking up the mountainside toward Tzur's position, carrying fifty-five-kilo (120-pound) backpacks.

I smiled when I thought of the look on the soldiers' faces when they would later open the backpacks. After a serious debate with the unit's doctor, I decided that Itach – our "commando chef," as we called him – would prepare a special meal of steak-in-a-pita. The doctor was right in his concern for the physical effects this might have on the soldiers, but I also wanted to achieve an effect of morale uplifting, by giving them a pleasant surprise and a good, hearty meal.

"Stopping in two minutes," Boaz reported.

"Got it." I raised my hand.

"This is it." Everyone crouched on the side of the path. This was our split-up point, where Oded's force took off to his separate mission.

"Good luck, see you before dawn."

Moving on. The dark night was green through the night-vision goggles, and we sensed the smells and sounds of the night. We half walked, half ran, passing in silence between houses and fields, climbing hills, crossing valleys. Once in a while we stopped and kneeled, took out a compass, regained our bearings, and pushed on. The load was heavy, and sweat was burning our eyes. We didn't stop to rest or drink, but each operator could sip water from his personal water pack.

I glanced at my watch, making out the time by the glowing green hands.

"Time is marginal," I made a point to myself. We had lost precious time circling in the Galilee Panhandle, waiting for approval to cross the border.

My mind was racing with calculations and speculations. Every segment of the mission had been carefully analyzed and tested, so I knew the soil type, distance, time, and angle of climb or descent of every segment, together with the weight of the operators and the equipment they carried.

Would we make it on time? We had already lost all the spare time that had been built in to the plan. We were literally running. Boaz and two soldiers in front, as a scouting and navigating advance team, and Eylon and Adam in the rear all understood the time constraints and were doing their best to keep us moving at top speed, as we made our way between LAF positions toward the enemy post at the top of the mountain.

Ambush!

"Gal, stop! Now!"

What was this? It wasn't coming from our internal communication, but from the FCG in Israel. I was still running, bypassing another boulder and leaping over a cluster of thorns.

"Gal, this is Nahum, stop where you are!" Colonel Nahum Lev was the commander of the Air Force special operations headquarters and my CO. I highly regarded him, although we had our differences.

I was very angry. Why was he making me stop? Had he any idea how pressed we were for time? But I forced myself to relax and think. Of course he knew. Nahum's voice was confident and calm, but I sensed a worried tone and thought that he might know something that we did not.

I raised my left hand. The operators froze and then dispersed, disappearing into the bushes. They were probably relieved, using the precious moments to catch their breath.

"What happened?" I asked Nahum.

"Ambush straight ahead, a few dozen meters, don't move, Gal!" Nahum instructed, almost pleading. A rush of cold sweat came over me.

I looked around and although I could see nothing suspicious, I knew that at headquarters they had a wide variety of sensors at their disposal, and one of them must have spotted the threat. Probably the LAF, having heard the helicopters earlier, had decided to take initiative.

I asked the commanders to join me quietly and consulted with them. I very much value a variety of opinions, although as a commander, I will always bear the loneliness of the ultimate decision.

"Without opposition," I used to say, "my decision-making process is not complete."

After a short consultation, I decided to proceed. Boaz would circumvent the ambush with his advance team, identify the enemy, and find an alternative route for us to follow. Dedication to the mission – this was our way.

I briefed the operators on the new route. They had all learned the way by heart, and would be surprised if we made an alteration without telling them. I then updated Nahum on my plan.

"Stand by," he said. I knew all the senior service commanders were by his side, and they were probably debating the issue. "The CGS is probably waking Minister of Defense Rabin," I thought, but then concluded that he probably had not slept that night.

While we waited for approval, I reorganized the force structure and briefed the other three team commanders over the radio about our route change. Tzur was already observing the guards at our target, and Dror was watching the compound from a different angle.

"Gal, it's a go," Nahum said, "but will you make it in time?"

I stood up and motioned the force to follow me.

"I'm on the move," I answered, avoiding a direct answer to his question. I did not share my doubts with Nahum. They all knew the timeline and how marginal it was, and anyway, I didn't want to overload the commanders at headquarters with all the peripheral coordination going on.

I thought of the various elements that had been put in place to assist us, including Ohad and his reinforcement team, who were surely airborne from the moment the enemy ambush was discovered. They were to circle over the Hula Valley and be ready for immediate intervention if necessary. They were reservists, the best of the best, and there was no force I would want more to come to our assistance, if it came to that.

We moved quietly in a circular pattern, up a thorny hill and around the enemy position, following Boaz's newly defined route.

"Boaz, stop." From our elevated position on a hill, I had seen something, using night-vision goggles, that made my blood freeze. Just a few dozen meters below us, a large enemy force was arranging itself for an ambush. Adam came to me and we both observed in silence, keeping low so as not to stand out in the skyline. He winked and I motioned with my head to indicate forward movement. We proceeded silently, distancing ourselves from the enemy ambush and trying not to lose precious time. We reached the first of three roads to be crossed, and did so easily, after positioning right and left cover elements in case a car came.

"Gal," an operator ran up and patted me on the shoulder, "stop."

"What is it now?"

"Roi sprained his ankle."

Just what we needed. The doctor quickly applied a compression wrap, and Roi's gear was taken by Adam without a word. As he hoisted the backpack I thought, *Oh, my God, he is now carrying more than 130 pounds!*

Roi was helped to his feet, and he motioned me with a nod that he was OK.

"What do you think, Doc?" I whispered.

"He'll hobble along with us, there's simply no choice," the doctor answered. I seriously considered leaving him behind with a small detachment, but knew this would complicate the mission and put headquarters under more pressure. Besides, Roi was an important operator, even with a limp, having a designated job to perform at the target.

We moved on, traversing hills and valleys and another road, after waiting for an enemy patrol to pass. We finally arrived at the "Motel" – a nickname we gave the foot of the cliff where our dangerous climb began. From this point we would now be observed by Tzur and Dror's forces, allowing them to secure and alert us if threats emerged.

We were a full hour behind schedule, and it was apparent by now that we would not be able to fully implement the plan. Change was inherent to the battlefield, as I learned in the paratroopers and taught in Shaldag. There is a constant need to improvise and persist with bold daring in fulfilling a mission.

I decided to cancel our scheduled rest before the climb. "They will make it," I thought. I had put them through very rigorous training in the last few months and I believed in them. *But is this responsible?* an inner voice asked. *They are not supermen. What if they collapse? What if their fatigue reduces their abilities? What if they pant, moan, or move rocks, and expose us as we approach the target?*

Dedication to the mission, another steady voice kept saying. *You don't return without carrying out the mission.*

Reach a decision, I pushed myself. No time, but rest is needed physiologically.

The enemy at the target must be alert, after hearing the helicopters in the beginning of the night and having already prepared an ambush for us. What else was waiting for us along the way?

"Moving on," I announced. "Tzur," I called over the radio, "keep an eye on us, will you?"

"You got it."

"We're going in faster than planned. Alert us if there's any movement of vehicles or guards. Nahum, we're at the Motel," I reported.

"Great!" came his enthusiastic answer, with joyous cries in the background, "very good." They seemed relieved, but I wondered if they remembered that the Motel only seemed close to the target but was actually a long and dangerous climb away.

"Are you crazy?" was the first response from Boaz, back when he had first seen my plan to approach the target this way.

No, I wasn't crazy. "It's not enough to attack them from afar," I insisted. We needed to reach the target and attack them from within. This would surprise and overwhelm them, reduce their self-confidence, and make them invest more energy in defense – ultimately resulting in fewer attacks on our forces.

I was very pleased when, after many meetings and heightened debates, the operation was finally approved.

Now Boaz was leading the force that penetrated the compound so skillfully. "What an amazing guy," I thought to myself.

"Nahum, this is Gal. Requesting assistance. We'll be acting fast due to time constraints, so we might be detected. I'll need fighter jets on immediate call for assistance."

"You got it."

It relieved me to know we had this backup at hand.

"One minute to rest," I told my men, "then we start climbing." We secured the dressing on Roi's sprained ankle, fastened the harnesses, and signaled Tzur that we were on the move.

"I have visual," he reported. "You look awesome," he added in his usual sarcastic way.

"OK, youngsters – here we go." I took out my compass. Together with Boaz and his navigators, we decided on the best route and began climbing.

This is mighty steep. Who was the crazy one that decided to do this? I thought cynically. *And at my age!*

The doctor and I were the oldest in the unit – "the golden age generation," as the young operators used to call us. Still, I set myself a rigorous daily training routine of both physical and combat training, and insisted on following it despite my busy schedule as the unit commander. Having a family was yet another constraint on my time, but it was very important for me to keep in shape and keep up with the younger operators.

I had made new regulations for physical and combat fitness in the unit, and established an Operator Physical Training that took place every Sunday at 11 AM, attended only by qualified operators who had graduated the course. It was an exhausting three hours, but this eventually became a permanent unit tradition of unification and integration. Throughout the week, personal and team training took place, and teams in preparation for a mission entered a designated and robust training routine, supervised by doctors, nutritionists, and physiologists.

Now I knew that the rigorous training had prepared these men for the challenge ahead, and I was confident that they would succeed in climbing the cliff and performing well under these harsh conditions. I knew they would be able to aim their weapons and hit the target accurately with the first bullet, even if they were out of breath, and I trusted them to make the right decisions under extreme pressure.

What made us a special unit was the combination of excellent people, superb weapons and equipment, strong unit spirit and traditions, and very high combat fitness.

We continued climbing, racing against time. When we were already inside the compound, the advance team stopped and Boaz motioned me to come to him. Faced with two very similar navigational points, he was not sure which one to choose. I understood his dilemma and took out my compass.

I had learned very early on that in critical navigation points, it was important to verify the azimuth, not only en route to the target, but in close proximity to it as well. We many times invest a lot of energy learning how to find the target area, but miss important features allowing us to navigate within the compound itself – and this is a mistake, for there lies the main purpose of the whole mission.

I checked my compass. "There, I think," I pointed.

Boaz nodded in agreement, and then added, "Thank you."

Tzur came on the radio and warned us that guards were approaching from the left. We froze. "OK, they turned away," said Tzur, so I gave the order to proceed.

"There's another one to your right." This time it was Dror, watching another segment of the compound. Again we stopped.

"Gone," reported Dror, allowing us to move forward.

While on the move and breathing heavily, I briefed Guy, a talented young team leader, whose mission was to secure the sapper team as they laid the explosive charges inside the compound and to warn them if threats emerged, neutralizing guards as a last resort. Guy confirmed that he understood. He would cover from the right, Adam took the left, and I covered from the center.

Now we faced another problem. An elevated mound near the junction we were to mine and booby-trap had been marked as a "possible bunker" by the photographic interpreters. As we approached it, there was no doubt – there was a big black entrance to a bunker, overlooking our main target. I consulted with Boaz, drew my silenced Beretta pistol, and said, "Let's go just you and I." We ordered the force to stay there, and crawled up the dirt embankment toward the entrance. Boaz kept pushing ahead of me, trying to be first in order to protect me, but I insisted on leading.

I would later be criticized for this by officers in the unit: "The unit commander should not be first in the line of fire in a case like this."

Let Me Do the Job!

We reached the bunker and Boaz peeked in, finding it to be more like a concrete cubbyhole than a bunker, with no one inside. But there was combat equipment on the floor, so we expected that sooner or later enemy fighters might return.

"Come on, Boaz, get everyone here and let's get to work," I patted him on the shoulder. "And hurry up, we haven't much time." The horizon was already showing vague signs of grayish first light. I was worried and knew that headquarters were extremely concerned, too.

"Gal, this is Nahum."

"Nahum, this is Gal, go ahead," I answered, knowing what was coming next.

"You are not going to make it in time for extraction, it's almost dawn."

Nahum spoke softly, but I could sense the tension in his voice. I knew he must be under much pressure from top brass.

"Nahum, I know it's late, but we will execute the mission. Plan on getting us out of here at the break of dawn," I said, doing my best to persuade him, as I saw my men working feverishly, digging in the hard soil and concealing the mines and charges.

"Gal, a guard is approaching from the left," Tzur whispered over the radio.

"Guy, be ready to take him out quietly."

Boaz heard this conversation and immediately concealed himself on the side of the road, ready for engagement with the enemy, or preferably letting him pass.

The work had been stopped, hints of grayish first light were increasing in the east, and my heart was pounding violently.

I am not returning without performing the mission, I thought.

"Gal from Nahum." I delayed answering.

"Gal from Nahum," came another, more emphatic call.

"Go ahead."

"Abort mission. Disengage from the target. Repeat – abort mission."

I was shocked and felt a chill come over me.

"Gal, the guard is getting close," Tzur warned. I alerted the operators and prepared my weapon.

"Nahum, let me do the job!" I begged. "We will make it on time to the extraction point. Besides, we took this scenario into consideration during our contingency planning, so I can implement the preplanned solutions. Let me do the job!"

I knew he wasn't the one making the decisions, and understood the pressure everyone must be under, having a small force in the heart of an enemy compound, under such extreme danger and marginal conditions, with nighttime running out and a soldier with a sprained ankle.

Oded's voice came on the radio and reported that vehicles were approaching his position and that he was planning to disengage, but also preparing for the possibility of engagement. That's all we needed.

I listened as he gave short and precise orders to his men, as well as coordinated with fighter pilots circling over the Mediterranean in case they were needed. I did not interfere – if he needed me, he would say so. Although they were only eight operators, they were – in Shaldag terms –a proficient and lethal fighting force.

"Gal, did you hear me?" Nahum demanded.

"I heard you, but still I . . ."

Boaz looked at me and motioned with his hand: *What should I do?* He had heard the order to abort, and understood the pressure I was under and the responsibility I bore. I touched my helmet with a clenched fist, signaling him to approach, and he quickly crawled to me.

"Hurry up and get the job done," I told him. "Guy will take down the guards if they get close, and we will hide their bodies on the side of the road. In the meantime you lay all the mines and charges as fast as you can, and then we will run to the closest extraction point."

As I said "run," I thought of the steep cliff and heavy brush on the way down, while navigating a completely new route. And we had the guards to deal with, and Oded, and Nahum pressuring over the radio. This was going to be tough.

Tzur and Dror watched us silently from their positions. Surely they, too, understood what was at stake and were under immense pressure, as was the entire unit's staff at the headquarters, and the rescue team inside the helicopter circling over the Hula Valley, ready to enter and assist us.

I was tired and sweaty, and felt the heavy burden of responsibility and accountability – to my commanders, to my men, to the mission, and for a fraction of a second to Donna and Meori. Donna had surely stayed up all night at our home at the Air Force base, waiting to hear the sound of the Yasurs bringing us home and dreading the sound of attack helicopters scrambled to assist, or utility helicopters sent to evacuate casualties.

"Gal from Nahum, abort mission, repeat, abort mission. That's an order!"

Boaz glanced at me again, while frantically digging into the stubborn soil.

How much longer? I asked him, using hand signals.

Fifteen to twenty minutes, he signaled back.

"Nahum, I need five minutes." Was I being disobedient, untrustworthy? Was I crossing the line of infidelity? Or was I upholding a sacred principle by which I was educated, and which I instilled in my soldiers and cadets at Bahad 1: devotion to the mission. *We do not return without performing the mission.*

"Gal, only five minutes and you're out of there," Nahum said.

I sent Adam from his position to assist Boaz, leaving one operator protecting the southern flank.

"What's with the guard, Tzur?"

"Standing still at the moment."

"Oded, how are you doing?"

"Still preparing here. I will report."

"Dror, report."

"A group of enemy fighters are convening in a parking lot with a few vehicles. Still heightened alert at the LAF positions: there's a tank moving and an antiaircraft gun turning."

It seemed that everyone was on high alert.

"Tzur, cover me on the way down as you did on the way up. We will be moving fast, unprotected. Bring in fighter jets and attack helicopters if necessary."

"Roger that," he answered calmly.

"Dror, prepare to attack any terrorists who attempt to move into or toward the compound. If I get into trouble or get stuck on the way to the LZ, you assist me with observation reporting and with fires."

"Got it," Dror whispered. Why was he whispering? I wondered if he saw someone approaching but avoided telling me, not wishing to add to my pressure. He had earlier entered the area professionally and quietly with a small team, and was now injecting vital information and protecting me from the north.

I was full of appreciation toward him, and toward Tzur, Oded, Doron, and the operators with me. A wave of warmth and love came over me.

"Gal from Oded, mission completed, enemy moving away, I am preparing my systems and about to make my way out. You won't be coming my way anymore."

"Good job," I said. "Prepare for independent disengagement."

"Gal, Nahum." My five minutes were up. "Abort mission immediately. Get out of there." I assumed that Nahum had been criticized for the extension he gave, and I also knew that we needed more time if we were to complete the mission.

My mind was calculating how to disengage, descend the cliff, cross the roads on the way, and reach the extraction point before daylight was upon us. At this point I decided not to answer Nahum in the following few minutes, fully aware that this was a severe and serious decision.

"Gal from Nahum. Abort mission," Nahum pleaded with me, but I did not answer, thinking that Nahum knew very well why. I decided to complete the mission, assuming that my plan was good and that I would make it on time for extraction at daybreak. I also fully trusted my forces, knowing that I would receive their utmost support. I also felt that I could count on the entire Air Force to assist, if necessary.

I fully comprehended the complications and consequences should my plan fail, and acknowledged that I was alone in taking this decision. There was no way I could share all my thoughts and considerations with headquarters.

I was fully aware that everyone was furious with me, and assumed that I would later pay a heavy personal price for this, but I felt confident with my decision. We were going to complete our mission. I did not have to take responsibility – for I had never given it away.

Time was ticking by, and the last checks were performed to see that all was in place and ready for activation.

Nahum wasn't calling me anymore, perhaps because he understood by now that I wasn't going to give up. I imagined that planning was underway for a big rescue operation.

Boaz came toward me, breathing heavily, followed by the entire sapper team.

"We're done."

"Show me five safety catches." This was a preplanned protocol we had set, for verification that all mines and charges were armed and ready.

Boaz exposed the five pins attached to ribbons with phosphorous numbers on them.

"Excellent. Two minutes for wrap-up. Guy and Eylon, approach."

The outskirt security team converged as we prepared for movement and made sure everyone was accounted for.

"Take everything from Roi except his Micro-Uzi."

"Gal, all clear," Tzur reported.

"Very good, moving out, heading to Mango LZ."

Mission Accomplished

Mango was relatively close, but required traversing rough terrain. We moved fast, navigating from memory, without opening maps.

"Oded, prepare for independent exit. Dror and Tzur, wait for me." Then I spoke to the commander of the rescue team in the circling helicopter: "On the move, leaving the compound, heading down fast."

I assumed that all other aerial assets were in place and eager to get us out safely.

"Noam," I called the Apache lead pilot, who was escorting the Yasur.

"Noam here. Go ahead."

"I'm running downward. Be ready to suppress enemy fire if we encounter trouble. Be advised: LZ changed to Mango."

"Wilco."

"Itay, do you copy?"

"Loud and clear, Gal." I could hear the sound of his rotor and knew he was airborne.

"Thirty minutes to Mango. Let's take the Alon route on the way out. Send your number 2 to get Oded."

"All taken care of. We are a formation of three. I'm coming to get you, and two and three will get the other forces."

I smiled as I ran, thinking how Nahum had implemented our contingency plans to the letter, just as we had practiced during the rehearsal.

"Nahum," I said heavily into the mic, but then I stopped, caught my breath, and said in a calm, clear voice: "Nahum from Gal."

Mofaz had taught us as young paratrooper company commanders that if you sound stressed and out of breath, it reflects negatively at headquarters and conveys a sense of losing control. "Speak in a pleasant voice," he demanded, "and resonate calmness."

"Go ahead, Gal," Nahum answered quietly. Was he angry? Or was he perhaps appreciative?

"Mission accomplished. We've been moving for ten minutes, running."

"Where exactly are you?" demanded Nahum, sounding a bit annoyed.

"Running like crazy up hills and down gullies," I answered humorously.

It was actually a pretty accurate description, for we were running over steep terrain, trying as much as possible to avoid thorny brush, occasionally falling and rising again. I was in the lead, navigating with Boaz, followed by the rest of the force, breathing hard.

My load was heavy, I didn't have enough air, nor enough light, and sweat was dripping down into my eyes, obstructing my vision. I was getting scratched from branches and thorns.

Suddenly someone spotted movement and we all froze, until it was declared a false alarm and we resumed our crazed run.

"Where in God's name is that LZ?"

By my calculations, it should have been right there on that ridge. A combined team of photographic interpreters, geologists, botanists, and pilots had designated the spot that ensured safe landing of the Yasur that was to take us home.

Home – what a sweet word.

During long nights of strenuous training, as we snuck by villages with blackened faces, straining under heavy loads, I would look at cars driving by and lights from houses, and think how unaware all those people were as to who was out here and what they were going through.

I swore that I would always remember this when I was fortunate enough to cuddle under a blanket during a cold night, or kiss my daughter as she slept peacefully. I would think of those who were out there in the dark and cold, tired and hungry, wet from rain and sweat, marching, climbing, hiding, their hearts beating fast and their emotions overflowing, whether from fear or longing to be home.

Boaz gave me the signal. I made two verification fixes with my compass. This was it.

"Nahum, we are at Mango."

"OK," he answered dryly.

"Itay, Gal." No answer.

"Itay, Gal, do you read me?" Still nothing.

I tried another radio and still received no reply. It was already daybreak.

Suddenly, I could feel it. You can sense the vibration of the huge rotor of the Yasur in your guts, before actually hearing it.

But why wasn't Itay answering me? Suddenly heavy gunfire exploded all around us. We dropped to the ground as the sky above was covered with green and red streaks of tracer bullets.

"Adam, to me." Adam leaped toward me. "Is everyone OK?" I asked, while verifying that I wasn't hit.

"Yes. It doesn't seem to be directed at us. As usual, they heard the helicopter and opened fire," Adam assessed correctly.

I raised myself enough to look around, and shuddered to see heavy fire from antiaircraft guns, right on our exit route, shooting in all directions.

The Alon route, which I had designated as the preferred exit route, was now seriously threatened.

"Itay," I tried again, "Itay, we cannot take Alon out! Do you copy?"

I could feel the vibration becoming stronger, but still there was no answer. I did hear a different pilot speaking to another ground force, but couldn't make out who it was.

I understood that Itay must have a communications malfunction, but trusted that he would arrive and take us. There was no time for inquiries with headquarters, as it was a matter of seconds.

"Prepare to board the Yasur. Adam, you count the operators on the ramp, while I run to the cockpit to alert them on the threatened exit route."

"Understood," Adam said.

I looked at my men, who were no doubt exhausted after the swift run through the brush, and I couldn't believe my eyes. They were recumbent on their backs, like overturned turtles, as if detached from the dramatic rescue that we were seconds away from.

What's going on here? What happened to operational alertness and peripheral protection? I ran toward them, furious. "On your feet, sluggards!" I snapped, surprising even myself with the harsh words I had uttered. They looked at me in shock at my aggression. I would later receive much criticism from operators who felt I was being too strict and unsupportive. But now they quickly responded, rolled over, and assumed operational mode.

The mission wasn't over yet. This was enemy territory, and it was a very dangerous and sensitive situation. We still needed to board the helicopter under heavy fire and make it out safely, while flying through dense antiaircraft gunfire.

Suddenly the shadow of the Yasur emerged from the ravine, creeping upward at a very low altitude. Its deafening noise pounded us, and we were bathed with dust as Itay put it down precisely on the designated spot.

I ran up the ramp and through the cabin, as Adam positioned himself on the ramp and began his head count. Assuming the helicopter had some kind of electrical malfunction, I didn't try the intercom, but grabbed Itay's helmet and screamed into his ear: "Don't take Alon out! Change route!" Itay raised his thumb and nodded.

The helicopter was usually dark during missions, but this time even the cockpit instrument lights were out. It was true – they had a total electrical failure. Itay had flown in to get us, risking himself and his crew, without navigational systems or radios, when he could have easily reported his malfunction and asked to be replaced by a backup helicopter. I felt a wave of warmth, from awe and appreciation.

The Yasur took off, and three operators took positions as gunners at the windows and the ramp. The airborne mechanic handed me a headset and I put it on.

"Itay?" I understood that the intercom must be working on the backup batteries.

"Hi, Gal, we don't have electricity so we're navigating without a navigation system and we have no communications. I understood not to take Alon, but we're not heading out anyway."

"What? Why?"

"Our number three had a malfunction so we need to get part of Oded's force. The first half was taken by number two."

"Way to go!" I complimented him.

We were flying low, and Itay was maneuvering the helicopter aggressively in order to dodge the bursts of antiaircraft fire all around us.

We were searching for a signal indicating the location of Oded and his four-man team, alone in enemy territory.

"I have a visual!" I heard the copilot call out. "Nine o'clock, four hundred meters." Itay turned sharply to the left and pitched up for a short final. Bullets flew all around us. I could see my soldiers were sitting on their helmets, for improved bottom protection.

It was a fast approach and landing, the airborne mechanic opening the ramp even before we touched down. Out of the darkness, Oded's operators came charging in, almost overrunning my men, who retracted inward, toward the cockpit, to make room for them.

"Inside, go!" the airborne mechanic reported, and we were jolted as the Yasur took off in a steep climb upward, at four thousand feet per minute.

"Great maneuver," I said, impressed.

"We're taking a high route back, out of effective range of antiaircraft fire, so it will take a bit longer," Itay apologized. I just wanted to hug him.

We talked about what had happened as we headed out west, over the Mediterranean. From the window, I could see the dim green lights of the Apache formation, led by Noam.

When we crossed the coastline, I let out a sigh of relief.

"Good job!" I congratulated the helicopter crew.

"No, you guys did a good job," answered Itay.

The lights of Israel could be seen in the distance, as Itay updated me that he had received an order to take me directly to the forward headquarters, and not home to the unit.

I understood what this meant. I was going to be rebuked for not aborting the mission as ordered. Or maybe – the thought crossed my mind – this was going to be more than just a reprimanding, but the end of my career. This would not be the first or last time that I was fully aware of this possibility, but I believe that there are decisions a leader must make that are worth such a sacrifice.

The CGS Is Waiting

The helicopter touched down. It felt so good to step out onto Israeli soil, in full daylight. I asked Adam to oversee the return home to the unit, where they would unpack, resume operational status, and catch some rest before initiating the debriefing and lessons-learned process.

I was originally supposed to join them for a short time at the unit, and then return to NORTHCOM to continue controlling our deployed forces, but was now directly taken to the forward headquarters.

On the outskirts of the landing pad, two brigadier generals shook my hand and said, "The CGS is waiting for you." I thought they both looked at me in a strange way, but I couldn't interpret what it meant. My face was blackened with makeup and I was filthy, smelly, and all scratched up.

"Wait a minute," I said, and stepped aside, removed the clip from my rifle, and cocked it to remove the round chambered in the barrel. I did the same with my pistol, then jumped into the car and said, "Let's go."

The CGS, LTG Amnon Lipkin-Shahak, looked up at me as I entered the brightly lit room. Beside him sat NORTHCOM commander MG Amiram Levin, his face revealing no emotion. Nahum and Herzl were absent, so I assumed they must still be in the operations room. But Colonel Eliezer Shkedi, head of the operations department, was there as the Air Force representative.

The CGS spoke first and began peppering me with harsh questions, mostly on why I did not abort as ordered. "It was that close to a major rescue operation," he remonstrated.

Amiram said nothing. Did he support me?

"I don't understand all this pressure!" I counterattacked. "We had a few more minutes of darkness to spare, and managed to complete the mission. Worst-case scenario, we could have hidden and waited for extraction the following night."

The CGS opened his mouth to speak, probably to scold me, but the door flung open and Nahum appeared.

"Come to the operations room!" he said, excited. "They're triggering the mines – we're seeing significant results. Our forces are attacking. You should come and see this."

As everyone jumped up and hurried out, Shkedi slapped me on the back of my neck, and Nahum winked. I remained sitting, stunned, my heart pounding. It crossed my mind that this might be what divine intervention looks like.

There would still be an incisive debriefing, where I would be criticized and reprimanded for "disappearing" off the radio channel, not sticking to the schedule, and disregarding the "abort" command.

But after the harsh words, the CGS would praise the actions of the force, the high professional level, the determination and devotion to the mission, and high combat fitness.

When he ended with "Well done," I breathed a sigh of relief.

I imagined what Amnon was going through. On the one hand, he needed to relate strongly to my violation of procedure, but on the other hand, he wanted to commend the importance of devotion to the mission. He had found the appropriate way to express his leadership while combining both messages.

LTG Amnon Lipkin-Shahak passed away in 2012. He is dearly remembered and honored by all as a unique and inspirational leader.

My attention now shifted to a new and challenging mission – the birth of our second child.

Born on a Full Moon

Donna was pregnant again. Combat officers are not always there at the right time, so it had taken six years of anticipation. We were very happy.

When Donna was eight months pregnant, I began to be very worried that I might miss my baby's birth because I was spending long nights away from home on missions across the border.

I expressed these concerns to one of the doctors in the unit.

"I have to be with Donna. I can't miss it."

"We will take care of it," he said. "Don't worry."

Shaldag has more than twenty reserve doctors, and they are Israel's finest, from a variety of medical fields. They are an extraordinary group of talented, capable, friendly, and brave professionals.

Donna and I went to Tel Hashomer Hospital to talk to the surgeon. Donna was in favor of a C-section because the first time with Meori had been complicated, and she didn't want to take any risks.

A group consultation addressed the situation and came up with a solution.

Dr. Korach said that we would perform a C-section at a time suitable operationally. Meori had also been born via C-section, so there was no reason not to proceed this way.

We opened a calendar with moon phases and scheduled the procedure for a full-moon night, thus minimizing the chances of me being away on a mission. It was also decided that two doctors from our unit would perform the C-section.

It became not only a family but a unit effort, giving the term "military life" a unique and deep perspective.

My daughter Ofri was born on a full-moon night. The first moon after the operation.

Chapter 6

From Within and Without

Earthquake

The Oslo Accord signed in 1993 was an attempt to resolve the Israeli-Palestinian conflict by recognizing the PLO as the legitimate representative of the Palestinian people and establishing an interim self-governing authority. The IDF withdrew from parts of Gaza and J&S, and Yasser Arafat's armed forces took control. The Israeli public was divided in accepting the process, which was a complete change in Israeli policy, negating any dialogue with the PLO terror organization. The fact that terror attacks increased throughout the negotiations and implementation contributed to the strong criticism of Yitzhak Rabin. The Israeli public was, and still is, torn between a deep and genuine wish for peace and an equally genuine wish to avoid the associated heavy price in concessions and security risks.

It was a rare evening of quiet, quality family time in our home on the base. The next morning I was to begin the brigade commanders' course. I had no idea how it would be possible to combine commanding the unit with the demanding curriculum of the course, but my superiors insisted.

"Start it, and if it doesn't work out – stop. The unit is first priority."

Meori was sleeping, and Donna and I were sitting on the rug, watching television. Outside, the sound of a landing helicopter muffled the steady beat of the sprinkler on the lawn.

At Kikar Malchei Yisrael in Tel Aviv there was a big rally in support of peace, attended by Prime Minister Yitzhak Rabin. I had heard that a few soldiers from the unit were participating.

Suddenly the regular TV broadcast was interrupted by confused and anxious reports.

"Shots fired at the square!"

"Rabin was unharmed," a woman was heard describing what had happened.

"There were gunshots but they missed," a reporter said.

Donna and I looked at each other in concern and disbelief.

A terror attack in the heart of Israel, I thought. Was it Hamas or Islamic Jihad? My mind was taking the obvious course. At first the reports were vague and even optimistic.

An unidentified extremist Jewish organization announced, "Next time we won't miss." But then there was: "The prime minister has been hit and he was taken to Ichilov Hospital in Tel Aviv."

I tried to collect information from the unit.

"Does anybody know what's going on? Do we have anyone at the square who can report?"

But we soon learned that Rabin had in fact been shot. Then came a dramatic announcement by the prime minister's bureau chief, Eitan Haber: "The government of Israel announces in consternation, in great sadness, and in deep sorrow, the death of Prime Minister and Minister of Defense Yitzhak Rabin, who was murdered by an assassin, tonight in Tel Aviv. May his memory be blessed."

We were both in total shock. Donna burst into tears and I covered my face with my hands.

Oh, my God – It was a Jewish, not an Arab assassin.

"Why couldn't they save him?" Donna cried out. "How can this be?"

Silence. Shock. Tears.

"What are we going to tell Meori?" she asked. "How can a child grasp such a thing?"

I called my deputy who lived next door.

"Adam, let's meet outside."

"What a blow, ah?" Adam said.

We stood under a lamppost, and I remember wondering how the sprinklers could go on with their clatter after such an earthquake.

"Adam, get down to the unit and issue orders for an early briefing tomorrow morning. We are going to be needed. There could be ripple effects from either Jewish extremists or terror organizations. There will of course be a funeral and the ISA Personal Security Unit will surely need reinforcement. So get down there and I'll join you shortly."

"You got it," Adam answered, walking toward the parking lot.

I went back inside as Channel 2's anchorman looked at his watch and said: "It is five minutes past eleven. Prime Minister Rabin has been assassinated. Also we here at the studio need to collect ourselves."

On screen there were photos from various points in Rabin's life. I couldn't believe it.

Yitzhak Rabin had been the minister of defense since I was a company commander, and I felt great appreciation and respect for him. He was extremely involved and used to come out to visit us in the field, knew minute details, and asked very good questions.

I trusted him. He had a unique connection with commanders and expressed not only genuine interest, but in-depth understanding. Above all, he demonstrated full support and backing for us, the field commanders.

In the morning, Donna woke up little Meori and tried to explain to her what had happened.

"What is 'murdered'?" she asked, stunned. "Why? And why didn't they take care of him? And who did it? The enemy?"

In the briefing room at the unit, all gathered in silence, officers and soldiers, operators and administrative personnel. I was not surprised to see many reservists who had come just to hear my morning briefing.

"What is to become of us?" I thought to myself. "What is to become of this country?"

I took my position at the podium, breathed deeply, and began.

"My prime minister was murdered. Rabin the minister, CGS, warrior, and friend..." My voice broke. I was silent for a moment and continued.

"This cannot happen to us. We cannot accept intolerance. If it happened last night, it can happen again. We will deal with every expression of violence, social and political. We will not allow subversion; we will not accept intolerance."

Throughout my career, I always addressed my unit as the direct representative of the prime minister himself. I thought it was my duty to reflect national-level directive and vision. Now the historic significance of the tragedy was clear, and I didn't know what ripple effects it might have. In the state of shock we were all in, there were unit commanders debating if life should or could go on. Air Force squadron commanders were asking whether they should take off for training missions.

I gave guidelines and orders for the day and talked about my prediction as to our assignments in the coming days. It was important for me to avoid a sense of vacuum, so I assigned officers to lead various missions and set a time-table for completion. I knew that as a leader, it was essential that I maintain continued movement and directionality. This was much needed in all times of uncertainty, certainly in a situation as crazy as this.

I drove to Glilot for the opening session of the brigade commanders' course. As I entered the main hall, a newspaper headline struck me: "Rabin Assassinated!" I felt as though it had slammed me back against the wall. It was as if I hadn't really absorbed it until seeing it in writing.

BG Efi Eitam, an instructor in the course, spoke: "Tough day, moving on." Then he did just that, and began briefing about the course.

Too fast, I thought, *at least for me.*

Someone shoved a note into my hand: "Call Air Force headquarters."

The Saddest Mission

Someone on the other side of the line briefed me concisely: "The funeral is tomorrow. Attendees are arriving from all over the world. Your unit will run the operation of flying them all from Ben-Gurion Airport to Jerusalem, and you will assist the ISA with personal security. Air Force operations branch chief will set up a headquarters on the roof of the Hilton. You are to coordinate with the Ministry of Foreign Affairs and other agencies. Recruit reservists if you need. Good luck."

I was on my way out when I got called to the course commander, MG Ivry Sukenik.

"You got orders?"

"I have."

"If we failed in protecting the PM, anything can happen. Do it right."

"Clear, thank you," I said, and hurried out.

Over VHF radio, I asked the unit headquarters to arrange for a helicopter to Jerusalem and to be joined by the operations officer. I also gave Adam preliminary instructions, covering various operational and ceremonial aspects, such as what uniform each team would wear. Our usual class B uniform would be fine for behind-the-scenes work, but those of us who would come in direct contact with heads of state should don class A.

"Get on the phone and call in bilingual reservists who also know their way around Jerusalem."

A Bell 206 Sayfan helicopter was waiting at Sde Dov Air Force Base. We flew to Jerusalem, where I searched from the air for appropriate landing sites that could be used for the large-scale flight operations scheduled to take place. I chose the YMCA, hospital landing pads, Beitar soccer stadium, and others. While still airborne, I relayed various instructions to the unit headquarters.

I understood that under my command was a large-scale logistical and security operation, involving numerous VIP delegations from around the world.

I gave special attention to command and control, by having all elements on a combined radio network and positioning a forward-deployed headquarters at Shaare Zedek Hospital, manned by representatives of all agencies involved. This site would also serve as the main landing pad, due to its proximity to Israel's national cemetery at Mount Herzl, where the funeral was to take place.

The idea was to disperse the landings as much as possible and have landing teams, security details, and snipers positioned at every landing location. We would also call in counterterror teams from Shaldag (the counterterror unit) and public order units. All areas around the landing pads would be combed by the police.

I scheduled a briefing for 5:00 PM, after which everyone would be flown to Jerusalem. I wanted all teams to deploy throughout the night and make the appropriate preparations before morning, when VIP delegations from all over the world would land at Ben-Gurion Airport and be shuttled by an armada of Air Force helicopters to Jerusalem.

When I landed back at the unit before the briefing, I was handed the operational order from the Air Force headquarters. The symbolic title of the operation stood out before my eyes: "Earthquake."

Morning dawned. At the soccer field at Shaare Zedek, we encountered an unexpected problem. The usher wouldn't open the gate. "What do you mean, helicopters?" he cried. "This belongs to Beitar soccer team!"

He was escorted away as we broke the locks and prepared the field. Soon after, helicopters began landing one after the other. Leaders were greeted by officers who saluted them and led them to an improvised terminal we had prepared in the locker rooms, by "remodeling" the interior walls. From there, they were escorted out to the limousines, lined up in a first-come, first-served fashion.

The prime minister of Turkey, Ms. Tansu Çiller, came running out of the helicopter and kissed a surprised Adam. This story would later be told and retold in the unit, for Adam was very proud.

"Did you see that big kiss she gave me? That wasn't just a polite kiss."

The constant influx of leaders caused a momentary loss of control in the headquarters on the roof of the Hilton.

"Who is on that helicopter that just landed?" BG Avner Naveh, head of Air Force Air Division, demanded to know.

"I really don't know. We lost control. They're simply flocking in."

"Well, ask them!"

The pilot instructed his airborne mechanic to ask his passenger for her identity.

"Excuse me, who are you?" he screamed at the distinguished-looking guest.

"I am the queen of the Netherlands!" she screamed back.

"Really?" the airborne mechanic looked surprised, and the queen nodded to assure him that she was indeed the queen. So the report went out: "We have someone who claims that she is the queen of the Netherlands."

The president of Georgia, Eduard Shevardnadze, was ushered to the locker rooms. It was getting very late, but there were no available limousines.

"How am I going to get him there?" asked the deputy minister of foreign affairs, Eli Dayan.

"Nehemiah, come here," I called to our trusty driver, who had been transporting Shaldag forces for many years in his run-down old truck. "Take Shevardnadze to Mount Herzl."

"Take who?"

"A very important man."

"No problem," Nehemiah winked, and led the president and his entourage to his truck, which was loaded with boxes and kitbags. Shevardnadze stood at the door and uttered a few sentences in Georgian. I assumed that he was not very impressed with the transportation we provided.

One of his assistants asked me something that I assumed to mean, "Is this taking us to the funeral?" so I answered, "*Da*." They all got on and Nehemiah took them to Mount Herzl.

I greeted King Hussein of Jordan with a salute. He stopped and stood at attention for a few seconds, then smiled and shook my hand warmly. A kind gesture by a king. Ehud Barak was leading him to his vehicle and grabbed me by the neck and shook my hand.

President of Egypt Hosni Mubarak came last.

"He comes only to funerals," I grumbled to my colleagues at the headquarters. I was resentful that otherwise he did not see fit to visit Israel, a country at peace with his.

"Welcome to Israel," I said sharply. With a frozen face, he shook my hand with his big hand, nodded, and entered his vehicle.

Then it was quiet. The leaders were all gone, and the soccer field was filled with silent helicopters.

"Bring all personnel out to the field," I ordered. "I want the pilots, mechanics, Shaldag operators, security detachments, and members of the Ministry of Foreign Affairs."

Minutes before the funeral was to begin, I improvised a ceremonial formation, lining up everyone without adhering to organizational affiliation or rank. My communications officer broadcasted the ceremony on Mount Herzl through the loudspeakers at the soccer field. We stood at attention facing Mount Herzl, and the officers saluted as the sound of a siren indicated the commencement of the ceremony. When the siren ended, I was overwhelmed with emotion and slipped away to my headquarters.

At Mount Herzl, CWO Yitzhak Taito, of Bahad 1, was crying for the first time during a ceremony. On the roof of the Hilton, BG Avner Naveh covered his face with his hands. When I heard Rabin's granddaughter Noa Ben-Artzi's eulogy, I could take it no more. I broke down in tears.

Earthquake.

In 2004 I inaugurated the Rabin memorial site at Bahad 1, consisting of personal photos, his life story, and a lecture hall bearing his name. I felt it was essential that the place that shapes the IDF's new leadership should be imbued with Rabin's presence and values.

I invited Dalia Rabin, Yitzhak's daughter, to the unveiling ceremony, along with the deputy minister of defense and Bedouin sheiks from the Negev. In front of all the cadets, we unveiled the plaque and planted olive trees for the memory of Yitzhak Rabin.

I ended my speech with my own twist on the words from the book of Exodus found in the Passover Haggadah: "And you shall tell your son that day, to never forget this man and his legacy, nor his assassination and the reason for it. And you shall tell your son that day, from generation to generation, for Israel's eternity."

Operation Grapes of Wrath

The everlasting tension in Lebanon violently erupted from time to time, with rockets and IEDs. Shaldag had contingency plans for when the Israeli government felt it was too much.

Generations of operators became qualified and concluded their service without carrying out these plans, and all were anxious to fulfill their mission. It was clear to all that it was a matter of time, and everyone knew from the lessons learned in Operation Accountability in 1993 that commando operations would play a significant role.

I knew we needed to take every mission, however distant or farfetched, and plan alertly with utmost seriousness. My experience has shown me that most plans are eventually actualized.

Many times, I found myself implementing preplanned scenarios, and thanking God and my talented subordinates for all our thought, preparation, and hard training, which allowed us to bring our capabilities to bear. We succeeded in being relevant. We were planning for future challenges, not wallowing in nostalgia and preparing for battles of the past.

I found myself constantly racking my brain, imagining, looking far and wide, and trying to predict or guess what the next campaign would look like and how events would unfold.

We worked in small teams, openly discussing, in a very broad and abstract way, what we could expect. We began by identifying and understanding the basic framework, analyzing the trends and potential of the rival system (that is, our enemies). From all these we built a general construct of understandings, which led to in-depth, practical military thinking. We then sat down and wrote first contingency plans, then specific orders, and finally mission briefings.

In April 1996, I was called to the Air Force headquarters in Tel Aviv. It had been very tense in the north for some time, with Katyusha rockets regularly hitting Israeli towns and villages. Time after time we had teams standing by for deployment to the northern border, expecting a large-scale operation, but they were always stood down, with no decision to act.

"A serious unit is accustomed to multiple cancellations," Nahum used to say. "That's just the way it is."

After a series of successful operations in Lebanon, including deep recon missions, we were very familiar with the terrain and the enemy's routine. We felt at home there. We had planned and trained using mockup terrain and excellent representation of the enemy. We had carefully analyzed and calculated all routes, slopes, vegetation, and terrain.

We were ready.

I received a thorough brief on the situation and was instructed to prepare internally, without calling in operators from their homes and without recruiting any reserves. But I sensed that this time it was different, so on the way back I gave instructions to call everyone, including the reserves, to come to the unit and prepare for battle.

It was the holiday of Passover, and many were planning family vacations and rest after hard and demanding work. But I felt that this was it – the government of Israel would not continue to tolerate the aggression, and would order us to covertly penetrate enemy territory and strike them as only we knew how, with sophistication and daring.

"Everyone report immediately to the unit," I ordered, and added, "Have the unit headquarters prepare all forces for takeoff."

"Wilco."

All at once, the unit was in a frenzy. All personnel were engaged in various forms of preparation. Dozens of phone calls were made, hangars sprang to life, and the air was filled with bustling sounds of laughter and excitement of operators anticipating the upcoming action.

Gunshots and various exploding sounds were heard from the nearby firing range, where our weapons were being tested and calibrated. Black drapes covered segments of the briefing rooms, due to careful attention to secrecy and compartmentalization, even within the unit. It was imperative that if operators fell into enemy hands, they could not disclose and endanger other teams.

It turned out I was right. Within a few hours, the unit headquarters received orders from above. This was it. We were activated. A short thrill of excitement was felt in my throat, my back, and my gut.

Large backpacks were carefully filled with all the fighting equipment, energy sources, and survival gear. I put special emphasis on force independence and sustainability – water, food, batteries, and ammunition.

"Gal, we have a problem."

"What is it?"

"The rabbi is all worked up."

I knew what this would be about. All IDF units observed the Jewish law of eating only matzah, an unleavened cracker-like bread, for the seven-day holiday of Passover.

"He won't allow Itach to bake bread. He wants us to take matzah on the mission. That's ridiculous!"

"Where is he?"

"Waiting for you near the unit headquarters."

On the way there, I met the first reservists who had arrived, and we exchanged greetings and pats on the shoulder.

I found the rabbi near my office, already confronted by a few young officers.

"Hello, Rabbi," I greeted him with a smile.

"Sir, please, it's Passover! You can't take bread!"

He looked very determined, and I could understand his convictions, but I was also extremely concerned as to the ramifications if we ate matzah in enemy territory.

"It'll be a mess," complained the commander of our logistics section. "We'll be leaving a trail of crumbs, it'll draw insects, and our forces will be exposed."

"Besides," added a reservist, "we will all suffer from stomachaches – not so good for operational readiness."

"Look," I said, after thinking the matter over for a few seconds. "The rabbi is perfectly right in his wish to observe Passover."

"What?" "Oh, come on!" "Really, Gal!" A chorus of angry voices erupted all around me.

"Wait," I continued. "But we also must take into account life-saving and operational considerations. So I approve buying bread in Jaffa or baking it here."

"I will take this to the chief rabbi of the Air Force!" said the angry rabbi.

"You do that," I answered him patiently, "and I will also speak to him and explain my considerations."

"And now, Itach," I turned to our cook, "please go and prepare the appropriate combat food for our operators."

Having solved this religious crisis, I called the commanders for a briefing, and shortly afterwards, our control teams were flown northward in helicopters, in order to prepare the radios, computers, and charts in our forward-deployed headquarters.

Where would I position myself? I debated. The unit was to be deployed in many teams, and if I were to join one of them, I would lose the big picture and my ability to affect the development of the battle.

"Stay at the headquarters," commanders pleaded with me. "Someone needs to synchronize it all."

"Don't disappear by joining a team," Nahum chimed in. "Just as we planned during training – you control the entire unit with all its forces."

I knew they were right, but I had never before sent soldiers into battle without me. I was criticized many times for insisting on leading missions myself.

Reason finally prevailed, but I promised myself that at the first chance I would get, I would go out with one of the forces, maybe on a specifically complicated mission.

"It's Not That I'm Scared"

I now faced a very disturbing situation.

Oval, a senior company commander, asked to speak with me urgently.

"Not now, Oval, we're really under a lot of pressure."

"It's extremely urgent, critical," he insisted.

"What is it?" I said and closed the door.

"I think we should abort my mission. It's too dangerous."

What? I was astounded. Oval was to lead a very important mission and attack a few enemy targets. The mission had been carefully analyzed, planned, trained, and rehearsed. Why was he bringing this up only now, hours before heading out?

"It's dangerous," he continued. "It's difficult to operate there, it's too close to the enemy, and it's irresponsible." Then he added, "It's not that I'm scared or anything."

I was faced with a serious dilemma. I didn't have time to make any changes. We were about to begin the final briefing, and then a helicopter was to take me to the headquarters. Soon after that, the forces would be crossing the border to their various missions.

"Oval, I can't make changes now. I trust you to carry out the mission as planned. We checked everything. The risk is reasonable, and all parameters were calculated and taken into consideration. We must carry out the mission."

"But – " he began again.

"No buts!" I was on the verge of exploding. What was going on here? I had never encountered such behavior in the unit. Could I replace him now? How would this affect the operators' morale? What impact would this have on the decision makers?

Our unit had always insisted on making courageous operational breakthroughs. It had taken time and many successful missions to build up our self-confidence, and the leadership's confidence in us to use our capabilities. I was concerned that this might set us back and shatter what we had worked so hard to achieve.

"Head out and perform your mission!"

Oval left the room, and I remained there a few more seconds before exiting. I walked over to where Oval's operators were preparing their gear and called his deputy, Guy.

Guy was a young and sharp-witted officer, and I trusted him.

"Guy, I want you to make sure that the mission is completed, is that clear?"

"Of course," he answered, puzzled at my unexpected request.

"You are heading out to a long period of fighting, where you will surely encounter difficulties and changes along the way. I want you to fulfill the mission, no matter what."

"Don't worry," he smiled, tight-lipped as usual.

I was extremely worried, but had no more time to deal with it. I gathered the commanders for final briefings, collected my personal gear, and headed out to the helicopter that would fly me up north.

My mind was filled with many stormy thoughts. I was praying, hoping, trusting, worrying, afraid, confident, and lonely – a tumultuous alloy of knowledge and emotions. That is what makes a commander.

At the forward headquarters, all was prepared and ready for action. We had practiced this so many times, it was almost automatic. At my disposal were communication links to other ground forces, artillery, fighter planes, attack helicopters, assault helicopters, Navy ships, unmanned aerial vehicles (UAVs), intel assets, and rescue forces. It was like conducting the best orchestra a commander could ever wish for.

All forces set out to their various missions. Some were flown by helicopter, and others penetrated enemy territory on foot. All was proceeding as planned in this initial commando phase, as other IDF forces were making final preparations for the operation against terror activity from Lebanon.

A silent, tense atmosphere surrounded us at the command post, as we monitored the proceeding forces. Real-time imagery was shown on the screens in front of us, and over the radio came whispered reports of progress.

I envisioned an escalation to a wider campaign, necessitating more forces, so although Air Force headquarters had not yet approved any actions, I had arranged for supplementary teams from the unit to be recruited and prepared. I knew that a commander's challenge is to be able to identify a developing and changing environment, and adapt accordingly.

"Gal, Oval wants you on the radio."

What could he want? They should have landed and made it to their target zone.

"Gal, I can't find my designated spot. This area won't do. I'm going to a nearby LZ for extraction."

I felt dizzy with rage and astonishment, and let out a curse.

"How could this happen to us? What a disgrace. Who will deal with the operational gap in the area he is deserting? What am I going to do?" I was whispering to myself.

"Hold it together," I told myself. "You are the unit commander."

"Stand by," I said quietly into the microphone. Then I walked out, grabbed a package of halvah, sat down on the stairs, and devoured two mouthfuls of the sweet sesame confection. I was thinking fast, my heart pounding. How could he do this? Why had I been so stupid as to have sent him out on the mission?

I reentered the command post. Inside there was a commotion, with people calling out, "The Air Force commander wants you!" and "NORTHCOM commander wants you!" I returned to my seat, took the microphone, and asked everyone to quiet down.

"Tell them to relax, that I'm dealing with the situation and I will update soon."

"Oval, this is Gal, let me speak to Guy," I said, making an exceptional request. I had no choice. The clock was ticking away and morning would not wait for us.

"He's in the rear. It'll take me time to reach him." He understood that I was circumventing him.

"Let me speak to Mendi." Mendi was a former company commander in the unit, who had joined our medical department after graduating from medical school. This way we gained a doctor with vast operational experience.

I asked Mendi to describe the situation and give me his evaluation, and he did. Then I called one of our analysts and asked him to urgently review the matter with his team and figure out where the force was and how to make it to their target. He ran to the other room, and I could see them feverishly tackling the task huddled over maps and imagery. He soon returned, spread out imagery of the area, and pointed.

"There's no problem, I know what I'm doing," he said with his strong Anglo-Saxon accent. "They are here, and they have to get to here. I don't understand what the problem is!"

Neither did I. I took the microphone again and guided the force meter by meter to their destination, using the material in front of me and visualizing the terrain. Finally, after nerve-racking minutes, Oval reported, "Found it! Beginning work."

I leaned back and exhaled loudly.

Two weeks later, I was leading a small commando team on a mission in the vicinity. I couldn't resist the temptation, so I slightly changed course and navigated to the spot that Oval had not been able to find. I fell upon it precisely with ease, let out a curse, and continued on my way.

We're Ready

As anticipated, the operation continued, amidst constant Katyusha rocket fire. Although we were hitting launchers and enemy fighters, they were able to make use of the long range and small size of their rockets to quickly reposition them and avoid detection. Rockets continued to fall on Israeli citizens until the very last of the sixteen days of Operation Grapes of Wrath.

The operation led to political processes that constructed new understandings, which redefined the rules of the game in the north. When fighting guerrilla forces and terror organizations, there cannot always be a decisive outcome. A military's task is to shape facts on the ground in a way that enables the political echelons to forge new and improved arrangements, while constantly learning from past experiences and using that new knowledge to improve performance.

As the operation raged on, I kept coming up with new ideas on how to bring to bear our commando capabilities in support of the overall mission. I presented new operational plans to the NORTHCOM commander, and called in reserve operators to begin preparation.

"Gal, you are disregarding what I said," lamented Nahum. "You have no authorization to recruit reserves."

I did not answer.

"Gal?"

"I understand, Nahum. Let's talk about it later." I consulted with Itzik, our special forces doctor, who assisted me in every field.

"It's your responsibility," he said. "You are the leader."

"Continue recruiting the reserve teams," I instructed the unit headquarters. I would pay a personal price for this after the operation. A day later, our assignments were approved.

"When can you be ready?" asked the NORTHCOM commander.

"We're ready."

"How can you be ready? You must recruit your forces and prepare them."

"We already did all that," I was able to say.

"Gal, I need your help," the commander of the Air Force control cell said, showing me a place on the map. "There's a mortar or rocket launcher down in this gully, constantly targeting the city of Nahariya. We can't seem to pinpoint it."

"Let me think," I said, and convened my planning team. We stood around an aerial image of the area and brainstormed what could be done.

"We need to send a recon team down there to locate the target," I said.

"We don't have any available forces now," an officer answered. "And to prepare a new team from the unit will take another day."

"We need this done tonight," pleaded the commander. "Nahariya is being hit constantly."

I racked my brain and came up with a plan to detach two operators from one of the forces deployed deep in enemy territory, who would navigate alone to a meeting point, where they would link up with three operators from another force. Together they would form a new task force and make it down the gully to find the enemy target.

"But who will command this mission?" someone asked.

I began scanning in my mind all the commanders currently deployed in the two forces, and chose Ram, a young, decisive, thoughtful, and extremely operationally oriented officer.

COL Amos, the newly appointed commander of Air Force special forces, who was a legendary warrior and an expert in commando operations, ran over to my table, leaned toward me and said angrily, "What are you doing? How can you send these people out like that, alone, in the middle of the night, in enemy territory?"

"It's a good, feasible, plan. The operators are well trained. I know them personally and it'll work."

"What do you mean it will work? Do these soldiers have two pairs of arms and two pairs of legs? Are they not human beings?"

Everyone was looking at us, tense. I waited for a moment, and then said, "We are Shaldag. These are elite operators, and the mission will be accomplished."

Faced with my determination, Amos straightened up, thought for a moment, looked me in the eye – and approved my plan.

That night, Ram and operators from two separate forces linked up and created a new task force. They set out to their recon assignment after Ram had briefed and prepared them silently at the meeting point, and redistributed the equipment they had brought in order to optimize weight and mission readiness.

Late that morning they spotted the mortar that had been targeting Nahariya and transmitted its precise location. In collaboration with aerial assets, it was destroyed along with its operators, using creative and clever improvisation.

That very night, Ram and his men moved on to other assignments within Lebanon.

Our teams were deployed undetected in various missions, and all performed well, demonstrating creative means in overcoming challenges. Some devised original methods to destroy targets, others decided to change their positions to optimize operational efficiency. These were things we had never specifically trained for, but this was precisely what we educated special operators to do – to think creatively, plan boldly, and act independently.

To our surprise, and completely contrary to Air Force forecasts, it snowed heavily, and the operators were faced with extreme conditions for which they were not equipped.

One of the teams identified enemy forces approaching their hidden position. They had not identified the soldiers, but accidentally walked right up to their position. The operators held their fire and their breath, hoping the enemy would pass them by, but one of them stepped on Sagi's foot and found himself looking into the eyes of an Israeli soldier. Left with no choice, Sagi opened fire, taking him down and alerting his friends, who opened fire. The battle lasted no more than thirty seconds, leaving the enemy fighters dead and our operators unharmed. But the incident exposed their position, and it was now a struggle to get them out of harm's way before reinforcements arrived.

I coordinated fighter planes to attack the team's surroundings, in order to conceal their location and divert attention from the extraction efforts. UAVs were diverted in order to supply us with full coverage of the area. An attack helicopter formation flew low over the team and gave close air support. Tzvika, my neighbor from the base, led the formation, and I trusted his talent and bravery to support Boaz's team and help them to get out safely.

In one of its first operational missions in the Israeli Air Force, a Black Hawk helicopter landed and safely extracted the team, with many Air Force assets airborne, the entire unit alert, and the whole IDF watching tensely.

We then witnessed the effects this incident had on the enemy. The number of rocket launches was reduced, and movement in the area was minimized and calculated. It demonstrated the effect commando operations can have on the enemy, not only when performing covert operations, but also when acting overtly, loudly, and aggressively. A mix of overt and covert operations produces disruption and deterrence, and forces the enemy to divert more attention to defensive measures.

The operation was broadening, and the unit was now employed and deployed at full capacity. Every day, helicopters were landing on the runway at our home base, loading teams and equipment, and heading northward. Occasionally I would fly back to the unit to prepare and brief a team before a mission, and then fly back to my headquarters at NORTHCOM.

I was running many days on little sleep, relying on adrenaline and my sense of responsibility to keep me going. I was constantly engaged in planning and assessing the situation, while trying to keep two steps ahead of events: shaping reality, instead of only responding to it as things unfolded.

I was called to the phone. Oval wanted to speak to me. After returning from his previous mission, he had been operationally grounded because of the fiasco on the first night.

"Gal, don't do this to me, let me go out there. I learned my lesson!"

I had serious doubts. Should I make an example of Oval and turn him into an educational monument on how not to behave on a mission, or should I give him a second chance?

"I will consider the matter and let you know."

A few hours later, I assigned him as mission commander for the next round of activities. He performed well, completed the mission, and with that was reinstalled to his operational status in the unit.

It was times like these, of heightened operational tempo, that allowed for bridging gaps, reconstructing loyalties, and mending rifts. I recalled all the reservists whom I had suspended after the "mutiny" at the beginning of my tenure, and assigned each and every one of them to a specific responsibility. They reported immediately and were integrated in the unit activity.

Our unit was united and morale was high.

On April 18, an Israeli artillery battery returned fire toward the source of a Hezbollah rocket launching, and mistakenly hit a UNIFIL compound at the village of Qana, killing many civilians who had taken shelter there. International shock and condemnation followed, focusing on the tragic outcome, but not on the fact that Hezbollah had been firing from this area. The operation was suspended but resumed the next day.

Toward the end of the operation, and after much consideration, I decided to lead an operation myself, and assigned Mickey Edelstein to take charge in my absence. It was a long and complicated mission, and I felt I needed to both set a positive example and better understand the operational environment.

On April 27, 1996, Operation Grapes of Wrath was over, with new understandings with Hezbollah bringing another period of relative calm, until the next time.

We were extracted by helicopter and flown directly to our home base. We landed on the runway, a place from which I had set out for many missions tense and excited, and returned tired and fulfilled.

As we walked down the ramp of the Yasur, we encountered much activity, as our teams were all returning from their various missions. One of our technical officers approached me and took a picture of me with the big backpack still on my back, filthy, blackened, and bearded. He then shook my hand warmly as did many others, with pats on the shoulder and hugs.

Adam took me in his car to the unit, and during that short ride it began to sink in – we made it. A huge chapter in our collective and personal lives had just concluded. We had performed well, fulfilled our missions, and made it back alive, without causalities. As we entered the unit compound, I was overwhelmed with emotion. A large sign greeted us, reading "Welcome back." Dozens of operators were busy disposing of their fighting gear, and among them circulated NCOs with food and cold beverages.

Every military unit has procedures on issuing and returning equipment, but with the intensity of the operation, we had lost track of who had what, so everyone simply dumped his equipment into the various labeled boxes.

As I myself was untying different pieces of gear and ammunition, I could hear the helicopters landing again and again, bringing all our operators back. Every few minutes another team entered the hangar, with smiling, tired, and dirty faces.

I called Donna from a nearby office.

"It's over. Everything is OK. I'll be home soon." I knew I would have a couple of hours to sleep before heading back to the unit for debriefings, reorganizing, and releasing the reserves.

At 4 AM we ate a wonderful dinner, fit for king. I praised our chefs, Itach and Nisim, who were happy to see us all return safely and proud of the meal they had prepared for us.

I was very hungry, but couldn't eat, for I felt my throat choking with excitement. I knew we had done something significant, but the most important thing was that our memorial room would not add more photographs on the wall and no operators were in hospitals.

In seventeen days of the operation, we performed thirty-seven successful commando operations. We operated covertly and lethally, and delivered a severe blow to the enemy, while disrupting rocket launches toward Israel. The results were phenomenal, and the deputy CGS later said that Shaldag had set an extremely high standard during the operation.

Commendations and Moving On

Some time after the operation, at the annual Air Force gathering, Shaldag was awarded the Air Force Commander Citation, commending our accomplishments during Operation Grapes of Wrath. In an impressive and touching ceremony, I was called up onstage to receive the award on behalf of the unit, as the crowd cheered. All the officers of the unit stood shoulder to shoulder and saluted.

As I descended from the stage, the minister of defense, Itzik Mordechai, approached me and led me to the president of the State of Israel, Ezer Weizman, who shook my hand. The CGS, LTG Amnon Lipkin-Shahak, addressed the audience and stated that this was a special occasion in which the Air Force was recognizing the outstanding achievements of its ground commando force.

It seemed like the cheering wouldn't stop. It was a special moment in the spotlight, after hundreds of hours in the darkness, in quiet operations behind enemy lines.

In the summer of 1996 I concluded my tenure as Shaldag commander. The operators threw me a farewell party, including speeches, great food, and even original songs and theatrical skits.

I addressed the entire unit and read words that I had written one night before a mission and fine-tuned as we flew up north and during the long, dark night behind enemy lines. I had written what would later become the unit's anthem.

I was now at a crossroads. I felt that after commanding Shaldag, it would be difficult to find challenges to match it. I was offered the opportunity to study for a master's degree in business administration without committing myself to more years of service, as usually required, and I agreed.

My studies at Tel Aviv University exposed me to advanced management tools, and I identified fields in which the IDF could benefit from integrating them.

In September 1996, during my studies, an entrance to the Western Wall Tunnel was opened in the Muslim Quarter in Jerusalem, igniting three days of violent riots by Palestinians in Gaza and J&S.

I had been planning for assignment to a new position on the Lebanon front, but the CGS, LTG Lipkin-Shahak, made it clear that I was needed in J&S, which was seen as the primary challenge the IDF would be facing.

"The peace process is fragile," he said, "and we need to prepare for war."

I wasn't happy with the idea, but as there were no available brigade commander billets open, I was temporarily assigned in 1997 as the chief of operations of the J&S Division in CENTCOM. I invested most of my time and energy in preparing the division for war, quite a challenging task when all around everyone was talking of the winds of peace.

I invested much effort in transforming the IDF HQ in J&S into an operational division, ready for war. I conducted significant organizational changes and introduced new methodologies and standards, such as Lebanon-style operations and special operations tactics. Some thought I was crazy, but I knew what needed to be done.

I was waiting to be assigned as a brigade commander, but things didn't work out exactly as I had expected.

Chapter 7
Ambush

"I Can't Breathe"

Words can't describe the tremendous blow I felt when the boulder came crashing down on my vehicle, crushing my shoulder, neck, and head.

I was driving a military vehicle near Birzeit, a Palestinian town north of Ramallah, when I encountered a well-planned ambush aimed to kill me. It almost succeeded.

I could feel my limbs being crushed and my bones cracking, as the roof of the car caved in, pinning me to the floor. I couldn't breathe, and foam sputtered from my mouth. This was it – I knew I was going to die.

"Hold it, hold it!" I managed to mumble through clenched lips, barely able to push out the air needed to make a sound. I could feel my consciousness slipping away and kept telling myself, "hold it, hold it," as in a difficult Krav Maga session or a fist fight during counterterror training.

In a split second it was clear to me that I was in critical condition. My head was throbbing and I couldn't move it because the roof of the car was crushed against my face. Out of the corner of my eye, I noticed my arm bent back awkwardly, barely connected to my body with what looked like fragments of tissue. I could not move it.

I tried to move my legs. *Oh, my God* – I realized in horror that the vehicle was rolling toward a cliff on the right. I heard screaming and shouting in Arabic around me, and realized they were coming to finish me off with a Molotov cocktail, as I have seen happen many times before. I wanted to reach for my weapon, but my arm did not respond. I reached with my left hand to grab my pistol. I was not going to die without a fight.

A strange sound came to my ears, as the car rolled downhill. With all the power I could muster, I used my legs to try to steer the car in order to avoid plunging over the cliff to the right. The vehicle did not respond, and neither did my legs. How could I stop the car?

I glanced to the right and saw the huge boulder that had crushed me, lying on the floor on the passenger side. It must have been launched from the huge Birzeit Bridge, as I passed underneath it.

Damage assessment. I was beginning to grasp my bleak situation. I could barely breathe, so my lungs must have been punctured. My shoulder and arm had been crushed, and I could feel a strange sensation in my pelvis and legs. I thought my spine must have been seriously damaged. My mouth was filled with blood, and I wondered if it was from my lungs, crushed jaw, broken teeth, or all the above.

I was lying on my back and managed to peek out and see a segment of the road ahead.

I succeeded somehow in steering the car with my legs toward the middle of the road, thinking I should block the way so no other vehicle could pass under the death trap at the bridge. I was hoping that someone would come and rescue me before my assailants succeeded in killing me.

I remembered that I had a Motorola radio, and knocked the microphone with my knee over to where I could grasp it with my left hand. I felt I hadn't enough air to speak.

"Ops room, can you hear me?" I knew I was speaking with my soldiers, and wondered if they would answer me before I passed out.

"Ops room, we hear you." I was so relieved.

"Bridge ... ambush ... wounded ... wounded ..." I muttered.

"Got it, Gal!" I heard the answer, then sounds of tense shouting, as the division operations room sprang to life.

"Bridge, bridge," I said, as blood and broken teeth poured down my throat, making it almost impossible to speak.

"Acknowledge – bridge," came the reply, and I knew, or rather hoped, that they had understood my exact location.

My mind was addressing wider considerations and I tried to relay them through the radio, grunting: "Close road. Forces to the bridge."

A car stopped in front of me and a man and a woman came running. I later found out that he was Elhanan Glat, a resident of the village Ofra.

"Stop the car," I whispered. He ran alongside the car, bent over, and pulled what was left of the broken handbrake handle, finally bringing the vehicle to a full stop.

"Take the phone, rifle, pistol, and bag of maps," I whispered, "and turn the phone off." I didn't want Donna to call me.

"I can't breathe." My arm seemed barely attached, hanging awkwardly to the side, and blood was coming out of my mouth. Elhanan reached over and wet my lips with cold grape juice. "Don't drink," he begged. "I don't know what your condition is."

The woman with him was a student who happened to hitch a ride with him. She was amazingly brave and calmly replaced Elhanan by my side.

"Take care of him," Elhanan directed, as he went over to his car to call for help. "They will be here shortly," he comforted me. "Hang in there."

"Block the road," I grunted, "so students don't pass under the bridge. And bring forces." I was extremely concerned that just as they had hit me, they could hit the school buses scheduled to pass by any minute.

"OK," answered Elhanan, and went to block the road with his car.

I could hear vehicles arriving, sirens wailing, and sounds of gunfire. The deputy division commander, COL Shlomo Oren, arrived and leaned over me.

"What's happening, Gal?"

"Shlomo, I need you to call Donna's office for me," I said. "Tell her boss what happened so he can tell her."

"You got it," he said, "just hang in there."

I couldn't breathe, and my legs and stomach felt extremely cold. There was a sickening feeling as if the last bit of energy was draining out of me.

"OK," Shlomo assured me, "just hold on."

Around me there were doctors, paramedics, and firefighters, all trying to pry me out of the mangled vehicle. I was finally extracted and placed on a spinal board, with a Philadelphia collar around my neck.

I could hear people talking.

"By helicopter or ambulance?"

"The helicopter is on its way."

"We might not make it, let's drive him fast!"

"Cover me, please." I was freezing, and could feel stiffness taking over, a sign of coming shock.

"Don't fall asleep," the doctor said. "Please don't fall asleep. That isn't good."

"How is he doing?" someone asked. There was no reply, so I gathered the question was answered with a hand gesture or expression. I knew I was in critical condition, and fought to hold on and stay conscious.

After initial treatment in the trauma room at the Hadassah Ein Kerem Hospital, I was wheeled to a series of X-rays. The movement of the bed sent spasmodic bolts of pain through my body. I didn't scream and did my best to stay strong, gnashing my teeth together until I thought they would break.

Between X-rays, I was turned over and over and the pain was so intense that I could take it no longer. I let out an anguished and broken scream. I felt I was passing out.

"Stay with us," pleaded Yoav, the division paramedic's officer. "Stay awake, Gal," he went on, as he hugged my head. I couldn't yell anymore, I felt a choking sensation and foam came out of my mouth again. What was happening to me?

I was paralyzed on the left side of my body. In a complicated operation, a titanium rod was inserted from my shoulder all the way through my shattered arm. My lungs were collapsed, I had broken ribs, a damaged jaw, head injuries, exposed nerves where teeth had been knocked out, a fractured spinal cord, and a shattered collar bone.

The worst thing was that my brachial plexus – the network of nerves in my right shoulder – had been practically torn away from my spine.

I was a mess, I couldn't breathe, and I was in excruciating pain.

I had three guardian angels – or rather, pilots – at my side. Noam, Roni H., and Roni O., all cobra pilots and neighbors at the base, spent long nights with me, sleeping on the floor, replacing urine bottles, and wiping sweat from my forehead.

One afternoon, I felt something was wrong. My head was foggy.

"I'm sinking," I told my Uncle Moishe, who was by my side, and then suddenly began acting aggressively toward my family.

"What's happening to him?" I could hear Donna asking.

"I'm sinking, I'm sinking," I said again, sensing that I was losing my grip on reality. Donna ran and called a doctor, and he came with an instrument to measure oxygen saturation in my blood.

"It can't be," the doctor said. "The device must be out of order." They were talking about seventy-six, which I later learned was a critical value. When a second device was brought in and showed the same figure, I could sense the pressure the staff was under and heard the doctor say: "Hurry, get him to intensive care."

A specialist arrived and leaned over me. "I see that you are someone I can explain things to," he said, and proceeded to explain the procedure he was about to perform, which included putting tubes down my throat. A few staff members stood around my bed and lifted me over to another one in order to wheel me to intensive care. It was extremely painful, and I was moaning and groaning.

"Where is Moshik?" My mother sounded angry. "Where is he?"

My brother Moshik came running in. "What is it? What happened?"

My mother was weeping, and Donna clung to me, her face close to mine, under an oxygen mask.

My bed was wheeled out into the hallway and toward the elevator, with the medical team running alongside. A big oxygen tank was leaning on my knees.

"What should I do?" Donna whispered in my ear.

"I don't know," I answered, by way of my facial expression.

"What did the doctor tell you?"

"All I know is that he didn't invite the *chevra kadisha* yet," I said, referring to the Jewish organization that arranges burial services.

Donna's contagious laughter was picked up by Dr. Zangvil, the division doctor who had been summoned.

Donna called MG Uzi Dayan. For some reason I felt he should be notified and I had asked Donna to do so.

"His situation has deteriorated," I overheard her saying, explaining my situation in brief sentences. "He is being taken to intensive care."

My bed was being rushed through the corridors, and just as we reached the elevator, it malfunctioned. Donna burst out laughing again. I was concerned, and the doctors were clearly stressed, but soon the elevator responded and we made it to the intensive care floor, continuing the fast movement down the hallways.

We stopped for a moment, as Avi Munis, the IDF Jump School CO, leaned over and kissed my forehead. I felt that he was saying good-bye forever.

The doctors managed to stabilize me, but my critical condition necessitated a prolonged stay in intensive care.

Friends and family from all over the country came to the hospital.

Bright lights illuminated the intensive care unit twenty-four hours a day. I lost sense of time, and could even barely make out whether it was night or day. I stared up at the ceiling and observed the medical staff as they treated me and other patients.

There was much time for contemplation, and I tried to arrange all the raging thoughts inside my head. How had I let them hurt me? How did this happen? After all these years out in the field, in combat. I felt humiliated. They succeeded, those bastards. What a failure!

One morning, I finally succeeded in sitting up. I was surrounded by tubes and devices, covered in black, blue, and orange spots, and had a hard time breathing. I finally was urinating on my own, after a day earlier I had forced the doctor to let me try. He was skeptical, but I succeeded in filling two urine bags autonomously, much to his surprise.

My father was arriving from abroad to see me that day. He was hesitant before coming in and actually stood outside my room for a few moments before taking a deep breath and getting up the nerve to enter.

When I was ten years old it had been the other way around. My father was seriously wounded, and I came to visit him in the hospital. I remember seeing him lying in a brightly lit room in the intensive care unit, looking awful.

"Daddy, Daddy!" I cried.

"Hi, Gali," he had answered wearily.

Now it was him coming to visit me, and he approached me with an unstable stride. He must have been shocked to see me in this awful state, with many wounds, medical devices, and a beard covering my torn face. I didn't care.

"Hi," I said simply. I was in much pain. My body was shaking. Tears filled my eyes.

During long nights when I couldn't sleep and found it hard to breathe, I would observe the medical staff as they treated other patients. Since I was under the effect of morphine, I can only remember broken spells of thought and visions. Once I awoke and found Yoli, who sat near my bed for a long time. I saw senior IDF officers sitting beside me, but I couldn't speak with them.

To Shoot, Hug, and Write

"He's concerned that he won't be able to operate his weapon again," Donna told Mofaz.

"Brigade commanders don't need to operate weapons," he answered, clearly only trying to make me feel better.

It was a difficult morning for me, and I was sitting up, breathing heavily with a swollen face.

I had been operated on that morning, and a few teeth had been removed. My mouth was stuffed with blood-soaked gauze.

"I must look awful," I whispered to Mofaz.

"You look fine," he declared, trying to conceal his emotions.

A group of joyful Shaldag officers appeared at the doorway, and Professor Libergal insisted that they come in one at a time. First to enter was S., a brave Air Force pilot who transitioned to Shaldag and became a tough operator who could look someone in the eye and kill him without hesitation if need be. He took one look at me, then passed out and dropped to the floor. I faintly called to Donna, and she summoned the medical team, who took care of him.

"It's hard for me to see him this way," he said when he came to. When he tried once more to enter my room, he passed out again.

My dear friend Shimon, who served in the Mossad, came to visit me and told me that the security guard had directed him to my room without even asking who he was looking for. "He said that hundreds of people come to see you every day, so he just directs them all to here," Shimon said.

My room was swarming with visitors all day long, and people filled the hallway and the whole ward. Family members, friends, subordinates, commanders, and friends from all over Israel and from overseas came to see me.

One night I opened my eyes to find a man with a long beard standing beside me. I thought he might be a rabbi.

"What is your name, son?" he asked.

"It's Gal," I whispered.

"Your name has been written," he said. "*Gal einai v'abitah nifla'ot mi'Toratecha*" (Open my eyes that I may see wonderful things in Your law), he said softly, and disappeared.

I later asked my friend Rabbi Tzahor to explain the source of the sentence. He brought me a photocopy of Psalm 119 and showed me verse 18, in which that quote appears. *Gal* in Hebrew has several meanings, and one of them is to reveal or expose.

I never found out who it was that came and quoted the Psalm for me.

I wanted to see my daughters Meori and Ofri, but I was afraid of their reaction to seeing me in this condition. I planned how to do it for a long time. I asked that colorful drawings made by the girls be hung over my bed. I practiced the sentences I would tell them when they entered my room, trying to keep my voice from shaking, and experimented with my blanket, having it cover as many of my ugly wounds as possible.

I asked to see my face in the mirror. I checked how long I could go without an oxygen mask and then asked that they be brought in to me. They came in accompanied by Donna's parents, Zehava and Shlomo, at whose home the girls were spending a lot of time. They came in showing much excitement.

Meori approached first. "Daddy!" she cried cheerfully, recoiled for a moment when she saw me, but then drew near. I couldn't hug her, so Shlomo raised her up enough to reach my face and kiss me. She began questioning me on many things, from my condition to what every appliance in the room was.

Ofri did not recognize me. She was quite frightened by all the commotion, and only after some time, after I whispered our special secret codes and jokes, she recognized me. She sat on the bed beside me and looked at me for a long time, her face expressing mixed emotions.

I cried. No one saw this – or at least so I thought – but I cried bitterly inside.

After a few more procedures and treatments, I was transferred to the rehabilitation ward at Tel Hashomer Hospital. I met Dr. Azaria, a rehabilitation expert who was a legend among injured IDF soldiers. I sat slumped over in a wheelchair and could hardly speak.

He examined my wounds, read my file very carefully, and looked at the X-rays sent by Professor Libergal.

"You sustained serious injuries," he concluded. I said nothing.

"Serious injuries," he said again. "Stay here for a few weeks, we will begin treatment, take it slowly." Then he looked at me and asked: "What are your objectives? What do you want to achieve in your rehabilitation?"

Suddenly, in a flash of thought, I could feel the essence of my being. I knew I wanted to operate my weapon, and I craved to hug the girls and Donna. I felt I couldn't live if I could not lift Ofri in my arms after she fell asleep, and carry her to her bed, kissing her the whole way and smelling her sweet, fresh scent.

I also wanted to write. I needed to learn and put into writing ideas and impressions. This was so important to me.

I looked my doctor in the eye and said resolutely: "I want to shoot, hug, and write."

Donna looked at me as I spoke, not at all surprised to hear that these were my goals.

"An extremely challenging plan, very ambitious for someone in your situation, but we will do everything we can to make it happen," said Dr. Azaria.

I knew he was skeptical. My right side was paralyzed. How would I ever hold a weapon?

"Let's get you admitted and start working," he said.

"No!" Donna intervened.

"What do you mean, no?"

"He isn't staying here," she said quietly, powerfully, leaving no room for doubt.

"His situation isn't good; he needs more time in the hospital."

"He will arrive here every morning and do all the treatments, but at night he will come home to the girls and me."

The doctor thought for a moment, looking at Donna. She didn't even blink.

"Very well," he said.

And so it was. A vehicle assigned by CENTCOM picked me up every morning and returned me to my family every night.

The Frog Screams

It was a year of strenuous rehabilitation.

My family had to adapt to functioning with a father with challenges. Donna insisted on eating a family dinner every evening when I got home from treatment. Then she bathed me, after carefully covering my bandages so they wouldn't get wet. I read bedtime stories to my girls and then spoke on the phone with colleagues, commanders, and friends, as Donna busily prepared the house for the morning rush. She had her own challenging day at her job, and then this full-time evening job, but she allowed us to function as a family, as if it were an island of tranquility amidst a raging storm.

On the weekends, our home was filled with visitors, and many people also came to see me during breaks at the hospital. It was so helpful and inspiring to receive so much encouragement and love.

But at night, I would moan with agonizing pain and prop myself up against a pile of pillows, trying to find a more comfortable angle. I would lie there, staring out the window, waiting for morning to come.

The days went by, and my pain was increasing, both physically and mentally. It is something that is hard to understand if you haven't gone through a serious injury. Amidst the horrible suffering, there is this huge frustration that builds up, and with it, a deep and fundamental sadness.

I forced myself to push on, grinding my teeth, not allowing myself to break down and give up.

During the first few days of my rehabilitation, Meori wouldn't go to school. She insisted on staying with Daddy, whether it be at home or at the hospital. She wouldn't listen to persuasion. She had made up her mind.

We walked out of the house together, me limping on crutches, and went to the playground at the end of the street. I tried to convince her to go to school, but she wouldn't give up. Crying bitterly, she explained that she didn't trust anyone, and that only she would take care of Daddy.

I understood that not only I carried scars, but that my family was also deeply affected. Donna and the girls went through challenging days and great suffering, and realizing this made me even more determined to fight, overcome obstacles, always find a way, raise my head high and smile, and choose life. This would be a daily choice and struggle – to strive for active and fruitful living – with my family, and for my family.

My rehabilitation reached a stagnation point, so I was flown to Paris, to be treated by the famous Dr. Alan Gilbert, who happened to be a relative of Yishai, Shaldag's doctor.

While I was preparing for the trip, Adam, my deputy from the paratroopers and Shaldag, suddenly showed up.

"What are you doing here?"

"I'm coming with you."

"Why? I'm going to a hospital."

"I never let you conduct cross-border operations without me. Paris is across the border, I believe."

When I returned to Israel, my recovery was still not progressing, and my treatment profile was updated. One evening, I could move a finger, and the next day, two. I was thrilled, and worked hard in treatment and training. I was going to be OK! Six months after my injury, my nervous system was beginning to regain functioning, and I could feel that I was on the way to recovery.

Until this day, I still live with sharp pain, a continuous burning sensation in my right arm. But when I work hard and everything hurts, it blurs the specific pain from the injury.

"We need to talk," the therapist at the rehabilitation center told me one day.

"What about?" I asked, curious.

"I'm not sure that everything is OK with you. Your rehabilitation is not complete. You aren't talking."

"Why do you say this?" I looked at her with concern. I had been working hard for ten months now, determined to return to operational duty. The IDF medical corps was giving me a rough time, and I heard that the chief surgeon himself objected. I knew that I would also need to convince Mofaz, and was determined to return as soon as I felt that I could operate a weapon.

"Look at your frog," she said, pointing at a clay frog that I had crafted during an occupational therapy session.

I looked at the frog. Three-year-old Ofri understood that Daddy needed to work with his fingers, so she instructed me what to make her during therapeutic ceramics sessions. The frog was one such "gift," along with a turtle, kitchen tools, and others.

"What about the frog?" I asked, puzzled.

"It is screaming from pain," she said quietly. "It is wounded and hurting and still has not made a full recovery."

She was right.

Chapter 8

The Journey to Operational Art

This New Beast within Me

In the mid 1990s, Western militaries began developing new concepts in operational art. In the IDF, this field was introduced in order to bridge between the highly developed tactical field and the realm of strategic thinking.

This chapter describes a tumultuous chapter in the history of the IDF, and the role I played in the eye of the storm. Although beginning chronologically, it references various periods throughout my career.

I believe that this chapter is especially important for military leaders and statesmen.

* * *

"I want you to start learning," MG Itzik Eitan told me.

He was the commander of J&S Division, and he came to visit me at home in Rosh Ha'ayin one afternoon. He found me in the yard, propped up against some pillows, breathing heavily and sighing quietly from pain.

"What do you mean, learn?" I said through clenched teeth.

"Between medical treatments, you should go to OTRI, the Operational Theory Research Institute. It'll do you good, and will serve the IDF's needs, too.

"Isn't it intended for division commanders?"

"It suits you. This isn't a matter of rank or position; you'll fit in."

"Itzik, I'm admitted in the hospital!"

"I talked to Mofaz about this and he totally agrees. Arrange it with the hospital."

I had heard about OTRI and the team that taught the course, with their newfangled, weird concepts. I had also attended one of their classes at the brigade commanders' course and resented the aggressive, blunt, and condescending attitude demonstrated by their lecturers. Why did I need this?

I began the course after a motivational discussion with its commander, BG (Res.) Dovik Tamari.

"Go to your treatments at midnight," he smiled. "We don't have time for these injuries. Have the hospital adapt their schedule to yours."

"I am more than 90 percent disabled," I protested. "It's hard for me to sit, and I can't write. I don't know how I will be able to learn here."

"Start and we shall see how it goes."

Studying took place using the Systemic Thought Generator software. Dr. Zvi Lanir, one of the founders of the course, sat with me and helped me with my research, injecting ideas and recommendations, using his vast experience.

Something was beginning to shift in my perception of the subject and the team, especially after hearing a lecture by Dr. Shimon Naveh. He was crude, rude, and impatient, but the effect his words had on me was electric, challenging all my preconceived notions and generating a storm within me.

My body was broken but I had wings. I could fly.

In the evening at the hospital, after the first day, overwhelmed with thoughts, I struggled to hold a pencil between my fingers and write down insights. It felt as if operational poetry was pouring out onto the paper. Here was the place for me to soar high. I was realizing that war can be waged as an art form, in its broadest context.

I had finally found an avenue through which my rich literary background could be utilized. My knowledge of the Bible, literature, and language skills were melding together in a fresh conceptualization. I had found a space where I could express operational ideas with a new clarity and depth.

I realized more than ever before that advanced military analysis cannot be developed using standard operating procedures and checklists alone. Another ingredient is needed, a different methodology and completely different way of learning. One must look at the current situation frame by frame, identifying all its elements in turn, naming the various phenomena and arriving at new findings and understandings.

My ability to concentrate and learn was increasing, and I felt that I understood the picture and processes faster and better. First came the analysis of reality in a broad context, then an in-depth look at different cases from various angles. After this came conceptualization and definitions. This all led to a new understanding of reality which allowed me to transition to planning and implementation.

But, once I'd formed plans, I'd look at them again with doubt and criticism, attacking my own analysis and reevaluating my assumptions. I'd restudy each plan from all directions and challenge it with further investigation.

Reality, the unfolding of events, the opponent's actions, weather, and friction all etch and burn previously acquired knowledge with a new scrutinizing flame. Soon, the newly constructed concept is tested and needs changing, tweaking, updating, reshaping – leading to a new concept, and then another and another.

I felt that I was dealing with advanced material, but I had doubts as to its practical applications. The methodology was indeed suited for dealing with ever-changing and adapting enemies, especially those acting in a decentralized manner, organized in cells, and learning quickly, such as terror organizations and guerilla fighters. But how would I convey these ideas to regular military units, which are based on standard operating procedures, checklists, orders, and themes such as simplicity and conformity? How would they adapt to high-tempo changes such as these? Did we even have a choice, if we wanted to remain relevant?

The investigative method I learned to implement systematically analyzed the gaps between my system and that of my rival, in a relevant context. These gaps necessitate new definitions, sometimes revolutionary. Here the need for new conceptualization may be crucial. Many times we find that existing terminology is not suitable and cannot appropriately describe reality and the measures needed to face it, so new and updated terms are born. It is impossible to fight current campaigns using the terminology of past wars.

New language creates new realities, and new realities create new terminology.

Many of us remember how we once needed to stand close to a wall in order to speak on the phone, simply because it was connected by wire to a socket. Then one day, someone coined the term "mobile phone," and our communication habits changed forever. I assume that the creator of the term was perceived at first as detached, delusional, and crazy.

The same process of inventing new terminology is required in fulfilling operational needs, especially when coping with terror and guerilla warfare, because the rival system is also flexible and constantly and rapidly changing.

The more I delved into this process, the more I found myself inventing new and exciting words and phrases to describe and define reality – both the threat and the operational response.

With time, some of my terms became a huge success and led to the introduction of meaningful content into the new term. The concept of "low signature" was adopted by me from the field of sonar and radar, to define operational patterns of ground forces using a different, lower profile. This led to the creation of highly successful new modes of operation, using different equipment, tactics, style, and force structure. Soon I wrote my first paper on "Low-Signature Operations," on behalf of the IDF Training and Doctrine Division. It became very influential and was widely adopted, from the tactical to the strategic and political echelons.

There were, of course, also failures. I coined the term *snailing* to describe an operational mode used by special forces, where the objective is not always to engage the enemy, but to disengage, dig in, and lie low – like a snail recoiling within its shell – and carry out a designated mission. This was not typical of "regular" military forces whose default mode of operations was to engage the enemy and reach a decisive victory. Though the tactic was extremely successful, the terminology was not: people want to be lions, not snails, and the term elicited a fair amount of objection.

Later on in my career I would implement this operational concept while dealing with multiple terror attacks in Benjamin Regional Brigade's area of responsibility in J&S. It was an extremely difficult time, for many terrorists were shooting along the roads and succeeding in killing civilians and seriously disrupting ordinary life.

I couldn't provide protection throughout the entire region with the limited resources at my disposal, so I designated specific routes for use by Israelis and focused operational efforts there. These routes became "protected sleeves," combining overt, high-signature forces, together with covert, low-signature forces. These were concealed forces, including recon, observation, and disguised forces.

We called this "combination of signatures," and the operational plan limiting Israelis to specific routes we called "the snailing plan." My idea was to minimize the territory requiring supervision, reduce friction, and protect our civilians.

There were many who did not recognize the fact that remaining relevant necessitated changing and reshaping the language. Not everyone understood the role language has so often played in revolutionizing a field. There was much ignorance and alienation, but I perceived this partly as my own failure. I should have led the revolution using different methods, which were more low key, quiet, sophisticated, and subversive. I should have led the train of change to its destination without sounding such a loud whistle and awakening those who prefer to sleep and wake up at the station.

At the Advanced Systemic Course, we carried out various exercises, and I clashed with my instructors daily. They did not fully grasp my ideas and were not patient in dealing with this new beast going wild within me.

"We didn't understand you," Dr. Naveh would tell me years later. "We didn't appreciate what we had in our hands."

I find tremendous value in professional skepticism and doubt, and realize the great importance of professional modesty. Just because something has been said or written does not mean it is correct. New and updated strategies and procedures can be developed to suit changing facts on the ground.

In my journey toward mastering operational art, I went from hearing to listening, from looking to observing, from a systematic approach to a critical one, from self-confidence to controlled humility, and from creative and flowing writing to the agony of getting it right.

The new methods demanded not just focusing on tidbits of information but grasping the wider context of events at the heart of the analysis. Objectives and targets have always been the stuff of military strategy, but in my course work I was learning how to manipulate effects.

I went from studying mechanical action patterns based on checklists to analysis of operational molds by their signatures – high, low, combined, controlled, and sub-low signatures. From classic advancement to subtly gradated concepts of permeation, diffusion, and infiltration. From old-school attack to nuances of pouncing, developing the cloud of wasps, and refinement of the concept of swarms.

You might say that as a commander, I had found a synergistic combination of field manuals and protocol with poetry and prose, or in management terminology, the importance of philosophy alongside that of business management. They each have their place, and I cannot do without either of them.

My very concept of the meaning of learning went through a process of refinement, and it became a focal point of my activity as a commander and a leader. I felt bound by my sense of duty: I am obligated to learn and develop my knowledge and that of my unit. It must be translated and instilled in my subordinates as well as my commanders. It is a constant quest to align my knowledge with the situation developing on the ground. An important task is also ensuring that the accumulated knowledge radiates outward to the entire organization.

There is also a huge effort to precede the precedents, to identify situations before they are actualized, to build an appropriate response to emerging threats while they are in their initial stages, even if they are not yet clear and identifiable. My task is to have one foot planted in the future. I must always be relevant!

To promote these ideas, I began to educate and encourage a "sensorial attitude," asking my subordinates to transform themselves into sensors. There is always movement and change, so a commander must constantly observe and evaluate firsthand, take in maximum inputs, observations, and insights, and identify, quantify, and label his findings to make sure that the interpretation is concise.

During those days, I began to understand principles of force application in greater depth than ever before – far beyond the linear, mechanical aspects. A force can be deployed using endless variations of functionality, profiles, and signatures, all tailored to the context and need.

The existence of a force does not necessitate its activation, for it may project its influence without taking any action (such a force is known as a "fleet in being"). And an enemy force may be defeated by learning its makeup and constructing a counterforce accordingly.

Operations at the Speed of Thought

Identifying changes, understanding them, and developing methods, capabilities, and mission forces to face them – these are preconditions to becoming a relevant organization.

A frantic reality has become a part of our lives. We confront daily uncertainties, which we must interpret and assess in order to come up with solutions. Most of the time, we react to the threat, but the challenge is to be able to create a relevant operational response, in a relevant time frame. We then must immediately go on to identify the next threat. In an era of speedy and frequent changes, this challenge is becoming more and more difficult.

In his book *Business at the Speed of Thought*, Bill Gates described the meaning of the "era of speed" and the need to prepare an appropriate business response in order to confront the high tempo of change: "If the 1980s were about quality and the 1990s were about reengineering, then the 2000s will be about velocity. About how quickly the nature of business will change. About how quickly business itself will be transacted." *

Unlike the business world, in the military realm, the "profit" is reflected by the ability to create an effective and timely operational response. This reality also influences the operational art of war, especially in limited conflicts, where the opponent is more flexible, agile, and challenging, and its intel/media footprint is immersed in a sea of information. He is difficult to identify. He operates using characteristics of underground cells, subversion, terror, and guerilla warfare. He is evasive by nature, low in profile and signature, and is also influenced by the era of speed. He also constantly learns and improves.

As a result, a military must maintain the following crucial capabilities, which it must constantly promote and enhance: the ability to identify a situation, the ability to maintain conceptual coherence, the ability to create a unit-community climate or combat community that stresses combat learning, the ability to create a rapid communication system to transmit information and knowledge, and the ability to create operational, mission-oriented formations.

Identifying a Situation

Changes within a system are not always noticeable and clear. Still, developing and materializing trends supply us with an abundance of clues, early signals, and indicative signs.

In the era of speed, a commander is required to collect, identify, and interpret these signals as "incipiency" – preliminary signs, attesting to a new trend in creation.

Identifying the situation requires a "sensorial attitude" – acute sensitivity to developments and changes, as minute as they may be. These must be reported quickly by all field and staff levels, and go through an evaluation process to determine whether these signals or signs are indeed indicative of a trend and reality change.

No less important, the new phenomenon should be named.

---

* Bill Gates, *Business at the Speed of Thought: Succeeding in the Digital Economy* (New York: Warner Books, 1999), xii.

Conceptualization – naming a new phenomenon, occurrence or trend – is the basis for creating a common language within our forces, and an efficient technique to clarify the operational concept and situation.

Creating new terminology for new concepts is an awe-inspiring, almost spiritual pursuit, like the first man naming the newly created animals in Genesis 2:19: "whatever the man would call every living creature, that was to be the name thereof."

Utilizing conceptualization requires extra caution, however, for words create reality, and creative metaphors can be confusing if used before all are familiar with them. There has to be a control mechanism that grants official authorization to a new term before instilling it throughout the force and enriching the military language with it.

Without proper control and authorization, new terms may create a Tower of Babel situation, where some forces implement the new terminology, while others have not yet been acquainted with it.

There can be no progress and improvement without change, and there can be no change without updating the military language, but it must be done with appropriate caution.

Maintaining Conceptual Coherence

We process the data that is continuously collected on the opponent and the environment and turn it into information, which is then analyzed and verified and turned into knowledge. This is the central and vital asset of any organization, especially in a military.

The situational assessment, representing the arena's characteristics and status as well as our forces' concept of operations and the main avenues of actualizing them, is referred to as a "knowledge map."

We usually think of maps as a visual representation of geographical data, but as social sciences professor Juval Portugali explains, "there are also other maps – maps of the mind, maps which reside, in a way that we cannot fully determine, inside the mind/brain. These are termed *mental* or *cognitive maps*. Though one cannot actually observe cognitive maps, they are of the utmost importance, as it is according to them that we navigate...our way." *

---

* Juval Portugali, *Implicate Relations: Society and Space in the Israeli-Palestinian Conflict* (Dordrecht, Netherlands: Kluwer Academic Publishers, 1993), 156.

This knowledge map includes the information that has been processed and analyzed, and the terms that have been identified and coined during the identification-interpretation-analysis-conceptualization process. It is the knowledge base of our force in constructing the appropriate operational response.

In order to promote the ability to shape and influence reality, we must adopt a preemptive attitude, which is activated before our opponent surprises us. So it is not a responsive action following the assessment of the situation, but understanding the potential and expected outcome from signals and incipiencies that have been identified and named. This allows us to construct, in advance, a comprehensive and suitable operational formation, which includes forces, movement routines, procedures, weapons, points of emphasis, and policy of force activation.

The term coined is "communal information." It accumulates a treasure of insights, information, and knowledge, and so it is also a common knowledge asset. There is always a chance that the new response we had constructed to counter the incipiencies identified is premature. It may have been constructed long before the opponent's potential has materialized. So there must be the appropriate sensitivity in determining the time and the method in which the new term will be launched.

Creating a Unit-Community Climate
These actions can only be taken using a unified terminology base – a situation where commanders know and understand the knowledge map, are aware of the process in which the trends and phenomena were identified and created, implement a cross-echelon discourse, understand the operational concept, and follow it in full unity.

The process of identification-interpretation-evaluation intrinsically incorporates criticism, and it necessitates brainstorming and an organizational climate that encourages open discourse, free from the fear of hierarchy. The communal style neutralizes the bureaucratic pressure that command echelons entail, and allows for the encouragement of open, critical, and creative thinking.

There is always tension between striving to germinate a new term and objection to its germination, but the operational community respects and nurtures the opposition. The clash of ideas within the organization is what creates the alloy of knowledge: the opposition forces are the ones who create the turbulence that leads to new opportunities.

Once created, a term must be distributed, incorporated, and absorbed in as many ways as possible, both organizationally (by military formats such as orders and staff papers) and via viral distribution by word of mouth.

A combat community both learns and teaches. It is like an absorbing tissue that knows to bring in units that have not yet been exposed to the new knowledge, teach them, change them if needed, and adapt them to their designated missions, using combat absorption and learning mechanisms such as teams that specialize in instilling knowledge, thorough familiarity with the operating arena, quick extraction, and utilization of lessons learned.

Striving to achieve order, and convergence and alignment into model units, is a common and understandable goal in all big organizations, especially militaries. There is constant tension accompanying the quest for creativity and agility (speed + flexibility) when it clashes with the pillars of the military: order and standardization.

Order and standardization are tools for achieving control and stability, but limited conflict – that is, small-scale conflict that involves operations rather than wars, targeting small and evolving terror groups rather than armies – and the era of speed require optimal and fast utilization of brain resources in the unit. A communal climate enables us to be up to speed with the speed of our enemy.

The agile rival, global changes that have led to "shrinking" of the world into a "global village," the Internet, the accessibility of the media and the constant demand of humanity for more information – all these necessitate change and realignment of the priorities of advanced units. In this new reality, only the fast survive. The rates of change require our operational systems to constantly evolve and remain relevant.

A modern operational unit is bound to function as a community, because it is an "information-based mechanism." Passing information fast enough for making timely decisions will not be possible in a climate of hierarchical bureaucracy.

An incident may be covered in real-time media worldwide, stirring public opinion and world leaders. Our political leaders are immediately required to respond, explain, and direct, but we, as a non-communal, hierarchal, and bureaucratic organization, cannot supply them with the facts they need in time, for we wait for the data to make its way up the multitiered chain of command.

This is especially true in a limited conflict, where tactical echelons have critical influences on the strategic ones. This phenomenon is characterized by the "strategic corporal," who may influence the course of a country with one tactical move.

A unit responding and retaliating after a serious terror attack may trigger a turning point in the entire campaign. Senior leadership must fully understand the environment and expected ramifications before employing a force or carrying out a move. It is therefore crucial to establish the flow of information in a speedy and complete manner, and not as in a broken telephone game.

If a commander in the field knows something and feels that he has an important insight to convey and clarify, will his unit encourage him to do so even if it goes against the flow? Will the organization understand that such inputs may reflect a fundamental change in the enemy's organization and that the whole reality may have changed? Does the unit have the strength and the methodologies to identify this change, name it, and develop an appropriate response, even if nonprocedural? Will this happen in time?

From Cargo Ships to Speed Boats: Creating a Rapid Communication System and Operational, Mission-Oriented Formations

The need to quickly transfer information and knowledge contradicts the need to preserve a hierarchal structure. In order to cope with this problem while fighting Palestinian terror, it was decided in CENTCOM that information and knowledge would be transferred unrelated to hierarchy, and to achieve this, the command could coordinate, if needed, directly with the battalions. At the same time it was also emphasized that no change was to take place in the hierarchal structure when it came to battle procedures and orders.

A military is a big and complex organization. The era of speed necessitates operating the organization like a fleet of speedboats, not massive, lumbering cargo ships. There must be unique maneuvering capabilities, military actions at the speed of thought, an organization harnessed to a database with common knowledge assets and equipped for structural changes, and the creation of task forces as quick as lightning. The speedboat organization understands that operational approaches are dynamic.

The operational community should be aware of the frenetic environment and the speed required, so it does not grumble and express criticism of frequent and rapid changes, and the scramble to incorporate new requirements.

It is natural that tensions will be created between these communal and military methods. It should be emphasized that a military organization should always be driven by orderly operational staff work. A unit's tactical commanders must maintain basic military methods, but at the same time, the operational structure should be temporary, dynamic, and flexible – a key challenge.

The communal unit builds itself as an agile operational structure. It educates its people in this spirit. It is constructed to develop knowledge and quickly disseminate it, while building a qualification and adaptation system. It is built for change and constant innovation. It may be a large operational framework, abundant with resources, equipment, weaponry, and forces – but although it is essentially a cargo ship, it behaves like a speed boat.

There is also a technological significance to enabling an operational community.

A fast communication network, internal information sharing protocols, conceptual coherence, and a communal climate all create the unified entity, the synergy, the connection between the various unit components, and the ability to respond effectively, promptly, accordingly, and relevantly.

Crazy Times Call for Crazy Organizations is the title of a book by business management expert Tom Peters. Operational forces too must hone their skills of swift adaptation to new environments and threats.

The traditional view is that armies are intended for confronting existential threats. According to the common wisdom, low-intensity conflicts (LIC) do not pose an existential threat. This confluence of beliefs leads to armies being left in their current structure. Moreover, armies usually do not develop for themselves terminology systems suitable for LIC and do not build forces, commanders, and soldiers in a dual configuration suited both to limited conflict and to fighting a regular army.

In order to adapt operational forces to a frenetic reality, a structural flexibility is needed. Assuming a country will not construct two separate armies, an army must possess the ability to build ad hoc forces, create unorthodox operational structures, and give them full support in training, logistics, weaponry, and legal cover, befitting the conditions and constraints of the operational arena. An army must also be able to carry out different missions simultaneously.

A unique example of rapid construction of flexible forces was seen during the preparation phase before the "Ebb and Flow" events that began in September 2000 (the Second Intifada). Having surmised a threat that gunmen might act within mass riots, the IDF built a full-spectrum response. "Riots with weapons present" was a new doctrine written even before the threat materialized, based solely on early identification. The doctrine was complete down to detailed tactics and techniques, accompanied by designated equipment and training modules. The operational construct entailed force amalgamation never before seen in the IDF.

All this robust investment in preparations proved vital when the Intifada broke out on the eve of the High Holidays, September 2000.

OTRI's Team

A commander who is actively engaged in learning, growing, and attempting reform sometimes encounters a painful experience. People resist change; they are not with you, and you are mocked and ridiculed. It is no longer the ordinary jealous rivalry among scholars but a cultural war between reactionaries and learners. This is also one of the prices of transformational leadership. It was not the first time that I moved against the current, against the wind. Changing, drilling, and breaking ground was always my way.

I can now say with the perspective of time that Dr. Shimon Naveh, Dr. Zvi Lanir, BG Dovik Tamari, and their partners, this special group who led IDF operational thinking, had a significant role in my life. Although there were also quite a few confrontations, they helped me realize my potential, helped me fly high and connect between operational art and strategy, and between operational art and tactics.

I also know that in their eyes, it was I who connected the deep insights and abstract knowledge to the practical world, to the operational world, to the field.

I believe that the work performed by OTRI was of great significance in shaping the future of the IDF and the defense of the State of Israel. Their deep influence on operational planning in all arenas, on the critical thinking of IDF commanders, and the construction of a vibrant and profound discourse in the military, will be fully appreciated only in years to come. Many IDF commanders were exposed to another important point of view on military thinking. They were now more prone to rethink, update, and clarify a situation in order to adapt it to the dynamic reality.

I am certain that successful confrontation with the Palestinian terror in CENTCOM is very much connected with the steps taken by OTRI. They influenced many other plans in other regions and fields. They triggered a deep process of analysis, discourse, and learning throughout the military. Their success can be attributed especially to intelligent and critical senior commanders who were willing to look at situations in the new perspectives provided by operational art.

A few months before the 2006 Second Lebanon War, the institute's prominence began to fade, for there were those who systematically acted to reduce its influence. It is true that Dr. Naveh and his people provoked substantial objection and even resentment by a senior group within the IDF. It was no longer an academic, idea-driven debate.

Because of this heightened cultural war, there were those who found ways to oust this group of scholars from within the ranks of the IDF, using various excuses. It was a sad and troubling move, and I believe also negative for the future of the IDF. Surely there were things to fix and change, but there was no reason to dispense with such a "turbo engine" from the Israeli defense establishment.

Many senior officers and prominent institutions from other countries value and adopt the unique ideas that emanated from OTRI, yet here in Israel we didn't seem to find room for them and their ideas.

A few weeks before the Second Lebanon War, I received a letter from one of OTRI's senior leaders, warning me that I was to be next, as the IDF senior leadership was tired of critical and transformational officers, representing the approach of OTRI. He warned that they would soon find a way to get rid of me and were only waiting for an opportunity.

Because I value these people and their approach, I am pleased to see this group back within the ranks these days, serving in IDF colleges, as I anticipated when I was writing the Hebrew edition of this book some years ago.

The ideas were – and still are – vital and viable, but I am convinced that their methods of getting them across were flawed. They showed no patience with those who did not keep up. They were callous and sometimes arrogant and distant. They did not have a "connecting" attitude toward the military's institutions. The content was superb, but the packaging was problematic both organizationally and from a marketing point of view.

I know that I share in both the accomplishment of developing this unique field and the failure to insert it into the IDF's genetic code. In fact, I served as the implementer of this method, and I believe it proved significantly successful in ways that I will describe.

But because there was not enough effort invested in patient integration, marketing, and attending to the politics of the processes of change, the wonderful accomplishments were overshadowed by a wave of friction and confrontation, so much so that the ideas themselves were no longer the main focus, but rather the struggle around them.

The systemic way of thinking became second nature to me, and, combined with methodologies I had learned at the school of business administration at Tel Aviv University, gave me powerful tools that influenced my conduct as a commander and future manager.

Years later, I would plan for the war in Lebanon assisted by the methodologies of operational art.

My Longest Mission

I continued to learn and rehabilitate. I underwent extremely painful treatments, but as soon as I began my studies, I decided to stop using painkillers, especially morphine. I suffered, but felt I must regain control. I did not want disability to be a major component in my life. I knew that if I could not fight in service of my country, I did not have a life. The truth is that I could not bear the thought that terrorists had cut my trajectory short.

For me, national and personal concerns were intertwined.

Every accomplishment in my rehabilitation was a reason for celebration. I managed to open the refrigerator with my right hand. I walked with more stability. In spite of excruciating pain, I cocked and fired my weapon. I walked long distances every day and underwent a variety of treatments and therapeutic activities: acupuncture, physiotherapy, swimming, clay therapy, and medications.

My rehabilitation was the longest mission I have ever performed.

I set myself a secondary target – I would not let this time go to waste but invest it in strengthening my capabilities, besides learning. Beyond in-depth learning of operational art and participation in CENTCOM think tanks, I adapted to a computerized environment and significantly improved my English. We decided to move, then located and bought a house – all within the same year.

Between hours of pain, medicine and needles, the painful paralysis lying like a cloud over the entire right side of my body, the cracked jaws, broken teeth, shattered shoulder blades, rehabilitating lungs, and broken spine – I set an azimuth and course, and set out in the direction of vitality.

I was discharged from the hospital on a Sunday, and reported to duty on the following Thursday. Exactly one year after my injury, I was wearing a ballistic vest in the Benjamin Mountains, the scene of my ambush.

CGS Mofaz had appointed me as Benjamin Brigade commander.

Chapter 9
Benjamin Brigade Commander

Building Relationships

Returning as a commander to the place where I was injured was symbolic and significant for me. It was important that everyone understood that we would not be broken with rocks and boulders.

There was a concern among the Palestinians that I might have returned to seek revenge and might not wish to implement the Oslo Accord policies.

I related to them with both kindliness and sternness. I prevented acts of violence. I fought stone throwing as if rocks were hand grenades. I embraced the settlers and worked effortlessly night and day to protect them. At the same time, I worked to implement the political directives mandated by the Oslo Accord. This balance wasn't easy, and there was a lot of tension.

In the brigade's area of responsibility, there were various populations, and I persevered to maintain close contact with them and strengthen their affiliation to Israel and Israeli society. I worked hard to connect the settler community to the brigade. We conducted various events together, and despite tension and doubts, we performed the annual memorial service for Yitzhak Rabin.

I made a special effort to connect the ultraorthodox community in Modiin Illit/Kiryat Sefer to the brigade's activities. I maintained close relations with the local leadership and visited people in their homes. The apex of this relationship was when I was invited to meet with Rabbi Yosef Shalom Elyashiv, considered by many to be the leading authority in Jewish law. I was the first military officer that the wise and elderly rabbi had invited to his Jerusalem home, and this unique experience is well engraved in my heart. Of course I was attacked in the media the following morning by left-wingers, claiming that it was inappropriate for a brigade commander to "seek blessings" from rabbis.

I invited nearby kibbutz members to participate in combined discussions with key figures in the settlements, and even made an effort to achieve reasonable communication with young activists known as the Hilltop Youth (so named because of their propensity to claim hilltops as their own and build unauthorized settlements there as part of their nationalist efforts at settling the land).

I maintained contact with then mayor of Jerusalem Ehud Olmert, because the northern part of the city overlapped the brigade's area of responsibility, and I saw the protection and fortification of Jerusalem as a fundamental part of my duty. I had different confrontations with every one of the populations, and there were always steps taken toward building relationships. My goal was maintaining a controlled balance, and I saw in all these interactions a national social start-up, bridging gaps and nurturing cooperation and understanding.

I kept continuous personal relations with my Palestinian colleague, brigade commander Abu al-Walid. Beyond our professional roles, I knew him as a person, and in this way I related to him. We broke bread together and exchanged holiday greetings. I expressed my condolences when children from his family drowned in Gaza beach. When a building in Ramallah collapsed, burying construction workers, he called me for help. I entered Ramallah with many brigade forces and called the excellent forces of the Home Front Command to assist in the rescue efforts. We worked together all day, lifting rubble and extracting survivors, until the work was done. Ramallah residents flocked to the site and supplied both Palestinian and Israeli rescuers with food and beverage.

There were also those who stoned our forces. International media accompanied me all day, covering the combined operation in live broadcasts.

It was a special and touching event. It showed we could work together to save lives.

One evening it came to my attention that Palestinian extremists were planning to riot on the following day, designated as a "Day of Rage" against the Israeli settlement policy.

It was expected, but I had an unexpected development. Donna and I had purchased tickets to a concert by George Martin, the legendary producer of the Beatles, performing in Jerusalem. We very much wanted to see it, and it was to be a rare occasion for us to spend time together.

I called Abu Firas, the Palestinian governor, and asked him about their plans for the big demonstration. I told him that if I didn't make it to the

George Martin concert, I would have my own little day of rage, and Donna might even get angrier than me.

"What Martin?" asked Abu Firas.

"An important musician," I explained.

"Don't worry," he said. "We will take the demonstrators to a distant place with buses and have them demonstrate near some olive trees. They will have their demonstration, some cameras, why not?"

"Demonstrate," I told him, "but finish on time."

Abu Firas laughed but kept his promise. Buses took a few hundred protestors far from the problematic friction points of Ramallah, where there would have been higher chances of things igniting into a real conflagration. After being confronted with determined action by the Israel Border Police, the demonstration dispersed.

Donna and I were late to the concert and were seated in the wings. During the break I received a call from the governor's assistant, inquiring whether "Colonel Gal managed to make it on time for that Martin."

Nakba Day, 2000

I invested most of my time in preparations for war. I did not believe in the stability of the peace process and prepared the Benjamin Brigade for battle.

I had a wonderful staff, unified and with a willingness to learn. We conducted continuous learning processes, assessments, and intensive preparations for war. We stayed closely coordinated with the civilian population and seriously addressed every incident of Palestinian terror or acts by extremists from both sides.

We carried out many combined activities and became a close and integrated team. I knew we would need this unity when we would be tested.

May 15, 2000. Ayosh Junction, north of Ramallah. It was the morning of Nakba Day – a commemoration day when Palestinians mark the establishment of the State of Israel as their tragedy (*nakba* means "catastrophe" in Arabic).

"Dadon," I called the Border Police force commander with a dry throat. "Dadon, come here." I also tapped my helmet with my fist, a signal for the commander to approach.

The heavy-built officer came running toward me, smiling. The noise of the roaring mob was getting louder and louder. Heavy smoke was billowing from burning tires, letting off much heat and a smell of burning rubber.

Smash! A Molotov cocktail landed at my feet, an explosion and a large flame, and I leaped back. My jeep driver, Levy, drove back a few meters, and the heavy vehicle squeaked.

"Come here, Dadon." I placed my hand on his shoulder and smiled at him, receiving a smile in return.

"Yes, Brigade Commander," he breathed heavily.

I could never convince him to call me by my name. For Dadon, I was, and still am to this day, the brigade commander.

I jumped up and down, and bent over in order to rearrange my heavy ballistic vest. I was perspiring heavily, after four intense hours of confrontation at the junction.

"Look, Dadon," I showed him, my right hand on his vest and the left pointing toward one of the Border Police platoons in a nearby alley, battling the masses in the junction.

"They are not operating well," I explained. "There's no cover from the left, they aren't working under the protection of protective barriers, and the whole neighborhood can open fire on them. It's a matter of seconds, you know."

It had been stone throwing, Molotov cocktails, and burning tires so far, but in the chaotic situation, I knew it could turn to live fire in a flash. We had been training for a long time on how to repel crowds of protesters using nonlethal weapons, while maintaining preparedness for instantaneous "table turning" to live fire. Even then, we would have to be very selective and sharp, and not serve the Palestinian propaganda machine by causing many casualties.

I tightened my grip on his shoulder.

"It very well may be that they open fire here today. Don't take it lightly; the situation will change within seconds. We haven't had a live-fire battle in J&S for years now, and we will need to adapt quickly, yes?"

"Right," he agreed with me.

The night before, my staff and I had hastened to the paratroopers' encampment at Nebi Musa in the Judean Desert to prepare them for Nakba Day. The situation assessment was that things were about to change. I had insisted on receiving reinforcements and received Paratroopers Battalion 202, my old battalion, commanded now by LTC Aaron Haliva. They were not prepared for this kind of fighting and continued to train for facing the Syrian army and Hezbollah. The Palestinian threat was not perceived at the time as posing a substantial challenge. Only the regular forces permanently positioned in J&S knew the drills, the codes, and the unique language developed in CENT-COM. Reserve and regular forces assigned in the region for operational duty received dedicated orientation training and briefings, in order to "recalibrate" them and adapt them to the sensitive complexities that were our share of the task on a day-to-day basis with the Palestinians.

At Nebi Musa, we had briefed the paratroopers and their commanders. Each of my staff officers had been assigned to a paratrooper company, to prepare them for the different kind of warfare we faced.

I had explained to them why it was essential to show restraint, calm things down, and cool the atmosphere, unless the tables turned. If the other side opened fire, a swift and lethal response was to follow, closing the incident quickly and preventing escalation to a broader confrontation that would disrupt the political echelon's efforts to achieve the awaited agreement with the Palestinians. We strongly emphasized the context of our actions, the need to act accordingly, not to overrun long months of political efforts with extensive force, and not to play into the hands of the Palestinians.

I would have wanted to train the 202nd for a few days, bringing them up to speed with the drills we had developed, but they had been assigned to me only on the eve of the Nakba Day. So I had not wanted to put them in front and decided to make them a backup and intervention force.

"We'll position Dadon's Border Police platoons in front," I had ordered my operations officer. "They're professionals. We'll also use our units like Duchifat, and ask for Duvdevan – they're practically locals."

We had been working closely with Duvdevan, under the command of LTC Mickey Edelstein, and since we were pressed for time, they were the best choice. Only if the situation escalated would we activate Aaron's paratroopers.

We had drilled them for a few hours and delivered appropriate equipment, which was also limited. The paratroopers had been loaded on trucks and headed to their positions.

At the brigade headquarters I had issued orders and given a brief. I used the battle layout sketched on aerial imagery to explain how to deploy the forces, rules of engagement, contingency plans, and commander's intent.

"Do you understand, Dadon?" I said, turning him sharply so he faced a tall building inside Area A – territory designated as controlled by Palestinians under the Oslo Accords.*

"Look at the paratroopers. They must also be warned and kept sharp."

Boom. An explosion and a shrieking sound, and Dadon dropped from under my hands, stumbling toward the road. I grabbed a strap from his vest and pulled him behind the jeep. He leaned on me, groaning.

"Medic!" I yelled, as a large blood stain spread on his pants and he moaned with pain.

"Shalit stations, this is Shalit Actual!" I barked into the radio. "Take cover; try to identify shooters; return fire; prepare for table-turning."

Two medics appeared with backpacks and a stretcher. Aaron, the paratrooper battalion commander, also came running with a group of soldiers.

"Are you OK?" he asked, concerned, looking at my hands, which were covered with blood.

I leaped over to the other side of the jeep as the medics began cutting open Dadon's pants, revealing a mass of flesh and blood.

"Aaron – spread out your battalion as planned and prepare for battle."

"Brigade Commander…" I heard Dadon moan. I leaned over him and stroked his face, as he lay on the stretcher, already bandaged.

"An evacuation vehicle is on its way," reported Asi, the health care administration officer, reading my mind.

"Brigade Commander," Dadon whispered to me. "They were aiming at you. That bullet was intended for you."

The rioting went on for several hours. Once in a while I ordered a swift advancement of the jeeps toward the crowd, simultaneous opening of the doors, and a combined salvo of tear gas and well-aimed rubber bullets. We called this combat technique Shock Horses. It was important that we push the crowd away from the junction, due to its proximity to IDF bases and to the only route connecting the village of Beit El to Jerusalem.

Of course we could not open fire to drive away the rioters. The limitations on using force in a democracy are the strength of the weak. We needed to juggle and maneuver while making careful use of nonlethal weapons, beside

* Area A includes the urban areas of Nablus, Jenin, Tulkarem, Qalqilya, Ramallah, Bethlehem, Jericho and 80 percent of Hebron. Israeli citizens are not allowed to enter Area A, with the exception of IDF forces.

pinpoint employment of precision munitions when it came to confronting armed gunmen. To describe this delicate balance I coined the term "riots in the presence of weapons."

There were great tensions between the conflicting interests in the day-to-day fighting, and we needed to carry out the missions in a way that would not contradict the intentions of the strategic echelon. This required constant inter-echelon discourse and inquiries between commanders in the field, senior leadership in the division headquarters, regional command, and the General Staff. Sometimes it was necessary to conduct direct, cross-echelon communication, in order to verify that there was a clear understanding what the appropriate mode of operation was, so the IDF would serve as a tool in the hands of the political echelons and not interfere or disrupt.

A reserve battalion of combat engineers moved forward to the junction, to replace Dadon's men. They were excellent, well-trained reservists.

Their line of jeeps aligned as they should, battalion commander in front. A hail of bricks, stones, and burning tires came down on them and they retreated slightly back, preparing for another charge forward.

I moved forward with a small team and positioned myself about thirty yards behind the battalion commander's jeep. I stood there, observing the roofs and windows of nearby houses. Suddenly I had an ominous feeling. Everything was too quiet.

Clang! I heard a bullet strike a street sign, a meter to my left. Then another clang and whistling sounds and a bullet ricocheted off the road.

"Fall back, take cover, table-turn, open fire!" I ordered.

I ran to the side, raising my weapon as I spotted someone in uniform carrying an AK-47 running between the tall building and a building near the Ramallah-Jerusalem road. He stopped for a moment, raised his weapon, and fired.

I raised my weapon – range about two hundred meters – and fired a few rounds toward him. He either fell or ducked to take cover.

"Actual," called the engineering battalion commander. "All the windows are shattered, I'm taking fire, pulling back, improving my position."

His forward jeeps were bulletproof, including their windows. Bullets had shattered the vehicle's windows and hit the armored plates protecting the engine. At times like this you realize how crucial the armor is.

My mouth was dry. Fear – I recognized this feeling. I knew I must act, fast.

I needed to organize the force. I was thinking fast, hearing shots from my soldiers behind me. I was in a forward position, in the middle of the junction, and my vehicle was sustaining direct hits.

"We need to improve our position!" Lior yelled.

"Wait a minute," I said, taking the microphone, and reminding myself to use a low and authoritative voice and structured orders, like in officers' training school.

"Shalit stations, this is Shalit Actual. Enemy contact straight ahead, 300, infantry and snipers." I deliberately chose standard enemy terminology to have my men act accordingly, as if they were confronting the Syrian army. After all, what was the Palestinian "Force 17" if not infantry?

"Assume firing positions, take out armed targets."

"Gal," Lior signaled me. Bullets were pounding the shelters around us. They probably knew it was my vehicle, for they had targeted me in the morning when they hit Dadon.

"Wait a minute," I signaled back, and continued my orders: "Sector division – road is center. Right boundary – antenna, left – DCO (district coordination office) hill. Duvdevan from the road and right; 202nd from the road and left; Border Police and engineering as backup, from current position. Acknowledge, over."

"This is Mickey, wilco."

"This is Aaron, wilco."

When all had approved, I took my command group and moved to the rear while covering. A wounded French journalist was being rescued under fire. The paratroopers were in great danger as they pulled him to the rear and treated him, while their friends supplied cover.

I assumed a position a bit south of the junction. Not the best spot, but there was no use in moving at this point.

I asked the deputy DCO commander to get me in touch with the Palestinian brigade commander, Sliman Hilas Abu al-Walid.

"Take him," he handed me the mobile phone.

"Abu al-Walid, you're shooting at us!" I said in Arabic.

"Yes," Abu al-Walid answered, embarrassed. "Things are out of control. Please do the best you can."

And that is what I did – the best I could!

My deputy Tzvika and I assessed the situation and gave the order to continue looking for gunmen and hitting them.

After a few hours of fighting, Shlomo, the division commander, arrived. I asked him to approve some kind of initiative action, such as taking over a hill in Area A or bringing in attack helicopters.

"There's no sense in just hammering each other. We have two hours until sundown. Let's hit them hard! Attack helicopters will bring quiet."

"Not yet," said Shlomo. "This is an incident that will end soon."

A bullet penetrated my jeep, grazing a soldier's forehead. He was lucky. A few minutes later, Mickey reported that he had a critically wounded soldier who had been shot in the neck. Without even waiting for Mickey to finish his report, Asi lunged out of the division headquarters gate with a protected jeep to extract the casualty.

Two years earlier, as the division's G3, I had begun promoting the training of Air Force pilots for fighting in J&S.

"Tanks and helicopters in J&S?" People claimed that I had lost my mind. Adopting capabilities that were used in the northern border to J&S was negatively perceived as "Lebanonization" of the situation.

I had also claimed that we should conduct brigade-level exercises for regional brigades dealing with routine security, preparing them for possible escalation to confrontation and combat.

Asymmetric warfare, facing an irregular enemy, necessitates the construction of a "wall" comprised of various bricks: police, security agencies, governmental ministries, military units, and different kinds of weapons and equipment. This is the only way to build an effective and relevant response.

Attack helicopter pilots needed to be trained and a collaborative database needed to be constructed. Because J&S was not covered by maps for use by both Air Force and ground forces, pilots could not find attack coordinates using a common language. It just didn't seem necessary during the days of peace negotiations.

I was accused by many of inciting war.

Now it was the Palestinians who were escalating.

I wanted to indicate to the Palestinians that I intended to escalate, so I scrambled two Cobras, which were soon in position, waiting to assist. I spoke briefly with the pilots, asking them to fly over the junction and then conduct another flyby while dispensing flares, to make it look as if they were shooting at something.

The message was extremely convincing, and hundreds of Palestinians ran in fear of the flare-dispensing helicopters.

I told Abu al-Walid on the phone that if his men did not cease fire, I would give the order to open fire and bring more helicopters. The commander of CENTCOM gave the same message to the Palestinian leadership.

It was finally quiet. I waited for nightfall and then approved the Palestinians' request to move about and collect their many casualties. At the same time, Paton tanks were making their way on tracks via the route to Ramallah, positioning themselves in ramps that we had prepared with bulldozers ahead of time, back when it was difficult to imagine tanks in the Palestinian arena.

Workshop at Lachish

From this battle in May 2000 until August 24 of that year, I worked feverishly to capture and implement lessons learned, and to prepare various classes and courses in coordination with the chief of Infantry and Paratroopers Corps headquarters. I trained and drilled many forces and worked hard to push the development of the new doctrine for fighting "riots in the presence of weapons," tailor-made for a complex urban environment.

The division and command accepted my rigorous approach of doctrine and training.

"You're the kind of commander who should be either encouraged or oppressed," joked BG Shlomo, the division commander. "As we prepare for war, I choose to encourage your activity."

He not only encouraged but vigorously supported my program by promoting (along with MG Itzik Eitan, commander of CENTCOM) the acquisition of protective equipment, funding of sniper courses, preparation of intel material, and advancement of the contingency plans.

On August 24, I led a workshop for fourteen hundred reserve and regular service officers, from company commander and up, in the CENTCOM training base in Lachish. We introduced the equipment and presented the newly written doctrine, with live demonstrations of various levels of escalation, including the employment of SOF and disguised operations, aerial assistance, and tank operations accompanied by Border Police jeeps. Indeed, the jeeps were a new mode of operations, aimed at preventing tanks from being struck by Molotov cocktails. Tanks could not be penetrated, of course, but it was perceptional rather than physical penetration that concerned me.

The highlight of the demonstration was the takeover of a Palestinian town. I already assumed things could escalate to our having no choice but to regain control of the whole West Bank. There were reservations related to this demonstration, as it was not our goal or intention to actually take over a town, certainly not while the peace process was underway. I insisted, however, due to the critical importance of preparedness. Finally we reached a compromise with senior IDF leadership – we would only demonstrate the takeover of a town's outskirts.

I agreed because even the outskirts would yield the required outcome. IDF officers would learn the required doctrine, and they would learn and remember that we were not merely riot police, but a fighting organization that knows how to engage in combat in an urban environment.

The classes and demonstrations were a great success and attracted much attention. It was all very realistic, with an abundance of effects and pyrotechnics, helicopter flybys and landings, tanks, APCs, bulldozers, engineering, Border Police, and disguised operators.

It was an impressive display of joint, coordinated, complex warfare, and people got the message.

During preparations for the workshop, I received word of the tragic death of Nahum Lev in a motorcycle accident. Nahum was a venerable leader and an asset to the IDF. He was courageous and wise, and encouraged initiative and open thought. He was a commander and a friend. I learned much from him, I respected him, and I miss him deeply.

Backing

As events unfolded, I found myself twice at Duvdevan commander Mickey Edelstein's side, advocating in his defense, when it seemed that the system was not backing him up and unjustly having him bear responsibility for events beyond his control.

One night in a village north of Ramallah, his unit raided the home of a wanted terror suspect. The soldiers had silently surrounded the house, when suddenly they began taking small arms fire from the roof.

One of the soldiers identified the source of the shooting, aimed his weapon, and accurately returned fire, killing the shooter. I rushed to the scene. The house was surrounded with additional forces that had been called in, and a PA system was calling to those inside to exit out to the yard. When we stormed into the home, we discovered that the shooter was an old man who had thought that thieves were breaking in to steal his family's possessions.

I saw his body and the loaded gun at his side on the roof. My heart went out to the family when I witnessed their sorrow, but I had no doubt that the force had acted correctly.

There was harsh public criticism of their actions. The incident was defined as a "reckless shooting" by soldiers with "itchy trigger fingers," and the media rushed to side with Palestinian claims of supposed recklessness that resulted in the death of an innocent, harmless old man.

I was livid. I prevented any outside contact with Mickey and took full responsibility myself.

I initiated a full investigation and declared on live television that I was the one who was in command of the operation, and that an armed old man is first and foremost armed and only then an old man.

I also adamantly reaffirmed to my CO – and when I was allowed to, on television and radio as well – that "when we are fired upon, we return fire and hit our targets."

I responded with an especially severe outburst toward an interviewer on Channel 2 when I was asked outrageously provoking questions. In a cynical rebuttal, I said, "If a soldier had been killed from the old man's fire, then I would certainly be here, answering other questions, right? There are no limits to hypocrisy."

I raised my stern opposition to MG Itzik Eitan concerning the commission of an examination committee, and I notified him that he could have me court martialed if he wanted to. He did not.

The second incident occurred on August 24, 2000. Duvdevan was operating in the village of Asira ash-Shamaliya, adjacent to Nablus (Shechem), in pursuit of the terrorist Mahmoud Abu Hanoud, a dangerous fugitive serial killer.

I was spending that weekend at the brigade headquarters in Beit El when I first received reports of an incident involving Duvdevan, north of Nablus in the neighboring regional brigade (the Samaria Brigade).

I was told that there were three fatalities. I rushed to get more details and called Shaldag commander Ronnie Numa, who had served in the past as my deputy in the unit.

"Mickey has fatalities and wounded in Asira ash-Shamaliya," I told him. "You should scramble with your helicopters immediately. They may need you."

Back when I was the Shaldag commander, I had decided that there would be an airborne commando force on alert for every mission that might require it, regardless of where it took place.

This decision was met with severe opposition. There were many who claimed that it was not necessary and that Yamam (the police's special counterterror unit) and Sayeret Matkal were sufficient.

I did not back down and presented my case to the CGS, LTG Amnon Lipkin-Shahak. I claimed that an Air Force commando force stationed on the same base with helicopters was capable of taking off far faster than any other unit. I was positive that there would be events that would require the force being activated. I was supported by Herzl Bodinger, the commander of the Air Force, and the CGS approved.

Sure enough, since we established the alert force, it has been called into action multiple times for urgent missions all over the country. This was the reason that Mickey was not surprised now, when three of his soldiers had been killed and Abu Hanoud had slipped away, that helicopters landed near him with his colleagues from Shaldag, who had come to provide him assistance.

The tragedy led to serious criticism and feelings of dejection. Mickey wanted to resign. He felt he had failed, as did the commander of the J&S Division, BG Shlomo Oren, who announced his resignation.

Mickey had been designated to replace Ronnie as the next commander of Shaldag, but the appointment was now put on hold, and it was decided that Mickey would be dismissed.

I had difficulty accepting Shlomo Oren's decision, and even more so, the behavior of his commanding officers, Generals Eitan and Mofaz (the CGS), who did not try to stop him.

My reservations were shared by the five other brigade commanders in the West Bank Division. I told Shlomo that he had to remain in his position and make needed reforms from a position of command, but he wasn't willing to stay. I saw that he felt he was not receiving support. Those under his command were behind him, but his COs were leaving him alone and exposed.

I expressed my unequivocal objection to Mickey's dismissal at every possible opportunity and personally spoke with the entire chain of command.

My message was harsh, but simple and true: *combat commanders need to be backed up*, even if the results are not positive, and even if they are severe! This is a difficult profession, characterized by the need for constant operational learning, facing an implacable enemy and multiple challenges. If we want field commanders who are leaders with stature, then they need to be given strong backing. The only exception is when a commander has failed in the realm of morals – for this there is no forgiveness and no atonement. Values and morals come first.

Mickey and Shlomo had been in the service of their country for many years. I pleaded that they be embraced and backed, but it was to no avail.

Several weeks later, fighting broke out in the West Bank and in the Gaza Strip, receiving the official operation name Ebb and Flow, but now known as the Second Intifada.

Shlomo was replaced by Benny Gantz, who arrived two days before the fighting began. Mickey, under my command, bravely led his unit in combat.

On one of the days of battle, Mofaz came to see me. As we descended from an observation point, I spoke to him words that were direct, honest, and scathing. I told him how Mickey had led Duvdevan in quality combat and that he needed to remain in command.

I told him that the military was not only built on success stories – there are achievements and errors, successes and failures. We know that in the IDF there are senior officers who have been able to walk through the sprinklers without getting wet. They have never crossed a border and never fought or commanded in battle, so naturally, they have also not erred. They may have only held staff positions, served only on training bases, or they may have been "politicians" – in other words, evasive sycophants. If we continued this way, I told Mofaz, we could find ourselves with only this type in leadership roles, and we had enough of them already.

Mofaz stared at me silently for a long time; he agreed.

Mickey completed his command according to schedule and went on to lead a remarkable career. Mofaz, and later Moshe "Bogie" Ya'alon, gave him the backing he deserved, and I was happy with his success.

The Tunnel to a Final Status Agreement

On September 29, 2000, the campaign confronting Palestinian terror broke out.

What began as a path toward a final agreement with the Palestinians turned into a campaign to systematically dismantle the terror infrastructure in all Palestinian territories, with a physical separation by means of a security fence on the seamline. These actions largely reflected despair of ever achieving a political agreement with the Palestinians.

The campaign in the Palestinian arena in CENTCOM went through a few development stages during the period of time between the beginning of implementation of the Oslo Accords, with the Israeli retreat from Gaza and Jericho in May 1994, until the height of the separation process and construction of the fence in July 2003. CENTCOM's operational concept developed as events unfolded, whether it be preceding them, aligned with them, or lagging behind and responding.

From a focused effort to realign Israeli presence in J&S (including the "Gaza and Jericho first" initiative, which promised partial withdrawal from Jericho and the Gaza Strip, and the Hebron agreement, which gave some autonomy to the Palestinians in Hebron and its environs), the main effort now shifted to a continuous campaign to confront Palestinian violence, mainly the wave of terror attacks against Israel.

As long as agreements between Israel and the Palestinians were being implemented, the operational effort was adapted to facilitate them and maintain the required atmosphere. The IDF dealt with shaping the new reality on the ground and assisted in establishing peace. The metaphor leading CENTCOM's operational concept was that the IDF and the Palestinians were building together a "tunnel toward the final agreement." There was a genuine effort to reinforce the tunnel, illuminate it, and allow free flow until implementation.

In order to allow for the construction of this metaphoric tunnel, CENTCOM emphasized the terms "preventing friction," "avoiding a sense of Israeli patronizing," and the development of a relationship based on an "interstate" logic. The idea was to force the Palestinians to assume responsibility and become a genuine factor in confronting security threats.

This concept of operations was translated into steps and operational terminology, and the tactical actions were used to implement the strategic directive. Thus there came about a variety of logics all intent on the need to transform the Palestinian Authority (PA) into an addressable state apparatus capable of realizing its responsibility.

As I was involved in the thought process, and having the appropriate operational tools to analyze the situation, I considered myself responsible for developing tactical tools derived from the variety of terms and piles of written material. It was not enough to coin terminology that described the current situation. There was a need to express the political directives as updated doctrine, with new operational concepts, techniques, and procedures that would reach all the way down to the soldiers.

I simply began to work on it. I could not leave a doctrine vacuum. The great achievements of early identification and classification of the new situation would remain meaningless without tactical implementation.

I was drawn to implementation in the field. I developed knowledge, learned what had been defined in CENTCOM and understood in the division, and transformed it from theory into practice. It was a period of great professional productivity. Shlomo (during his term), Itzik, and Bogie encouraged learning and assuming responsibility. Mofaz adopted the understandings and added his own points of emphasis. We also saw results in the field. We became an effective combat community. We were relevant.

Thus "preventing friction" and "avoiding a sense of patronizing" were translated into low-signature operations and a change in the operational mode from prominent to covert. Additionally, friction was reduced by reduction in roadblocks and turning some of them into checkpoints.

"Development of a relationship based on interstate logic" was translated into tightening of coordination and liaison activity with the Palestinians, and the operational mode was defined as a "cooling" approach, striving to neutralize friction points (and extreme elements who might sabotage the process), control the level of violence, and contain the situation.

The containment idea was intended to ensure that the security situation stayed under control and did not hinder the main political effort of reaching a peace agreement with the Palestinians. Relevant terms were "the strategic corporal" and "the dual soldier," the first relating to the strategic impact one soldier might have with seemingly tactical actions, and the second implying that a soldier must understand the "cooling" approach and act in a restrained manner. The key is to know how to identify a table-turning situation, and then spring into action, strive to engage, take out the terrorist, and remove the threat.

While sincerely trying to facilitate the establishment of the political agenda, the IDF also underwent wide preparations for a crisis situation, in case the negotiations collapsed and violence escalated dramatically. The situational assessment for the year 2000 clearly identified a Palestinian aspiration to construct a state with a "blood and fire" narrative.

We had earlier indications of such large scale violence, as for example in September 1996, when riots broke out after the opening of the Western Wall Tunnel and three days of live-fire fighting took place throughout J&S and Gaza. Since then, there has been occasional large-scale violence and a relatively low and stable level of terrorism, mainly carried out by terror organizations such as Hamas, Islamic Jihad, and others.

IDF preparation included force buildup, headquarters training, and development of doctrine and procedures developed for the Palestinian arena – a theater with civilian population, urban environment, and popular resistance using stones, Molotov cocktails, and cold weapons, combined with firearms, explosive charges, antitank weaponry, and snipers.

The Air Force was integrated into preparations for the campaign. Appropriate acquisitions were made and rigorous training was conducted in the various military schools.

I was one of the brigade commanders, but my position as an exploratory, pioneering, and innovative leader was well accepted, and I enjoyed real cooperation.

This was a time for leadership.

The period of supporting agreements while preparing for escalation had continued until May 15, 2000, with the eruption of violence on Nakba Day, which I described earlier. After a day of clashes then, the fire subsided and the political process resumed, leading to the Camp David Summit in July. It was a relatively quiet period and was used by the IDF for a more focused preparation in light of the lessons learned in May.

The fighting had instilled an armed struggle agenda within the Palestinians, however, and for the first time, the Tanzim, a militant faction of the Fatah, was allowed to openly use its weapons.

The Fighting Phase

Although Ebb and Flow was not defined as a war, it was in fact a war in the full sense of the word, and may even be officially defined as such in the future. It was the first time the IDF encountered an asymmetric confrontation in high intensity.

From September 2000 the agenda was no longer arrangements and agreements but confronting and countering violence and terror. The development of our operational concepts can schematically be described as follows:

The **containment phase** (May 2000 until the beginning of 2001), the interim period of **continuous pressure** (2001), the period of **systematic dismantling** of terror infrastructure (January–March 2002), the counterstrike of **Operation Defensive Shield** (March 28, 2002), the security control phase of **Operation Determined Path** (June 2002–May 2003), and lastly, the phase of **operational stabilization and arrangement** (second quarter of 2003 and on), during which the security fence was erected.

This was a complex phase, involving simultaneous fighting and negotiations, restraint and offensive action. The Palestinian side initiated popular resistance combined with wide-scale armed activity. The campaign was also conducted in the perceptional arena – mainly through the media, but also physically, on the ground.

The Oslo Accords negotiations between Israel and the Palestinians continued, while on the ground there was intense fighting on the outskirts of cities and along transportation routes. The coordination mechanisms were still fully functional, so in fact both sides were talking and shooting at the same time.

The relevant terms used at the time stemmed mainly from the early preparations for the outbreak of hostilities. Doctrine was mostly focused on riots and disruption of public order, combined with use of weapons in urban areas. The IDF used two kinds of weapons – nonlethal weapons and regular firearms, mostly snipers and precision fires. There was also use of tanks, antitank rockets, and attack helicopters. It was a new phenomenon: the "mixed battlefield."

During this phase, Israel still honored Palestinian sovereignty, by not acting within Area A. Coordination meetings with the Palestinians continued and rules of engagement (ROE) remained strict and stringent.

After about two months, in December, the riots subsided, probably due to our efficient operational countermeasures, and the terrorists diverted their efforts to attacking civilians and military personnel traveling on the roads, as well as indirect firing into villages and military bases. There were also increased terror attacks in central high-population areas within Israel.

The strategic directive continued to maintain containment as the main operative pattern, while striving to prevent internationalization of the conflict (i.e., active international intervention, whether from Arab countries or others). We also had to make all efforts to stabilize the situation and avoid escalation.

In the perceptional arena there were many complications. The Palestinians positioned themselves as David versus the Israeli Goliath.

While commanding the Benjamin Brigade in battle, I was also positioned as a "media warrior," and was sent again and again to counter the Palestinian propaganda in international media. My exposure was very high, in Israel and worldwide.

"You will ultimately pay a high price for this exposure," an experienced media person told me.

Harsh images were etched in the international perception, such as the iconic death of twelve-year-old Muhammad al-Durrah in Gaza (the IDF was accused of having shot him, and although exhaustive investigations proved this was false, the image persisted), and stone throwers confronting tanks.

The picture in the perceptional arena was somewhat balanced in what later became known as the Ramallah lynching. Two IDF reserve staff sergeants entered Ramallah accidently and were detained by Palestinian policemen and taken to the Ramallah police station. A mob of more than a thousand Palestinians brutally murdered them and indescribably mutilated their bodies.

Upon first notification, I tried to assess the situation, drove to the ISA headquarters for updates, and then headed toward J&S Junction to prepare a breaching force, but the incident was over thirty-seven minutes after the initial information, as a Palestinian vehicle brought the victims to the DCO. The sight of their barbarically mangled bodies was horrific.

Shortly after, helicopters attacked and destroyed the police station in Ramallah. The situation was severely deteriorating.

I was an experienced warhorse and had seen my share of terrible sights, yet I took this incident to heart. I felt the same way when a sixteen-year-old Israeli was lured by a Palestinian female terrorist via the internet, and driven to the outskirts of Ramallah, where he was murdered in cold blood.

The massacres carried out by the Palestinians made me skeptical as to the existence of a worthy partner on the other side. During the clashes and battles in the Benjamin Brigade arena, I became convinced that nothing could be settled, even with the Palestinian brigade commander or governor. During local cease-fire arrangements, we would vacate certain buildings and ridges to allow casualty evacuation and to quiet the situation, but we would have to retake these places the next day. I did not always have patience for these games. I was also very resolute in my discourse with our leadership and stubbornly campaigned to keep control of every hill or building captured by my forces.

I clearly understood that this was a cultural clash and a deep-rooted hatred that defied definition. I knew that therefore we must be strong, determined, and steadfast. This will not end in our generation. The term *solution* is irrelevant, so we must buy long periods of time. We can negotiate, but we must resist getting carried away by illusions. There is great uncertainty, so we cannot lose a moment and must build, create, and strengthen ourselves and our hold on our land. Period.

The Palestinians continued to use the situation to their advantage with much sophistication. In order to confront this, I established an Information and Documentation Branch at CENTCOM, which supplied vital material from the battlefield, in near real time.

We experienced the limited extent to which Israel could operate powerful conventional forces during limited conflict. In this phase, it was essential to operate a new, special combination of forces, in order to fight in a mixed arena. Our ability to confront an enemy that employed various patterns of terror, urban guerilla warfare, and increasing civil disobedience became better and better.

Understandable considerations of restraint and fighting ethics led the IDF to strict proportionality. Every retaliatory action was implemented only after measuring its value as opposed to its inherent risks. An effort was made to ensure that our force's signature, or footprint, would be minimal – not in order to reduce friction and a sense of patronizing, but due to perceptional considerations, so our actions would be "under the radar" (or rather, under the camera) to neutralize the underdog effect. So quiet raids, preemptive strikes, lethal and focused intel-based missions, and SOF were preferred in Palestinian territories, in order to diminish the insult of challenging Palestinian sovereignty.

The assumption at the time was that we were facing a centralized Palestinian system that promotes, enables, and controls these manifestations of armed violence.

Therefore, CENTCOM redefined its operational concept as "leveraging," meaning "continuous pressure on the Palestinian Authority, in order to coerce them into preventing terror themselves."

Chapter 10
Operation Defensive Shield

Leveraging

The updated political-strategic directive led to a change in our pattern of operations, and there were also personal ramifications for me.

Bogie asked me to assume the position of chief of operations (J3) at CENTCOM, a position usually attained after two terms as brigade commander, and known to be a stepping point to division commander. The request was repeated by his successor, MG Itzik Eitan. They both stressed the importance of transitioning the command from defense to offense.

CENTCOM needed to be led to a change in its operational pattern and mindset. We needed to initiate and attack, to adopt an offensive state of mind – not just to focus on defense – and to be ready to do so by preparing a wide array of operational plans. I agreed to take the position.

I was already contemplating two main plans. The first was perceived at the time as unthinkable – to fully take control of the West Bank in an operation that would later be called Defensive Shield. The second was an idea that had been debated in the past: to construct an effective physical barrier between central population areas in Israel and J&S. I assessed the situation as critical and called for a hasty implementation of a security separation, lacking any other solution at the time. I perceived this as strictly an operational measure, not a political statement. I believed that in addition to the barrier and separation, a comprehensive response had to be put in place in order to secure the roads, settlement blocs, and specific villages, some of which would be challenging due to a complete lack of defenses. I had a lot of work cut out for me.

After a period of fierce fighting, I concluded my position in Binyamin

Brigade and moved to CENTCOM headquarters at Fort Nehemiah, in the northern outskirts of Jerusalem, near Ramallah.

Negotiations through open channels ceased, and operational activity was directed toward the Palestinian Authority, being the governmental system that bore responsibility for the acts of terror and violence and maintained affiliation with terror organizations. The dual-hatted system – maintaining both a diplomatic appearance and terroristic activity – was no longer tolerated as a phenomenon of a system in its establishment phase. The Palestinian Authority became a target and an opponent, but for some reason was not yet officially declared an enemy.

Because there was no intention to negate the Palestinian Authority's sovereignty or damage their civil mechanisms, there was a need for an operational concept of applying varied levels of pressure and different extents of visibility. For this, I assembled an operational tool box containing an array of pressure actions.

At Kibbutz Ma'ale Hahamisha we held a systemic operation design (SOD) session, which is a form of situational assessment and knowledge-development meeting. It was chaired by J&S Division commander BG Benny Gantz, who would later become the IDF's twentieth CGS.

I led the development of the toolbox for realizing the principle of leveraging, and called this approach TSSBBE, standing for **tightening** (the grip around the PA territories), **shaping** (engineering projects intended to improve defenses, construct new roads, block routes, "re-obstacalize" the area, and encircle towns that served as launch sites for terror activities), **stings** (short-term raids with small- and low-signature forces), **butts** (heavy, high-signature, armored raids, usually lasting for one night), **bites** (high-signature raids, intended to grab and hold areas for longer periods of time), and **easing** (so as not to drag the entire Palestinian population into a full-scale popular struggle, there was a need to funnel pressure and make it easier on those members of the population who were not involved in terror).

The operational concept was implemented tactically by conducting repeated penetrations into PA territory in all regions.

The targets were PA assets – usually buildings, positions, and barriers used by their armed forces. We also conducted arrest operations inside Palestinian territories, and intel-based joint operations with ISA. Other activities took place with the assistance of the civil administration and Israel Police. Military commanders in J&S were not only required to act as a joint force, but to integrate with interagency elements, such as civil administration, the ministry of defense (MOD), and other governmental offices.

I found it very difficult to drive the operational system of CENTCOM toward change from the containment situation and into various forms of initiated strikes.

I gathered around me a perceptive, razor-sharp team. The most dominant in the group was Oded, a young intel officer who actually became the intel officer of CENTCOM's operations branch. I needed a field intel officer who was operational, creative, daring, and fast, and Oded was exactly all these things. He was a young lieutenant who created miracles, generated targets, investigated sources, initiated and raised new ideas without fearing hierarchy or bureaucracy. He had chutzpah. He worked twenty-four hours a day. I was deeply impressed with him, and despite his young age we became close friends. He would later become Shaldag's intel officer and my business partner when we both became civilians.

The operational concept of leveraging held for a few months. The idea was that applying pressure in various intensities would convince the Palestinian system to act, whether via deterrence or by acknowledging that this could promote their objectives. This was the essence of the leveraging concept – applying pressure in order to attain a result. Under this policy, hundreds of initiatives were carried out, and with time and accumulated operational experience, more and more IDF units took part.

Our actions were always proportionate. Most were carried out as a retaliatory response to Palestinian terror attacks, and every step was evaluated for its context and extent, as well as for value versus risk. The mechanisms for approving operational plans continued to be robust, and every entrance to Area A required approval by the General Staff.

Missions were conducted pursuant to the principle of low signature. Although raid forces included tanks, APCs, and bulldozers, most activities were carried out at night and limited in scope. The intent at the time was still to limit as much as possible the conspicuousness of our actions and the media resonance, which is naturally negative, and even more so when it comes to military actions in an urban environment.

The scope of our force's actions increased as time passed, and the more the Palestinians escalated their actions.

On May 18, 2001, after a deadly terror attack in a Netanya mall, Air Force fighter planes struck the prison building in Nablus, which was used as a terror compound. It was the first time fighter jets had been used in J&S. Following a murderous terror attack in Hadera on January 17, 2002, the IDF carried out extensive operational initiatives, including the destruction of the Palestinian Broadcasting Corporation installations in Ramallah, and taking control of the Palestinian town of Tulkarem for the first time.

The leveraging idea had dominated until increasing terror, such as the murder of Minister Rehavam "Gandhi" Ze'evi on October 16, 2001, led to the conclusion that the continuous pressure was not fruitful, and there really was no one to leverage.

At this point an understanding was reached that the campaign against terror had to be waged by our forces alone, for the PA would not do it. The operational concept of CENTCOM was updated and became "systematic dismantling of terror infrastructure throughout the region." The peak in this implementation was Operation Defensive Shield.

Systematic Dismantling of Terror Infrastructure

It had become very clear to Israel that there is a deep linkage between the official Palestinian system and terror organizations. Official Palestinian forces were directly involved in carrying out attacks, and suicide terrorism became a widespread phenomenon.

A turning point came with the horrendous terror attacks in the United States on September 11, 2001. Suddenly, Israel was no longer the focal point. Our counterterror efforts assumed a global context, and the IDF received extensive legitimacy for continuous and systematic actions within Palestinian territory. This influenced mission target choices, such as the large-scale raid on Balata refugee camp in February 2002, as well as the nature and pattern of force activation – activities were more extensive and with an increasingly higher signature.

When I worked on planning the first operation in a refugee camp, we designated Balata, near Nablus, as the objective. The ISA's recommendation was a leading factor, and ISA director Avi Dichter pushed for crossing the psychological barrier. Up until then it had been considered practically impossible to penetrate refugee camps, which are some of the most densely populated areas in the world.

The name of the operation was the title of the book my daughter Ofri was reading at the time, *The Colors Hike*, but soon before issuing the operation orders, I changed it to the Colors Journey. I had experienced missions that did not end up fitting their names, and I expected heavy fighting and consequences. So the trip became a journey, and the mission was initiated.

The mission was successful and delivered not only a physical blow to terrorists and their infrastructure, but an important psychological message that no place was safe for them, and the IDF would reach them anywhere.

A principal integrated in the "systematic dismantling" concept was "blurring of colors." The Oslo Accord maps indicated the zones (Areas A, B, and C) with different colors, but now only operational considerations would dictate where and how the IDF operated, not the colors on the maps. Palestinian sovereignty as defined by the zones was dismissed from the set of considerations.

The systematic approach was reflected both operationally and tactically. Every place that had a sufficient intel picture was attacked, and whole areas were combed, in some cases even from house to house. The Palestinians used homes, schools, and mosques as terror strongholds and weapons caches, hoping Israel would refrain from targeting such places, and using their civilian population as human shields.

At a certain point, after I had gained more experience, I arrived at the decision that the time had come for deep attacks in Palestinian towns, to the point of gaining control over them. After the devastating murderous attack on a bat mitzvah party in Hadera, I ran to the CENTCOM commander, and from him to the General Staff, with a plan for a controlled takeover of the city of Tulkarem. I viewed this as an essential move, to send a message, deliver a blow to terror infrastructure, and prepare ourselves for an overall takeover of the West Bank.

I attended the operations and sorties meeting – a weekly session led by the CGS and attended by members of the General Staff and senior intel officials, where all IDF operational activities are approved and synchronized. As soon as I introduced the concept, I was met with serious objections, for the dominant approach was not to escalate our actions. But I spread out the maps and passionately explained my plan and opinion.

"Will this solve the problem?" LTG Mofaz asked provocatively.

"No, but this is what should be done when civilians are murdered in Hadera. We need to escalate!" I answered angrily.

A heightened argument developed, and it seemed that everyone in the room was against me, but I didn't care and insisted. I thought we should take over Tulkarem, kill terrorists, comb the place, and show them that from now on Palestinian cities would not be immune from attack or serve as safe havens for terrorists.

The room fell silent for the CGS's decision, and to my surprise, he approved the operation. I exited the room and breathed in deeply, trying to lower my racing pulse.

The head of the Planning Directorate, MG Giora Eiland, came out of the room and approached me.

"What just happened?" I asked.

Giora smiled. "Entering Palestinian towns was out of the question until now, but you convinced the CGS."

I called MG Eitan on a secure line and updated him, then conveyed orders to the operations center. The operations officer was excited, wanting to know, "How did you convince them?"

I then called Nahal Brigade commander COL Yair Golan, whom I had already designated for the mission. I wanted to personally explain the outline of the order and deliver preliminary planning guidance. It was important for me that he understand the atmosphere and spirit of the order, and that in light of all the arguments and concerns, it had to work. You simply cannot explain such things in written documents.

After the Tulkarem operation, this method was expanded, and more preemptive strikes were carried out. March 2002 was the deadliest as far as terror attacks, and the systematic dismantling reached its peak.

Without authorization or approval, I began to prepare the operation to take over the whole West Bank. There was a concern that such an act might destabilize the entire Middle East.

I concluded that it would take no fewer than five divisions and understood this would require large-scale reserve recruitment. There was no doubt that a serious preparation process was called for. I summoned representatives from the General Staff and the divisions. We conducted an initial situational assessment, and the battle procedure was underway. The General Staff completely rejected the overall concept, and specifically objected to the order of battle I asked for. I attributed this to a lack of identification of the changed situation, together with gaps between the perspectives of the General Staff and the command, but I assumed that as time passed and the planning progressed, our interests and viewpoints would converge.

My firm approach triggered harsh responses. At a commanders meeting chaired by Mofaz, he asked to be briefed by senior commanders from the command. When my turn came, I presented my opinion clearly – that there was no point in continuing the current policy, that Palestinian terror would continue and escalate, and that we should carry out a large-scale operation to take over the entire West Bank. I argued that this drastic move would reshape the arena and even restructure the entire region geopolitically.

The commander of the armored "Steel Division," BG Udi Adam, jumped up and angrily demanded that I be restrained, for it was not the place of colonels to speak of region shaping and geopolitics. I concluded my presentation and sat down.

"I did not ask you to stop," said Mofaz.

"I finished what I had to say. My position is clear, and I stand behind it."

My mind was set on continuing preparations for the campaign, and I received support from Itzik, the CENTCOM commander.

I set a six-month schedule and devoted substantial portions of my time to these preparations. I saw great importance in connecting and sharing the valuable knowledge that was accumulating with the command commander and the entire General Staff up to the CGS.

We began to conduct planning groups, allocate the forces, prepare intelligence material, and include other services, such as the Air Force, in the preparations. Order groups were conducted, and plans were reviewed and approved.

The feverish attitude with which we worked was not shared by all, for there were those who still thought that the planning was based on my own unrealistic fantasies.

A New Strategic Debate

On March 27, 2002, a Palestinian suicide bomber murdered thirty people attending the festive Passover meal at Park Hotel in Netanya.

I was called to the HQ in Tel Aviv, where I immediately suggested activation of our plan to take control of the entire West Bank. We were authorized to begin with Ramallah and continue incrementally. On the way to Jerusalem, I knew that the time had come. We were going to defeat the Palestinian terror.

The command's war room called me to ask what would be the name of the operation. I thought of the words of the poem "Between Borders" by Israeli songwriter Haim Hefer, ending with "For the impoverished and the old, we will be a defensive wall!" I had been thinking of the words "defensive wall" for some time, and believed they expressed the defensive aspect embodied in an offensive operation.

"The operation is called Defensive Wall," I informed the war room.

Operation Defensive Shield (as it was dubbed in English) commenced on March 29, and became the largest IDF campaign in the West Bank since the Six-Day War in 1967. The extent of the terrorist acts that had been perpetrated gave the legitimization needed to embark on such a large-scale operation.

It was a massive, simultaneous strike, attacking all Palestinian armed infrastructures, combing all refugee camps, arresting and interrogating thousands of people, collecting thousands of weapons, destroying bomb labs and headquarters, and targeting hundreds of terrorists. It was aimed at breaking the Palestinian rationale and creating new security conditions for a new situation. Operation Defensive Shield should be seen, therefore, as a move to cripple the Palestinian system that supported and nurtured terror. The operation was meant to create an effect of shock and paralysis throughout the area, particularly on terrorist organizations.

Palestinian security apparatuses were removed from the cities, eliminating threats and barriers limiting our forces' activity, and setting optimal operational conditions, enabling prolonged preemptive missions and security control by our forces without needing to impose martial law or civil administration.

The blow that the Palestinian Authority suffered, including the physical isolation of Yasser Arafat, laid the foundations for a new strategic debate on the image of the Palestinian mechanism. In this sense, it may be seen as accomplishing the goals of Operation Defensive Shield. I have found that continuous strikes have an effect that may certainly be perceived as a form of decisive outcome in asymmetric warfare.

The effects of Defensive Shield diminished within a few months.

Maintaining the operational momentum and suppression of terror necessitated continuous action and full security control on the ground. Usually such campaigns are aimed at serving a political purpose, but in this case a diplomatic opportunity did not arise, and there was no other Palestinian partner to hand over control to. There was a need to continue preemptive operations throughout the area, because "blurring the colors" and IDF presence in the cities made the rural areas relevant for terror activity, including places that had not been perceived in the past as natural terror habitats.

Such actions are intel based, feasible only with an intel grip perfected to the point of dominance in the Palestinian arena. In places lacking such a hold, disruptive measures are needed, preventing the active Palestinian terror infrastructure from carrying out attacks, or at least interfering with their execution. For this, military actions are needed, in a combined high and low signature. Without intel input, these activities are implemented according to situational assessment.

In this situation of security control, there is also a need for broad feint and deception activities, aimed at intensifying the uncertainty among terror cells, as well as deterrence, and a perceptional campaign aimed at various target audiences. The main campaign was aimed at deflecting the Palestinian public away from suicide terrorism, and was implemented by public diplomacy efforts and psychological warfare, deploying pamphlets, and also by direct targeting of suicide terrorists, their supporters, and their houses.

It should be mentioned that while carrying out high- and low-signature activities, there can also be covert, indiscernible activities, carried out by special forces and governmental agencies.

Identifying and defining the situation is a central and constant challenge for commanders and senior staff officers. I saw this as a key issue in CENT-COM throughout my three positions there. Remaining pertinent, and not overly obsessed with past battles, necessitated advanced processes for knowledge development and for operational planning.

I believe the analytical methods we developed were efficient and advanced, and enriched the standard assessment processes. These methods would later prove vital in the Galilee Division and in the Depth Command.

Still, it should honestly be said that these are difficult missions for every leader, even an experienced one. It is hard to perform magic.

Operational Politics

Toward the summer of 2003, MG Moshe Kaplinski (Kaplan) was appointed to replace Itzik Eitan as the commander of CENTCOM.

Kaplan and I had known each other for many years, and our relationship was quite complex. I viewed him as one of the commanders who had greatly influenced and shaped me when I was the 202nd Battalion commander and he was my brigade commander. He had vast experience in routine security operations, and was injured twice in Lebanon. His attitude toward my battalion was both good-natured and demanding. Over the years, however, our relationship became murkier.

We renewed our connection after a few years, when he was appointed as the prime minister's military secretary. He had accumulated much power and was clearly influence by political agenda. Kaplan called me to his office in Tel Aviv, where we discussed current events and analyzed the situation in J&S. He explained the prime minister's policy and asked me to keep in touch and to keep him posted.

Our interaction became more frequent and close, but then came the affair of my appointment as the Paratroopers Brigade commander.

MG Eitan had already notified me that I was to replace COL Aviv Kochavi as the Paratroopers Brigade commander. During a meeting with Bogie, after his selection as the next CGS, he confirmed my nomination.

But Kaplan had other plans.

I started to worry when the CGS, Mofaz, changed IDF protocol and delegated the authority to select colonels to the commander of the Ground Forces Command.

When Kaplan was confirmed as the new commander of CENTCOM, it was already clear to me that things had changed. I was called to an interview with him at the prime minister's office in Jerusalem. It was a warm conversation, but I felt it was just for the sake of protocol. When Kaplan used the term "candidate" to describe my position, it became obvious to me that he was building a case to rebuke my nomination.

At the time all this was taking place, I was at the height of my strength, and I was highly regarded throughout the force and government for influencing the IDF's moves and the success of Operation Defensive Shield.

But rumors were being deliberately circulated and messages conveyed about me, and I learned of a new allegation: that I ostensibly did not go enough into detail. I had already become known for my adoption of operational art, but this did not diminish my attention to tactical details, as I had demonstrated in all my positions up to J3 CENTCOM.

Delegitimization, sullying, slandering, spreading rumors, and using the media were common and dominant internecine tactics in the IDF at the time. This was downright politicization, with scary norms, methods, and practices of "erasing" people who did not belong to the right team. Frankly, I was a fighter, and not equipped to deal with this.

For the first time, I discovered the invention common to some senior commanders in the IDF of portraying merits as disadvantages. Thus intelligence turned overnight into a handicap, and intellectualism became "lack of combativeness."

The promotion and assignment process in the IDF was helplessly fettered to this evil spirit, so promotion depended on affiliation with the right group.

The complaints on sophisticated language, detachment from the field, and nicknames such as "astronaut" and "daydreamer" had acquired a foothold. They had a clear objective – to prevent me from making it to the top.

Because I captured lessons learned from my forces in the field and transferred them to the military schools, I became known as a man of the book (*safra*), not the sword (*sayfa*). My propensity to write articles and brief senior foreign generals in English was considered by some a disadvantage.

On the other hand, Bogie saw these abilities of mine as an advantage, calling my lexical skill "the wisdom of action." He encouraged me to continue initiating and writing as much as I could. "Your writings are already being learned in a few military schools," he said.

But his view was not typical of our organizational culture, which made a clear distinction between thinkers and practitioners. It was one or the other. He who held a pen could not hold a sword; speaking English, using correct Hebrew, and reading books made you a philosophizer, detached from details.

Sadly, there were also the masqueraders, secretly thinking and writing, but concealing it so as not to fall into the "detached" category. It was not in my nature to be secretive in this way, and I paid the price for my lack of attention to internal politics.

In my second meeting with Kaplan, he informed me of his decision to appoint COL Dror Weinberg as Paratroopers Brigade commander.

I spoke at length with Bogie, who was already the CGS. He was clearly disappointed with what had taken place and suggested that I command the officer school, emphasizing that this would be a stepping point toward division commander.

I viewed the phenomenon as shameful, and expressed my disappointment in the process. I notified the chief of Infantry and Paratroopers Corps, BG Gadi Shamni, of my decision to withdraw my candidacy for Paratroopers Brigade commander, as the process was artificial and the decision had already been made. Gadi tried to dissuade me, saying it was a vote of no-confidence. That was certainly what I felt.

Many viewed the appointment of the Paratroopers Brigade commander as it really was – a political act.

There were those who recommended that I resign, but I refused.

"Of course not!" I protested. "CENTCOM doesn't belong to Kaplan, but to the Israeli people, and I will bear my responsibilities until the end."

I was invested in vigorously promoting the construction of the security fence, approving new operational plans, carrying out special missions, and protecting villages. I wasn't going anywhere.

I arranged for a meeting with Kaplan and told him how I felt. I also told him I would continue to serve as a dominant J3 and that I would never mix personal issues with professional considerations.

Our relations were usually OK. I tried to align myself with Kaplan's style, which was quite different from that of his predecessor.

Kaplan brought much knowledge from his experience in Lebanon. We began pushing for a more advanced headquarters, to accelerate the construction of the fence and the protection of the villages.

He had a good influence on various issues that arose in the field, and I listened and learned from him, but did not become his yes-man. I believed that the command was moving forward but at the same time backward in many aspects, especially in operational design and planning, as instilled by Bogie and Itzik Eitan.

I told him many times that he was feared by staff officers and commanders, in a way that oppressed open thinking.

One day, during a meeting on the command's operational concepts, we were discussing strategic-operational level issues and Kaplan instructed that from then on I was not to use words with more than two syllables. It was not clear whether he was serious or joking.

"Is that clear?"

"Yes, Kaplan, why not? We'll use only two-syllable words."

His style was both friendly and aggressive. Kaplan has a special talent for being friendly, one of the guys, but then flipping in an instant and yelling furiously. It wasn't very pleasant.

I was very concerned by the tendency of some staff officers to kowtow to him. A staff officer in a regional command has great responsibility and is obligated to express independent opinions before his commander without hesitation or fear of personal consequences. This is why most staff officers in a command are full colonels – to enable their independent posture before a charismatic or even terrifying CO.

Facing Kaplan, there were those who mumbled, whispered, and just said the minimum. Some of them held critical positions in the command!

I believe that Kaplan valued my directness but did not like it. We shared moments of candidness, and in one of them Kaplan told me that if he were CGS, he would want me as his chief of the Planning Directorate (J5). He declared that after my tenure as commandant of the officers' training school, he would want me back as a division commander in CENTCOM, while he was still commander.

Despite all the tensions, the operations branch under my command continued to lead and act vibrantly. We were incessantly hit on the head and smacked on the wrist by Kaplan, but I held talks with my staff, and calmed and directed them toward implementing the commander's intent.

I was making a big effort to remain loyal.

Amidst those stormy days, the eye of the storm was at home, our peaceful sanctuary of warmth and togetherness. Donna was pregnant and we were anxiously expecting our next child during the difficult days of the campaign against terror, the fighting in Defensive Shield and the operations that followed. When Nir was born, we were overwhelmed with joy. All around were battles, fighting, stress, and historic events, but at home there was a little girl whose smile illuminated our lives and reminded us of the really important things in life.

The Security Barrier

A central strategic effort at this point was the arrangement with the Palestinian leadership. This would require the definition of territories and construction of long-term infrastructure, including barriers – all elements characteristic of agreements between countries. But it seemed that all attempts to engage a Palestinian partner for dialogue were futile. Without an agreement, it was essential to impose security arrangements, mainly building the seamline barrier and strengthening the security of Jewish villages in J&S. The experiences gained from constructing the fence in the Gaza Strip and knowing the effectiveness of barriers in other places, such as Lebanon and the Jordan Valley, assisted in the propulsion of the resource-demanding project named "The Other Way" – construction of the seam-line barrier. Although it is known internationally as "the wall," only 3 percent of the barrier is made up of a wall.

I devoted myself to this meticulous project. It was staff work of the most complex nature, combining all IDF services and departments, most governmental offices, and other agencies. Our groundwork laid the foundation for what would eventually be the role of a designated administration in the ministry of defense.

One evening, Kaplan and I presented the outline of the project to the CGS, LTG Bogie Ya'alon. I explained in detail all the components of the project, including the idea of differentiation between Palestinian population that supports terror and that which seeks normal life. When I used the Hebrew term for differentiation (*bidul*), Bogie interrupted and said: "What do you mean by *bidul*?"

I explained the concept.

"So you really mean *differentziatziah*."

"That is correct, sir," I said, sneaking a smile at Kaplan. "But my commander forbids me to use more than two-syllable words."

Worshipers' Alley

On November 15, 2002, during a battle following an ambush by terrorists along the "protected" Worshipers' Alley in Hebron that leads to the Cave of the Patriarchs, Colonel Dror Weinberg, the commander of the regional Judea Brigade, was killed, along with eleven more soldiers, police officers, and civilians.

Although I was toward the end of my tenure as J3 and had already served as a regional brigade commander, I immediately suggested to Kaplan that I take over the brigade.

"What for?" he asked. I guess he thought it would negatively influence the nomination for Paratroopers Brigade commander – the position that had been taken from me in such an ugly way.

He did not accept my offer, and quickly appointed COL Hagai Mordechai, who was called back from studying in the United States. Soon after that, Mordechai was also appointed the next Paratroopers Brigade commander. But the nomination was later revoked, after two security guards were mistakenly killed by IDF forces in the Judea Brigade area, under COL Mordechai's overall responsibility.

In his place was appointed COL Yossi Bachar.

Yossi, a decent and honest person, called me and expressed his discomfort.

"You are more senior than me and more suitable for the position. I feel bad about this."

I was already on my way to Bahad 1. I congratulated him, expressed my support, told him how much I appreciated his integrity, and wished him all the best in his position.

Chapter 11
Commandant

Safra and *Sayfa*, Doubtful and Determined

Bahad 1 is not just another unit, but a national institution, serving as a beacon to all officers, the entire military, and the Israeli society as a whole.

It is a unique privilege to assume command of such an institution. Although it trains a multitude of officers, it makes a point of maintaining high standards, and the results have been demonstrated in many battlefields throughout the years. I believe that an IDF officer is worthy of appreciation first and foremost because he or she chose not only to serve the nation, but to serve in a greater capacity – to add another term of service, and assume more duties and responsibilities. These are far from trivialities.

It was a significant closing of a circle, returning as commandant to the place where I had been qualified as an officer nineteen years earlier.

I aspired to educate cadets who would always strive to broaden their education and knowledge. We encouraged curiosity and set a goal to build erudite officers who combined the book and the sword – *"safra v'sayfa,"* as the Aramaic saying puts it.

An Israeli officer must be skeptical, incisive, and critical, but these attributes must be accompanied by genteelness, attentiveness, and a polite manner of speech.

Being an officer is a way of life, joining the collective of the few who make decisions and bear responsibility. Only those who choose to lead, and are chosen to lead, should serve as a generative force, and the passion of leadership should be like a fire in their bones. With them it is first "us" and only then "me."

I believe with all my heart in the need to promote the inclusion of women in all significant national positions and most positions in the IDF. Therefore, I felt it was essential to convey the value of equality to the military and entire nation.

Until then, most training courses for women were conducted in Bahad 12. I objected to this separation, and was happy when we finally succeeded in dismantling Bahad 12 and integrating women into the courses at Bahad 1, despite the difficulties.

The school was now comprised of the following components:

- Gefen battalion – infantry complementary course, the jewel in the crown
- Lahav course – basic qualification of all ground forces officers
- Maoz course – qualification of combat support officers
- Nachshon course – all staff and administration officer training

In Lahav, Maoz, and Nachshon, men and women were fully integrated. Only the dormitories were separate.

Integration of women was a significant challenge. It introduced natural tensions and sensitivities between men and women, and created many concerns – especially for the religious leadership in Israel. The debate and process were also joined by women's rights organizations.

There was a need to determine and define how to train new officers in a fully integrated and joint manner.

The Ground Forces Command led the Appropriate Integration Directive (Hashiluv Hara'ui) in the service. Together we dealt with implementing these principles in Bahad 1, and I made it possible to live together, religious and secular, Jews and non-Jews, women and men – based on mutual respect, strict discipline, and clear rules. I suffered scathing media criticism after I dismissed a cadet who made out with a female soldier, in public, on base. I delivered severe punishments for sexist remarks.

I was trying to set the tone for the long run and knew that if we failed, there might not be a second chance for correction.

It was a complicated organizational change, aimed at meeting the IDF's modern operational challenges, while carefully addressing religious sensitivities that have always been complicated in Israel. Those who understand the depth and difficulty of these issues in the history of our country can comprehend the magnitude of the revolution the institution went through during my tenure as commandant. I felt it was a unique, one-time opportunity, and I understood the enormity of the responsibility. This was not merely a military issue, but a national one.

Singing the National Anthem

There were many confrontations surrounding my rule that no cadet was to be accepted unless he or she knew our national anthem – "Hatikvah" – by heart. I also dismissed cadets who failed basic exams testing their knowledge of the history of Israel and the Jewish people, which I viewed as a minimum requirement. I believed that the intellectual and spiritual foundation of an officer was essential, not only for his or her role in the IDF, but in future leadership positions as a civilian.

I wanted to initiate a program that would develop Bahad 1 into a full-fledged military academy, and I began coordination with the academic establishment for recognizing studies as accreditation toward an academic degree. To this end, I met with the president of Ben-Gurion University, Professor Avishay Braverman. I also began planning a basic Judaism course in collaboration with the president of Bar-Ilan University, Professor Moshe Kaveh.

I set high standards and forced units to select and send only those capable of passing the exams. This also drove units to invest in educating their soldiers, to make them eligible. This all bore fruit, and gradually there was a clear indication that the level of cadets was rising.

We wrote publications on battle heritage, Jewish heritage, and basic concepts in Judaism, making them preliminary learning material for officer candidates when they were still in their units. The word spread in the IDF that Bahad 1 was seriously dealing with education, and this had a positive ripple effect throughout the force. I doubled the education terms of the course and added subjects dealing with the Negev Desert (in which Bahad 1 resided), under the name "Ramon File."

I made a great effort to promote the idea of creating an integrated, joint, multi-service officer training course, which would introduce the basic skills and elements such as education, navigation, physical training, and operational art. I believed in the need to have a joint phase of officer training for all IDF personnel, and then have each branch and service lead its own designated course, such as the Air Force Academy and the Naval Officer Course. This concept never materialized, due to the aloofness and stubbornness of the services, wishing to keep their independence.

I still firmly believe in the need for joint cooperation, and would also promote the idea of constructing an interagency officer course, integrating all national security agencies.

I insisted on accepting the best platoon commanders as instructors in the course, contrary to the unit's natural tendency to keep the best to themselves. My approach was accepted and backed by the commander of the Ground Forces Command and the CGS. Within a few months the change was apparent, and the school's staff was constructed of elite officers – the best of the best.

My "activist" approach was widely covered by the media. Sadly, I discovered that every internal session with my cadets was being leaked to each unit's "home journalist." This happened also after each evaluation board, where as commander, I assessed the suitability of some cadets and decided whether they would be expelled from the course or passed on to the next year. During these boards, I had the opportunity to set standards and send a message to the entire military, but I also remembered that I was dealing with individual people, eager to succeed. I felt that in a way, I was conducting a dialogue with the entire Israeli society, not only the military.

I found it imperative to publish points of emphasis and clarifications to the cadets and their commanders: for instance, the difference between mistakes that result from erroneous judgment and those that entail negligence or even malice. From these definitions it is clear that because we are only human, we may all make mistakes in judgment, and this should not necessarily lead to disciplinary consequences. But it should lead to something extremely important – a mistake is an opportunity, allowing a continuous process of improvement.

Willingness to accept mistakes is a critical component in developing responsibility and encouraging initiative. Still, mistakes should be evaluated in context. It is easier to forgive professional mistakes, and harder to forgive mistakes related to values.

On the other hand, mistakes that result from negligence or malice violate the military's basic foundations of code of conduct, discipline, and values. If done intentionally this constitutes a crime, and should be treated as such. I dismissed cadets who committed such mistakes.

I refused to compromise when it came to lack of credibility. Those who lied, cheated on tests, or deceived in any way were removed permanently. Cadets whose professional achievements were not sufficient were given a second chance to learn and pass the exams; if they still couldn't pass, I made them start over again with the next entering class.

There were also contemporary issues of importance to the IDF that needed attention. There was a widespread phenomenon of weapons being lost or stolen. I made it known that abandoning a personal weapon would lead to standing before an evaluation board, and – if negligence was proven – dismissal from the course.

There was one case where I decided to return a cadet to the course rather than dismiss him. A paratrooper cadet had reported to his commander that he had forgotten his weapon in his tent before navigation training. He had returned to retrieve it and headed out to the field, and could have easily gotten away with it had he kept it to himself. I saw this as a positive example of personal integrity, and I circulated the story to all the staff and cadets. The cadet stood before me in an evaluation board, and I decided to return him to the course with words of praise, but also a note of warning in his personal record.

During my tenure we began preparations for the disengagement from Gush Katif, the Jewish settlement in the Gaza Strip, where Jewish presence dates back to biblical times. It had been captured in the 1967 Six-Day War after a lengthy Jewish exile from the area and was resettled. Prime Minister Ariel Sharon's government decided that Israel would completely withdraw from the Gaza Strip and vacate all Israeli presence. The IDF was appointed as the leading force for implementation. The "Disengagement Plan" became one of the most controversial and sensitive events in Israel's history, and its ramifications are apparent until this day.

I did not like the plan or its implementation, but it was absolutely clear to me that IDF soldiers must carry out legitimate orders. During one of the discussions we conducted with the cadets before the disengagement, a cadet declared that he did not intend to take part, and that he intended to disobey orders.

His commanders brought him before me, and we had a discussion, in which he reiterated his intention to disobey orders. I found no justification to make him into an officer. An officer can never choose his missions according to his political or religious beliefs.

Because the IDF's main missions during that era were confronting terrorism and guerilla warfare in low-intensity conflicts, I updated the course curriculum to reflect these kinds of challenges, with less emphasis on fighting regular armies. It is the commandant's responsibility to set the appropriate balance, reflecting the times.

I did not tolerate disrespectful speech, street talk, or profanity, and emphasized this while insisting on correct Hebrew in every class and debate. A cadet who referenced the minister of defense using a disrespectful slang term was brought before the evaluation board, where I demanded that he take back his words. He refused, saying, "But that's what I think about him."

I explained that I have personal views on a few politicians, but as an officer I do not expose them – surely not using vile language. When he persisted, I understood that he was not mature enough and had him removed from the course. The next day, the case was debated in the Knesset, but for me this was merely a professional issue, not personal or political.

I encouraged the cadets to take upon themselves personal assignments aimed at influencing and assisting the community. Some adopted a school in the Negev, others a hostel for rehabilitating drug addicts.

Because I wanted personal connection with the cadets, I decided to teach some of the classes myself, and this way each cadet met me in person at least six times during the course. I asked that cadets give me written feedback, as they would for any other instructor, relating to my methods, conduct, and influence. I also received sociometric ratings from all students. Sometimes I got hammered, but I am very proud of the positive 99 percent.

Many people and organizations tried to intervene with what happened at Bahad 1. On the issue of inclusion of women, there were, unfortunately, rabbis who tried to initiate separation of a religious battalion. There were also rabbis who attempted to get involved in the regulations of conduct of the prayers on base. I refused and suffered the blowback from the religious newspapers. I left it up to CWO Taito, who coordinated it with the IDF chief rabbi. I stood my ground even when senior leadership recommended not opposing the rabbis.

One-Millimeter Leadership

More than anything, an officer is a leader. His ultimate test is his ability to lead people and motivate them to fulfill the mission. A good officer need not emphasize rank. His authority is expressed by his conduct, professionalism, and values.

In operational units, the commander should be observed by his soldiers as he shares with them all their experiences – eating, sleeping, working, and training. He is close to them and inspects their actions from within, while setting a positive example in everything he does. Operational activity will lead to shared experiences of long days in an APC, in observation points, and on patrols, where he is always one of the soldiers but special at the same time. This fits the ancient theme of "primus inter pares" – first among equals.

During operational activities, the combat leader should identify "leadership intervention points," identifying a decline in the level of performance, pointing it out immediately, and initiating strict corrective action. He will identify violations to norms and values and react strictly, including punishment. If he discovers compromises in the required standards or finds that over-closeness is leading to a breakdown in his authority, a leader must fearlessly reposition borders, even at the cost of losing popularity.

He will intervene and clarify, controlling his temper, language, and conduct, maintaining a reserved and restrained manner, and reminding all that this is a military unit committed to its mission and that he is nobody's friend, but rather their commander. A commander cannot allow the creation of an erosive togetherness environment. Good atmosphere and sense of unity, yes, but most certainly not compromising discipline or blurring the thin line between a commander and his subordinates. This is what I call "one-millimeter leadership."

If not on constant guard, a leader might experience a moral deterioration and degradation in his unit. A soldier must understand why something should be done and how to do it, both from the point of view of military doctrine and according to moral standards. In a democracy like Israel, neither of these can stand on its own.

Fighting, especially the continuous asymmetric warfare we are engaged in, necessitating extended presence in disputed territories in J&S and Gaza, leads to difficult tests of values such as facing helpless civilian population, prisoners, and detainees. Moral backbone necessitates that a commander speak words that are not always popular or easy. The effective commander does not "go with the flow." His words must be profound and direct, and spoken decisively and with perseverance.

First and foremost, human dignity begins within the platoon. A commander must foster an environment of mutual respect, and eliminate negative norms such as class distinctions and abusing rookies. For when this is breached and a free rein given, unfortunate deeds typical of godless people prevail.

A commander's authority emanates to a large extent from his perceived professionalism. Out of responsibility to the missions and his soldiers, a commander should demonstrate curiosity and a constant desire to learn and improve, and he should instill confidence within his subordinates that he can teach them, guide them, and assist them professionally. He must be proficient in the art of war as is required by his position, lead toward the target, fulfill the mission, and return the force home even if things get complicated. And his troops should have full confidence that if, God forbid, soldiers are hurt, he will never leave them behind.

It is extremely important for me to emphasize the need for a commander to see two simultaneous pictures: the picture of what exists in the present, and at the same time a picture of what should be – the desired way the unit should be conducted. The gap between these two pictures in the leader's mind creates a constant dissonance until the gap is eliminated and the present state and the desired state become one.

A commander's professionalism and values enable him to identify the gap, and the means to narrow it and bridge it, ultimately merging the pictures.

Am Yisrael Chai (The Nation of Israel Lives)

In November 2004 I was invited to Germany by my friend Eitan Drori, from Keren Hayesod (United Israel Appeal), to participate in a few events commemorating Kristallnacht. I hesitated. I knew Germany was now our ally and I occasionally hosted cadet delegations from Germany at Bahad 1 for joint learning events. But I had an unclear, primal, perhaps genetic resistance to setting foot on German soil.

I finally agreed and combined the trip with a visit to the German officer school at Dresden. Donna joined me so we could spend time together.

My first lecture was especially challenging. Eitan had arranged with the German government that I would speak before hundreds of young academics at Dachau concentration camp, on the anniversary of Kristallnacht. I consulted with my friend Arye Barnea, a brilliant expert on the Holocaust, but I found it difficult to prepare my speech.

"So don't," Donna said decisively. "After visiting the site, you will speak from your heart. You will know what to say."

We walked through the paths of the camp, between the buildings, and still I didn't know what to say. Meanwhile, more than a thousand Germans gathered to hear me.

I entered the gas chamber, from there to the crematorium, then out to the pile of ashes. I was shaken. With frozen fingers, I pulled out my notebook and wrote like a man possessed – the words were practically writing themselves. I straightened my beret and my uniform, took a deep breath, and spoke.

I later published my speech for the cadets at Bahad 1.

Commander's Bulletin Number 2

Eve of Yom Hashoah (Holocaust Remembrance Day), fifty-five years after Israel's independence and resurrection of the Jewish people.

In 1972, during the Munich Olympic Games, eleven Israeli athletes were murdered by a Palestinian terror organization. The murder was committed on German soil, twenty-eight years after the Second World War and the Holocaust.

No matter where they hid, the initiators and planners of the attack were eliminated, one by one, by the long arm of Israel.

Because the Jews have a state.

In 1976 an Air France airliner was hijacked by Palestinian and German terrorists. Jews and Israelis were separated from the rest of the passengers, reminiscent of the selections carried out thirty-two years earlier in the Holocaust.

IDF special forces landed at Entebbe by night, killed the terrorists, and brought the hostages back home to Israel.

Because the Jews have a state.

In 1981 terrorists entered a baby dormitory in Kibbutz Misgav Am and murdered a two-year-old baby, a kibbutz member, and a soldier. The IDF arrived on the scene and engaged the terrorists, killing them and freeing the hostage children.

Because the Jews have a state.

In 1991 when the Jews of Ethiopia were in distress, IDF and El Al planes with Shaldag operators flew to Addis Ababa. Within twenty-four hours, fifteen thousand Jews were brought to Israel. Out of the depths they cried for help, and in blue and white planes they were rescued.

Because the Jews have a state.

In 1999 the earth shook in Turkey and buildings collapsed. IDF teams rescued an Israeli girl – Shiran Franco – from the wreckage.

Because the Jews have a state.

And when terror intensified during the last two years, we rose up like lions to position a Defensive Shield between terror and the citizens of Israel.

ISA, Israel Police, IDF – we rose in these cases and in many more, to protect, because Jewish blood is not cheap. And there is a State of Israel.

On the eve of our Independence Day, we remember the millions who were murdered. They were victims of a systematic, planned, efficient process to commit genocide.

It did not happen thousands of years ago, and was not perpetrated by some desolate and uncivilized tribe.

It happened not long ago. The survivors and their scars are still among us, and the blood of our brothers and sisters cries up to us from the earth.

It happened, and we did not have a state and we did not have defensive forces.

In every generation there are those who seek to destroy us. We are the IDF, the strong hand and outstretched arm.

We remember our brothers today – children, families, elders – a wonderful human treasure that has been murdered and lost.

And we shall remember the bravery, the endurance, the determination to live, the courage to cope, and the bravery to rebel and fight in ghettos and forests, with the partisans, in the ranks of the Allied forces, and as parachutists from Mandate Palestine in the ranks of the British Army. Jewish valor has risen.

As Hannah Senesh (who parachuted into Yugoslavia in order to assist Hungarian Jews and was captured and executed) wrote: "Fortunate is the match that burns and kindles the flames. Fortunate is the flame that burns inside the hearts."

We are here, a lively and vibrant nation. "In your blood, live," Ezekiel (16:6) told us. "In your blood, live." And we live and remember everything, bleeding, scarred, and strong, and nothing is forgotten.

For we have a state and we have a purpose, and the Jewish nation lives.

Officers of the IDF are those who were inculcated with the responsibility and commitment to the State of Israel, to the Israeli society, and to the Jewish people.

An everlasting commitment lives within us for all generations. In fire we have been forged. We, the IDF soldiers, cadets, and officers-to-be, are entrusted with the eternity of Israel.

Many times an officer, soldier, or combat commander asks himself: "What am I doing here?" and usually it takes time – minutes, even hours – until he has the answer, and he puts on his combat vest and heavy backpack and carries on. After visiting Dachau, and even more so after Auschwitz, I knew the answers within split seconds.

In January 2005, the president of Israel led a delegation to Poland for an event commemorating sixty years since the liberation of Auschwitz. I led the IDF contingent, comprised of representation from Bahad 1 cadets, Air Force Academy cadets, and Naval Officer School cadets.

It was a harsh, snowy, and stormy winter, and during a short but meaningful and eventful visit, we represented the IDF and the State of Israel. The first thing we did upon arrival was to visit a large cemetery near Krakow, where we lay wreaths and flags of Israel on the graves of soldiers who fought in the Jewish Brigade of the British Army in World War II.

In snow and freezing cold, we conducted a meticulous military ceremony, which was also broadcast live on Israel radio. I addressed the formation of soldiers and said that we had come to Poland – a young and strong Israeli generation, with Adi, Matan, Gal, and Yuval – to express our respect to Peretz, Yaacov, and Salim. I meant to contrast our fresh and so Israeli Sabra names with the more traditional names of former generations.

I ended the ceremony and the radio broadcast with the words: "Good morning, Israel. *Am Yisrael chai.*" My words were repeatedly broadcast during the next few days.

It was the eve before the main ceremony at Auschwitz, and I wanted to visit the Auschwitz 1 camp with the cadets that very night. It was a long ride due to heavy snowfall, but we finally made it there and entered, marching in formation, raising the flags of Israel and the IDF. We passed between the piles of shoes, clothes, hair, and Zyklon B canisters, and left with our heads held high, marching as an army.

During breakfast the following morning, we spoke to Holocaust survivor Miriam Yahav. It is an important custom to have a Holocaust survivor join each delegation in order to serve as a "witness" and give firsthand testimony as to what took place.

"I'm furious," she said. "What are all of these countries doing here now for the Auschwitz liberation celebrations? They're taking advantage of us! When we were being murdered, they did nothing. I think I should do something about it."

I did not anticipate what she would do that evening, during the ceremony, in front of the entire world.

In the afternoon I convened all the cadets in the hotel lobby, and we were joined by IDF chief rabbi BG Israel Weiss, with whom I was very friendly.

We sat in a circle and I asked that each cadet tell us about himself, his family, and how he related to the experiences we had encountered. A touching discussion developed, and we shared magical moments of openness. I told them my life story and so did the chief rabbi, who was moved by the cadets' behavior and reflections.

Rabbi Weiss asked that we all stand, and he prayed for the welfare of the State of Israel, the IDF, and all of us. It was a moment that all who attended will cherish forever.

That evening, we set out to attend the international ceremony at Auschwitz-Birkenau. We marched through the death camp, toward the demolished crematorium, and the concourse where the ceremony was to take place, but an unpleasant surprise awaited us. The IDF delegation had been issued an "outer circle" badge, preventing us from approaching the assembly of the senior international delegations. Our arguments and protests were futile and we were, in fact, excluded from the ceremony itself, and out of view of the cameras broadcasting it worldwide and home – to Israel.

I was furious and decided I would not give up. I asked an Israeli with an "inner circle" badge to pass it through the fence once he was in. One of my cadets used it to get in and then passed it back out to us. This method was used to let in about half of our delegation, but we were soon found out and thrown out, frustrated and hurt, as the Polish organizers' loud reproach echoed throughout the ceremony area.

I still wasn't going to give up. As soon as the ceremony had begun, I took advantage of the diverted attention toward the podium, and repeated the badge drill. In no time we were all on the inside, and began infiltrating toward the front row, step by step, through the crowd, carrying the flags of Israel and the IDF. Holocaust survivors were excited to see us, and made way for us to push forward, but there were also Polish invitees who grumbled and complained that we were blocking their view with our flags.

"You should have thought of that sixty years ago," Rabbi Weiss muttered quietly. "If you had prevented this place from existing, we wouldn't be blocking your view."

We finally reached the front row, proudly flying our flags, as the president of the State of Israel began his speech. Suddenly, Miriam Yahav broke out of the crowd and ran toward the podium, passing through security barriers by raising her voice at the security personnel towering over her. She finally reached the podium and positioned herself behind the president, who was addressing the audience. She stood out in her white sweater with a big Star of David pinned to it.

When the president concluded, she approached the podium with great confidence and began to speak in Polish, her voice breaking from time to time. She rolled up her sleeve and showed the audience the number tattooed on her arm by the Nazis. When she finished speaking, the crowd applauded, and she came back to us and stood proudly among our flag bearers.

Then the second part of the ceremony commenced, in which heads of state walked solemnly, with heads bowed, and placed candles on the memorial site, surrounded by cameramen.

Meanwhile I had made a decision, first hesitantly, but then decisively.

I ordered the flag bearers, with two Air Force cadets, four infantry cadets, and the chief rabbi, to follow me in a left-right-left march, as soon as our president was called to place his candle.

They quickly got into formation and when the president was called, we marched with him, as if this was part of the planned ceremony. When he placed the candle, I saluted, and the flag bearers lowered their flags in salute.

"Beautiful," whispered the chief rabbi, excited.

"Cool," said the cadets.

"Israeli chutzpah," an Israeli television reporter said.

The Polish authorities were outraged, calling it a "diplomatic scandal," but all the front pages in Israel showed the president in Auschwitz, standing with IDF and Israeli flags and saluting cadets. I knew that, in a way, we had been rude and deviated from protocol, but I was proud of what we had done.

Moving On

It was extremely difficult for me to leave Bahad 1, which I regarded as the peak of my service and a mission of national significance. My voice shook as I addressed the cadets and the staff for the last time.

My tenure had been a continuum of breakthroughs, storms, shaping and changing, and constant in-depth treatment of sensitive issues. It had been a highly demanding mission, and I had given it my best. I was also willing to pay the heavy price of pushing and promoting what I saw as national interests, without regard to personal or political considerations.

As the years go by, I look back at the various positions I have held and I know two things: I always did the best I could, with devotion, hard work, and striving toward perfection. And second, I know that if I could do it again, the outcome would be much better.

Experience, maturity, and the ability to change one's viewpoint as circumstances and experience dictate are all assets to a commander. When I was a company commander, I already realized that I could have been a better platoon commander, and this enabled me to teach the platoon commanders under me. When I was a battalion commander, I saw company commanders who were better than I had been, and I knew how to assist them in becoming even better. After my injury, I became more sensitive to people and a much better commander. Each experience in a commander's career pushes him to grow and improve, moving him closer to becoming the leader he is destined to be.

Part 2

War

In honor of my brothers-in-arms,

the heroes who fell in battle in the 2006 Second Lebanon War

for the protection of the State of Israel

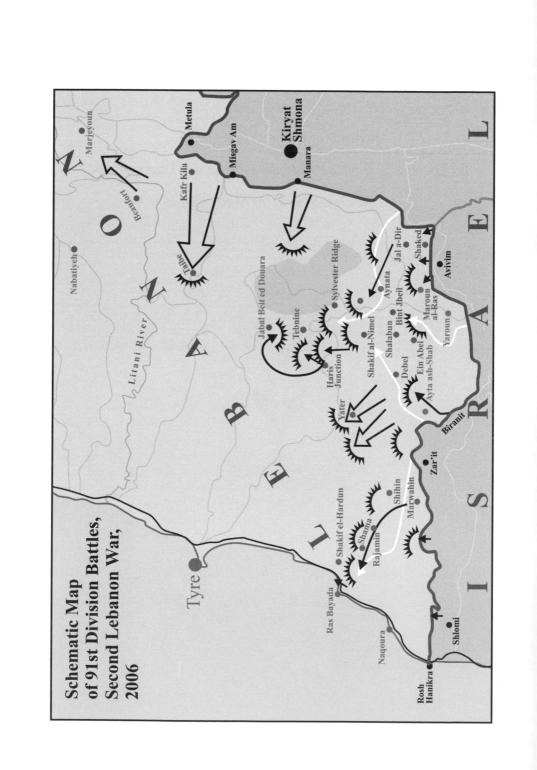

Schematic Map of 91st Division Battles, Second Lebanon War, 2006

Chapter 12
The Galilee Division

The Northern Arena – Syria and Hezbollah

Many Palestinians who had fled from the Gaza Strip and J&S during the Six-Day War had settled in refugee camps in neighboring Arab countries. Until the beginning of the 1970s, Palestinian terror organizations launched murderous attacks in central populated areas within Israel from their bases in Jordan. IDF campaigns against terror infrastructure within the Hashemite Kingdom and against the Palestinians' subversive activities within Jordan led to the events of Black September and the expulsion of the PLO and thousands of Palestinians from Lebanon.

The PLO operated their terror bases from Lebanon for more than a decade of bloody attacks on Israeli and on Jewish targets worldwide, as well as internal sectarian tension and violence. In 1982, Israel invaded Lebanon after an attack on a senior Israeli diplomat by Palestinian terrorists. This resulted in the PLO's expulsion from Lebanon to Tunis.

The vacuum left after the ousting of the PLO was filled by Hezbollah – an authentic, homegrown Shiite organization, whose roots began during the Lebanese civil war, but whose subsequent growth and development were mainly based on the opposition to Israel's deployment in southern Lebanon. Hezbollah maintains a strong connection with the local population as protector of the south and as an organization that defines the Shiite identity in Lebanon.

Hezbollah's strategy strictly maintains its dual-hatted position: a political party that promotes its agenda, as well as a subversive military force.

Moreover, it has external affiliations: Syria maintained a close connection with Hezbollah in its first steps and activated it as a proxy force in the confrontation with Israel. With time, a strong cultural and operational connection developed with Iran, allowing Iran to export their Islamic revolution agenda toward the west and sustain a "hot" border with Israel.

This served mainly as a conventional deterrent against Israel, in order to prevent it from attacking their newly created military nuclear program.

This reality changed after Syria's withdrawal from Lebanon in mid-2005, following international pressure after the assassination of Lebanon's prime minister, Rafic Hariri. These circumstances were only some of the significant changes that took place internally, regionally, and globally: the passing of Syria's President Assad and his son's inheritance of power; Israel's withdrawal from Lebanon, thereby weakening Syria's influence on Hezbollah; the evolution of the Israeli-Palestinian conflict; Yasser Arafat's death; Israel's withdrawal from the Gaza Strip in the Disengagement Plan and Hamas's subsequent rise to power; the 9/11 terror attacks in the US and the initiation of the Global War on Terror (GWOT); and the US-led campaign in Afghanistan and later in Iraq.

These conditions brought about a transformation in the Syrian-Lebanese-Iranian strategic system and the strengthening of Hezbollah's position in Lebanon.

Israel's withdrawal from Lebanon in 2000 left Hezbollah in a problematic situation. Its identity had been established around the concept of resistance to Israeli presence in Lebanon, but was now questioned and challenged. Aside from a narrative of victory with Israel's withdrawal, the organization was left without a main component of self-definition. On the one hand, internal changes in Lebanon strengthened its power as a political party, even though there was growing pressure to disarm, and on the other hand, the Syrian withdrawal left Hezbollah as the only non-state entity bearing arms in Lebanon.

During this time, the organization reshaped its image as carrying the flag of the Islamic and Arab fight against Israel, while ramping up attrition tactics against Israel. Hezbollah's relationship with Syria changed to an ally status, and Iranian narratives of Shiite Islam were stressed.

Hezbollah's objective was to sustain a level of action and conflict with Israel, without crossing the threshold of inviting wide-scale retaliation. But the organization also prepared for escalation of the conflict by assimilating lessons learned from the IDF and other armies in asymmetric warfare scenarios. Based on these lessons, and under Iranian directive, it built its infrastructure.

From Israeli maneuvers in Lebanon (Operation Litani in 1978, the First

Lebanon War in 1982), the organization learned about the characteristics of Israeli advancement battle, which included a forward armored force moving mainly on roads with aerial support, followed by a logistic "tail," and head-quarters and fighting forces in administrative movement. It was the Israeli version of the German Blitzkrieg.

From Israeli fire-based campaigns (Operation Accountability in 1993 and Grapes of Wrath in 1996), the organization learned the need to decentralize and disperse its capabilities and fighters, in order to create redundancy and to avoid being targeted by Israeli special forces or air strikes.

Lessons learned from the Israeli-Palestinian conflict taught Hezbollah the need to deploy in rural areas and villages in order to inflict more damage on the attacking forces. The organization also identified the advantages of forcing the IDF to operate amidst civilian population, a situation that makes it extremely difficult to differentiate between innocent civilians and enemy fighters, and poses many moral dilemmas to the army of a democratic state.

Hezbollah prepared itself to limit the maneuvering potential of the mod-ern Israeli army and prevent it from fully utilizing advanced operational capabilities and intel. The IDF was therefore pushed and channeled toward alleys, burrows, mountainous trails, and other terrain that would limit the operational effectiveness to only its most forward element.

From the American campaigns in Iraq and Afghanistan, Hezbollah learned about a Western army's capabilities of combining intel and firepower, allowing real-time targeting. We call this command, control, communications, com-puters, intelligence, surveillance, and reconnaissance (C4ISR).

Utilizing all these concepts, the organization constructed its operational defensive concept:

- Conducting simultaneous efforts using guerilla and urban warfare tactics, while employing a barrage of high-trajectory fire aimed at Israel's home front. Retreating along the roads helped buy time for the launching teams and enabled sustained launching periods.
- Enabling strategic durability by creating long-term stockpiles and addi-tional decentralization and redundancy of ammunition and weaponry in the fighting region.
- Creating an operational depth facing an Israeli ground maneuver, enabling the organization to operate from most of Lebanon's territory, not only from the front, by using an array of weapons with various ranges.

- Supporting the local population, deployment according to villages and towns, and reliance on them for logistical support as well as using them as human shields.
- Eroding the IDF's advantages in firepower and maneuverability by creating a force well supplied with antitank and antiaircraft capabilities.

As a result of these understandings, the organization's forces were deployed functionally, in a few operational regions.

Force Activation Policy

Since the 1970s, Israel has maintained a strict policy of not giving in to terror. "We don't negotiate with terrorists" describes the Israeli mindset. But our enemies know that Israel has conflicting values, and they have exerted much effort over the years to abduct soldiers as bargaining chips and as a means of gaining publicity. Israel has paid a heavy strategic price both in the internal debate and pressure, and ultimately in the release of terrorists in exchange for soldiers, alive or dead. Due to this obvious pressure point exploited by our enemies, Israel invests enormous efforts in preventing abductions.

When I assumed command of the 91st Division in April 2005, Hezbollah was deployed throughout southern Lebanon, including all along the border with Israel, with heavily fortified outposts and much activity. I already knew the organization to be an advanced, well-equipped and well-trained terror and guerilla organization. It relied heavily on Lebanon, Syria, and Iran and was a tough opponent, as the IDF had known from its long presence in the security belt in Lebanon until May 2000.

The operational reality became even more difficult and complicated after the IDF withdrew to the international border. Hezbollah was now deployed along the line, only a few meters from the fence, IDF forces, and Israeli civilians.

I called this situation "immediately accessible enemy."

I was directed to adopt a restrained policy, aimed at minimizing friction and depriving Hezbollah of excuses to attack – even when Hezbollah initiated a provocation! This policy of maintaining quiet in the north was articulated to me on various occasions by NORTHCOM commanders Gantz and Adam, and chiefs of the General Staff Ya'alon and Halutz.

Reality on the ground was extremely difficult, but IDF leadership strongly stressed implementation of the policy as dictated by the government.

Realizing my responsibility as the regional commander, I repeatedly presented my position and asked my commanders to reconsider and enable taking initiative. At the same time, I implemented the directed policy and prepared the forces for action within the defined guidelines.

There were cases when opportunities for preemptive strikes and over-the-border attack initiatives were denied, and my recommendation to better our deterrence by widening our fire retaliation to the entire region after incidents was strongly negated. It was decided that our response following Hezbollah attacks would be localized in scope, area, and time, requiring us to respond rapidly and proportionally.

Opposite us emerged an Islamic-Iranian-Syrian power with substantial operational capabilities, and we were required to exercise extreme sensitivity and careful control at the height of the conflagration in confronting it. This caution was necessitated because of the constant possibility of escalation. Keeping our response low key was considered (wrongly, in my opinion) especially important because of the Palestinian arena, which was defined as the main effort.

My division continued to raise new operational ideas. Because across-the-border operations were limited, we developed an array of capabilities to activate standoff fires, from afar. A new defense operational plan was written and new tactics and techniques were developed. The purpose was to try to operate from the border zone, on our side, adhering to the policy of not acting beyond the border or too aggressively.

My constant demand to widen the scope of our response when Hezbollah initiated attacks was not approved, and every single operation beyond the border required direct approval by the General Staff.

Intel, Forces, and Resources

Throughout the time I served under MG Gantz, he defined the status of our intel as "incomplete." It was in fact due to insufficient intel infrastructure.

We seriously lacked early-warning intel, and the gaps were presented and well known throughout the chain of command. After MG Amos Yadlin assumed his position as head of Israel Defense Intelligence (IDI), I initiated a meeting with him in which I conveyed my assessment of the ramifications of the present policy, and my reservations, as I saw them.

But first and foremost, I embraced my responsibility as the regional commander and implemented policies aimed at closing the gaps and improving the available intel – all closely coordinated with various units in the intelligence community. We improved the division's observation capabilities and products, tightened work relations with professional intel units, and conducted interagency roundtable discussions, in order to make the best of the situation.

Because of the binding restrictions, the division's intel team developed a method based on thorough analysis of all collected data (in order to ensure full utilization of all available resources and sources) and building a relevant operational framework.

We faced many threats, the main one being the possibility of abduction.

In order to prepare the forces properly for war, the division – together with NORTHCOM and the command's training base at Elyakim – built a mock-up of the outskirts of a Lebanese village, nicknamed "nature reserves" due to the dense vegetation. Such locations were identified as underground operational strongholds of Hezbollah, used to conceal weapons and launch rockets toward Israel. They were heavily concealed by thick brush, making them difficult to locate and attack. The division – together with other IDF units designated to be allocated to fight in Lebanon – rotated through the new training facility, where they learned and practiced tactics, techniques, and procedures.

Since the withdrawal of the IDF from Lebanon, there had been a substantial decrease in the number of forces allocated to defend the border region. The impact of the reduction in defense resources was so severe that I not only strongly expressed my concerns to the NORTHCOM commander, but met personally with the head of the Operations Division at the General Staff and asked for reinforcements. There was also a constant dialogue with the deputy CGS on the gaps in means and forces, and he was personally informed that "the division has reached its skeletal ORBAT [order of battle]," i.e., an organization and distribution of forces and resources that is insufficient to enable effective operational posture without enforcement.

The budgetary situation was also devastating, and operational construction was limited to dealing only with Mount Dov and the village of Ghajar.

As always, I not only expressed demands and complaints, but made the best of available resources, including by prioritizing resource allocation to the most critical operational areas.

I also continued to initiate operational actions, update tactics, techniques, and procedures (TTPs), and set priorities and principles for reinforcements that I hoped would arrive when needed.

Preparedness in a Low-Priority Environment

Today this may seem crazy, but back then, the Lebanese border was defined as a region with a priority equivalent to that of the border with Egypt or even less (medium-level priority). The Palestinian arena was distinctly defined as the highest.

With meager resources and under strict limitations, it was necessary to juggle and be extremely creative. We had to clearly define the threats in order to set our priorities. I decided that the division's main effort would be to deny Hezbollah operational success – mainly abductions – and to prepare for war, which I knew would follow a successful abduction.

I defined the identified threats as follows:

- Abduction.
- Penetration – above or underground, from the sea and from the air.
- Attack – with a variety of means, from line-of-sight small arms fires, to high-trajectory threats and IEDs.
- Escalation scenarios leading to an all-out war.

When I assumed command of the division, the routine security measures related to the technical fence as a "killing zone." Therefore, it was not patrolled systematically as had been common in the past, but protected using other methods, mostly observation from afar. After assessing the situation and analyzing the developing threat, I concluded that the plans were neither efficient nor sufficient.

I decided to strengthen and add to our plans, and wrote "Kartago" – a contingency plan (CONPLAN) aimed mainly at preventing and thwarting abductions, without diminishing our preparedness for other threats. Due to the sensitivity of the situation, I sat down and wrote the outline of the plan myself, and then had my staff broaden it into a full-fledged CONPLAN.

The plan was approved at all levels and translated into orders and training sessions. Many forces operated in accordance with Kartago, and it even withstood the test during battle days with Hezbollah, managing to thwart a few abduction attempts.

There was constant tension between trying to prepare the appropriate response to various threats and the limited means and resources at our disposal. For example, when we had to defend villages with soldiers, they were exposed to enemy fire and were also not able to spend their time training for war.

This continued to be my major concern, and I found myself constantly engaging various levels of leadership and different units and organizations, in order to shift priorities and allocate what I felt was crucial for fulfilling the mission.

In my campaign to influence prioritization, I also circumvented my chain of command, engaging directly with the highest levels at the General Staff. I uncovered deficiencies in the border protection systems and presented gaps in command and control and information collection technologies. I continued to request changes in force and resource allocation, such as diverting capabilities from J&S and Gaza to my area of responsibility.

In August 2005, I spoke to the head of the Administration for the Development of Weapons and Technological Infrastructure (abbreviated "Mafat" in Hebrew) at MOD and began working with his organization on improving capabilities in the north. They became involved in training and exercising in order to understand the gaps and test new ways to bridge them. I also initiated cooperation with the Department of Armament in the Ground Forces Command.

Iran was building up Hezbollah's capabilities, and I was doing my best to keep up, under far-from-optimal conditions.

Some of my efforts were successful, others were rejected, and some decisions only took effect after the Second Lebanon War.

In order to maintain a high level of readiness and constant operational tension, we devised and implemented a detailed training plan at Elyakim. A procedure was installed by which the commander of the training facility approved the qualification of each and every unit after it had completed the entire scope of training. The curriculum included learning and practicing the Kartago plan, counter-abduction methods, fence penetration procedures, etc.

In essence it was a certification process, approving force readiness.

Because the pastoral atmosphere around the northern border was misleading and dangerous, the division and force commanders constantly conducted exercises, surprise drills, inspections, and briefings, always extracting and implementing lessons learned.

An unexpected inspection was conducted by higher headquarters, praising the division and finding it qualified and ready for its missions. Operational results spoke for themselves, as we were tested more than once during battle days with Hezbollah and successfully resisted abduction attempts.

Still, I repeatedly told my soldiers: "We cannot be complacent. The next confrontation is on its way." It was obvious that Hezbollah was highly motivated to preserve its vitality by achieving an operational success, preferably the abduction of a soldier. There was no doubt that they would continue trying.

The "War Machine"

Because I put special emphasis on preventing abductions, I decided that we were to prepare for one as we would for any operation. Every week we convened planning and learning groups to evaluate possible scenarios – from an isolated event to escalation toward an all out war. From the outcome, we derived plans and orders implemented in the field, and these led to thwarting abduction attempts.

I personally led battalion and company commander gatherings, which were held on a regular basis, where we thoroughly briefed, learned, and discussed lessons. Special seminars on routine security were held for all forces deployed in our region or those who were scheduled to arrive.

During the preparation processes for war, a designated team conducted weekly brainstorming sessions addressing systemic needs, from conceptualization to operational representation, in tactical structures and battle techniques. Assisted by the expert Gadi Sneh, we used software tools in order to capture the ideas generated and allow for their refinement into implementable ideas in the field, using clear military terminology.

These meetings raised again and again the understanding that in our northern border, as in any campaign, we were operating within a unique context, and it was essential to build a tailor-made package suitable for the situation. We codenamed our response toward the threat of war "War Machine," and built separate "machines," or operational solutions, for each segment along the border.

Our war machine had a few basic characteristics:

- Its logic was context related – different contexts led to different types of machines, and besides being an organizational framework, it was also ready to assimilate and adapt to specific contexts, and could become an autonomous system for a given context and specific need.

- It could operate in changing and complex signatures. It sustained multi-dimensional regional control, blended into the environment, and could create a situational picture in all dimensions of the campaign (air, sea, land, space, and media) anytime, and from any place and dimension, within the framework of the campaign.
- Its organization was versatile and modular – in different contexts it would be able to absorb changes in its formation and types of resources, both from a command standpoint and as related to coordination and imple-mentation of the maneuver.

Uniquely adapted operational formations were implemented in every geo-graphical area that I defined. The companies and battalions put together operational sets of doctrine and equipment, suitable for the unique nature of their area of responsibility (AOR). When operated, these war machines were very successful, and I was happy to see them become adaptive learning systems under the division's directive.

Informing the Public

Because my reservations on the policy of containment led to no change, I requested and was allowed to bring the situation to the attention of the public. Media tours in my region were escorted by IDF Spokesperson's Office per-sonnel. Israeli civilians suddenly realized that the soldiers they were waving to when driving along the North Road were in fact Hezbollah operatives, not IDF soldiers. There they were, overlooking our soldiers and civilians, a few meters from the fence. This was the policy.

After the war, I drew up and submitted to the Winograd Commission a document listing all the incidents that had occurred.

Battle Days and Incidents

Thwarting Abductions

- July 2005 incident at Mount Dov – A senior Hezbollah commander was killed while conducting recon with a terrorist squad.
- November 2005 incident in Ghajar – Four Hezbollah operatives were killed during an abduction attempt. An intense fighting day ensued, and the northern part of the village was captured. The abduction attempt failed.

- February 2006 abduction attempt – Wide region.
- April–May 2006 abduction attempt – Wide region. Two abduction attempts were thwarted by appropriate deployment and preparation.

Incidents and Battle Days, 2005 (from April)
- April 24 – Discovered an IED arena on a road junction (Mount Dov).
- May 11 (Independence Day) – Rocket hit the town of Shlomi.
- May 12 – Battle day and high-trajectory fire toward outposts at Mount Dov (no casualties).
- May 13 – Battle day, with continuation of direct and indirect fires toward Mount Dov outposts.
- May 21 – High-trajectory firing in Mount Dov region.
- June 28 – Engagement with Hezbollah squad in Wadi Mrar. Egoz and Maglan forces killed senior Hezbollah operative.
- July 12 – Fire exchange between Hezbollah and IDF forces at Rosh Hanikra outpost, following the opening of fire at our forces.
- August 25 – Impact of a flak rocket at Kibbutz Margalion (no casualties).
- November 11 – Thwarting of an abduction attempt at Ghajar.
- November 23 – Israeli civilian parachutist landed in Lebanese territory and was rescued by IDF forces under fire.
- December 26 – Border crossing by a Lebanese man and an Israeli criminal (both caught).
- December 27 – Three rockets hit the city of Kiryat Shmona (no casualties).

Incidents in 2006
- February 1 – Armed man crossed the Blue Line into Israel in Mount Dov region. After IDF troops fired at him, a battle day developed and high-trajectory fire hit IDF outposts in Mount Dov region.
- May 28 – Following the killing of a Hezbollah operative in Sidon, shots were fired toward Mount Meron and sniper fire was conducted toward an IDF soldier at Kibbutz Manara. In retaliation, Hezbollah outposts all along the border were destroyed.

"Why Can't Dad Come Home with Us?"
Donna and the girls would usually come to me on Fridays, to the division headquarters, after a long ride from our home at Rosh Ha'ayin (east of Tel Aviv). We would participate in the traditional Shabbat dinner with the soldiers,

and I would deliver the commander's address on current affairs. Then they would play with my staff members, who were like family to us, and later we would head out to Moshav She'ar Yashuv, to Suzi and Shlomo Hayun, a warm family who had adopted us. There we would spend the day, with dogs, horses, orchards, a tractor, and a small guest room. This was how we maintained our family life when I wasn't home. From time to time during these visits I would get called away to the border and then return when all was back to normal.

During quiet days, we would hike in the north, walking the trails descending from Nebi Yosha, telling the tales of how the Palmach fought. We scrutinized the ground to get to know every flower and every snail, climbed the Sulam Ridge to see the sunset, ascended to Tel Azazyat to observe the Hula Valley, and rode quietly around the Hula Lake to watch flocks of migrating birds.

While traveling on the northern road, we were accompanied by a security detail, just in case. Hezbollah controlled our villages and the road from its "nature reserves," and all our moves, especially mine, were monitored from fortified observation towers near the border.

On the weekends, I made a point of spending time with my family not only at She'ar Yashuv, but at other kibbutz hotels and guesthouses. It was important for me that people see "their" division commander and his family in their midst. I insisted on always paying the full price for our lodging, despite generous offers to host us for free. I felt that this was our contribution to the local community and the bond between the citizens and the IDF.

It was our homeland, and we experienced our love for the people and the land together with our girls. We would use the entire day, and after Shabbat, at sundown, the girls would depart with hugs and kisses and make the long trip home, without Dad.

"When will you come home with us, Dad?" little Nir would pressure me, clinging to me in an unbreakable hug.

"Your father will come to visit this week," said Donna, attempting to appease her.

"But he comes at night and leaves at night!" Nir protested. "We don't have time to be together."

This was the nature of our conversations for years.

"When will you come to stay with us?" Meori used to ask, teary-eyed, back when I was 202nd Battalion commander, and she was a young child at

Kibbutz Ma'ale Hahamisha. She thought that she and her mother had their home at the kibbutz, and Dad lived in a tent, in Nablus, the Golan Heights, and Lebanon.

"Why can't Dad come home with us?" Ofri would ask when we parted on Saturday nights.

"Dad can't come because he is protecting our country," Donna explained.

"Why?"

"Because there are those who want to take it from us."

"Why?"

"Because…"

These conversations would go on and on, and then we would part with a heavy heart, my family heading home on the dark roads, and me back to my headquarters, command post, or tent, missing them dearly.

One Saturday morning, a month before the war, I awoke early in our room at She'ar Yashuv. My family had joined me, as usual, because I had to stay in the region. I woke Donna up and gave her a short letter I had written to her, carefully choosing every word. I had felt a need to express my feelings in writing and not only spoken words. I wanted Donna to know that an abduction was imminent, and a war would follow, and our life was about to change.

Tense Times

These were very tense days. Only a short time before, on May 28, we had had a tough and intense battle, and the line of fortified Hezbollah posts was destroyed in a series of actions that had been planned and practiced much in advance.

It began with a mysterious targeted strike that took out a senior Hezbollah operative in Sidon. Hezbollah responded with rocket firing toward Mount Meron, after which the IAF carried out air strikes in Beirut and the Beqaa Valley. Then, as expected, Hezbollah began carrying out sniper activity all along the border, attempting to find easy prey, such as a soldier or farmer.

I transferred the division to a predefined and thoroughly rehearsed state of "zero targets," which essentially deprived Hezbollah of potential targets, preventing them from carrying out their plan.

At the same time, I positioned our entire force, including antitank missiles and tanks, in a concealed reverse slope. Snipers, artillery, and fighter jets were all on immediate alert. I waited for the moment we would have a cause to strike.

The opportunity came unexpectedly. Two IAF soldiers arrived at the garage of Kibbutz Manara to check a fire truck, unaware of the sensitive situation and without coordination with regional forces. They were targeted by a Hezbollah sniper from the Lebanese side, and one soldier was critically wounded. Nahal Brigade soldiers rescued him under fire and saved his life.

I was notified within moments, and without seeking approval from my superiors, I immediately gave the order to unleash a massive and wide-scale attack from the Mediterranean to Mount Dov. Hezbollah operatives were shocked by the devastating precision, and within a short time most of their infrastructure along the line had been crippled.

Compliments were heard from all over. The new minister of defense, Mr. Amir Peretz, proffered an abundance of superlatives. When I met the CGS at the command headquarters, he walked up to me smiling, cuddled my face in his hands and said, "Well done, well done." The officers present were astounded at the affection and appreciation he displayed toward me.

I was very worried. I remembered the hits we had sustained at Mount Meron and the intensity of the antitank missile (ATM) attacks on our forces during the thwarted abduction attempt at Ghajar in November 2005.

Hezbollah quickly rebuilt their damaged positions, and I estimated that their motivation to abduct a soldier was still there, and that it was only a matter of time.

In the months since the Ghajar incident, we had worked hard implementing sophisticated and determined tactics and techniques in order to thwart additional abduction attempts. Backed by the policy of NORTHCOM under MG Udi Adam, we managed to foil Hezbollah abduction attempts in February, and then in April and May 2006.

It was nerve-racking, but more than that, I understood and openly stated that I could not ensure constant successes.

I continued to show, in every forum, photos of Hezbollah operatives standing in their positions on the border, observing the northern road from ten meters away. I knew that under these conditions, if we were to sustain a surprise attack without early warning, we could not prevent an abduction. We had villages all along the border – Zar'it, Misgav Am, Idmit, Shtula, Manara, and others. I could not leave them unprotected, for we were the Israel Defense Force, and protecting them was our mission.

It has been said many times: "Defense lines ultimately get breached." A contact line is not an impassible wall. I had more than a hundred kilometers (sixty miles) to defend, with dozens of villages and hundreds of kilometers of civilian roads near the border.

I didn't have a chance of creating a strong defense line everywhere without pinpoint intel. In allowing Hezbollah to build a continuous and strong array along the border, our policy had rendered my division's operational efforts ineffective. It was impossible to be strong everywhere at once.

Moreover, every few weeks we suffered new budget cuts. Various forces were deleted from the division's ORBAT and from the border, and transferred to Gaza, J&S, or even the Golan Heights.

I endured bitter struggles over every soldier, every artillery piece or tank. Sometimes I was successful, but mostly I was not.

Against this backdrop, I decided to make harsh decisions. I had no doubt that an abduction would come, followed by war. My time was split between acting to prevent an abduction and preparing for the war that would follow.

I ordered the closure of outposts, one after the other, removing mainly those most exposed to enemy attacks. There was no way to hold the many outposts we had, with the dwindling of forces.

It didn't make sense to stretch one company's deployment to six outposts, when it was structured to operate from two. This would lead to very few soldiers in each outpost, exposed to attacks and abduction attempts and without enough manpower to carry out other operational initiatives. Moreover, routine combat activity necessitated rotating soldiers though vacations and training, and there were the usual constraints such as soldiers on medical leave.

Additionally, worried that we might be surprised, I decided to transfer most of the division's forces from the weak spots – visible, high-signature outposts and patrols – to low-signature operations, out in the field.

We called this concept by the code name "Thicket," indicative of the nature of operations, which included many days out in the brush, conducting observations and ambushes. We concealed the tanks, ready for immediate operations, and integrated technological elements in various formats of activity.

Over and over, we practiced force activation during an abduction. There were constantly areas closed to traffic, surrounded and observed by covert forces, using day- or night-vision binoculars. We conducted our activities using a technique we called "distort-distorted," creating a posture that distorted the enemy's plans, and a distorted posture that made it hard for him to build operational plans.

Routine became an abominable term. Commanders constantly reviewed their actions in order to ensure they were not repeating a pattern. I did not want a Hezbollah commander to be able to identify such a pattern and exploit it to initiate an attack. I personally evaluated our operations along the line every few hours. We had inspections, examinations, training and exercises, and situational assessments twice a day, analyzing every bit of information. Sometimes we even conducted them every few hours. It was very difficult and stressful.

I understood that if we did not change our operational policy, Hezbollah would take advantage of its being an "immediate access enemy" and would find a target for attack and abduction. I ruled out the idea of resigning, viewing this as escape from responsibility. I did not spare harsh words when expressing my opinion to my superiors, but I never transferred my responsibility, upwards or downwards. I utilized all my strength, experience, and capabilities to prevent and preempt more and more abductions.

Learning, Change, and Responsibility

Operational learning is dynamic and requires constant change. A country and an army must change too. At the tactical level, we never ceased to change, so much so that the phenomenon was criticized by some in my staff. They did not believe that their subordinates could adapt to the high rate of change. But it worked against Hezbollah, and it usually succeeded. When strategy *doesn't* change, operations and tactics have limited capabilities.

Some of the reasons for the dissonance between the learning rates of different echelons were related to the changes the IDF underwent when CGS Ya'alon retired. During his tenure, the IDF had maintained a learning network throughout essential parts of the force, and the knowledge was continuously maintained. In my view, LTG Halutz preserved neither the same learning tempo nor the learning methods.

In the absence of strategic footholds in the learning process, operational and tactical learning is conducted in a disconnected space of its own. We did our best, but unfortunately our state of mind was disconnected from the strategic level.

There was another worry at the back of my mind.

Since we had already witnessed in Israel the phenomenon of blaming a scapegoat for systemic failures, I was concerned that I might not be backed up if an abduction took place, especially due to the extent of the blow the "system" would sustain.

I was concerned that the upper levels of command would seek a head to lop off, and it would ultimately be mine.

The division was well prepared for war, but it would not face this alone. Many forces would be augmented, regular and reserve, many of whom were not familiar with the doctrine we had developed. There would be many reservists, some of whom would not be tolerant of overly creative or complex plans. They would arrive for a short time and seek simplicity.

I had experienced this in the Benjamin Brigade, in confronting Palestinian terror. Not all my methods were well received, especially among reservists. But there were also wonderful units who liked and embraced my approach and looked upon continuous learning as a healthy organizational approach, as they would apply to their civilian businesses.

I did my best to prepare the entire army, not only my own division, for the challenges ahead in the northern arena. Of course, my main focus was inward, on the 91st Division.

I invested much energy in "centers of gravity" such as the Command and Staff College, division staffs, instructor staffs of battalion and company commanders' courses, and the staff of the national reserve training center in Tze'elim. But I was concerned that maybe it wasn't enough, and it wouldn't be fully implemented and assimilated throughout the IDF. We invested in all of these many long days of study, training, instruction, and mentoring – mostly to units and organizations that were not under my command. I did all this from a broad interpretation of the term *responsibility*.

Chapter 13

The Abduction Incident

Keeping the Reserves Ready

There were usually regular forces deployed along the northern border, but for a few weeks each year, reserve battalions would take their place. The General Staff would dictate their identity and time of replacement.

I made a point of demanding that we receive only designated elite infantry battalions, or organic reserve units from my division, with whom I was intimately familiar.

All units reporting to my region would undergo intensive specified training at NORTHCOM's training center at the Elyakim military base before deployment and were certified to perform routine security activity as well as wartime fighting under the 91st Division.

Elyakim base was not officially under my command, but I visited there frequently, and influenced the training material and concepts that were taught.

The period of reserve service is relatively short – three weeks – so the ability of the receiving regional brigade to influence the soldiers is very limited. This is why it is essential to rely on the original home unit to supply battalions with high standards and good discipline and operational culture.

During the operational deployment of a reserve battalion, the regional brigade must focus mainly on operational dimensions, which are by themselves laden with procedure and details.

Throughout my tenure as 91st Division commander, I delivered special directives in times when reserve battalions were deployed. They were aimed at assimilating and implementing my demand that each soldier must be prepared for an abrupt and sharp transition from routine security to intense fighting, within a short time – which I estimated as three minutes – in which the enemy would try to abduct a soldier and transfer him to enemy territory.

I assumed we would have approximately another thirty minutes to conduct pursuit, attack, and perform other complementary operations, followed by no more than three hours of NORTHCOM and General Staff level actions, until the incident would be extinguished. This assuming the enemy failed – for if not, an abduction would surely trigger a larger escalation.

I stood by my estimation. I believed it would take the enemy just three minutes. That's how close they were to us. The concept, coined "3-30-3," became known and used throughout the division and in the command headquarters.

Operating in the pastoral Galilee, with its green hills and orchards, yet so close to the border and Hezbollah, necessitated very high alertness and personal discipline. Every training and briefing stressed the need for a can-do, out-of-the-box approach, from soldier to patrol commander and all the way up the chain of command. This emphasis enabled mission completion and successful thwarting of abduction attempts. Although battalions are not directly subordinate to the division commander, I worked directly with them in the field, as I did with the reserve battalion that would ultimately sustain the abduction that would trigger the war.

5th Brigade's Reserve Battalion
I knew the 5th Brigade from its operations in CENTCOM.

Its commanders underwent a seminar on the Kartago plan, and the entire battalion allocated to Regional Brigade 300 underwent training and qualification before combat and at Elyakim base. Brigade 300 commander COL Chen Livni received clear instructions from me during a situational assessment, including specific points of emphasis about the battalion he was receiving. I allocated Herev ("sword" in Hebrew), the Druze battalion, which was in its training phase, as a regional reinforcement.

The reserve battalion from 5th Brigade had a command staff of skilled professionals who had been through all IDF command levels and been involved in many operational activities. I was satisfied that the battalion underwent a full and efficient array of preparatory actions before deployment.

Based on the alert situation we were in, and in light of the fact that there was a regular, qualified battalion in training near the border (Herev), I demanded from NORTHCOM to replace the reserve battalion with a regular one. I did not wait for approval and summoned Herev Battalion commander LTC Wajdi Sahran to a briefing with me before the expected replacement.

I thought it was not reasonable that during tense days such as those, we should have reservists, who were less trained, deployed along the border, when there was a better, available alternative – a regular elite battalion that knew the routine security thoroughly.

I fought for this replacement all the way up to the head of the Operations Division at the General Staff. It goes without saying that the highly motivated reservists objected to being replaced.

When the replacement wasn't approved, I again briefed the brigade commander, COL Livni, on how to deal with the battalion. Talking to him made it clear to me that Brigade 300 was implementing all of its responsibilities and capabilities.

On June 21, 2006, CGS Halutz visited the division. During the closing session, I told him that I feared an abduction could take place in my area of responsibility. I expressed my critiques on the ORBAT allocated on the northern border and stressed the problems with intel alerts and the states of readiness.

I told Halutz that the division had reached its skeletal position. Without sufficient resources, I explained, we relied on intel alerts for diverting and reinforcing forces. Without such an alert, we could not ensure success in thwarting an abduction.

"You know I never ask for extra resources unless I really need them," I said.

"I know," answered Halutz, "and I am grateful to you for this."

"So please understand that the situation is critical. Without reinforcements I cannot hold the line."

I and the other attending commanders – the NORTHCOM commander and the head of the Northern Arena at the General Staff – all requested to discuss "the day after" an abduction, but Halutz reiterated the issue of prevention, clarified that he was fully aware of the situation of missing ORBAT, and stated that the responsibility was his.

On June 25, 2006, Hamas militants carried out an attack on an IDF force near the Gaza Strip, killing two soldiers and abducting CPL Gilad Schalit.

I immediately convened a lesson-learning forum, using all the information we could gather from the Gaza Division. I conveyed instructions to the units and raised the alert status, not based on any specific information, but from knowing Hezbollah.

I visited the units and gathered the battalion commanders in each brigade for a special briefing. I also visited the reserve battalion of 5th Brigade at Zar'it. Inspections were made and designated instructions were given to the brigade commanders.

Another consultation was conducted on July 3, 2006, with the deputy CGS, MG Moshe Kaplinski, during a visit at the division. We held a discussion on the appropriate measures in order to avoid an abduction and how to respond if it were to happen. I again stated that we had a lack of forces in the division. In a debate on the question of pursuit after an abduction took place, we all agreed that it was essential to pursue, contrary to the Schalit abduction in Gaza where nothing was done.

I conducted constant situational assessments, following IDF doctrine and in accordance with accepted methodologies. In every situation, I chose to apply more strictness than defined by the General Staff. I carefully verified that all relevant information was made available to me; I even sent my intel officers to IDI bases, in order to confirm that not one bit of information was withheld. I then redefined the alert status of the division.

On July 10, I reassessed the intel situation and reached the conclusion that it was possible to lower the high alert status that I had declared after the abduction of Gilad Schalit. I hadn't any information to suggest otherwise. Only in hindsight do I now know that such information was already in the hands of IDI but never reached me. NORTHCOM had already lowered the alert a few days earlier.

After giving various instructions, I approved going ahead with the replacement of the reserve battalion with Herev Battalion the following day. Reduced alert status also would allow for opening the roads that had been closed for a long time, and we could also launch the special operations that I had planned to conduct.

I asked my deputy, Dror, to replace me for one night. After a long and stressful period of heightened alert, on Tuesday night, July 11, I felt it was possible to allow myself to spend a few hours at home.

The Night before the Storm

I spent time talking to the girls. Seventeen-year-old Meori told me about her studies at Herzliya Gymnasium. She was highly involved as an instructor at SHELACH (the Israeli land, heritage, and current affairs curriculum in high schools), and we discussed leadership and initiative dilemmas.

Eleven-year-old Ofri updated me on her progress at tennis practice, a field she had recently picked up. She also showed me stories she had recently written. Four-year-old Nir cuddled with me like a little puppy, not budging from me the whole evening.

"Will you also have some time for me?" Donna asked, smiling. "I missed you."

I had a little chat with our Labrador, Shoko ("chocolate milk" in Hebrew). I kept peeking at my pager for updates, and the phone kept ringing. From time to time I was called to the red phone installed in my home for classified calls. I browsed through e-mails and regular mail accumulated over the past few weeks. Then I looked at the stuck shutter that I had promised to fix, and remembered the electricity problem in the yard.

"I'll deal with it later," I promised myself. But when would "later" be?

After a family dinner, an important ritual for us whenever I was home, the girls retired to their rooms to prepare for school and kindergarten. The phone calls kept coming in – a problem with personnel, a meeting to schedule, and updates from the field.

"Dad?"

"Coming," I answered, and ran to read Nir her bedtime story, said good night to Ofri, and hugged Meori. It was midnight when Donna and I finally sat down to a quiet talk. After so many days of only phone conversations, there was much catching up to do, and Donna had prepared a long list of things to be discussed.

The kindergarten, the neighborhood, Donna's job, different arrangements and chores to be done, bills to pay, medical tests, family news . . . While making coffee, I updated Donna on the tense situation at the division in the past few weeks, following the abduction of Gilad Schalit.

"I called Yael, Aviv Kochavi's wife," Donna said.

I had been thinking of the difficult days he was going through as the Gaza Division commander, and I had sent him strengthening messages. I knew him from years of service together in the paratroopers; he was a devoted commander. An abduction like this was something that happens sometimes to commanders facing the enemy. You can't always thwart such occurrences.

My eyes were drooping. "Let's go to sleep," I said, "it's already 2 AM. I'm leaving at 5 for an operational exercise. I must personally oversee the preparations for the operation."

In the girls' room there was a soft light and gentle sounds of breathing. I awoke from the buzz of a mosquito. Nir was already bitten. Now it was a chase after mosquitoes. At 3 AM Donna fell asleep.

Another phone call from the NORTHCOM intel officer and an update on an incident in Gaza raised a doubt whether this might have ramifications to our region.

"Update me on the outcome of the incident," I requested. "If we think this may influence Hezbollah, we will resume heightened alert status."

At 3:30 AM there was another call: "No influence, nothing is happening in Lebanon by intel estimates, and the incident in Gaza isn't as substantial as we initially thought."

I thought about it for a few minutes, passing through my mind various scenarios, and conducted more consultations over the phone.

"Nothing's happening," my staff told me again. "See you at the exercise in the morning."

"Get some sleep," Donna mumbled.

At 4 AM I put my head down on the pillow. I had one hour before the regular awakening call from Or, my devoted driver, who would always call me before picking me up at home. I tried to catch a quick sleep.

Abduction

On the morning of July 12, 2006, while I was monitoring the training of a force from Maglan, my aide-de-camp, Tal, came running up.

"They are attacking the division headquarters!"

I made my way back to the division as fast as I could, and while en route gave orders to open fire and to attack Hezbollah positions across the division's entire region.

When I reached the headquarters, I realized that the attack was not confined, but spanned forty kilometers (twenty-five miles) – from Rosh Hanikra on the coastline to the vicinity of Dovev. They attacked in complete surprise and with immense firepower. Direct fire and mortars were being fired in massive quantities at IDF positions and forces throughout the region, as well as at communities and farmers adjacent to the border.

Hezbollah had certainly been planning this for a long time.

In the operations room I was trying to piece the puzzle together and clarify the situational picture.

It looked like the main enemy effort was taking place in the 300th Brigade's region. The commander, COL Livni, was away, so I called him and filled him in.

I collected all the information I could get from my staff officers.

Avi, the intel officer, leaned over and whispered intel reports into my ear. I'd been in intel darkness for months, fighting for every bit of information; suddenly it was flowing.

"Is this an abduction attempt?"

"It looks like it; doesn't look like just another battle day."

"Are we missing anybody?"

"We don't know."

Reports were coming in from the field, indicating that maybe one of our patrols was under fire.

Someone reported that he had heard "Engagement, engagement!" over the radio.

"No answer from one of the patrols."

We had two Humvees patrolling on the northern road between Shtula and Zar'it.

"What about attack helicopters?"

"Scrambled. They just took off, so it will take a few more minutes."

"Initiate the Abduction Prevention Procedure," I instructed, triggering a series of activities.

"The general wants you, and the head of the Operations Division wants you."

"Tell them I don't have a complete picture yet. I will update them soon."

"Two Humvees burning," came the report from the field, then confirmed by the helicopter pilots.

"See if anyone is missing!"

"Casualties at the scene."

I commanded the operation of air, sea, and land forces according to previously prepared plans, and ordered the attack and destruction of all Hezbollah positions that had been identified along the border.

"Report status of attacked Hezbollah posts along the border; tell me where the fighter jets are; bomb the bridges and junctions and isolate the area."

What if I am wrong? I thought. What a huge responsibility. I had just launched a massive attack with devastating ramifications on infrastructure inside Lebanon. What if no soldier had been abducted?

"How is it that I don't have any available artillery at my disposal?" I said to myself. "Cutbacks, this is the price of the cutbacks," I grumbled quietly, and let out a curse.

An artillery battery that had operated in my region had been reassigned elsewhere, and the few mortars in the 300th Brigade's sector were not enough to hinder enemy actions.

It was difficult to contact the forces in the field, and I needed to know exactly what was going on. I asked Nimmer, our experienced chief tracking officer, to make his way to the abduction point and report directly to me.

"I want airborne intervention forces from Shaldag and Egoz standing by."

Egoz was an elite infantry unit in the Golani Brigade, dedicated for guerilla warfare in NORTHCOM.

"Prepare for a pursuit, the entry point is 105. Isolate Ayta ash-Shab village, including a larger circle of villages."

Reports kept coming in.

"There are KIAs and a soldier is missing, maybe two."

"We found two, one is missing."

"Three are missing."

The reports were confusing, broken, and contradictory. We listened to the radio frequencies of the battalion and companies, and tried to reach the commanders.

"How much time has passed?"

"About half an hour."

"Have Wajdi [the Herev Battalion commander] get there himself with his forces and start a pursuit."

"Chen is on the phone."

"Move inward to better positions, block the exits from Ayta. It isn't too late. Watch out for IEDs on their escape route. If it looks like this is the case, do not pursue on the escape route!"

Sure enough, there were powerful IEDs planted on the escape route.

Nimmer reported from the field. "Sir," he panted, "three soldiers killed, two wounded, and two are missing. Hezbollah fired lots of missiles, blew out the fence, and took two soldiers out of one of the Humvees. They actually came into Israel – the ambush wasn't on the fence but on the northern road itself! The area is still being targeted with mortars."

Nimmer sounded riled and upset.

"Chen – pursue in the direction of the Flag Hill!" This was a controlling area – that is, an area from which the surroundings could be seen and controlled, and from which, potentially, the escape could be thwarted.

"Make sure that tanks and infantry are coordinated with the attack helicopters. Prepare the entire region for a battle day. Fill me in on the bombing and blocking situation."

"NORTHCOM commander is on the line. He needs you right away for an update."

"Udi, it's an abduction; looks like two are missing. The escape was probably in the direction of Ayta ash-Shab. Preparing forces for pursuit. No artillery here. We need all the help we can get."

"Don't just run into Lebanon."

"We're not just running in. It's a controlled pursuit. I am halting the full activation of the Abduction Prevention Procedure and executing only crucial and required elements. I have to try to save them!"

The issue of pursuit after abduction had been widely discussed on all levels, including with the chief of General Staff himself. The plan always contained weak points and threats to the pursuing forces, especially in light of the enemy's advanced capabilities.

The Abduction Prevention Procedure was a comprehensive plan in which everything would be done in order to thwart and disrupt abduction attempts.

The importance of the pursuit was emphasized, in spite of the inherent dangers.

After it became clear that two soldiers had in fact been abducted into Lebanon, I analyzed the terrain I knew so well and assessed the enemy's expected actions. My conclusion was that the appropriate thing to do – from a professional standpoint and certainly from a moral one – was to stop the abductors or disrupt their plans as outlined by the Abduction Prevention Procedure.

I ordered a force comprised of a tank and infantry, under the command of an armored battalion commander, to enter Lebanon and reach a specific point which controlled the area. They were supported and covered by attack helicopters, ground forces, and intel assets on the ground and in the air.

I hoped that if the abductors' plan was disrupted and their escape delayed, we could use reinforcements to lockdown the entire area and then search for the abductors and retrieve our soldiers.

After issuing the order, I dashed to the abduction point with my FCG. The place was still under heavy fire, so we dismounted at a distance and I led my team on a grueling twenty-minute walk up a gully leading to the fence. As we arrived at the scene, still under fire, I received word that the pursuing force had been hit.

They had set out with great determination and reached the designated spot. While the tank was maneuvering, it passed over a concealed belly charge, containing hundreds of kilograms of explosives. The explosion killed all four crew members. The force would later be attacked by mortars, killing another soldier from the Nahal Brigade.

From this point on, I gave orders to rescue the wounded and the KIAs, continue searching at the location of the abduction, and continue combat operations along the entire region.

From the beginning of the abduction incident until the end of the war thirty-three days later, the fighting never stopped.

The fate of the two abducted reserve soldiers – SFC Ehud Goldwasser and SFC Eldad Regev – was unclear for a long time.

According to forensic evidence collected by specialists from the MIA locating unit, we assumed that both were critically injured, or even worse.

Their bodies would be returned to Israel in 2008, in exchange for Hezbollah operatives and bodies.

First Day of Combat

We returned to the headquarters, but after updates and issuing instructions, I soon felt that my place was back out in the field.

"FCG personnel, prepare to move out. We are skipping over to the 300th Brigade." I had to meet Chen at his command center, speak with his staff, and support them. The day had been full of tough combat for us all, but the 300th was in the center of it all.

I still had to make a decision on how to extract the four bodies from the crippled tank. The terrain was a downward slope toward Lebanese territory and exposed to enemy fire. The recovery of the bodies would be difficult – but I could not allow the bodies, or body parts, to be taken by Hezbollah.

The bodies needed to be removed quickly to restore the continuity of fire over the entire sector in order to finish destroying Hezbollah's infrastructure along the border, but mainly to be able to plan for the next stage.

I knew this was going to be war.

I repeated my demand to call up reserve forces and ordered to immediately call up the headquarters personnel of the reserve brigades assigned to my division so they could begin planning. I also gave instructions to prepare a plan for a counterattack.

I decided to give the mission of searching for the tank crew's bodies to Maglan, which was allocated to me. If no major campaign did develop and this turned out to be only a bloody battle day, then at least the best soldiers I had would carry out what had become the most sensitive and critical mission.

I knew that they would accomplish it.

"Set up a meeting with Eliezer, Maglan commander, at the 300th Brigade; I will brief him there."

Finding the bodies of the tank crew was now the highest priority. At least the abduction of these bodies would be thwarted, and we knew from past experience that Hezbollah considered corpses as valuable an asset as live soldiers.

A secondary concern was that if parts of the Merkava tank fell into the hands of the enemy, sensitive technical information would be compromised (and there would also be severe damage to our image). We needed to go there, to search, and to find – and then I would decide on how to continue.

I got up from the chair in the operations room and took the microphone. The room became silent, and my voice was heard throughout the complex. I wanted to strengthen my people.

"It is going to be hard. We have suffered a harsh and difficult blow, and challenging combat awaits us. I appreciate what you have done until now, and believe you will continue to perform well in the future. No one can defend the north better than we can, and the responsibility lies with us. Later this evening we will assess the situation and send out divisional orders."

Everyone there was looking at me, their faces attentive and anxious. Some were still in shock from the overwhelming events of recent hours. But as I spoke, I could see smiles appearing and knew that I was getting through to them.

Practical orders were being assigned, telephones were answered calmly, and instructions void of anxiety were sent out through the radio.

The division is so well trained, I thought to myself. *We have undergone battle days, thwarted abductions; we have done exercise after exercise…*

"There is going to be war," I had repeated over and over again for more than a year. "Don't get drawn into this deceptive calm. There is going to be war."

The operations room was filling up. I felt a hand on my shoulder. It was COL Mickey Edelstein, the Nahal Brigade commander.

Mickey had served under my command for many years. We had planned and executed scores of operations together – always together and always understanding each other without words.

"What's happening, Mickey?"

"What's happening, Gal?"

"What's happening? War!"

Chapter 14

The Strategic Picture

The Challenges We Faced

In retrospect, with the detailed preparations we had made, nothing should have surprised us in this campaign.

From the long days of studying intel material and observations in the field, I was under the impression that Hezbollah was preparing for a confrontation with a 1982 version of the IDF – columns of armored vehicles on the roads combined with massive use of airpower.

Hezbollah had become more confident in its assessment of the IDF in light of the American maneuvers in Operation Iraqi Freedom. We had seen that the Arab armies that took part in the First Gulf War learned a lot about US doctrine, and they believed that Israel was "an American reflection." Maybe with a touch of Israeli cleverness and sophistication, but basically implementing similar doctrine.

I saw confirmation of this in the organizational structure of Hezbollah forces, which contained large numbers of IEDs, snipers, and antitank weapons, along with thousands of rockets and missiles. They planned to "pop" us on the roads, to sneak up from behind our logistical convoys and fight us by employing methodical retreat and delay tactics, while launching rockets into Israel. They would fire anything they could get their hands on – with more and more advanced rockets – deeper into Israel, and not only on the northern towns.

It was clear that the launchings would not stop unless we achieved control of the area, along with massive international pressure. This pressure needed to serve as leverage against Iran, Hezbollah, Syria, and Lebanon. Each one of these players could stop the rockets whenever they wanted, either due to international pressure or because they would not have a choice – because we would be there with our boots on the ground.

Just to make things clear, there is a solution to rocket fire! *We are absolutely capable of overcoming this threat and reducing the number of launches to zero*, but it involves a government decision enabling us to achieve *complete control* of the area. When we do not conquer and hold the Gaza Strip, the firing continues on the communities in the south for many years. When we do not have control in areas of Lebanon, large areas of Israel are under rocket threat, depending on the range. In J&S, rockets are not launched since we have complete operational and intelligence control of the area. There were attempts to develop launching capabilities of locally made Qassam rockets, but we thwarted them after taking vigorous action. I was chief of operations of CENTCOM at the time, and it was joint operations carried out by the ISA and the IDF that prevented this capability from ever evolving. As long as we continued to control the West Bank and let the ISA perform their intel-gathering activities, we were able to eradicate all launching capabilities.

We can also counter this threat by intercepting rockets during launch or in flight, as demonstrated by Israel's latest developed active defense systems (ADS): Iron Dome, David's Sling, and the Arrow. It is also always wise to continue investing in passive protection. But threats constantly evolve, and we cannot assume that we will always possess fail-safe defense systems for all types of threats. Interestingly, one of the most primitive weapons we face – mortar fire – still poses a serious threat and challenge.

In many ways, the existence of advanced defense systems opened up an array of possibilities for Israeli decision makers. It is obvious that without the Iron Dome, for example, Israel would have certainly maneuvered into Gaza during the conflict in the summer of 2014 (Operation Protective Edge), just as was done in Lebanon in 1982 and 2006.

My assessment at the time was that it would be impossible to reach an agreement on the Lebanese border, and without such an agreement, we would have to create a new arrangement. In other words, we needed to enforce our will over the rival system and shape a new reality.

Every new incident that occurs is like a coded message – a situation that must be clarified, interpreted, and labeled.

When the situation is identified as a dead end, I believe that the system needs new energy, a new move, a different type of vector. This means to proverbially break up billiard balls laid out in a certain pattern on the table, to rearrange them, to move the elements of a jammed-up system in order to create a new, realigned situation that buys time.

A dynamic situation such as this does not always follow the stable pattern of established Western codes of behavior, with clear, functional, orderly agreements.

It is actually the conflict between irregular forces and countries that necessitates reshuffling of the situation from time to time.

This is different from classical warfare, and has been given many names: asymmetric warfare, low-intensity or limited conflict, routine security, operational deployment, line deployment, and many more. Everybody understands the meaning of the word *war*, but when you need so many terms to describe a situation, this underlines the perplexity of generals and leaders. It is a strange condition that is neither peace nor war, and cannot be arranged in the template of a "solved system."

The familiar classical warfare has been studied and experienced for thousands of years; it has been "solved" – that is, documented and clarified. Advancement here is nothing more than linear and structured development. Even the concept that was prevalent at the end of the nineties, Revolution in Military Affairs (RMA), was nothing more, in my opinion, than novel commentary, and methods and possibilities enabled by technological innovations.

There is a significant difference between classical warfare involving regular armies of countries and asymmetric conflicts. The conflict between irregular forces and national institutions (the country's regular military and security services) requires continuous interpretation, continuous creation of solutions, and continuous development of capabilities. The fight against evasive-subversive elements includes many difficulties because the violence, terror, or guerrilla warfare it carries out is dependent on the civilian population, on national institutions (even though they themselves are being attacked), and on the shelter provided by the institutions, the law, culture, and the population.

This is Hezbollah: a terror and guerrilla organization being built by its patrons (Iran) as a military, but dependent on the population and the national (Lebanese) institutions that protect it. When it acts against another country (Israel), it also takes full advantage of its weak points – such as freedom of speech, access to information, and laws, procedures, morals, and values.

From my experience I have found that this kind of situation requires continuous impulsion of the system – the continuous movement of the billiard balls on the table. In order to reduce the advantage of the evasive, undermining opponent (guerrilla warfare or terror), a country must also know how to shake up, change, evade, undermine, construct, and deconstruct as much as it can in the face of the enemy. This is a difficult enough situation for a military, which is naturally large, awkward, and cumbersome.

But rapid reform approaches the impossible when dealing with national public institutions. Bureaucrats and typical, conservative officers find it difficult to accept change and evolution as a way of life. They resent the frequent changes and what they perceive as the "madness" of an unpredictable situation. Cynicism takes hold everywhere. The new language that is created to relate to these changes requires agility – a combination of speed and flexibility – which is anathema to bureaucracy. As a result, the new language is not implemented fast enough; those who are fluent in it are few, and they are weakened when faced with lumbering, cumbersome bureaucratic mechanisms.

With all of my experience, I have yet to find a solution other than maintaining cyclic processes of learning-changing-learning, with increasing speed, in order to baffle the enemy.

A heavy price of unpopularity is sometimes paid for implementing these changes (change is usually not popular), but they buy critical time for staying a step ahead of the enemy.

And if you manage to confuse the enemy by being different and unpredictable, even though you are a sovereign country, and at the same time you are wise enough not to arouse national bureaucracy or the juntas made up of those who believe that "no day was better than yesterday," then you deserve to be congratulated. You have survived.

I have described earlier in the book how I evaluate a new system using operational tools. I disconnect from the ground and hover in the air. The system's components, its intrinsic attributes and those which may evolve, seem so much clearer to me – as if they are calling me to come and rearrange them.

I deeply investigate, examine, throw away, create, generate imaginary motion in my mind with the system's raw materials, and eventually reach plausible courses of action.

I need a long time to translate this elevated perspective and this observation into a language fit for all.

Hezbollah, Lebanon, the Syrians, the Lebanese Army, UNIFIL, ourselves, the weather, the mood – ingredients such as these, colliding with each other, turn into a whole concoction, creating the "soup" known as reality.

When I observed the situation we faced in Lebanon, I sadly concluded that we were treating it in an irrelevant, linear, mechanical way, which was unsuitable for the entangled system that existed there.

It has been called a "complex system," and that is a mistake! The correct definition is an "entangled system." Complex systems can be broken down, but entanglement is a kind of amalgamation that cannot be separated into component parts – it must be dealt with as is!

During discussions back in 2004, I had suggested the term "frightening" to describe the trigger needed to produce an international intervention for an "arrangement" – another term I suggested back in the J&S Division (for other needs).

I assessed that the goal of a ground operation in Lebanon would be to deliver a substantial blow – a vector-countering vector – which would curb the enemy's logic and force them to realign. This would shuffle the cards so the intolerable situation in the north would be arranged differently. I thought that for this kind of arrangement, external intervention was required, and we had no need to fear it. I was under the impression that not every level of force operation would activate the international community to instill a different reality in Lebanon, and so the "frightening" move was required in order to trigger an arrangement that would create a new situation that would suit us better.

The alternative was to take control of the area, and by means of this domination reduce the number of launches even to complete cessation. However we knew that due to their range, the rockets could be launched from deep inside Lebanon, so a more extensive and longer operation was required.

During the two years preceding the war, the message was repeated over and over again, at the highest levels, that there was no intention to fight against the rockets. Rather, we needed to reach a direct and face-to-face confrontation with Hezbollah, and since the number of its activists at the time was not large, each activist taken out was significant and would bring a decline in the organization's effectiveness.

In other words, killing as many enemy fighters as possible would serve the rationale of direct contact with Hezbollah and reduction of its effectiveness.

There was also the assessment that the Air Force would be better at coping with the heavy launch vehicles –which are easier to identify prior to their launch or following their first one – while the smaller rockets which are harder to identify would be dealt with by ground operations. Most of them were in the vicinity of the Litani River, and it was to there that our ground operation was directed.

Moreover, the plan was to combine all effects, and by means of an integration of attacks from the air and sea, raids by special forces, and crippling of Hezbollah's southern unit's area of operation, which was spread out mainly from the Litani southward, the "frightening" would take effect, and Hezbollah would suffer a huge setback, leading to international pressure for a new arrangement.

Hezbollah would be removed from the border, the Lebanese military would be deployed there, and Lebanon would assume national responsibility. In the long term, I personally wanted UNIFIL to leave Lebanon as well, because I did not believe that there could be any chance that national responsibility would be taken by the Lebanese government as long as they were still in Lebanon.

The understanding that pursuing the launchers was not effective was also expressed in General Staff documents, and it was even said that there was a need to prepare the home front for continued incoming fire that could last for several weeks. I directed the division to prepare plans for a short and effective campaign. I was concerned that the campaign would be brought to a premature conclusion, both because of international pressure and from internal public pressure stemming from extended stays of civilians in bomb shelters. For many other reasons, I felt that a prolonged campaign would negate our gains from initiating the offensive and would allow Hezbollah to better utilize their abilities as a guerilla force against a cumbersome regular army.

Operation Grapes of Wrath in 1996 had seasoned me. Up until the seventeenth and final day of that operation, rockets were continuously being fired into Israel. By the way, the launching continued while NORTHCOM was operating under the command of people who would later lavishly criticize the handling of the Second Lebanon War, being especially critical of the fact that the rocket launchings were not stopped.

But now, ten years later, the Iranian involvement was much more pronounced. We had seen them and followed their movements in southern

Lebanon. Arming was on a large scale – the best weapons were supplied to Hezbollah, and they held continuous training sessions for their regular and reserve forces. We were, in fact, facing an Iranian front, in the full sense of the word, operated by proxy.

The number of rockets was estimated to be between thirteen and fifteen thousand, and that of antitank weapons equaled that of a regular military. For some reason during that time, an attitude developed that "It's true, there are many rockets, but we will make them rust…"

I was of the opinion that if weapons had been stockpiled, especially conventional ones, they would eventually be put to use.

The "Lebanese trauma" was especially salient at that time – a result of eighteen years of remaining in the "Lebanese mud." The pressures that were put on society and on the IDF surrounding the withdrawal from Lebanon, the losses prior to the withdrawal – and especially the way it was photographed as fleeing shamefully – all introduced conscious apprehension as to the option of a ground operation in Lebanon. The estimation was that even Prime Minister Sharon would be the last to enter Lebanon again after suffering political setbacks and being branded as the one who had led us there the first time in 1982.

When I presented the billiard table allegory to the new CGS, LTG Dan Halutz, I made it clear to him that in my opinion it was no longer in his hands, and the cue ball was already on its way once an abduction incident occurred. After it hit the stationary balls aligned on the table (the current reality), we would no longer be able to predict where the balls would eventually go. A chain reaction would begin leading to an uncontrolled situation – war.

Halutz pondered this for a moment and replied, "Make sure the table is as small as possible and the balls don't fall off the table." I took this to mean: act to limit and contain the incident and do what is needed to prevent losing control or further deterioration. In my opinion, this was an unrealistic expectation, and I told him so more than once.

Magen Ha'aretz Timrun Acher (MHTA)

The original CONPLAN for Lebanon was called Magen Ha'aretz (Defender of the Land). The main component of the plan, a relic from the past, was pressuring Syrian forces so they would apply pressure to Hezbollah, who would stop the shooting of rockets.

Since the Syrians had withdrawn from Lebanon in 2005, this was no longer effective. Conditions called for change, mainly moving from armored maneuvers to infiltration and swarms. This led to an adapted version of our original CONPLAN: we called it Magen Ha'aretz Timrun Acher (MHTA), Defender of the Land – A Different Maneuver.

I found MG Eyal Ben-Reuven to be a great partner for promoting my ideas and maintaining the momentum of preparations for a campaign in Lebanon. Despite not having enough resources and equipment, along with the threat of cutbacks and unit closures, Eyal pushed forward, and with a highly talented and tight-knit team, he performed structured procedures for the authorization and creation of operational plans.

I recommended substantial changes in the plan. These included a large infantry maneuver with commando forces deep into Lebanese territory, enhancement of the command over controlling areas within one or two nights of operation, and then securing logistical routes for every brigade, while carrying out meticulous search missions in the "nature reserves" and villages according to predefined priorities.

I also requested an infiltration of thousands of infantry soldiers during the first and second nights, which would be accompanied by "all-encompassing artillery attacks" from the air and sea, controlled by the division's artillery center.

I expected that the collective result of all of these would be a sort of multidirectional, multidimensional "buzz," an unending, irritating, and bothersome "noise," making it difficult for Hezbollah to identify our strategy and successfully cope with it.

I found it appropriate to adapt to the expected nature of the confrontation with Hezbollah, concerning acquisition, training, and force buildup.

I see commandos as the official military version of insurgency and subversion. I saw a way to combat the asymmetric situation by creating a kind of symmetric one. You confront us with guerilla warfare? We will come with infantry, special forces, artillery, and perception-shaping efforts – all combined into one. The combination of them all would create an effect on the opponent that would attain a substantial result. I did not believe in perception efforts alone: these forces needed to capture territory – swiftly and quietly – while destroying as many enemy fighters as possible.

Hezbollah's apparent advantages would be eroded when they were attacked using their own skills and methods, in a commando-type move that would counter their guerilla warfare.

I requested precision-guided munitions (PGM) for hitting quality targets. This contradicted the widespread perception that they should be preserved for a "real" war, but I believed that the real war was the one we were now facing.

I thought we needed modified logistical procedures, to better align with the plan and adapt according to our enemy's capabilities. This meant that there would be a lot of equipment on the soldiers' backs, a lot of equipment that would be flown in by helicopter, and the rest would be inside the armored vehicles, which were to enter a day or two later. I did not believe in supply convoys made up of trucks in the initial stages of combat, and furthermore, as experienced veterans of combat in Lebanon, we envisioned only a small number of heavy armored vehicles could maneuver in this type of combat.

I envisioned tanks carrying out fast armored patrol missions, with a relatively small number of forces. This was not the place to engage them in the existing models of a traditional tank company or armored battalion.

We planned to operate the brigade's forward command centers based on the excellent outpost infrastructure that had been built during the withdrawal from Lebanon, which could provide the communications we required. I also put on the table that humanitarian aid, media aspects, public relations, and information security all needed to be taken into consideration. To meet these demands, we broadened the concept of the "new staff body" that had been created in division headquarters during training sessions over the last year; it included the planning and operation of the professions of spokesperson, operational security specialist, liaison officer to the civilian population, and more.

This was war, I had no doubt.

This was an intermediate and fluid situation. I was asked many times what my goal was, and I replied, "To buy time." More time, and then more time, but it was clear – this was a volatile situation, we were "riding the tiger." Hezbollah was gnawing away at the current arrangement and was building itself a mighty combat force.

Lebanon had never stabilized, and I saw no reason that under the current conditions it ever would. I did not buy into all the fairy tales saying that "the situation is slowly stabilizing." In my opinion, Hezbollah is a generator of instability on a global scale, not just on a regional one.

I regularly voiced my reservations about the current policy of containment and reluctance to take the fight to the enemy, and was repeatedly reprimanded for this.

I was severely rebuked for my opinion and for my words. I was the one who had expressed my reservations so many times in the past, but now I was berated for my "irresponsibility and lack of restraint." I once again asked myself if this was a situation where one resigns, but I rejected the idea right away. Where was the wisdom in resignation, in leaving my people alone to face this threat, in rejecting the way that decisions are made in the highest levels of the organization in which I had grown up?

Many steps were taken by senior officials, but the root of the problem – the cause of the difficult equation on the northern border – they were powerless to change. This had been the policy of the Israeli government since the withdrawal from Lebanon and up to the Second Lebanon War. Iran had slowly built up Hezbollah's strength. Hezbollah had gone and positioned itself directly along the border, and the policy was to contain the situation and maintain the quiet. Period.

The priority at that time was neither the northern border nor investing heavily in preparing for a war in Lebanon. Most of the attention was being given to the fight against Palestinian terror in the West Bank and in the Gaza Strip. In the north, the pastoral atmosphere, the economic prosperity, and the high occupancy rates in the northern guest rooms needed to be preserved.

In spite of all of this, I had to be diligent and advance as much as possible a set of down-to-earth ideas and understandings. I had to train my troops, to plan, to develop methods, to coordinate our preparations with the ground forces and the regional command, to equip our forces, to learn, and more – much more. The scope of activities was huge, very intensive, and the heaviness of solitude weighed heavily on me.

I felt great loneliness.

"There are problems you solve," my blessed grandmother would say to me, "and there are those that you live with . . ." I chose to continue to try to influence decision makers, to prepare for a conflict with my strengths and abilities, to make my voice heard and hope for the best.

While preparing my division for war, I also prepared myself. I read a lot about what had taken place during the Yom Kippur War among the divisions, and between the divisions and the regional command. I discovered that warfare was full of intrigues and politics, and I wondered how it was possible to fight an enemy in such an environment.

The kind of attitude reflected in remarks such as "We will not return to the Lebanese mud" was deeply rooted up to the point that I believed it emasculated pure political-military thinking.

I heard that "It needs to be prevented by any means possible," as if Lebanon were an area in which a ground maneuver was prohibited, and as if preparations for war were ongoing only because a military needed to have plans, even if they would never be approved.

This reminded me of the fixation of thought in J&S prior to Defensive Shield. Due to the conditions and atmosphere that were prevalent following the Oslo Accords, decisions concerning military operations in the Palestinian-controlled areas were only made after the Israeli public paid an exorbitant price. There were those who said we mustn't carry out operations in Bethlehem and Beit Jala, in spite of the fact that it was from there that Jerusalem, the capital of Israel, was the target of sniper and mortar fire.

"If we do that," said the pessimists, "the entire Middle East could go up in flames."

The decision to enter into Area A came after many months of civilian losses and preparing the hearts of the public, but mostly of the leaders – both in the military and in the government – to cross this psychological barrier of the "sacredness" of the Oslo Accords.

Now the same thing was happening in Lebanon.

I knew from experience that crossing this threshold could be very costly for us, since we did not – and would not – have a choice. In these circumstances, it was inevitable, but I continued to be perceived as the "alarmist."

I tried to influence NORTHCOM, the Ground Forces Command, and the General Staff. I was, after all, aware of the paramount role my division would play in the event of a war. I decided to prepare for it in the best way possible, a challenging task since there was no sufficient budget for training. New legal restraints prohibited calling up reservists for periods of service that had been acceptable in the past. This was worrisome, since most of the division's combat forces were reserve soldiers.

I could not call them up for enough days to perform the enormous amount of work that we needed to get done:

- I was determined to unify the division's intel and fires centers (the fires center is the staff body that coordinates and employs all forms of lethal capabilities from land, sea, and air), in order to enhance sensor-to-shooter capabilities for coping with evasive, time-sensitive targets, characteristic of countering guerilla warfare.
- I needed to complete the establishment of the staff body (the fifth center) that combined the fields of media, perception, regional defense, operational security, etc.
- Our Merkava tank brigade needed to adapt from traditional doctrine to fighting guerillas in Lebanon.
- The division's artillery brigade needed to acquire the capability to perform counter-guerilla strikes, to prepare for counter-battery fire (artillery versus artillery), and to be ready for working under a heavy workload for several days at a time.

I was also concerned because the newly established regional logistics brigade (headquarters for organizing delivery of supplies) had yet to complete its preparations and force buildup, and the division no longer had its own logistics brigade.

Carmeli Brigade (reserve infantry) and Alexandroni Brigade (mechanized infantry) were both posted under my command during wartime, and I needed to prepare them for missions with "Lebanon characteristics," such as traversing long distances on foot, infiltration, capturing controlling areas, and cleansing complex tangled and urban areas.

I needed to work fast – who knew when war would break out in Lebanon?

As a truly experimental unit, the Druze Herev Battalion spearheaded the preparations for war and development of appropriate doctrine, such as the classic "swarm" mission profile.

Our combat intelligence collection unit had already completed their transformation to a light, long-distance infantry force that could travel on foot, identify targets, and destroy them.

I assumed the Golani Brigade would be allocated under my command, so I invested a lot in the training of this unit and was able to change the training session of the brigade's headquarters into a format that would be carried out the exact same way during the war.

"I don't have enough infantry," I said over and over, continuing to approach my commanding officers. I was eventually successful in having the Givati Brigade allocated to the division's ORBAT in the event of war, and managed to train some of their officers. As it turned out, however, most of the Givati Brigade was not assigned to me in the war.

Actually it was the Paratroopers Brigade (which had not exercised with us even once) and the Golani Brigade who fought with the division throughout the war. I realized we could not count on specific organization ahead of time, but I estimated that we could maintain our organic units if we initiated the war. This is critical when time is short, uncertainty is prevalent, and a common language is required.

I knew that war would break out following an abduction and insisted on kicking off every NORTHCOM or General Staff exercise with a horrifying abduction scenario. I invested a lot of time in helping commanders and staff officers internalize what would happen to us in the hours and days after an abduction. I also used previous abduction cases to learn how commanders felt and how they acted.

"It is going to be extremely tough," I said over and over to my people. "We are going to enter the fight with a sense of failure, and still function!"

I was no stranger to Hezbollah: I had been fighting them since my days as a company commander. I began the preparations for war with a three-day workshop for the division's commanding officers – both from the regular service and from the reserves. I began with a personal description of my combat experience against the Hezbollah, this bitter opponent, and the Law and Order experience I previously mentioned. It was important for me to share my personal experience, and to teach them about the determination of this enemy and the challenge it presented.

After the war, there were those who claimed that the unsatisfactory results were related to a lack of training and preparations. These claims are of course ridiculous.

The preparations went way beyond the framework of the division. We also went to great lengths to influence large parts of the IDF, mainly its training centers and facilities for training units and commanders. I was not obligated to do this, but I wanted to make an impact and prepare as many troops and commanders as possible for war.

Division Exercise – Three Weeks before the War

From Mount Carmel we were overlooking the Jezreel Valley laid out beneath us. MG Udi Adam had joined my command team, along with several of his staff officers.

Forces from my division were in motion, maneuvering from the Carmel region northward. We were in the midst of a large command-level exercise simulating war. The scenario began with soldiers being abducted by Hezbollah and developed into a broad aerial campaign in Lebanon. As time went on, an order was given to capture key controlling areas along the border and the northern road.

Regular and reserve soldiers reached the division and were processed and equipped, and we planned for an attack deep into Lebanese territory. A day later, combat operations began in a city simulating Bint Jbeil, and later in a city resembling the Tebnine region.

Forces were flown in by helicopter, but mostly traveled on foot, infiltrating the controlling areas and "freezing" Hezbollah's freedom of movement between the villages.

In some parts of the exercise, we operated with all of our forces to examine the schedule and the performance of larger units. Supply problems were revealed, and we discovered that the large capacity backpacks we had purchased overseas, using our own budget, were a significant solution to this type of combat. Lessons learned by the British in the Falklands and my experience in Shaldag operations had proven that a large backpack would serve the troops well over time.

We also practiced helicopter operations, including massive logistic airlifting and dozens of medevacs. We had already witnessed in earlier exercises the challenges of resupplying troops in this type of combat against guerilla warfare in the mountains of Lebanon, when the roads are booby-trapped and the region is full of antitank threats.

I also saw the difficulty in evacuating the wounded and made a point of training various scenarios, including on foot and evacuation by Merkava tanks in areas that only they could reach.

I was not planning on a massive armored operation due to the large number of antitank weapons and the hilly and tangled terrain of southern Lebanon. I was afraid that this would play into the hands of Hezbollah and make the tanks more of a burden than an asset. We trained our own "Steel Chariots" reserve Merkava brigade accordingly, operating with combat teams consisting of a pair of tanks, or possibly a team of four.

I had defined a number of areas to be developed a year prior to the large exercise and thirteen months before the war:

- The brigade was to learn and then teach the rest of the division's forces how to breech and hold a logistical corridor.
- They were to develop capabilities to destroy antitank teams according to a designated force we called armored hunting team (AHT), which acquires a target and moves to destroy it by utilizing its strengths of armor, protection, maneuvering speed, and firepower – all of which work together to form a shock effect on the antitank squad.
- We also decided to change the composition of the ammunition carried by the tanks to dual-purpose ammunition, mainly suited for combat against infantry.

"You are actually performing decentralized combat," Udi Adam said after ponderous thought. "This is decentralized warfare in high friction."

"Well put." I was happy with Udi's conceptualization.

"Nice," he added, and gave a few more instructions, after thoroughly checking – as he is known to do – and inspiring a positive and pleasant environment.

It was indeed decentralized warfare – a growing concept that was becoming more and more well known in modern military thinking. The claim was that a team could do today what a battalion used to be capable of in the past. Especially if it controls a certain area of territory and can attack the enemy with precision and standoff firepower, from the sea, air, and ground.

When these forces are small and bear a low signature, they can successfully infiltrate enemy territory without any needless friction and prevent casualties; with superior communication capabilities, they can be very effective. As Shaldag commander, I agreed with this approach and had already executed it, but several changes needed to be made.

In the division we discovered that it was not enough to control terrain in order to hit an enemy operating as guerilla fighters in tunnels, in the brush, and in densely populated urban areas. There needed to be a push for friction, engagement, and combat. Therefore I believed in sending in platoon- or company-size forces on foot or by helicopter in order to capture dominating areas and then proceed toward an engagement, utilizing our technological advantages – night vision, precision fires, protective equipment, electronic warfare, computerization, and available intel.

The exercise progressed well, but some difficulties also surfaced: the helicopters had difficulty flying in areas where Amnon, commander of our fires center, was unleashing salvos from the artillery brigade. There were challenges in evacuating the wounded, the communications were not always continuous with all the units, and the troops were getting worn down and needed to be relieved. The number of rockets and missiles simulated to be hitting the northern villages and cities were in numbers that looked surreal to some of us. The scenario was that civilians had been in shelters for several long days, and we were in preparations for the capture of the city simulating Bint Jbeil.

The exercise battles that took place in this city were long and hard, as expected when fighting guerillas dug deep into bunkers. We were not surprised.

A Fire-Based Campaign and Counterattacks

Just three weeks after that exercise, it was all starting for real. Within hours of the abduction, the division quickly transitioned into contingency mode, combat formation, and implementation of the defense plan.

During the day, the division changed from battle-day mode in the routine-security operations room to deployment in "centers" – our war mode of operations. This is a complex process in which the division changes its entire command and control structure, from physical deployment to procedure and personnel. But we were experienced, having drilled the process many times.

I put in a request to implement NORTHCOM's contingency plan and mobilize reservists right away, but these requests were not fully approved, and I was allowed to call only up to thirty people at the most!

I demanded to initiate and engage the enemy across the border (the area was already under fire and the residents were in the shelters) – but this too was refused.

I initiated missions and activities that were only partially and gradually approved (in Ghajar, Jabal Blat, and Marwahin). The directive was that a fire campaign was underway, and I was explicitly told that there would be no ground maneuver.

Throughout the day, I could see the gap in understanding the situation. This gap would unfortunately continue for many days.

I gave the order to prepare the activation of the divisional counterattack plan aimed at capturing areas controlling the northern villages and road, but authorization was not given until the morning of July 19 – an entire week later.

We are stabilized, we are doing OK, moving on, was the thought that ran through my head.

Avi, the division intel officer, ran up behind me, tapped me on the shoulder, and hugged me while walking.

"I was very impressed by your conduct today," he said, as we walked through the bunker's hall. "I just wanted to tell you this."

"Thank you, Avi. We have a war in front of us – I place my trust in you."

I knew that Avi was feeling bad following the abduction that had resulted from an absence of valid intel, and I wanted to support him.

My personal assistant (PA), Tal, had already changed my "light" forward command post – my unprotected jeep – to a wartime secured division commander convoy, just as we had done in training.

Outside there was the pounding of artillery fire, the thunder of shells impacting, and smoke. There was a strong smell, and the heat of a mid-afternoon sun.

And there was war.

After darkness fell, I finished briefing Chen Livni's Brigade 300 forces. I put special emphasis on Maglan, commanded by Eliezer. The approach was business-like, short, and to the point. Eliezer understood that this was the division's prime mission: they were the ones who were to search for the bodies of the soldiers who were in the tank that exploded while in pursuit of the abductors.

I still did not know if my belief that this was war would be accepted. I knew there was the chance that everything would stop after the Air Force bombing sorties deep in Lebanon. I could not wait and leave the possibility open that Hezbollah would grab the bodies of the tank crew.

It was a controversial issue, discussed at length in the IDF and in public forums. Was it right to risk soldiers' lives in order to bring home the dead for burial? Was it right to swap live prisoners for dead soldiers? My opinion was clear. This standard had been set in the IDF. We search even if it's for a fragment of a soldier, in order to bring him home for burial according to Jewish tradition.

Israelis vividly remember the pictures of IDF soldiers crawling on hands and knees in the sand in the southern Gaza Strip looking for human remains after an APC loaded with explosives blew up in May 2004. I was deeply moved by this, as I saw it as a sort of educational image for an entire nation – the power of friendship, in life and in death.

On the way back to the division headquarters, I received updates on the massive attack that the Air Force was about to launch at any moment in the center of Beirut. I understood the implications and what it would do to Hezbollah.

"Get me the regional civil defense officer," I ordered, and when I had him on the line, I asked him, "Moti, is everyone in the shelters?"

"Yes."

"Verify it. Hezbollah is going to attack the home front."

In the division's region, the civilian population was my responsibility. This definition includes all of the isolated villages located right on the border fence.

"Moti, speak to all heads of municipalities. Make sure that they are ready for a long round this time."

At the entrance to the division's war room, I stopped for a second, hearing a familiar scary and sickening shrieking sound. I became tense, and then came an enormous explosion – BOOOOOM! Flames, smoke, and a shockwave hurled us inside the command post.

"Mortars!" someone yelled.

Direct impacts shook the division's command center, and the smell of gunpowder and smoke overwhelmed us. I tried to make it to the communication systems in the command post.

The heavy structure of the bunker repeatedly rattled. The electricity was cut, the radio became silent, the computer screens went blank, thick darkness was all around, and the din of screams assaulted my ears.

"Bring me a megaphone!"

"Here."

"OK, people," I said in jest to those around me, "this is why we get field pay."

Alex, the division's communications officer, came in breathing heavily.

"The generator is out, and the reserve generator too – direct hits."

"All right," I said, calming him, "prepare the mobile forward command post to move out. We may move our operations to another location." It was clear that the division headquarters would be under fire – for it was right there, located front and center on the battlefield.

"Udi, we are sustaining fire," I updated my commander. "Direct hits, there is some damage, and we might leave this position. I am not sure I can command from here. It is completely targeted."

Over the sounds of explosions, I listened to Udi's voice, trying to assess whether NORTHCOM understood that we were at war. They did not!

"In one hour we will lose what energy is left," Alex informed me. The fans weren't working anymore, the oxygen was getting thin, and it was suffocating in the operations room.

"I understand. We're moving to another position with the mobile forward command post, just like we worked on in training."

"Where to?"

"We will move to Bravo." It was far enough away to prepare the division for the morning in relative quiet. I was not sure that Hezbollah would already be able to shoot that night at the towns deeper into Israel.

"OK, let's go! Sprint outside bent over, toward the vehicles!" Everyone ran toward the exits.

While we ran, a salvo of shells fell and a series of powerful explosions shook the compound. There was a flash of blinding light and a flurry of shrapnel.

My security detail shoved me back inside and someone yelled, "Your forward command post has been hit!"

"We will try to repair the generators," Alex said apologetically. "In the meantime use portable equipment."

"No problem, we won't move out; we don't have a mobile forward command unit. Monir, ask the command to allocate the general's command vehicle to us."

"The command has approved," he updated. "It will be here tomorrow."

"Good."

The firing abated. Reports came in from Eliezer, Maglan commander. They had found strewn human remains, and a wallet with blood stains. Everything was being carefully collected.

"We need at least one drop of blood from each of them," Asher, the division's rabbi, requested, "so we can give them a Jewish burial."

"Continue, Eliezer."

"We won't stop. Getting shot at sporadically. Working under fire."

"We will help you in any way we can."

"The attack helicopters you allocated are doing a great job and everything is fine," he said calmly.

Avi came in panting. "Now I am really going to give it to them, those bastards!"

"What is it?" I wondered.

"A direct hit on our quarters; my room was destroyed."

"Don't worry about it."

"Don't worry?" he snapped back. "The roof collapsed on my bicycle. There's a limit to what I am willing to take. The division, the region – I don't mind. But my bike?"

A day went by and the fighting continued.

"The CGS wants you."

"Put him through."

"How's it going?" We knew each other well, back from when he was my CO in the Air Force.

"How are you, sir?"

"I'm fine, and you?"

"Tough things to get over, but we are moving ahead. The division is hard at work."

"I just wanted to tell you to hang in there; it was a tough incident, but ..."

"Halutz, I am OK and we are all doing fine. Just let us do the job. Let us cross the border; it's impossible to fight without crossing the fence to the other side."

"Not now. What forces do you want to take over there?"

"Special forces in the meantime – small units; capture controlling areas; identify enemy fighters; counterattack and strive to engage. It can't all be done from the air."

"We will see. We'll think about it."

"Sir, at least let me send in small forces to seal off the western sector. We have a plan for this, and I can execute it with a fraction of the original forces."

"We'll think about it. Bye."

"Good-bye, sir."

After a while, Udi arrived at the division's operations room, where he received an update and then sat with me for a short conversation. I sensed that he was angry and a bit distanced – not at all characteristic of the warm and curious person I knew.

We spoke about the abduction and the harsh result. I told him straightforwardly that I was responsible for everything that happened in my area of responsibility. I said that this was a failure, although the result did not come as a surprise to anyone and I hoped it did not surprise him either.

"No," he answered, shaking his head. But he didn't sound very convincing.

Defense and Combat Learning

As the fighting progressed, I studied, analyzed, and labeled the enemy. The intel coverage we had on Hezbollah up until that point was practically irrelevant.

I knew Hezbollah intimately, but as soon as contact was made and there was friction, the method and scope of learning totally changed. There were gaps in understanding their tactical behavior, level of motivation, and skill in using their personal equipment. Visual contact and physical engagement enables a kind of "palpation" that is beyond intel. This is called developing combat knowledge, and its products are called operational combat knowledge.

Not much knowledge was developed about Hezbollah during the first week of the war. At any rate, nothing pointed to anything different from the existing intel material. There were exchanges of fire, mainly by high-trajectory mortars and rockets, and there were battles where contact was made with machine guns, artillery, and missiles.

I was not at all surprised that Hezbollah fired directly at civilian towns inside Israel. We knew that they had some fifteen thousand rockets and many mortars, and no moral barrier preventing their use against civilians.

At the same time, I understood that my plans were valid and it was the right thing to put them into motion as soon as possible. Under the restrictions in which we operated at the time, I applied our defensive plan, while incessantly pushing to receive a green light for the counterattack plan.

Even though I did not receive approval, I requested mobilization of all the division's units and implementation of the plans: the counterattack for capturing the areas that controlled the northern road and civilian communities

My grandmother Leah, grandfather Marco, and mother Rachel (holding me), pioneers in the desert, Arad, 1965

My cousin, LT Amnon Hager, 1977

Bar mitzvah at the top of Masada, 1977

As a cadet at the military academy, 1978

Team leader in the Paratroopers' Sayeret, 1985

On patrol in Lebanon, 1982 (photo: Bamahane)

Equipment check formation before a patrol in Lebanon, 1989 (photo: Shlomo Ben-Torah)

Commander of the combat engineering unit of the Paratroopers, 1988 (photo: IDF Spokesperson)

"Gal force" in the Beqaa Valley in Lebanon during Operation Law and Order, 1988 (photo: Yuval Navon, IDF Spokesperson)

Donna joins me during the Paratroopers' beret march, 1988 (photo: IDF Spokesperson)

As the 202nd Paratroopers Battalion commander, with my daughter Meori on the Lebanese border, 1992

Fighting in the brush on the northern border, 1993 (photo: IDF Spokesperson)

With Minister of Defense Yitzhak Rabin in Nablus, 1992 (photo: IDF Spokesperson)

As Shaldag commander, Operation Had Hushim, 1991

Air Force Commander Citation awarded by MG Herzl Bodinger to Shaldag after Operation Grapes of Wrath, 1996 (photo: IAF)

Briefing before a special operation with Shaldag (photo: IAF)

Shaldag commandos boarding
helicopters (photo: IAF)

Operational movement (photo: Ziv Koren)

Counterterror training (photo: Ziv Koren)

Fighting Palestinian terror: raiding a
terrorist's house (photo: Ziv Koren)

Our snipers in action (photo: Ziv Koren)

As Shaldag CO, returning from enemy territory, 1996 (photo: IAF)

My rescue from the damaged vehicle after the ambush, 1998 (photo: Avigdor Shatz)

The crippled car and the boulder that had been hurled from the bridge, 1998 (photo: Avigdor Shatz)

From the hospital to Benjamin Brigade –
promotion ceremony presided over by the
CGS, LTG Shaul Mofaz, 1998 (photo: IDF
Spokesperson)

Benjamin Brigade commander, 1999
(photo: IDF Spokesperson)

Battles in Ramallah, Nakba Day, 2000 (photo:
IDF Spokesperson)

With CNN correspondent Bob Simon, 2000
(photo: IDF Spokesperson)

Visiting Rabbi Elyashiv, 2001

Work meeting with the Palestinian governor of Ramallah, 1999 (photo: Benjamin Brigade)

In the field with Benjamin Brigade staff, 2000 (photo: Benjamin Brigade)

With Prime Minister Ehud Barak in Ramallah, 2001 (photo: Benjamin Brigade)

Battle day in Benjamin Brigade, 2000 (photo: Gilad Goldberg)

At CENTCOM war room as chief of operations (J3), Operation Defensive Shield, 2002

With General Moshe "Bogie" Ya'alon at my appointment as Bahad 1 commandant, 2003 (photo: IDF Spokesperson)

Bahad 1 commandant, 2004 (photo: Bahad 1)

Commander of IDF delegation to
Auschwitz, with IDF Chief Rabbi BG
Israel Weiss, 2005

Meeting with Bedouin Sheikh Al-Atrash,
2004 (photo: Bahad 1)

With cadets from the German
Bundeswehr, as commandant of Bahad 1,
2005 (photo: Bahad 1)

Promotion ceremony – BG rank pinned on
by Donna and the CGS, LTG Moshe (Bogie)
Ya'alon, 2005 (photo: IDF Spokesperson)

My daughters Meori, Ofri, and Nir visiting me at the 91st Division, 2005

Division war room during the Second Lebanon War, 2006 (photo: Tal Miller)

Blessing on the wine during a Sabbath meal, Second Lebanon War, 2006 (photo: Tal Miller)

Inside a Lebanese house, 2006 (photo: Tal Miller)

Briefing before a raid on Bint Jbeil, 2006
(photo: Tal Miller)

Regional Brigade 300's FCG during
the battle at Maroun al-Ras, Second
Lebanon War, 2006 (photo: Tal Miller)

Briefing at Carmeli Brigade's FCG during
the battle at Ayta ash-Shab, 2006 (photo:
Tal Miller)

Consulting with 300 Brigade's FCG between
battles, 2006 (photo: Tal Miller)

Visit of the CGS, LTG Dan Halutz, accompanied by Ground Forces CO MG Benny Gantz, Second Lebanon War, 2006 (photo: IDF Spokesperson)

During the war, 2006 (photo: Haim Azulai)

On the Lebanese border at the end of the war, 2006 (photo: Tal Miller)

Chairman of Defensive Shield, at the International Institute for Counter-Terrorism (ICT), IDC Herzliya, 2015

With Judge Mishael Cheshin, 2015

Change of
command
ceremony at the
Depth Command,
with the CGS, LTG
Gadi Eizenkot, 2015

My dear family, *right to left*: Donna, Meori, Nir, Ofri and myself, 2013

With my mother, Rachel, and Nir on the day I became a general, 2005

My father, Yitzhak Hirsch, and the girls, 2010

Pinning on Ofri's officer rank, with commander of the Air Force MG Amir Eshel, 2015

Ofri receives her officer rank, 2015 (*from right to left*: Meori, Ofri, and Nir)

Commandant of Bahad 1 and I pin on
Meori's lieutenant rank, 2012

Armored brigade during
the Second Lebanon War,
2006 (photo: Ziv Koren)

Leaving Lebanon, 2006
(photo: Ziv Koren)

it led to, and transition to the offensive plan, MHTA, using the method we had worked on for more than a year – the "swarm" tactic of decentralized attacks with high levels of friction.

My estimation was that the more friction from intensive engagement, the more there would be targets to attack.

Unfortunately, during the first days of the war, both NORTHCOM and the General Staff lacked any motivation to push for friction with Hezbollah. There was a feeling of satisfaction with the results from air strikes against long- and intermediate-range rockets, and from the effects of the attack on the Dahieh Quarter of Beirut.

It did not appear that there was any inclination toward a ground confrontation.

The pressure I applied for authorizing cross-border operations achieved only minor results, such as allowing us to take over the northern part of Ghajar.

The Operation in Ghajar

The operation in the village of Ghajar was carried out with combined forces from the Israel Police's elite counterterror unit (Yamam), Egoz, and Shaldag.

Ever since the abduction attempt in Ghajar in November 2005, I had assessed that proactively overtaking the northern part of Ghajar would be the first move in any escalation scenario. The lives of the residents of the divided village were intolerable; there was a constant danger of abduction, and the threats in the vicinity of the village were substantial, as there was no fence or obstacle between us and the Hezbollah there. I wanted to take advantage of any situation where there was a conflict to reshape the reality on the ground – or at least try.

The operation included not only conquering and destroying Hezbollah outposts adjacent to the village, but also apprehending people who were in contact with Hezbollah or involved in criminal activity. I needed the Israel Police with us in order to arrest Israeli citizens, even though they lived in Lebanese territory (as a result of the village's division during the 2000 IDF withdrawal). I received Yamam, their elite counterterror unit.

In spite of the type of hostilities that were ongoing throughout the region, we were required to follow routine procedures, including my detailed authorization of the plans and presenting them to NORTHCOM.

"This is ridiculous," I grumbled. "We are at war. We can't conduct things as if it's a routine mission."

"This is the way we are doing it," was the answer from higher headquarters. The authorizations at this time went all the way up to the CGS. The IDF was unable to detach from standard, routine, ceremonious mission-approval procedure, almost until the end of the war.

I was also amazed to discover that NORTHCOM had sent me a "mentor" for the execution of the Ghajar operation. It was a relatively small-scale operation, comprised of a number of small teams, yet an armored division commander was sent to observe and inspect. After just a few moments on the job, embarrassed, he asked to be relieved of this duty. "This is ridiculous," he said, and left.

The operation was a success, and I broadened it with follow-up searches and raids in the area. Several Hezbollah operatives were killed while scouting near one of the villages. A Shaldag force destroyed a truck loaded with rockets and assisted attack helicopters in taking out additional enemy squads. Forces that the 769th Brigade commander had pulled out of their usual sector of operations carried out smaller searches in suspicious pockets of Lebanese territory adjacent to the fence, but this was not enough.

The shelling and the rocket launches continued. The plan that had been built exactly for the kind of situation we were now facing had been exercised many times before, but the stubbornness of the higher echelons not to authorize an operation over the border was still in force.

There was concern that Hezbollah might carry out "surprise" operations – attempts to attack or overrun a civilian community, capture an outpost, or infiltrate the divisional headquarters.

"You must invest in defense," Udi insisted.

"We have to go on the offensive; we must call up reserves, to reinforce!" I replied adamantly.

It was to no avail. All eyes were on the air strikes and the naval blockade of Lebanese ports. It was disheartening to see the cloud of the kidnapping incident still hanging over NORTHCOM. It was a painful series of events – kidnapped soldiers, KIAs, and an exploded tank – but in spite of the fact that we had trained and discussed incidents such as these on numerous occasions prior to their actual occurrence, when they did happen, they had a paralyzing affect.

The division was already at war; NORTHCOM – not yet.

I insisted on receiving reinforcements. One battalion arrived and was allocated to defend the region, but was spread out from the sea to the Golan Heights, under direct orders from the NORTHCOM commander.

Udi thought there was a real threat of Syrian intervention.

"OK," I said, "it certainly is possible, but if that is the case, what is one lone paratrooper company going to help?"

"That's all there is."

In the meantime, the firing increased in the area of Moshav Avivim and Kibbutz Yiron. I ordered tank reinforcements. On my way to one of the units, I saw two Merkava tanks moving on the northern road, cautiously edging their way toward Sasa Junction.

Two civilian vehicles were on the road ahead of them. The civilians got out to look at this surreal scene of tanks driving on the road. They waved enthusiastically to the tank crew, and one of the tank commanders stood up straight in the turret and waved back with a gloved hand. Then he dropped back down the hatch and the tanks turned left and continued their movement toward Kibbutz Baram.

I was reminded of the book *The Heights of Courage: A Tank Leader's War on the Golan* (Praeger, 1992), by BG Avigdor Kahalani, about the Yom Kippur War in 1973. He described his dilemmas in the initial stages of the war – whether to drive his tanks on roads and ruin them, and through fields where irrigation lines would be trampled. What if this were just another battle day and not war? Was it worth all the damage to civilian infrastructure?

I wanted my people to assume a war mindset, so I gave an order ahead of time: "The tanks will travel on the main roads, and there are no other considerations. This is war. When it is over, we will repair what needs to be repaired." I now saw that my instructions were being carried out. I was satisfied that my soldiers quickly understood the situation and acted accordingly.

This mode shift did not occur at NORTHCOM, the General Staff, or on the political level.

In one of the first nights of the battles, I was summoned to a commander's meeting with the minister of defense and the prime minister. I met Minister Peretz in the hallway. He shook my hand and voiced his support after the terrible abduction event. I appreciated this.

During the meeting, I became very worried. After the updates and briefings,

I heard Peretz tell Prime Minister Olmert that his intention was to declare a "special situation on the home front," a natural course of action in light of the heavy firing throughout northern Israel. The prime minister's response surprised me: he told him to wait because there were serious economic and other implications. As to my request to take the offensive and initiate a ground maneuver in Lebanon, the answer I received was weak and dismissive. I realized that the political level was also not in the mode or mood for war.

The dominant offensive mission that took place at that time was "razing" the line of Hezbollah outposts by bulldozers. But the bulldozers were few, and a large number of the outposts were booby-trapped with hundreds of kilograms of explosives. One bulldozer was hit and overturned near Mount Manor, and it was a miracle that the vehicle's crew was only slightly injured. The operation also progressed slowly because it was not possible to secure the engineering teams from within Lebanese territory, and providing effective protection from the other side of the fence was never approved. The situation was frustrating. The bulldozers and tanks that worked on the line in an attempt to erase Hezbollah infrastructure took continuous fire from Lebanese territory, and they couldn't be helped by infantry forces who were – according to our carefully laid but now ignored plans – supposed to capture controlling areas across the border some time before the heavy vehicles started working.

"Let me deploy forces inside to protect the razing operation," I requested.

"No," was the answer, "we are not entering Lebanon."

When in spite of this I ordered to go in, they ordered me to exit immediately.

"Why isn't the razing operation going faster?" they asked from NORTH-COM, from Tel Aviv, and from every place possible.

"It is progressing; it takes time."

"It isn't going fast enough."

"There are not enough bulldozers, no security, there is enemy fire, and everything is booby-trapped. Enough!" I shot back angrily.

The 35th Brigade's excellent headquarters arrived, led by COL Hagai Mordechai, the brigade commander. This was a brigade headquarters, but I didn't have any troops to place under its command. A day later, part of the Paratrooper Recon Battalion arrived from the West Bank.

The main mission at that point was of course the razing of Hezbollah infrastructure, and it was being carried out under fire in the region of the

Sulam Ridge, overlooking Rosh Hanikra, a very problematic location. There still wasn't authorization for offensive actions.

"Hagai," I said to COL Mordechai, "go over there and command the sector. We will reduce the area of the 300th Brigade. Carry out the razing, put in small forces for protecting the bulldozers' operation, deploy in Hanita."

"Wilco."

Chapter 15

First Forces Enter Lebanon

Making Do

As time passed, and I exerted more and more pressure on my superiors, including direct and difficult conversations with both the CGS and his deputy, I began to receive approvals to mobilize small forces toward the border.

"There aren't larger forces to allocate for a counterattack. Will you make do with this?" I was asked.

"Small forces are fine. Just let us get to work."

"No forces…" I mumbled to myself, "how could that be?" A few days had passed, the firing continued, the combat continued, and the priorities had yet to change! There were still quality forces in Gaza and the West Bank, and evidently that was where the priorities lay. I was still without reserves, had almost no reinforcements – and those that did arrive were thinly spread throughout the sector by orders of NORTHCOM. What was going on here? After all, it couldn't be that we were the only ones who were behaving as if it was war.

"That's all there is," I repeated to myself. "We need to engage the enemy, friction is needed, we need to initiate contact and disrupt their basic plan. We need to stop being targets."

In order to create contact with the enemy and take control of the ridges controlling the northern border, I put several special forces into operation, and by July 18, I had already transferred hundreds of soldiers onto Lebanese soil, most of them Shaldag, Egoz, and Maglan, to assist in defending the towns and villages, to protect the northern road, and to locate enemy targets to be attacked.

The first force's crossing was delayed for a full day since I still did not have Sayeret Yael (a special unit from the Engineering Corps that mainly dealt with explosives) to forge an opening through the minefield.

Sayeret Yael soldiers experienced a horrific night in the heart of a minefield. The outdated maps made it difficult to find mines in the thicket of the old minefield, while on the ground behind them Shaldag operators crouched and waited for a clear passage.

Prior to the war, I had urged my superiors many times to clear paths through the minefields, in order to prepare for the launching of a ground maneuver. It had not been approved.

The forces moved silently and covertly toward Lebanese territory from the slopes of Mount Dov, through Kafr Kila, Nabi el-Awadi, Jabal Blat, and other routes. The search operations carried out by Herev, the Druze battalion, in the village of Marwahin resulted in the destruction of a Hezbollah car, and ammunition stockpiles were found in the village mosque.

"Great!" Halutz said excitedly, "bring pictures, lots of pictures."

Slowly but surely the maps filled up with blue arrows of our forces' positions beyond the border, in controlling areas.

According to our contingency plans, the Steel Division was intended to receive responsibility over the eastern region. But since this had not yet been approved, my division was stretched along the entire line, dozens of kilometers from the sea all the way to Mount Dov.

"Call up my reserves," I requested again and again. "There are many missions to carry out. Recruit my division or send me reinforcements."

"Just Like in Gaza"

One night I was summoned urgently to NORTHCOM headquarters, and a confrontation erupted between the CGS and me. I was adamant that we should begin a ground maneuver in Lebanon, and stated in no uncertain terms that air and sea attacks would not be enough.

"There will not be a ground maneuver!" Halutz insisted.

I persisted. I told him that I was interested in a broad division-sized maneuver with several brigades, fully utilizing the division's capabilities. The small forces that were already operating inside Lebanon were not enough to bring about a change in the situation. The shooting into the north continued – nothing would change without a broad ground maneuver, something I also knew from my experience in J&S. The international community would not move or interfere if there were not a frightening and dramatic ground move. Counterfire would not suffice in this drama, and we already knew it.

We needed to create an "effect of presence" in enemy territory and explain the new situation to the world and its leaders.

"Maybe there will be approval for a brigade combat team (BCT)," Halutz said during one of our disagreements.

"It won't help," I insisted. I knew why he was locked onto the BCT concept. He was thinking about the model we used in Gaza. The Air Force was also mesmerized by the magic of the Yemei Teshuvah (Days of Penitence) operation; everyone loved the BCTs, and the saying "just like in Gaza" was coined. But this was not Gaza; we were in Lebanon!

"So maybe a double BCT ..." Halutz offered.

"A double BCT is a division," I clarified, exposing Halutz's "cleverness."

"I have restraints concerning the formations," he said during NORTH-COM's situation assessment forum, at the peak of the argument between us. I leaned back and listened.

This was a moment of candor from him. Could it be that the political echelon was limiting the scope of forces he could use? Were they dictating to the CGS whether he would put a BCT or division into action?

The arguments between us continued. I knew that I was considered a troublemaker, but I couldn't stop. I felt a responsibility to stick to my guns and not to be a yes-man.

I was angry at the downpour of foolish and inappropriate directives we were receiving: not to fight in the "nature reserves"; to stop combat during the day; not to call up reserve units; not to involve reserve units in combat; to allocate drones only to the brigades and not to the division ("just like in Gaza"); not to drive tanks on asphalt roads...

I was bitter and aggressive. How much arguing were we capable of?

In those times when I acted without asking for permission (since I was afraid of the response I would receive), NORTHCOM or the General Staff quickly discovered my actions and ordered me to stop. This was what happened concerning the combat in the "nature reserves" and on other occasions. I knew that a change involved direct contact with the enemy. This was what we had said and written; this was what we had trained for before the war.

It was not always like this, but I decided, for the most part, not to act contrary to the orders from NORTHCOM, as I wished to avoid repeating the fiasco of the Sharon-Gorodish clash during the Yom Kippur War in 1973. I had studied that war long and hard, and made up my mind that I would not break the chain of command. I also knew that there could be a personal price to pay for this loyalty.

I decided to act according to my own logic and situational assessment, while adhering to the *spirit* of the orders I received – not necessarily following them to the letter. But when NORTHCOM's orders clearly contradicted mine, I invested great effort – at times hours and even days, to argue my point. This led, at times, to real disputes.

Despite my oppositional conduct, I also knew when to back down, as my experience of serving in a regional command during combat assisted me to understand what was going through the minds of the echelons above me. As soon as I realized that the discussion was over, I acted according to the orders and what they represented, while trying to find new places for interpretation and new initiatives in the field without asking too many additional questions. I knew that if you asked questions, you might get answers, and I did not want to hear all the answers.

Those were very difficult days, when my loyalty to my superiors was being constantly tested. However, I managed things in such a way that the tactical combat level working with me had no idea of the conflicts between myself and higher authorities.

I suffered extreme loneliness, but to my subordinates, I reflected only a continuous, professional, and unified command authority. To them, the steady voice of "Sela Actual" over the radio represented everything.

"I can't continue like this," I told Eyal Ben-Reuven, who had just come back from overseas directly to combat. I was bitter, hurt, and frustrated. The pressure was unbearable, and the pestering from NORTHCOM never ceased. There was intervention into marginal issues while we were dealing with unremitting war. We had been in combat since July 12, at 13:00. NORTHCOM, on the other hand, was not. There were talented officers there – many of whom I knew well and respected – but at that time, their state of mind was totally different from ours.

"I'll deal with it," Eyal promised.

We had worked long and hard together for an entire year before the war, and we had a close and trusting relationship.

After some time, I began to see the effects of Eyal's intervention. He was a seasoned commander who had experienced the 1973 Yom Kippur War, served as a battalion commander in the First Lebanon War, and was now assisting

NORTHCOM in stabilizing the situation. He was a level-headed, quiet leader – and he helped Udi a lot. His arrival was actually the reinstatement of the corps operational organizational structure that we had trained with, but which had subsequently been dismantled. Eyal actually returned to be my corps commander and gave me fast and direct access in real and relevant time to a senior commander with authority, for consultation and for coordination and approval. As time passed, the relationship with Udi also improved and stabilized – but not before we experienced the "first battle effect," in Shaked and in Maroun al-Ras.

Shaked

In the meantime the firing continued on the villages and towns adjacent to the border. In Avivim, an artillery round scored a direct hit on a building and set it on fire, and rockets fell incessantly. This just could not go on. My pressure mounted on NORTHCOM to allow me to seize controlling areas inside Lebanon.

On July 19, I ordered the attack and takeover of the area of Maroun al-Ras-Shaked. It was from here that both high- and low-trajectory fire was being unleashed toward northern Israel and IDF forces.

On that same day, Maglan troops were inserted into the Shaked area in an attempt to destroy the recoilless artillery and rockets that persistently targeted Avivim from controlling positions. They reached their positions, but in the morning found themselves in the heart of a "nature reserve," directly over the openings of shafts leading down to a vast underground complex.

I had not even known this specific nature reserve existed, but we would later learn that IDI knew and never informed us.

I realized that either we initiated and engaged, or the enemy would. I wanted to avoid our team being ambushed from a hidden position or crenel. I directed the brigade commander to initiate – to slip hand grenades into the openings and destroy the positions. All the time they were covered by observation points, intense firepower, and nearby reinforcements if needed.

I was seeking that friction, for I knew that Hezbollah would be thrown off balance as soon as they were attacked and suffered casualties. As long as we only fired from standoff positions, they were able to hide in their underground infrastructure, but when they realized that we were already on top of them, their behavior would change.

This is exactly what happened. Direct engagement now forced Hezbollah to become mobile, to request assistance, and to deal with casualties, creating targets that could be attacked.

All at once the fighting transformed.

Although two soldiers had been killed during the battle, the unit maintained contact and remained in combat while they were joined by backup tanks and fire support.

By this time I had already made the decision that later that night, larger forces would ascend and assume positions inside Lebanon, securing our side of the border. These were the positions that had been analyzed for controlling the northern villages and road. The division's special forces were already widely employed there.

During the battle in Shaked, our peripheral support forces attacked and destroyed enemy vehicles and positions, and hit many of their fighters. They had moved in response to calls from their comrades at Shaked, and due to their understanding that there were now Israeli forces on Lebanese territory. We had been waiting for this, and the division's intel and fires centers were now seeing an abundance of potential targets; their hands were full.

That's how it goes – friction always creates targets.

As opposed to this positive operational development and the feeling that things were "finally beginning to move," there was also, unfortunately, needless hysteria, mainly following the casualties suffered in the battle. Someone apparently was operating under the assumption that we were facing cardboard targets, and that there are wars of luxury, devoid of casualties. I am a battle-seasoned soldier and I have lost many of my commanders, subordinates, and friends. Each man lost is a devastating blow and an eternal wound to my soul. But even in our day of technological advancement, we can never guarantee zero casualties.

A wave of rumors and deliberate leaks to the media ensued.

The battle was described as an erroneous "encounter" with the enemy. The mission that had been personally authorized by the CGS was made into an "irresponsible initiative by Gal Hirsch." Although it took place merely a few hundred meters from the fence, and was backed up by four Merkava tanks, seventy-six soldiers on immediate rescue and evacuation alert, and a comprehensive envelope of observation points, artillery, helicopters, and missiles, it was turned into an "improvised mission without backup."

I was flabbergasted when Kaplan met me in the hallway at NORTHCOM and bluntly criticized me: "This is how you go on an operation?! Without any backup? Without any cover? Without approval? With such a small force?"

"That is totally incorrect," I replied defensively, tired, and in shock. "Who told you that?"

"That is what I know."

"Well, it seems like you simply don't know!" I shot back angrily, as I left the room and dashed back to the division.

The next day Kaplan called me in a different mood and asked: "Are you and I OK?" This was the familiar pattern: anger, leaks, absurd accusations, and flying off the handle, followed a day or two later by words of "togetherness" and reconciliation. I did not have time to understand what was taking place behind my back. I did not know at the time that there had been several attempts to appoint someone in my place. Those who didn't like my appointment as 91st Division commander in the first place were seeking every way to impeach me.

During the war, and mostly afterwards, I was told about the initiative to dismiss me. I also learned about the adamant opposition by Generals Ben-Reuven and Adam, who claimed that there was absolutely no reason or justification to take such measures.

Meanwhile, the battle in Shaked ended with good results, and the fire on Avivim stopped. For the first time, pictures of the Hezbollah underground infrastructure were distributed throughout the IDF. We could finally understand firsthand what the nature reserves looked like. Completely undetected from the air, these were immense underground facilities, equipped with electricity, communications, and supplies. An interconnecting network of tunnels enabled flexibility and mobility, making it extremely difficult to tackle. The only way to operationally confront the nature reserves was to send soldiers down into them – an extremely dangerous and complicated mission, but a necessity. Captured equipment was taken for further research. We released photos and blueprints to all the headquarters and units of the IDF, in case they would be allocated to us in the war.

In my area of responsibility, Hezbollah began to lose their equilibrium; they began to move, reinforce units, and make mistakes.

I planned that the continuation of the initiative would be an attack that night on Maroun al-Ras, Shaked, and additional ridges, which would shove

Hezbollah back from the current line of contact and expel them from areas controlling our villages.

Maroun al-Ras

"When was the last time you conducted a battalion exercise?" I asked LTC Nimrod Aloni, commander of the Paratrooper Recon Battalion.

"Never," he replied. It turned out that like most of the battalion commanders who fought in this war, Nimrod had never commanded a battalion exercise with his unit, due to budgetary cutbacks and operational tempo in J&S. He had once done a withdrawal maneuver exercise in the Command and Staff course – but that was it.

After the commanders went to an observation point with Chen, received support forces, were briefed, presented an order, and had their plans approved, the forces went out on the operation.

Nimrod captured Maroun al-Ras using a tank company, artillery, combat engineers, attack helicopters, and observer teams – following only several hours of preparations, while fully coordinating with two additional battalions and the 300th Brigade headquarters. The results of the battle were conclusive: the enemy was vanquished.

The battle in Maroun al-Ras was impressive tactically, morally, and certainly with regard to the results. Still, it was the first battle, and mistakes were made.

During the battle, the southern flank of the Paratrooper Recon Battalion was exposed to enemy fire. Tanks were called into action too quickly, immediately after the paratroopers had taken control of the outskirts, but before they had destroyed the RPG squads. Two tanks were hit and several soldiers were injured, but the battle went on.

Close-range combat developed in between the houses while Hezbollah attempted to organize a counterattack. During the battle, enemy fighters also closed in on a group of houses where Nimrod's Sayeret soldiers were located.

The enemy was taken out, fast and professionally.

For the first time during the war, I could clearly say that we had a definite advantage over Hezbollah in face to face combat. Although Hezbollah was organized and highly motivated, it was apparent that there was a huge gap between the quality of their fighters and the level of IDF soldiers.

After capturing the houses in the higher, controlling areas of the village,

Nimrod prepared to engage in indirect fire. He directed artillery and made good use of the attack helicopters that were allocated to his brigade by the division. Hezbollah suffered heavy losses, and division intel reported that the enemy was showing signs of pressure – there were reports of their fighters fleeing, and their wounded were being evacuated to hospitals in Bint Jbeil. Because of the previous day's attack on Shaked, the enemy mistakenly understood that our ground maneuver in Lebanon had begun.

The activity of the Paratrooper Recon Battalion coincided with the armor and infantry maneuvers of the 82nd Battalion (Merkava tanks) on the Jal a-Dir Ridge. The force, led by commander of the 82nd Battalion LTC Oded Basiuk, quickly took control of the ridge line and engaged the area in the vicinity of the village of Aytarun and the city of Bint Jbeil. While this was taking place, Maglan continued its operations of clearing the Shaked nature reserve, between Maroun al-Ras and Jal a-Dir. The supporting forces surrounding the area of the operation contained two artillery batteries, an observation company, an antitank company, and additional forces.

After a short time, I brought in the reduced engineering battalion under the command of LTC Amir Olo, a wonderful officer with whom I had worked in the past in CENTCOM. Amir had lost his leg years earlier, but in spite of his disability, he continued to fight until the strain of combat wore him down several weeks later. His battalion did everything: fought, evacuated the wounded, performed engineering missions, cleared urban areas – and never stopped until the end of the war.

Activation of the Egoz Backup Force

The attack went well, and the enemy sustained much damage. In short-range combat, many Hezbollah fighters were killed, among them their regional commander. In the morning, we identified an opportunity to preserve the momentum.

I asked that another force be allocated to the 300th Brigade as reserve. I was given the Egoz unit and transferred it to the commander of 300th Brigade for infantry missions. Chen saw an opportunity to complete the maneuver and decisively defeat the enemy forces in the area. He decided to employ Egoz in the western side of the village. The force was deployed after a few hours of preparations, in broad daylight. They reached their destination without casualties.

Next, a secondary Egoz force set out in pursuit of an enemy vehicle. They were exposed on a forward slope, and after hitting the Hezbollah vehicle, they returned to the high ground. But on their way back, they were hit by enemy antitank missiles, probably from long range. Four were killed, including a company commander. Another soldier was killed entering a house harboring Hezbollah fighters. We had one MIA, after a wall hit by a missile collapsed on him. But his body was recovered the following day in a combined effort of the MIA unit and a talented UAV operator.

Demoralized by Victory

Udi was pretty shaken up from the incident with Egoz and responded severely. My team updated me that he was on his way to Chen Livni's FCG.

"Udi, don't go to Chen. You're going to finish him. He is stressed as it is. Leave it to me," I requested, almost pleading.

"No!" Udi snapped, "I'm not finishing anybody. I'm the commander, I'll go wherever I please."

The FCG's heavy jeeps made their way uphill to the division's headquarters, led in advance by a protective detail of soldiers. I was in the center, with a small command element. Another vehicle was in the rear of our small convoy, with staff officers and security personnel. I had just exited Chen's headquarters. I analyzed the situation quickly. Chen was very tired, and the hardships of the past few days were clearly apparent on him. I planned to return to him later that night to be beside him and help him, but the entire region was still on my shoulders.

BG Guy Tzur's Steel Division had not yet arrived to assume responsibility over the eastern sector as planned. I never liked the idea of giving part of "my" area of responsibility to another commander, but this was the plan made before the war. Indeed, as the days went by and the battle raged on, it became apparent that it was appropriate to divide the region and allocate part of it to another division, possibly even to more than one. The burden was extremely heavy, and there were different characteristics in each area along the border, requiring special attention by a senior commander.

The jeeps roared on the winding road. I had to reach the division headquarters in order to get an update from my staff, perform a situational assessment, give out directives and orders, and return to Chen. I had been out in the field all day with the battalion and brigade commanders.

"It can't go on like this," I was scolded gently by COL (Res.) Chaim Avital, our chief of staff. "We need you here, and you're running around in the field with the FCG. You may lose the divisional picture."

I called my commander again over the secure radio. "Udi," I said, "I ask you to be gentle with Chen. He's OK, just don't pressure him. I'm coming over as soon as I can; let me talk to you first. There are many things to discuss."

I knew that the report about the casualties and MIA was leading to this pressure. I had seen this before with the abduction, the rescue attempt, and Shaked. Every report on casualties led to a storm. I was in pain too, of course, and shuddered with every report on a fatality or serious casualty, but this was war, and we needed to push on.

"OK," Udi brushed me off, "I'll meet you there." Then he suddenly raised his voice: "We need to do something about this battle at Maroun al-Ras. What are we doing there?!" he said furiously, "Run away from there, retreat!"

I was stunned and furious, but tried to remain quiet and cool.

"I'm not running away from anywhere!" I said. "Sorry, but I have no intention of moving backwards. If you want, I will move forward. Maroun al-Ras is an important and dominant place, from which we have been fired upon for a few days. You yourself have seen the houses being hit in our villages along the border. It's good that we captured Maroun al-Ras, and I'm not coming down from there."

"Gal," Udi said, infuriated, "we're losing too many people in this fight." I thought that he must still be processing the scope of our casualties, and the transition from routine to war.

"It is not true," I tried to reply. "This is war, there are casualties." At this point in the war, we had already sustained civilian casualties, and as an officer in the IDF this troubled me deeply. I saw it as my mission to protect the citizens; unfortunately we lose soldiers in fulfilling this mission.

Udi answered me, but the reception was weak and I couldn't make out what he said.

"Udi, I'll join you at Chen's headquarters. I'll just give instructions to the division and I'll be on my way. I ask you to please wait for me there!"

"He will wait for you there," I heard another voice answer, probably Boaz, the Command's chief of operations (J3). Udi probably needed to take another call.

I was very worried by Udi's words. I thought he might issue an official order to retreat, and I had no intention to carry it out. After the achievement of capturing this key area, there was no way I would leave it.

I arrived at the division headquarters in total darkness. Dror, my longtime driver, brought the vehicle right up to the entrance, allowing me to leap with relative safety into the protected structure. Mortar rounds were falling all over, and from time to time there was the shriek of a rocket and the distant thunder of Amnon's artillery.

If this isn't war, I thought to myself, *what is?*

Boom! A shell impacted close, shaking my command group, a rain of metal shrapnel tearing through nearby vehicles and hitting close positions. Thick smoke...

I entered the dimly lit bunker, where dozens of soldiers were sitting or lying on mattresses along the walls.

"This looks like a submarine," said Dror, my deputy.

He was right. We also used the "hot bed" method in which soldiers take turns sleeping and the beds are always warm, as it was very crowded and there weren't enough beds for everyone. The air was stuffy, and from time to time a frightened scream was heard when the building shook from an impact.

"The division commander is here," I heard soldiers saying, "Gal's here." I walked through the corridors, my helmet in hand, stepping over people. "Make way for him."

"Hi, guys, how are you doing?" I tried to smile to the men and women I met.

Near the war room, three female soldiers sat embracing each other. One of them was crying bitterly. I recognized her as a computer specialist who had participated in the division's exercise before the war.

"What happened?" I asked her.

"Gal, hurry!" Lutfi, the division's operations officer, urged me.

"A moment," I signaled him. "Let me take care of something."

"What's happening?" I crouched near the weeping soldier, as loud explosions shook the building and dust came down on us from the ceiling.

"I can't take it anymore, I want this to end already!" she said, crying.

"She'll be OK," her friend told me, stroking her hair.

"You know what?" I said, smiling, trying to overcome the noise of mortars impacting outside, "I'm working on making this stop. I'm on it, OK?"

She smiled and wiped her tears.

"We need to hang in there a bit longer. You're all doing a great job, under extreme conditions of war, and I'm really proud of you."

I saw smiles, and returned a smile.

"Gal," Lutfi grumbled.

"I'm coming," I said, and dived into the war room.

An emergency light and computer screens shed a dim light, soft voices spoke into receivers and microphones, and crackling sounds were heard over the radios.

"It's good that you're here," Monir, our chief of operations (G3), greeted me. "We need to conduct a situational assessment and deal with a few issues."

"I'm not here for long. We need to stabilize the situation at Maroun al-Ras and see what's happening in the rest of the arena."

"On the whole we're doing fine," said Avi, our intel officer (G2), who had approached quietly from behind, laying his hand on my shoulder.

I liked hearing his assessments, and I liked even more to contradict them. This was the way to generate quality thinking.

"Approved opposition" is my way of leadership and command. I do not like staff officers or subordinates who do not argue with me. Of course the commander ultimately makes a decision, but it should be in light of other ideas from people who are not afraid to present a contradicting opinion.

Avi excelled at this. Our high-pitched arguments were well known, but we always ended them with words of comradeship and appreciation between comrades and true friends.

"Doing fine?" I teased. "What is this idyll?"

"Hezbollah has sustained bitter blows and is flustered. They are moving, making mistakes, creating an 'intel footprint.' We even see signs of panic and stress. They are bringing in reinforcements. Obviously, our attacks on Maroun al-Ras and Shaked took them by surprise. They thought we were going to continue airstrikes. This is an opportunity, and we should take advantage of the momentum."

"Gal," said Monir, "we are still missing an Egoz soldier. We have four fatalities from the rocket attack at the village outskirts, and two Maglan operators were killed taking over the recoilless gun compound at Shaked. That makes six fatalities in one day!"

I am aware of this," I said sharply. "This is war, and we will unfortunately sustain more casualties, but we must strike Hezbollah. Now let me sit down.

I want a situational assessment in three minutes. We are not going to conduct this war by hallway discussions. Monir, take the microphone and get people over here, let's go!" I concluded with a somewhat tough tone. I needed to verify that things were in order and on track.

A commander's intonation has great importance, especially during a war. This is true in the field, over the radio, and in the command post. Sometimes he is soft and empathic, sometimes decisive and scathing, and sometimes demanding and uncompromising. The entire division calibrates itself to the leadership of one person who stands alone: the commander.

I felt extremely tired, this being the seventh day with hardly any sleep or time to eat. I slumped into my fleece jacket and closed my eyes for a minute.

"Gal," Amnon yanked me out of my jacket.

"Yes, Amnon," I managed a smile. He returned a smile, his face smutty as a result of skipping back and forth between the artillery batteries and the division's fires center.

"We have located the pieces shooting at us, and are returning fire, but a lot of it is coming from within villages," he said. "Can I bring down artillery there too?"

"Only PGMs," I ordered. "Attack helicopters, too, but we are not going to bring down artillery salvos inside villages," I said again for emphasis. I was not about to oversee random accidental killings of Lebanese villagers from using such heavy armaments. "We did not relinquish the Spirit of the IDF, morals, and values here." The people around me nodded in consent.

"Yes," insisted Amnon, "but at the same time they are firing at the division headquarters and our villages." He was right. It was a difficult dilemma.

"I know," I ruled, "but firing into villages is with my approval only, and for now we are only using PGMs, and only toward sources of fire. This is what I want from you. And now," I remembered, "what about that situational assessment?"

"We're beginning," said Monir. "Gentlemen, we are commencing the situational assessment. The order of speakers will be as follows..."

The division entered into a process of assessing the situation, following a protocol that we had devised and practiced many times during the past year. It was aimed at making the required information accessible to the commander in a condensed and clear form. Anyone who took too long or diverted from the main point of the discussion would be rushed and reproached: "Focus, focus!"

I looked at my staff. All were concentrating, learning, and getting updated.

We were lucky to be convening at a time when many staff officers were at the end of their tour of duty, so we had with us both the acting officers and the incoming replacements or those who had just been replaced. This enabled us to conduct shifts between "twins."

Beside Gil, our medical officer, there was Michael, his successor. Alex, our communications officer, had with him his replacement Lior. Our munitions officer Moti's "twin" was his successor Ofer. And Nir, our operations security (OPSEC) officer, had Danny with him, who had been recently replaced.

Our personnel were extremely diverse, due to the IDF's unique method of gathering people during wartime to join the fight. University students stop their studies and report to predefined positions or their old units. Operational officers serving in noncombat positions, such as training and instructing, are assigned secondary appointments for wartime. Reservists are of course the backbone of the IDF. And there are even old-timers who simply show up unofficially.

We benefited from capable and committed officers in key positions. COL Eldad Peled, commander of the basic training base, was appointed by me to a secondary role as commander of the division's SOF cell and had already trained with us a few times before the war. Before the war, I appointed LTC (Res.) Shalom Dahan, who served as a judge in the military court, as head of the new fifth center, together with Nir.

COL Ofek Buchris, who was set to replace Chen Livni as commander of 300th Brigade, assisted me in briefing forces and introducing them into battle. Another asset that I highly appreciated was the presence of the Headquarters Training Center instructors, led by COL Eyal Weinstock. They had trained in our headquarters before the war, and simply showed up, uninvited, as soon as it broke out. This meant every staff officer now had a capable instructor by his side.

I was surrounded by excellent, well-trained and goodwilled people.

It was time to give my closing remarks: "We are at war," I emphasized again. "Please place a sign on the wall behind me, reading 'War,' so every video conference we hold with NORTHCOM or the General Staff conveys the message that the 91st Division is at war. Put up another sign that says 'Time is running out.' I am concerned that an imposed cease-fire will be declared before we have reached an optimal outcome."

As I spoke, I looked around the room, making sure that my words were sinking in.

I began to describe the situation as I saw it: "For seven days now, we have been attacking from the air, land, and sea. But the enemy's firepower, although affected, still continues.

"Only today did we launch our counterattacks. It is only these last twenty-four hours that have shaken Hezbollah and thrown it off balance. We attacked the areas overlooking our villages and the northern road. We are acting to kill Hezbollah fighters and to bring an end to the attacks on our villages. We have suffered casualties, but there are also substantial gains.

"Our plans have changed, but remember: we stick to the mission, not to a plan. This is what we have taught and learned in the IDF for many years – first the mission. The plan can, and sometimes must, change.

"We have not received all the forces we needed for the counterattack. We improvised and changed our plans accordingly, but the missions have been carried out, and that is what's important!"

"Gal, in the papers they are saying that the battle at Shaked and Maroun al-Ras was an unplanned encounter with the enemy," said Maayan, our public affairs officer, holding up a newspaper, whose headline read: "Ambush for the Rocket Hunters."

"Listen up," I said. "There's a limit to how much we can affect the media. We will do our best, but focus on fighting."

"But they're already talking about the Maroun al-Ras battle as a screwup!" said Nir.

"Nir," I said calmly, "we cannot fight for the headlines. If we can influence them, good – and if not, we will fix it later. We know Maroun al-Ras was a successful battle. Look at how many enemy fighters we killed, and notice that we are now holding the key positions controlling our villages. They are not being fired upon anymore."

Nir still looked concerned. I made a mental note to take care of this later. No time now. I still needed to run over to Chen's headquarters to talk to Udi. Apparently, even my own commander, charged with leading the entire northern front, needed to be coaxed into seeing the situation as it really was.

What was going on here? the thought came to my mind. Why wasn't it clear to NORTHCOM what was going on? This was war, as we had anticipated for years, and this was the counterattack we had planned for so long. Why all the endless pestering on every casualty and every tank that was hit? How could we fight like this? And if our own command didn't get it, how in the world could we expect politicians in Jerusalem, the media, or the public to understand?

Obviously they were still in routine security mode, so every battle was an "unplanned encounter," every casualty was a "screwup," and every tank hit was an "incident."

I summed up the intel and operational picture, defined the priority intelligence requirements (PIR), and defined the missions for the next twenty-four hours. I also addressed long-term issues and gave an order to prepare for a divisional offensive maneuver.

"Continue to insist on recruiting all the reserves."

"They are still only approving thirty people!" said Yaron, the division's personnel officer (G1), cynically.

"Continue to recruit," I said. "This is a war, and eventually everyone will be here. I approve recruiting the brigade headquarters."

"We can't," Yaron tried to interrupt me.

"Recruit!" I ordered. "Find a way. We must at least prepare the commanders for their missions until the General Staff approves recruitment. I told you a week ago to prepare the counterattack, and today we have executed it. Prepare the division's offensive plan which we practiced in the Galilee."

I then ordered to open sensitive intel material which was set aside to be opened only for the next steps.

"There is no authorization for this," came the answer.

"There will be!" I said, impatiently. "They will eventually understand."

I continued and gave out instructions to the various centers – fires, logistics, manpower, and command, control, communications, computers, and intelligence (C4I). I gave instructions to Moti, the regional civil defense officer: "Set up a meeting with municipality and village leaders. I want to 'feel' them and strengthen them."

I said a few words to the operations center – the biggest and most dominant center in the division. I then addressed Tal, my PA: "Prepare the FCG to move out; we're going to Chen."

"The guys are dozing off in the vehicle," he smiled. "They're pretty exhausted after a week on the road."

"Wake them," I said. "Can I have a bottle of water?" I asked one of the radio operators. I felt dehydrated.

As I was leaving, many officers approached me, shook my hand, patted me on the shoulder, asked me "just a little question," or said words of encouragement.

"You have to sleep, Gal," said BG (Res.) Avigdor Klein, the former chief armor officer, who had independently put on his uniform and come to help. "It isn't smart to wear yourself down. You have the whole division on your shoulders."

"You're right," said I. "You know what? As soon as I get back from the 300th Brigade, I'll catch a couple of hours of sleep."

"Yeah, right," mocked Avigdor. "As soon as you get back. We'll see when you get back and what happens by then. And Gal," he pulled me aside, "keep calm with Udi. Don't explode!"

"He's killing me!" I allowed myself a few moments of candidness with Avigdor, a trustworthy, mature, and experienced officer. "He isn't identifying the situation," I said, frustrated and angry.

"Eyal will help," he said, referring to MG Eyal Ben-Reuven. "He understands you and what is going on here."

"Gal." Lutfi was persistent. "They're waiting for you."

Skipping over sleeping soldiers, we made our way out and ran to the vehicles.

"Gal," Tal said, nudging me with his elbow, "tons of people are looking for you! There are piles of messages; what should I do?"

"We'll talk about it later," I promised. "Send Donna a message that I am fine. Tell her to hug the girls for me, and that I will call when I can."

"I will," Tal promised.

"Just a second," I requested. I retraced my steps and asked to speak with Benny Gantz on the phone, and then spoke with Kaplan, providing him with updates. I also spoke with Ronnie Numa, assistant to the CGS, and asked for his help.

"Don't let them tell me to retreat," I urged him. "Udi may be considering it, and we can't let that happen!" It was out of the ordinary, and only happened once during the war, but I felt that I must directly engage the General Staff in order to influence against Udi's position on retreating from Maroun al-Ras. His oversensitivity to casualties was unbalanced and counterproductive during wartime.

"Let's run," I told Tal. Two security guards cleared the way ahead of me. A beer-bellied reserve soldier came to embrace me and give me a shot in the arm. A friendly NCO gave me a huge nectarine, as big as a grapefruit. "It's from my farm," he said. I gave a quick wave to soldiers manning one of the centers, and we were on our way.

Friction

In the 300th Brigade's mobile FCG near Yaroun, below Maroun al-Ras, there was a large commotion. The brigade commander's FCG was positioned in a small tent set up beside a command car, and the units participating in the battle set up their rear command posts around it, linked to it by cables. It was kind of like a "control center cluster" comprised of all the combat units.

I liked the idea, but not the ruckus – neither the large number of vehicles, nor the many people who were there.

"We have to get things straightened out here!" I said, grasping an officer from the 300th Brigade. Rockets were falling close by. The enemy had identified the preparations of the command posts and was launching toward us. "Not good," I said to myself, "not good."

I moved the tent flap aside and walked toward the CO's table. Looking exhausted, Chen explained what was happening on the battlefield. The MIA had not been found yet, and they were evacuating the wounded Egoz soldiers. The Paratrooper Recon Battalion was still clearing the village of Hezbollah fighters, and the 82nd Battalion was engaging antitank squads in the area of Bint Jbeil, from the dominating Shaked Ridge it had captured earlier in the morning.

"Are the battalion commanders speaking with each other?"

"Yes," Chen replied. His people looked at me with expectation. It was obvious that they were extremely tired. Chen dozed off for an instant and then looked embarrassedly at me with his bloodshot eyes, his face garnished with several days' stubble.

"Come with me," I said, and stepped outside. Chen got up and followed.

"Take command for a few minutes," I told Major Shaadi, the brigade's operations officer, "I'll be right back." He nodded in agreement.

"How are you holding up?" I rested my hand on Chen's shoulder.

"Fine," he said. "The NORTHCOM commander was here, and he is waiting for you over there," he said, gesturing.

"And...?" I asked.

"Listen," Chen started, "I understand the pressure... but even so, listen..."
He turned his head away, his eyes red from exhaustion.

"Come with me." I led him to the FCG Humvee and opened the door.
"Get in."

"What?" Chen asked in surprise.

"Kfir, bring a sleeping bag," I said, sending my security guard to look for one. I covered Chen with it. "Rest for an hour. I will wake you up."

"No," he got up and wanted to leave the Humvee.

"Chen, shut up and go to sleep. I will replace you. Don't you trust me for one hour?" He leaned back and fell asleep immediately.

"Look after him and make sure it is quiet around here," I instructed Buskila, Chen's radio operator.

"Even if there's noise, it won't wake him up," he said, smiling.

"Watch over him, there is shooting around here. And don't let him out of the Humvee without my permission."

I entered the FCG. Shai, the general's aid, approached me and said: "Gal, Udi is waiting for you."

"I remember, give me a few more minutes," I asked.

I gave Lutfi an order to convene the division's staff officers and to set up my FCG next to the 300th Brigade's. I told Eyal, the intel officer, and Shaadi to remain in the tent. I had my staff join us and conducted a quick situational analysis session. I also spoke over the radio with the battalion commanders operating under the 300th Brigade. To complete the picture, I would later go out and observe the field with night-vision equipment. I understood the updated picture of battle. Only a few changes had taken place in the few hours since I had been there last.

The battalion commanders sounded OK, and they were happy to hear my voice. Two of them even put in an effort to add an inflection of calm in their voices. But the tension was clear. I would speak to them again soon.

I issued several orders, asked Shaadi to stay alert, and instructed Lutfi to move forces and attack the targets I had requested.

"No problem," Shaadi said. "I'm with you."

Deep down, I knew this, I thought, as I went outside – but how long could he hold on? He had also been awake for the past eight days.

"How are you, Gal?" Udi asked, leaning on a truck. He always tried to be polite, even in the tensest of situations.

"I am fine, thanks."

"Listen," he burst out, "what is going on here is unacceptable!" Then he rattled off a few scattered instructions.

"Udi," I said, trying to calm things down, "you're misunderstanding the current situation."

"No," he cut me off, "*you* are mistaken and you will do what I tell you; we have too many casualties!"

"Listen!" Now it was my turn to burst out. "Listen to me and listen well – we will have 250 fatalities and another fifteen hundred wounded soldiers in this war. Let those numbers sink in – that's what happens in war. Stop calling me after every casualty; you are hampering my efforts to fight. In war there's no need to talk every time a tank throws a tread. I'm going to stop answering you on the radio. You're driving me crazy!"

"*You* are driving *me* crazy," Udi shot back. "Be disciplined. Taking initiatives isn't the only thing that is important."

"Overall I am disciplined," I replied. "After the war you can dismiss me."

"I haven't made a decision about that yet," Udi said.

"OK," I muttered, "decide later. Now we have the momentum. I am personally taking command of the battle of 300th Brigade. I sent Chen to sleep a bit. Soon I will reinforce the village. I am going to bring in more air support and activate artillery. We will find the MIA. I called the MIA Unit. We are holding the dominating areas. The division is on the offensive and we have control of a one-hundred-kilometer [sixty-mile] strip, from within Lebanon. The situation is under control. Calm down."

"Don't tell me to calm down!"

"Yes, I will tell you to calm down. And one more thing." I felt that I had already crossed the line, but I couldn't stop the hurt and frustration. "Udi, this is not the first time I've been in combat. There are going to be losses; get used to it!" I looked him in the eye, trying to breach him. "Udi, I don't want to be in a situation like Ariel Sharon was, confronting Gorodish in 1973. I don't want to break the system. I don't want to break the chain of command. I want to continue to speak with you and maintain the system. Help me!"

Udi looked at me, perhaps shocked at the harshness of my words, and opened his mouth to speak.

"General, the CGS wants you," Boaz, his J3, called him to the phone.

Udi turned his back and was gone.

"What's up, brother?" An arm hugged me, and the smiling face of BG Eli Reiter beamed at me in the dark, illuminated by a flare. He was commander of the Armored Ga'ash Division, deployed on the Golan Heights.

"Aren't you cold, Gal?" I had left my fleece jacket in the war room, so the night chill penetrated my bones and my teeth were chattering.

"Take it," he said, offering me his own jacket and wrapping it around me. "It's the same rank."

"At this rate, they will soon rip them off of me," I said, while zipping up the coat. "Thanks, brother."

"Can I help you with anything?" Eli asked. "The Syrians refuse to attack and I have nothing to do. Now tell me what is going on."

"I don't have time," I said apologetically. I shook his hand and ran to the FCG.

Be disciplined... Udi's words echoed in my head.

I passed quickly by a group of excited Maglan soldiers. I waved to them, smiled, and said, "Way to go, guys – good luck!"

"Thank you, sir," they called back. "Thanks, Commandant," a team leader said, shaking my hand. He had been my cadet at officers' training school, so to him I would always be the commandant of Bahad 1.

Be disciplined! The words struck me again. I was trying to recall when I had first met those words in the past. And then I remembered, as if it had just happened yesterday, in that operation beyond the border, ten years earlier, when I refused to abort the mission as directed.

I dove back into Chen's FCG and called the 300th Brigade staff and several of the division's core staff officers, who were with me wherever I went. In this unique situation, I decided to command the major battle from a forward position, assisted by a combined staff from both the division and the brigade.

"We need to continue to take control of Maroun al-Ras, to build on the achievements of the Paratrooper Recon Battalion and the 82nd Battalion. We need to complete the destruction of the nature reserve by Maglan and to transfer Eliezer's Maglan forces, in order to maintain the momentum of the attack on the village itself."

By morning, I wanted our forces in better positions, holding all of the important territory, and Egoz's situation improved, so that with the help of the MIA Unit we would find our missing soldier.

I needed additional forces in the center of the village. From a quick glance at an aerial photo, observation reports, and a consultation with Nimrod on the encrypted phone, I understood that the correct thing to do would be to tighten the control over the village itself with additional forces, to reinforce the hold of the Paratrooper Recon Battalion, and to move into additional pockets of territory. I called Eliezer and gave him the mission. He was to move on foot with a small number of troops, coordinating with Nimrod and with Oded, the tank battalion commander. I wanted to take control of as many key areas of the village as I could by first light. I indicated groups of buildings to him on the aerial photo – those I had analyzed with intel.

Eliezer asked several questions, received his orders, and moved out. Several hours later he reported that he had reached all of his objectives, and was about to rendezvous with the paratroopers with whom they were operating in full coordination. The village was relatively quiet; Maroun al-Ras was under our complete control. A long time passed before we would complete checking all the village homes, but as far as I was concerned, the village was captured. I could move on.

Udi came back and called me aside again. "OK, we are continuing," he said. I did not know what had happened in the conversation he had been called to, but he seemed more relaxed now. I updated him on my intentions and plans, we agreed on our priorities for the coming hours, and we parted with a handshake.

The next day, the paratroopers' FCG would arrive here from Ayta ash-Shab, relieve Chen, and complete the search to clear and disarm the village. Hagai prepared for future missions in the area. I thought that they might allow me to go to Bint Jbeil, Tebnine, and Jabal Amel. Maybe we would finally start to implement MHTA.

Maroun al-Ras was key territory for the division, for it controlled Hezbollah's entire operational sector in the area. Now we had it under our control, the firing had ceased, and there was quiet in the villages along the northern border. On this basis the division began to engage in the region of Aytarun-Bint Jbeil, and to attack additional enemy forces. Large amounts of captured enemy equipment were taken from the area of Maroun al-Ras, including an entire enemy operations room.

The mission – even though not executed according to prearranged plans – had been completely fulfilled!

The "First Battle Effect" and Combat Learning

The "first battle effect" is a phenomenon experienced by all armies. It is the effect of the first physical friction between your forces and the enemy. For the first time, concepts, perception, plans, doctrine, weaponry, and training all collide with reality and with the rival. Friction created during the first battle strongly impacts the entire campaign. The way in which the enemy is seen shapes the perception of our forces throughout the war. Lessons and knowledge extracted from this first real encounter influence decision making and state of mind – including public perception – for a long time. Therefore, there is great significance to the way in which a force enters the first battle, and it is highly important to succeed.

The battles at Maroun al-Ras and Shaked were significant as the first battles during this war. The 91st Division was the first to learn and the first to teach. We knew how to develop knowledge and learn fast. With talented officers like Ofek Buchris and others, we disseminated acquired knowledge among the division's units and throughout the IDF using the Ground Forces Command.

From this point forward, the division methodically improved as a result of "combat learning" up to the end of the war, even though the combat was not devoid of errors.

Because all the divisions that joined the fight came through us to be allocated a sector, they also received briefings as to what we had already learned. I believe that this saved many lives, as the efficiency of the forces was increased dramatically and they were able to hit the ground running.

I learned a great deal about Hezbollah during these battles – the scope and use of their weaponry, how they operated their forces, the structure of their tactical units, and the extent of their initiative, such as their attempts to develop local counterattacks.

I knew Hezbollah well from methodical learning processes and intel material, but there's nothing like the first real encounter. On the whole, my assessments were confirmed – Hezbollah was a trained and capable force, with a determination to fight. They operated like guerillas, but at the same time were well organized and relied on their fortification line. Still, they did not come close to our force in quality and capabilities.

I realized that they were handicapped and ineffective when it came to night fighting, and that they clung to plans and usually did not improvise when plans failed. They relied heavily on advanced antitank weaponry and high-trajectory fires. I learned that they were deployed according to an operational infrastructure that had been put in place over many years – tunnels, burrows, belly charges, weapons caches, and fortified launch sites – what became known as the "nature reserves."

My original plan was that the decentralized "swarms" maneuver would result in a quick takeover of most of the dominating areas. The idea was to cast sort of a "blanket" over the fire and suffocate it by creating multiple friction points with as many enemy fighters as possible, leading to the suppression of the operating capabilities of the organization.

We knew that for a relatively small organization like Hezbollah, every downed fighter would be irreplaceable. So we tried to create friction in as many areas as possible, by controlling the entrances to towns and villages as well as the nature reserves, which relied on the town for logistics and for protection by hiding behind civilian cover. The plan was to systematically comb and clear, starting some time after the completion of the takeover, in order to focus our efforts according to situational assessments pertaining to every area or village. We knew there was no way to clear the entire area within a few days, and the plans reflected this by allocating several weeks for this mission.

During the battle at Maroun al-Ras, the enemy rival system became more and more clear. I understood that it was important to confront it as such and turn it into a collection of separately addressed segments in order to neutralize it. It wasn't enough to only create friction and kill enemy fighters.

I understood that a blanket, swarms, and fire strikes alone were not enough. I realized that it would take a combination of efforts: to dissect the system; to flood the area; to spread out quickly throughout most of the region and thrust wedges between the villages and the nature reserves, between the villages themselves, and from the Litani region to the front line of the battle. Additionally, I concluded that wherever we created effective friction with fire, launches toward Israel subsided, and wherever IDF boots were on the ground, enemy activity moved northward.

In a situational assessment, I decided to update the maneuver plan. Friction and seeking engagement were appropriate, but I thought we should create correlation with the original plan – and that maximum forces should move swiftly to engage Hezbollah's depth formations.

I needed to bridge between two conflicting rationales: killing as many enemy fighters as possible by creating friction, but also the need to swiftly advance inland in order to stop the rockets.

This is how I solved it: Where time and space were constrained, I planned to use helicopters. I wanted simultaneous activation of artillery and sea- and air-based fires. I would try to seize key locations such as the Jabal Amel region, Sylvester Ridge (a ridge spanning from Barachit to the mountain of Shakif al-Nimel), Nakura Ridge and Jabal Beit ed Douara, in order to dismantle the rival system and disconnect their rear from the forces in the front.

Now it also became clear to me where those wedges needed to be inserted. Our "palpation" was working. I was feeling Hezbollah much better now.

We constantly learned new lessons, and from every error we came out stronger. I was happy to see steady improvement in the performance of battalion and brigade commanders, as well as the auxiliary forces. I also noticed that I was getting better and better.

Despite our mistakes, which we analyzed and learned during the debriefings, I was happy to see the professionalism and determination of Nimrod's recon battalion, Eliezer's Maglan, Kahana's Egoz, Oded's 82nd Battalion, Amir's engineering battalion, and other peripheral and augmented forces. They all performed well, and I was extremely proud of them.

The problem was that my lessons and insights from Shaked and Maroun al-Ras could not yet be implemented. NORTHCOM didn't want to take over many areas and did not want to push forward. It did not want to dismantle the Hezbollah system, only confront it.

All NORTHCOM wanted was raids leaving dead Hezbollah operatives. I believe that even at this point, the command had not yet shifted to a mindset of war. Perhaps they perceived the situation as a collection of "battle days," or as a prolonged clash and no more. From my point of view, it was a war from day one. The result was that the command and the division were operating under completely different operational logics. I was finding it extremely difficult to combine the two.

Chapter 16

Iron Web – The Raids Phase

The First Division-Level Battle – Bint Jbeil

The battle at Maroun al-Ras was fully utilized, and the region was under our control. It only remained to clear the area, but this was left to a later stage. I wanted to take advantage of the situation and proceed toward the Bint Jbeil region, to capture Sylvester Ridge and continue to a key location: Jabal Amel and Tebnine – the Shiite stronghold and the heart of Hezbollah's operational area. I also wanted to continue to move westward toward the coastline and threaten the area of the city of Tyre. I believed that applying pressure on these two regions would create the appropriate effect, which had been discussed many times before the war.

At the meeting led by the CGS, a heated debate took place between the attending generals. There were those who were still traumatized from the outcome of the first battle at Maroun al-Ras and Shaked. They were influenced by the painful atmosphere due to the losses we suffered, without examining the results in perspective, and without taking into consideration the severe blow to Hezbollah.

I claimed that we should push on and attack. My position was supported by the J3, MG Gadi Eizenkot. He believed that NORTHCOM should utilize its forces to the fullest immediately, in one concentrated effort, and objected to NORTHCOM's course of action of simultaneous efforts in multiple regions where we had already made significant achievements.

Golani Brigade, en route from Gaza to the north, was preparing to deploy to the Taibe region, while I was allocated a small paratrooper force for conducting some sort of limited and focused raid at Bint Jbeil. I objected to this.

Gadi assessed the situation correctly, and strongly argued that Maroun al-Ras, with dozens of dead Hezbollah fighters, should be seen as an accomplishment, and that we had proved our complete superiority over the enemy. He demanded that I be allocated the Golani Brigade in order to conquer the Bint Jbeil region.

The CGS settled the argument by deciding to carry out a central divisional effort, as a model demonstration of IDF capabilities and strength, in one designated and symbolic point: Bint Jbeil. This was where Hasan Nasrallah, secretary general of Hezbollah, had delivered his "spider web" speech in 2000, after Israel had withdrawn from Lebanon. Nasrallah had equated Israel's power to that of a spider web which can be easily torn.

I was given forty-eight hours to prepare, including suppression with artillery and attacking designated targets in the area, as well as other actions intended to set optimal conditions for our forces. I thought it was enough time. The paratroopers were already in Maroun al-Ras and seasoned in battle; Golani is an excellent brigade and had just arrived from Gaza; and I was planning to also deploy 7th Armored Brigade's headquarters in the region. Everyone involved knew how to be ready for combat in forty-eight hours.

I set out happily and dashed to the division headquarters, relaying orders over the radio en route to save time. I convened the Golani Brigade commander, the paratroopers' chief of staff, the 7th Brigade commander, and the division staff. It was for issuing an advance order, but in fact, as was my approach, I also made it into a combined planning session. I enjoyed the combined planning with commanders, as well as their company.

Together we formed the operational concept. I knew Bint Jbeil very well from previous assignments. It was clear to me, from intel and assessment, that the fighting at Maroun al-Ras had attracted many enemy fighters to the region, and I was glad this was so. Before the war, we had stressed many times the need to engage the enemy directly and inflict as much damage as possible, so I saw the convergence of forces at Bint Jbeil as an opportunity to make the best of this friction.

It was clear to me that Hezbollah was aligning itself in a defensive posture, and I did not want to allow it to focus its efforts in one location, so I decided to attack from several directions. A gripping maneuver would place 7th Brigade as the anvil at Maroun al-Ras and the southern ridges, while the two hammers would be the paratroopers flanking from the south and Golani from the north. We were to infiltrate into the high grounds based on the urban space, strike the enemy, and continue in a controlled manner toward the heart of the city – the casbah. All this would be accompanied by massive precision fires and suppression of nature reserves and high-value targets.

I assigned responsibility for encircling the city and closing the entry and exit points toward the Sylvester Ridge, and began determining tasks for the various division centers, so that they might contribute to our maneuvers and collectively create one comprehensive divisional effort.

While we were at work, an order came from NORTHCOM: "No conquering, only taking control." Then while updating the plan came another: "No taking control, only encircling," and later yet another.

The following morning, on July 23, NORTHCOM commander MG Udi Adam made it clear to me before we set out to battle that we were "not to conquer Bint Jbeil, but *seize* it." He also added that the mission was limited to a forty-eight-hour window. In fact, the general defined the mission as a "raid," aimed at severely damaging the enemy and its infrastructure in the Bint Jbeil region.

Needless to say, these frequent changes hindered our preparation process. The biggest difficulty was the advancement of the attack from the 24th to the 23rd of July, which was relayed to us only on the morning of the 23rd. This not only compromised our preparations, but significantly reduced the suppression phase and psychological operations on enemy targets in the city and the surrounding area.

I clarified every one of these points to my superiors and conducted a constant dialogue on the ramifications with the various components at the command.

All brigades allocated to me – paratroopers, Golani, and 300th – were in fact reduced, as not all battalions made it in time from J&S and Gaza. I was also given 7th Brigade headquarters with a few small forces.

Beginning on July 21, the division was also engaged in handing over the eastern sector to the Steel Division.

Our hands were full.

Final Briefings to the Forces

Amidst the hectic preparations, I received word that Golani commanders, including LTC Mordechai Kahana, Egoz commander, had given media interviews criticizing the way the forces were being deployed and the decision making at Maroun al-Ras. I also heard of an invidious interview by COL Tamir

Yadai, Golani Brigade commander, in which he directly attacked the "swarms" concept. It was certainly disturbing. I made up my mind to disregard these acts, but I realized that an evil seed of rumors and slander had been sowed.

I heard criticism about sending Egoz forces into Maroun al-Ras in daylight, and also anger and stressful feelings directed at me because of our accumulated casualties from the beginning of the war.

The dramatic changes in the objective of the mission and the twenty-four-hour advancement of the execution led me to a decision that I would directly influence the short battle procedures at the battalions and personally brief all commanders from platoon level and up. This put me and my staff under extreme pressure, and we dashed from one staging area to another.

I explained the situation as I saw it, emphasized that this was war, reminded them of the rockets striking our civilians, and encouraged them to hit the enemy hard and disrupt its capabilities in order to allow Israeli citizens to leave the shelters.

As I spoke, I could see determined and attentive looks, and their body language showed that they were with me. I could see that they understood.

On the night of July 23, the attack commenced, and the mission was completed the next evening, within sixteen hours.

My gripping maneuver did not unfold as I had planned. Golani performed well and on time, while the paratroopers did not complete their mission during the first night. When I ordered them to continue moving during the day, General Adam intervened and overruled me, ordering the forces to stay in place.

The fierce argument that followed did not do any good. The exaggerated media effect of Egoz's daytime battle at Maroun al-Ras was interfering with the battle that morning, and would continue to do so throughout the war. "No fighting in daylight" was an unprofessional and hysterical statement that critically crippled our operational abilities.

After nightfall, the paratroopers completed their mission, and during this time all forces continued to hit enemy fighters.

Unfortunately, Golani forces were involved in a friendly fire incident. Misidentification led to opening fire, and there were casualties. Battalion commander LTC Guy Kavili dashed in with his brave tankers to retrieve the wounded, but they were struck by a powerful belly charge on the way back. A bitter rescue operation ensued, during which two armored soldiers were killed.

The following day, July 25, the results were encouraging. Commanders

reported between sixteen and twenty dead Hezbollah fighters, many infrastructures were destroyed, and much equipment was captured, including a
complete Hezbollah operations room.

MG Adam declared that the objective had been reached and ordered us
to withdraw to the Maroun al-Ras line that very evening, forty-eight hours
after the operation had begun.

But I wasn't content with the results and thought we could and should have
achieved more. I repeatedly requested to stay and complete the conquering
of Bint Jbeil, in order to strengthen the achievement as originally planned
and approved by the CGS.

Still, I began preparing my forces for this task. A situational assessment
was held around noontime, and NORTHCOM staff attended via video
conference. The forces were prepared for withdrawal at nightfall, as ordered.

On July 25, I was asked by an IDF spokesperson to brief the media prior to
pulling back our forces from Bint Jbeil. I did so near the Israeli village of Matat,
near the border, and spoke in Hebrew and in English. Unfortunately, I was
later quoted and criticized for saying "Bint Jbeil is in our hands," when in fact
I had never said it; rather another brigadier general in a different briefing had
uttered those words. The facts didn't matter. It's what they said on the news.

Change of Assignment

When I concluded the short media brief, which was held only minutes away
from the division headquarters, I was called urgently to the radio and was
told that we were to stop the retreat from Bint Jbeil and hold our ground. MG
Adam came on seconds later, sounding angry, and confirmed: "You're staying
in Bint Jbeil, but not conquering it."

I told him I thought it was a wise decision and asked for clarifications. I
also emphasized that we could not remain static because our forces would be
attacked. Udi approved local advancements in order to improve our positions,
but stressed that we were not to enter the red polygon.

Our charts had the city outlined by a black polygon, while the heart of
the city, the casbah, was depicted in red.

I could tell he was angry at the decision that had apparently been imposed
upon him from above, but at this point I was not yet aware of the tremendous
tension between NORTHCOM and the General Staff.

It was already evening; the forces were minutes away from the previously planned retreat from Bint Jbeil; I needed to stop them and issue new orders – fast! I dashed to the division headquarters, ran through the hallways, and burst into the war room.

"We're not leaving, stop them, not leaving!" I yelled, as my staff looked at me in disbelief. Questions came flying from all over.

I caught my breath, grabbed the microphone, and began relaying orders and clarifications. I gave directives to the commanders and defined the tasks for the night. I hadn't a clue what the mission was going to be, but it was clear that the night should be used for improving positions and assuming key ambush positions in the urban area, so we could attack enemy targets at dawn, as we had done the day before.

The following morning, Golani's 51st Battalion lost eight men in combat, demonstrating many heroic acts, at the battle of the "black polygon."

The Battle at the "Black Polygon"

Troubling fragmented reports reached me before dawn, initially talking of some twenty-three Golani KIAs and dozens of wounded. I quickly headed out to join Tamir at his headquarters at Malkia, near Kiryat Shmona. Together we tried to build a concise picture, listening over the radio as LTC Yaniv Asor commanded the difficult battle his 51st Battalion waged in the alleys of the black polygon (the outline of the city on the map).

Using aerial imagery downlinked from a UAV, and closely coordinating with the Air Force component at NORTHCOM, we carried out a complicated mission to extract the casualties.

The battle had taken place before sunrise, and we could not wait the many hours until darkness to take out the casualties, so we operated in broad daylight. In true acts of heroism, Golani soldiers brought their wounded to improvised LZs at the outskirts of the town, where they were airlifted by daring Blackhawk crews, under cover of attack helicopters, fighter jets, artillery and tank shells, and smoke screens. I also ordered Hagai to attack the casbah with his paratroopers from the opposite side in order to engage Hezbollah and force it to split their efforts. Coordinating all land and air assets was extremely complicated.

Risking their own lives, warriors on the ground and in the air extracted all the casualties under fire, as the battle in the alleys ensued. Many medals were rightfully awarded for the acts carried out that day. It was the same fighting spirit and sense of sacrifice that had characterized the IDF in past battles – in Jerusalem, the Suez Canal, Maydun, Beirut, and many other places.

MG Benny Gantz, commander of the Ground Forces Command, arrived during the battle. Trying to assist, he called out words of encouragement and leaned over the aerial picture I was working on, showing me with hand gestures which tactic he thought was appropriate.

"That's exactly what I'm trying to do," I said impatiently. I didn't intend to insult him, but I was under extreme pressure, commanding a complex situation.

Once the wounded were all out, we were left with the bodies of the fallen still with our forces in their positions. The battle raged on, and I ordered that they be carried out at night on stretchers, without disrupting the operational momentum. I hoped that now we would finally receive approval to capture the whole city. A decisive decision was needed.

As I exited the tiny room from which the rescue operation was coordinated, I was called to the phone to speak to the CGS and Minister of Defense. They spoke words of encouragement, and for some reason found it necessary to remind me that casualties were part of war, and that we needed to push on despite the losses. On the one hand, I was happy to learn that they had finally come to this realization after two weeks of war. But on the other hand, the fact that they had called to "encourage" me was a troubling hint that senior echelons were in fact demoralized by the accumulating casualty count.

From this point on, for three days, different and conflicting orders came down on me – altogether seven written changes of assignments, together with additional oral instructions that never made it to written orders.

I wasn't aware of the extent of the clash between NORTHCOM and the General Staff over the mission at Bint Jbeil. I was ordered to "conquer," "defend stubbornly," "take control," "retreat," and "stay" – leading up to the night between 28 and 29 July. Throughout this time, the division continued to fight and kill enemy fighters, while carrying out defense and attack operations throughout the breadth of our region.

On the 28th of July, I spoke with MG Adam.

"You were right," he said candidly. "This is a war. We are recruiting all our forces, including the reserves, and preparing for a full NORTHCOM maneuver."

I felt a sense of relief. Could it be that from now on we would operate under the same situational assessment? But then Udi added the following directive: "I want you to take your division and retreat to the Maroun al-Ras line."

I objected, claiming that if we were to carry out a command-level maneuver, we would need to reclaim all the areas we had already conquered and paid for at such a bloody price. My objection was to no avail. Udi was merely conveying the orders issued by the GS – to retreat from Bint Jbeil to the Maroun al-Ras line, and commence the battle procedure for a wide-scale maneuver in southern Lebanon.

On the night of July 28, Hezbollah's special force (which had conducted the abduction) was severely hit in a battle with the Paratroopers Brigade, leaving twenty-six Hezbollah fighters dead and many wounded.

The fighting continued throughout the region, but I accompanied this specific battle personally, including speaking personally over the radio to Hagai and the battalion commanders. The division was supposed to retreat that night, but due to the battle that developed, I decided to delay it. Many decisions had to be made, fast. The paratroopers of the 101st and 890th Battalions fought Hezbollah's special force at close ranges. The enemy suffered many casualties, but they insisted on coming back again and again to rescue their comrades, leading to more and more casualties.

Our absolute advantage over Hezbollah in night combat in urban terrain was once again demonstrated. As the hours passed, Hezbollah's body count was rising, but it would soon be dawn and we had not yet extracted our forces as ordered.

We were now fighting between the houses. There were serious dilemmas, and the most challenging one I now faced was the severe injuries sustained by one of our paratroopers. I knew his precise location, but assessed that a helicopter attempting to land there risked being lost with all its crew. In other instances that night I approved such helicopter extractions, but here I needed to choose between the life of one soldier and the lives of his rescuers. I consulted the division's doctors, Gil and Michael, and understood that the soldier stood a chance, although his wounds were severe. The debate was cold, technical, and professional. I spoke with Hagai and decided not to send in the helicopter. I prayed that he would hang in there and make it. It was one of the toughest decisions I had ever made.

A few hours later, the situation on the ground changed, and I approved to send in a Black Hawk. After hours of pain and suffering, he was in the hospital. His life was saved.

On July 29 in the morning we concluded the operation at Bint Jbeil and retreated to the line of Maroun al-Ras-Shaked. Our forces had suffered a few casualties, and Hezbollah's special force had been destroyed.

Throughout the mission, I expressed strongly but appropriately my professional opinion about the frequent mission changes and operational plan of NORTHCOM. Conquering – and not raiding – would have allowed the division to act according to plans that had been practiced; to utilize the tanks, fires, and infantry; and to breach new logistic routes (for bringing in supplies and so on). My demands were not approved, and my repeated requests for recruitment of reserves were only fulfilled on July 29, seventeen days into the war.

The 91st Division fulfilled its mission, although not according to the plan. The instability emanated, according to my understanding, from the relations between NORTHCOM and the General Staff.

Eleven soldiers were killed in this battle over the course of six days from July 23 to July 29. The forces operated professionally, and many acts of bravery were carried out. More than a hundred enemy fighters were killed throughout the six days of the battle, and Hezbollah's special force was practically wiped out. Vehicles and infrastructure were damaged, and a massive effect of presence in the region was achieved, as dictated by NORTHCOM.

Throughout the mission, as in the ones before and those to follow, I never pointed out to my subordinates that the commanding echelon was the one making all the frequent changes, so commanders in the field thought that I was the one generating all the mayhem. I believed that it was important to maintain loyalty and exemplify a high level of ethics and leadership, as expected from a senior IDF officer. Over the radio there was only one commanding authority, one voice, and one call sign: "Sela Actual."

After the war, I learned during the debriefings that everything that had taken place had been attributed to me. The criticism was all directed toward me, and none of my superiors found it appropriate to set the factual record straight (most of them until today).

Horses Uphill

Hagai, Tamir, Amnon, and Chen, the four Bint Jbeil battle brigade commanders, entered the little shack at Shomera.

I was angry about the extraction of the forces from Bint Jbeil, about the way things had been handled during the past few days, about the frequent changes to the mission and the clash between the generals. I felt it was all on my back, during combat.

There was also something else troubling me. The CGS had given an interview to *Maariv* newspaper, and when asked by the reporter, Chen Kotes, about "difficulties in the performance of the Galilee brigade commander," instead of answering "What are you talking about?" he said, "You don't replace your horses uphill."

"Nonsense!" I said to those who showed me the newspaper headlines. I brushed it off as nothing, but the words circulated among commanders. "Combat gossip" was at play, and people were saying that the CGS actually meant that he intended to replace me when we reached "the top of the hill."

"It isn't nonsense," insisted my staff officers. "You must do something about this."

After the last soldier had exited the area of Bint Jbeil, I turned to deal with this annoying matter.

"Roni, I wish to speak to the CGS," I asked the chief's assistant.

"Not now. I'll connect you with him when he's available."

"It's urgent, Roni!"

"He isn't available now."

Roni had not revealed to me that Halutz had been hospitalized for tests after suffering from fatigue.

"Roni, what is this about not replacing horses at the top of the hill? What does Halutz want with me?"

"It's nothing, Gal. I don't know of any such intention."

"This is serious, Roni. I need to know what is going on. Everyone is talking about it. How can we fight like this?"

"I'll try to connect you with him, and if not – speak to him tomorrow when he comes to visit the 300th Brigade. Arrange a meeting with your brigade commanders."

Halutz arrived the following morning. We exchanged greetings and shook hands, and I led him to where the brigade commanders were waiting. They told Halutz of their experiences and presented questions: "What did you want to achieve?" "What is the meaning of these orders?" "Why were we pulled out after entering?" etc.

The CGS replied: "The public wants another twenty-six dead Hezbollah fighters [as we saw on July 29] and more such successes," he said, referring to the previous night's battle where paratroopers destroyed the special force of Hezbollah.

"It isn't my job to define your mission...," he continued. "It isn't my job to tell you how to do it...; it isn't my job..."

He continued with more and more sentences beginning with the same leading statement. I couldn't believe it. If it wasn't his job, whose was it? So this was what he meant about the "horses uphill" – rolling all the responsibility onto me.

I was furious, amazed, and felt a tremble go through me. This couldn't be happening. I debated what to do. Should I lash out at him in front of the brigade commanders? So far, I had been persistent in backing up my superiors and reflected to my subordinates only one voice – mine – "Sela Actual," making it so the entire hullabaloo was attributed only to me.

I decided not to confront Halutz publicly and to discuss things with him privately.

The meeting ended, and I quickly briefed the brigade commanders: "Go out to the staging areas; prepare according to the orders given. There are more big raids planned, but there is also massive reserve recruitment expected, and it very well may be that we will implement one of our contingency attack plans in Lebanon. You must be prepared for a lot of changes," I warned them, "including in the definition of the mission. That's just the way it is."

My brigade commanders nodded. We all got up; there were smiles, handshakes, and slaps on the back.

The CGS and I moved over into Chen's office.

"How are you, Gal?"

"I wish to understand the meaning of this sentence of yours."

"I heard something about it. What did I say?" Halutz played innocent.

"You said that horses should not be replaced uphill, and I want to understand: When is the top of the hill reached, when am I to be replaced, and what is it that you want from me?" I said with pain.

"It was an unsuccessful statement," admitted Halutz.

"So correct it!"

He disregarded my request and said, "I had complaints on the way NORTHCOM performed."

"So what do you want from me? Have you asked me what is going on between me and NORTHCOM?"

"Is there tension between you and the command?"

"You know there is."

I knew that he knew. Why was he playing this game with me?

"What about?"

I elaborated about the disagreements, the arguments over the definition of the situation, over force allocation, over endless orders of peacetime nature, and over interfering with minute details. I reminded him again of the need to fight a ground offensive inside Lebanon – a decisive, definite, and deep maneuver, as we had trained for.

He nodded.

"You need to cease this foolishness of having NORTHCOM conduct this alone, as a theater of operations, while the GS stays in Tel Aviv to deal with the entire Middle East as a theater of war," I said. "The war is here and now. Have the entire IDF come up here, including you."

I hoped I wasn't crossing the line, but he had to hear it from me. Who else would tell him? I already knew of the tension between Eizenkot and Adam, and between NORTHCOM and the General Staff.

"I get that now," he answered. "NORTHCOM is now the main effort, and the General Staff will be more involved."

I looked at his face and thought what he must be going through. I decided not to continue with the conversation, so I said nothing else. He stood, as did I, and we said good-bye.

I went to a small grove near the village Even Menachem, where I met Chen, Basiuk, and a few junior officers. We sat down to talk. They seemed very tired, their faces unshaved and their hair matted. I updated them on the situation, asked them how they were doing, and then something extraordinary happened – they stood up and hugged me. A strong embrace of comradeship.

"Good-bye!"

"Good-bye, Gal."

Even company commanders were using my first name. "It's a good sign," I thought, as I climbed into the vehicle. I never liked formality. My leadership style was that of closeness, not distancing. This is how I had educated my subordinates and my officer cadets for years.

The Battles at Bint Jbeil – Systemic Analysis

An asymmetric rival does not collapse when its capital is captured or its leaders are killed. As long as it is motivated, manned, knowledgeable, and resourced, it may push forward relentlessly.

This is why I did not believe it was wise to operate on centers of gravity, and I did not think that bombing the Dahieh – Hezbollah's main compound in Beirut – would topple the organization. I assessed that wide-scale, multifarious takeover operations, in as many areas as possible, while creating a constant "buzz," could neutralize the opponent and inflict severe losses.

We did focus our efforts at Bint Jbeil as if it were a center of gravity, but the rationale here was our wish to demonstrate the IDF's capabilities, at least in one place, because it was unclear whether the campaign would continue.

The convergence of Hezbollah forces at Bint Jbeil was an opportunity to target a large number of them. Such a blow could deliver a shock – even if not decisive – that would create a suitable perceptional effect and instill confidence among our decision makers. This was exactly what took place. But the indecisiveness, unprofessionalism, and arguments and clashes between NORTHCOM and the General Staff led to the withdrawal of our forces, and a missed opportunity in the first battle of Bint Jbeil.

We would later need to retake the same places again. The moment the decision to take Bint Jbeil was made, the division focused its efforts, and within eighteen hours the town and its surroundings were in our hands, and the entire 3rd Hezbollah Regional Command (HRC) had collapsed. This was supposed to enable our further advancement toward Jabal Amel, but a political decision halted us. The entire momentum would be brought to a standstill, with large forces accumulated in the field for the attack remaining in place and becoming targets. Only later would the division complete its mission, MHTA, when the decision was finally made to "unleash the Rottweiler."

Chapter 17
Change of Direction

From "Raids" to "Special Security Perimeter"

Just when we received the order to leave the Bint Jbeil region, the recruiting of reserve forces was finally approved, two and a half weeks after the commencement of the war.

Now Dror, my deputy, was coordinating the complex task of recruiting thousands of soldiers. Within hours, they came through the emergency warehouses, where they were received, registered, and equipped. Tanks came out of their storage, as did APCs, trucks, radios, and weapons. How fortunate it was that we had persistently prepared and trained for this before the war.

The idea of defense and raids, as well as the concept of dominating the battle space from the air, had been exhausted. The operational rationale at last began to change.

The mobilization of reserve units was a catalyst for operational planning based on existing contingency plans (such as Magen Ha'aretz), but since approval had not been given to go on the offensive, orders continued to be issued under the "raids" rationale.

The result was that during the operational planning for taking control of pockets of Lebanese territory and creating a special security perimeter (SSP), the operational planning for raids in the sector continued uninterrupted.

This produced a burdensome amount of operational planning, both for the larger plan based on reserve forces and preparations for war, as well as for the smaller plans – the raids. At the same time, the division was extremely busy with the preparations for various operations with different levels of importance, logistics, and magnitude of forces, but mainly with the uncertainty of which plan would eventually be put into action.

"Gal, Boaz (NORTHCOM J3) wants you."

"This is Gal."

"Gal, there's a problem, we have a situation in Qana; a bomb hit a group of civilians, and a lot of people were killed!"

"You can't be serious!"

"I am. It's true!"

"In Qana? The village of Qana?!" I asked. I could not believe what I was hearing. Could history be repeating itself? It was only a decade ago, during Operation Grapes of Wrath, that the first Qana incident had taken place.

"It's Qana again, and this time the war is ending; a cease-fire is expected this evening. It's a done deal, the world is angry at us, and it's a catastrophe. There are many dead children!"

"OK." I waited for what would follow after his dramatic introduction.

"Udi wants you to push the timetable up for your operations and put everything you planned into action tonight."

"Boaz," I said, "we are planning a number of things at once. You want me to put two raids into action in Ayta ash-Shab and Majdal Zoun in order to take out as many Hezbollah fighters as possible. You want me to prepare a Magen Ha'aretz-style offensive, for which reserves are now being recruited and a battle procedure is underway. If that's not enough, we are also continuing standoff fires from air, sea, and artillery, defending the border from inside Lebanon, and dealing with the civilian rear near the border. Have you decided what you are doing?"

I understood the pressure NORTHCOM was under. This was exactly what had happened to me as CENTCOM J3 during the period that preceded Operation Defensive Shield, and especially during the operation itself – the pressure, the ever-changing orders and missions, and the drive to prepare everything fast and in the best way possible.

To implement all this, I simultaneously prepared the division for *three* operational options. The division's operations department was buckling under the staggering load. The brigade commanders complained to me, "What's going on here?" But I knew the division needed to create flexibility for NORTHCOM and not weigh heavily on them.

I also grumbled a little to myself, but toward NORTHCOM I tried to project cooperation and partnership. The repercussions of the first week were still being felt, but I also saw that Udi had started to understand that I was not his problem. There was understanding, there was coordination, and there was a common goal. Although there was something distant between us, Udi was still the general I respected.

"Look, Gal, at least the operation in Ayta [ash-Shab] has to be moved up," Boaz said quietly.

"But Hagai is only being extracted tonight from Bint Jbeil, and there is a battle procedure for a raid on Ayta." And what if my plans for a large-scale ground maneuver to take Jabal Amel did materialize?

"We know, but no one knows what the future holds, and we need to do all we can before it's over."

A classic example of uncertainty, I thought.

"I'll check what plans can be launched tonight, before the cease-fire, and let you know."

"Thanks."

"What Can We Carry out Tonight?"

"Find Hagai!" I called out to my staff.

"They are at the Sea of Galilee."

"What?!"

"They were taken there to reorganize. NORTHCOM said so."

"So why did we agree? What is this, Club Med?! This is war!"

"They couldn't find another place."

"Check out this nonsense with our logistics and personnel center. They are responsible. It shouldn't be this way!"

I was in disbelief. "The Sea of Galilee," I fumed to myself. How can you send soldiers who fought at Bint Jbeil right back into the fight after being at the beach? We had planned before the war that units would be extracted to the rear for reorganization during battle – we had even practiced it in a division exercise – but to a hotel on the beach?!

This was not going to go over well.

"What's up, Gal?" Hagai sounded very tired, and he had also caught a cold.

"What can we carry out tonight in Ayta?" I asked, and told him what had happened at Qana.

"Are you serious?" He also found it hard to believe.

"Totally. What can we get done tonight? I know the troops are exhausted, and that they were only pulled out the night before from Bint Jbeil, but your recon battalion was removed first. Can it be activated to carry out the preliminary operations?"

"Nimrod, yes," Hagai said, thinking out loud, "and what do you want to achieve in Ayta?"

"In the order I issued to you I wrote 'raid' and we have already spoken about that."

"Right."

"But you are not raiding! I want you to conquer, understand?"

"Understand completely."

Hagai also understood that after the yoyo we had gone through in Bint Jbeil, my first priority was a mission with all the loose ends tied up – capturing controlling territory so we would have it in our hands, engage the casbah, and kill the enemy. I wanted to put some certainty into the operation and leave nothing open for interpretation. I was actually concerned with NORTH-COM's behavior that they might pull more back and forth like it had been with Bint Jbeil.

"After taking control of the territory, if they tell us to go back, we'll go back. A raid is an offensive and overtaking of territory for a limited time," I said, explaining my intentions to Hagai and making clear to him the future implications. "And if the progressive battle from Magen Ha'aretz is put into action toward Bint Jbeil (again) and Jabal Amel, I will take you out of Ayta so you can start to move forward gradually toward the controlling areas."

"I understand; give me a few minutes."

"You got it."

True to his word, he was back on the phone with me after just a few minutes.

"OK, Gal, tonight we will deploy all of the forward, recon, and observation forces, and will make contact with the target area. If we are halted because of Qana, then we will stop. If you instruct us to attack Ayta, then I am going to introduce the battalions to attack according to the plan you approved. If you need anything else, we'll do that too."

"Thanks, Hagai, I need the recon battalion's deployment to be supportive of a progressive battle toward Shakif al-Nimel, the Sylvester Ridge, and A-Taire. Let Nimrod secure the flank north of the combat in Ayta and at the same time be ready to serve as front guard when we maneuver toward Bint Jbeil."

"Roger."

"Good luck."

"Monir, update NORTHCOM. We will set the operation in motion tonight in the area of Ayta. We'll see how it goes," I ordered.

In any case, in spite of the uncertainty, we prepared several options, and I felt satisfied that we would know how to operate in any situation and following any decision.

That same night, after exploring the feasibility and following a situation analysis, the division began an operation in Ayta with the objective of killing scores of enemy fighters and crippling Hezbollah's infrastructure in the region.

In the midst of the operation in Ayta (by the paratroopers), I was ordered by NORTHCOM to commence a separate offensive under the name of Change of Direction (COD) 8.

This was actually the same operation that I had initiated – a broad-scoped, division-sized maneuver with seven brigades attacking simultaneously. The main force was to surround Bint Jbeil, and the secondary effort was aimed at the western region (the coast), while combining naval and air forces.

Change of Direction (COD) 8

The directive was to reach areas controlling the city of Bint Jbeil from the west, and the region of Rajamin in the western sector, with the goal of taking control of vast areas in southern Lebanon and creating a special security perimeter (SSP).

I broadened the scope of the division's operation and defined the ruse and the operational concept of a tight encirclement of Bint Jbeil from the east (by the 7th Armor Brigade) and from the west (by the Paratroopers Brigade). I ordered the reserve Alexandroni Brigade to reorganize after its previous mission (border defense) and to occupy the western sector (Rajamin and then Ras el-Bayada), in order to pose a threat to Tyre from the south, and initiate engagement.

As expected, due to the fact that the Alexandroni had been spread out from Mount Dov to the shoreline, it would take a long time to reassemble it back into a combat force.

I ordered the Carmeli Brigade to replace the paratroopers in Ayta (so they could carry out their mission in Bint Jbeil) and continue the operation in the village. I gave the 300th Brigade missions along the southern Lebanese road, and of course protecting the border and the villages in the area. I also issued orders to the artillery brigade, the logistic units, and all support forces, including naval and air forces.

The Raids Cease and the Offensive Begins

The battle in Ayta began as part of the raid rationale and at the same time, exactly as I had planned, served as the preface for the option that NORTH-COM would approve the initiation of an advance to contact maneuver into Lebanon, to go beyond the ridge of Bint Jbeil and Jabal Amel and reach areas that controlled Tyre. The battle evolved. Troops from the paratroopers already held most of the controlling areas and were engaged in fierce combat in the casbah. In their battles that day, the paratroopers lost four men.

In the first stage, Hagai set up his FCG next to mine. Within a two-minute walking distance, he could oversee most of his area of operations. For better or for worse, the division was positioned right on the front line, and Hagai had set up his headquarters correctly. He would later move to Talat Abu Tweil, a controlling area next to the village.

I arrived at his forward element at a difficult time for him. There were reports of casualties, and the pressure was immense. Near the brigade commander's table were small screens receiving UAV downlinks, showing a vertical perspective of his forces in real time. After the war these screens would receive the derogatory label of "plasmas," and the commanding officers observing them from the battlefield would be called "plasma officers," supposedly for violating the IDF value of leading from the front. But this criticism was unfounded, unprofessional, ugly, and lacking integrity.

Hagai's staff now concentrated on directing artillery and air-based fire support, as well as reinforcement and evacuation forces. I tried to inspire confidence, and when I began to feel that I was infringing on his independence, I left, but not before emphasizing several points to Hagai. I felt that mentoring was an ongoing process, even during combat.

I verified that all orally given orders in the commanders' axis were backed up by officially written orders in the operational staff axis.

My FCG followed with me whenever I left the division headquarters. My orders were all documented and relayed to the division's situation room. They would also send out a written order or document while I traveled in the field or visited various units.

Hagai and I had spoken, and it was apparent that he understood the situation well, but there is no substitute for a written, official, and obligating order. An order synchronizes all of the division's centers and units and focuses them on the commander's instructions and intentions. Speaking is important, but a written order is binding.

Advance to Contact – The Plan

This was it. We had reached the moment of truth. In order to realize the plan, I now needed to move large units, some of them reserves, and set the plan in motion already by the night of August 1. Indeed a huge task.

I directed Hagai to take over the areas controlling Bint Jbeil from the west. He had been there before and was familiar with the area. I decided to assign the Alexandroni Brigade's forces (led by COL Shlomi Cohen) along with the Navy units to the western sector – HRC 1. I wanted them to flank the two nature reserves near the border and approach them from the rear.

Rockets were being fired from there, and I wanted to engage Tyre by fire and observation. As it was such a central city, I was convinced that putting pressure on Tyre and its surroundings would reduce the pressure on Israeli northern communities in the western sector. Along the way there, it was also important to take control of the Rajamin intersection and to search and clear enemy fighters from the villages in the area.

From the east, we needed to flank Bint Jbeil and reach the Sylvester ridge. This was where HRC 3 operated – a unit that had been seasoned in combat against us during the battles in Maroun al-Ras and Bint Jbeil.

I knew they had suffered heavy casualties – more than one hundred killed and dozens injured – but I still considered them a highly motivated and organized unit, possessing modern equipment. For this mission I decided to activate the 7th Brigade from one flank, and the paratroopers from the other – and to completely surround them. The enemy forces defending that area would thus come under multidirectional pressure, allowing us to engage the Jabal Amel and Tebnine regions relatively quickly.

I tried to convince MG Ben-Reuven: "Let's go straight to Tebnine and the Haris Junction, just like in the plan." But he refused.

"We have no intention of reaching there; not now, anyway. Let me try to get your eastern maneuver approved," Eyal said. He would have to convince NORTHCOM and the GS of my claims that it was incorrect to move only along the western flank as I had been ordered. Pressure on HRC 3 from only one side would allow their people to move effortlessly to the other side – this was clear and elementary.

Soon Eyal got back to me: "OK, you can attack from the east as well." The maneuver of the 7th Brigade was approved.

Now I needed to keep the foothold created for the division in the Maroun al-Ras–Jal a-Dir (Shaked) region. The 7th Brigade had held the area since the division had conquered it.

"Eyal, I am counting on Finkel to replace Amnon in the Dovev-Shaked region. Please let me have him."

COL Meir Finkel's Steel Chariots reserve Merkava brigade was in the process of recruitment. It was well trained and prepared for war. The problem was that NORTHCOM had yet to officially allocate it to a division. Another difficulty was that NORTHCOM had a method of force allocation that drove me out of my mind: from every battalion that arrived, a company would be automatically extracted and allocated to another division. Every brigade would be split among the divisions as some kind of ostensible "social justice," which severely broke the organic nature of units. I already envisioned how we would later need to gather fragmented forces from all corners of the land.

"Isn't it simpler to allocate organic forces?!" I burst out toward Boaz, the J3. But he apparently had his own considerations.

"Don't forget that you were once the J3 of a regional command," he replied.

I tried a couple more times to convince NORTHCOM that it was wrong to break up forces, but then I gave up. I understood that a division commander needed to manage the time spent for disagreements and arguments, certainly during wartime.

"Gal, don't leave me like this with other divisions – take me with you!" pleaded COL Ilan Atias, commander of Carmeli Brigade. His brigade had trained with me in preparation for the war, and even though it was not an organic part of the division, it certainly felt that way by now.

Carmeli was recruited along with other reserve brigades and was getting organized in their emergency depot. My request from NORTHCOM to allocate it to me, as it appeared in the CONPLANs, had been refused. Contrary to the plan, Carmeli was not allocated to any division, but designated as a general reserve brigade. Unwisely, they were sent down south to Tze'elim, the national training base, for pre-combat training. The long trip from the recruitment facility in the north to southern Israel severely hindered the brigade's preparations. Only after I repeatedly demanded that they be posted in my division was Carmeli Brigade finally ordered back to the north. My request to have them flown by C-130s was turned down, so they were forced to make the long trip back north with buses.

"If you get Carmeli, what are you going to do with it?" Eyal Ben-Reuven asked.

"They were originally planned to operate in the Kafra-Yater region."

"That area won't be under your responsibility. Eyal Eizenberg's airborne division will be operating there."

"What sense does that make? My division planned that area, and it is a natural continuation to the operations being conducted at the Sylvester, Shakif al-Nimel, and Bint Jbeil region."

"That is the decision. Carry out the missions you were given. You have enough as it is."

"But Eyal – "

Eyal did all he could to maneuver between me – the commander in the field – and his need to represent NORTHCOM and the GS. I felt that his heart went out to me and that he had been supporting my views for some time, but he also was bound to his position in NORTHCOM.

"Leave it alone, Gal. The fact is that we wanted Eyal to operate somewhere elsc, according to the CONPLAN, and then make contact with you..."

"That's right."

"But we didn't receive approval for that, so we are giving him the Kafra-Yater region, and having him pass through your forces to reach it."

"What's this, social justice? Their mission wasn't approved, so they get a consolation prize to work in my AOR?" I lashed out, but was immediately sorry I did. It sounded childish.

"This won't be the last change, believe me," said Eyal.

I was quite familiar with these frequent changes. Every few hours the commanders of the division's units would be called to briefing rooms in order to hear that "the orders have changed." Cynicism and humor took the place of tense pre-battle readiness.

The various brigade headquarters' staffs were in the division's dining room studying the new order when Eyal received a message and grimaced.

"Well, disapproved; we're going with an even more reduced version. You are to continue up to where we agreed upon, to the ridges that control Bint Jbeil and all the way to the Rajamin Junction to the west."

"Eyal, that's like doing half a job. Let me at least go up to Sylvester, which dominates our current position. I should hold it so I can threaten Tebnine by firepower. And what do I need Rajamin for? I want to engage Tyre with fire; that's where Acre is being targeted from!" My voice was hoarse, and I was overwhelmed with frustration.

"I understand you, but that is all they are giving me. Explain to me again – what is Carmeli's mission at Ayta?"

"I need Hagai up forward toward A-Taire, west of Bint Jbeil. When Ilan replaces him in the Ayta region, he will isolate it, occupy it, and prevent any trouble from there. We need to perform an advance to contact maneuver now, and Ilan will secure the flank of the advancing forces," I explained. And then I added, "Eyal, one more thing."

"Yes?"

I had wanted to tell him something personal for a long time. "You have a very important role here in this war, and I really appreciate what you are doing, Eyal," I said honestly, without hesitation. It was the truth. He had been putting things in order, he was decisive, quiet, and level-headed. He was a leader. Commanders who were battle-seasoned apparently see things differently.

"Thanks," he said with a smile, and then he gave me a pat on the shoulder and hurried to NORTHCOM.

Meanwhile I had many orders to give.

"Listen, Monir, I want Amnon to carry out a right wing flanking maneuver, through the Manhalah Ridge, and come around from the east. He has his recon battalion and tanks, and also give him one of Carmeli's battalions. Issue an alert order to Amnon. When can we get the first planning group together for the offensive?"

Monir looked at his watch. "Maybe at one o'clock?"

"One it is." And he was off to prepare while I moved on to the next order. "Tal, come over here, call the FCG staff. I want to get to an observation point and see from up close what is going on. Come on!"

I took the time to check my cell phone and found a text message that Ofri had sent the night before: "I will not go to sleep. I am awake all the time with the cell phone in my hand, waiting for you to write me something."

Ofri, my dearest Ofri, who was born after that operation in Lebanon, on a full moon.

"Swarms" – Planning the Offensive

Everyone met in the division's dining room for the orders group, with the echo of explosions and impacts all around. Not far away, Amnon's artillery brigade was firing at the source of the incoming fire, trying to silence it.

As the nerve center of combat, the division headquarters was all astir, teeming with people and vehicles, coming and going. Multiple units came to get updated, to be assisted by information, knowledge, intel aids, and equipment. Merkava tanks traversed inside the headquarters compound, occasionally shooting at various targets and changing positions. Nearby artillery batteries fired at the enemy and were themselves being targeted.

Just a few days before, we had suffered a direct hit to the fires center's vehicles, and a soldier had been critically wounded. I had been commanding a battle when it happened, and while the division kept performing its operational processes, the wounded soldier was quickly dragged to a small niche near my command post. A large piece of shrapnel from an incoming projectile had shattered his throat, and large jets of blood spurted from it. Our doctor, Gil, was an experienced surgeon, and within seconds, he made the decision to perform an emergency field operation. From the corner of my eye I watched how he handled the scalpel, successfully inserted a tube into the soldier's airway, and stabilized him. When the firing subsided a bit, the injured man was evacuated on a stretcher from the bunker to a helicopter that had been scrambled and landed within the division compound. His life was saved.

He was not the last casualty we suffered within the division headquarters itself. Our division was an easy target for the enemy, since we were located right on the border and literally shared a fence with the Israeli-Lebanese border.

We had deliberated a lot about moving to a more protected location. The high cost was somewhat of a deterrent, but the main consideration was setting an example to the civilian population. After all, many towns and villages were located right on the front line, as a matter of Zionistic values of conquering the frontier and physically defining Israel's borders. Could we, the IDF, relocate to the rear and leave the civilians we served and defended on the front line? Our position exemplified the famous IDF creed "Follow me!" and the division headquarters at Biranit had always been a national symbol.

On the other hand, there were many who were amazed to see us situated directly on the front line, as if we were one of the tactical units. "You guys are crazy!" a visiting foreign general once told me with a strange look on his face.

"You are right about that," I replied.

Aerial photographs and maps were hung on the walls, and someone even positioned a video camera for documenting the session.

"Tonight is a decisive night," I began. "I know there have been many changes, but this will not be a long briefing. The basic situation is changing. From defense and raids, we are now transitioning to an offensive maneuver."

I looked at my people. They were attuned, despite extreme fatigue following long days of fighting. I thought to myself that it had been two and a half weeks of fighting until the division was finally allowed to attack, as planned for over a year.

"Orders will soon be issued. You will receive intel and professional annexes [documents with additional information]; I will answer your questions and then give my final remarks. Time is short, but I also want this structured. I also want to put together an orders group 2 today."

The session proceeded in order and the missions were clarified: Shlomi, commander of Alexandroni, would collect his brigade (which had already assembled) and attack westwards into the heart of HRC 1, to Rajamin Junction. I wanted him to achieve fire and visual dominance over the city of Tyre.

"No approval for this yet, Shlomi, but this is your expected mission."

"Clear." He nodded.

The paratroopers were to leave a battalion at Ayta until Carmeli Brigade took up positions there, while the rest of the brigade moved forward to the ridges overlooking Bint Jbeil from the west and the south. Hagai had already proceeded with some repositioning as we had agreed, and had moved his recon battalion (commanded by LTC Nimrod Aloni) and a company from the 890th Battalion (commanded by CAP Yoav Bruner) forward to better positions.

Earlier, I had met the commanders of the 890th at their makeshift FCG at the village of Even Menachem, after the battle at Ayta. I spoke with Kobi, the battalion commander, and the company commanders. Despite their losses, I encountered a strong battalion, calm commanders, and a battalion commander who was a leader.

Amnon, 7th Brigade commander, asked: "What are the main and secondary efforts?"

He was right to ask, but in the kind of maneuver I intended to perform, there was no classic answer.

"There aren't only two efforts here, Amnon. It is a plan intended to 'extinguish' the area as soon as possible, flood it from multiple directions, engage and kill as many enemy fighters as possible, and control key areas in a short time. The idea is to cast a cloud of swarming wasps over the entire area. This is the essence of the Magen Ha'aretz plan using the 'swarm' method.

"The main effort is around HRC 3, around Bint Jbeil, but in practice, at the division level, we have three, or even more, main efforts. They are relatively balanced, and within them there are many secondary efforts. These are the 'swarms,' which Hezbollah will find impossible to cope with. They are waiting for us on the roads, but we will come at them from many directions—on foot, at night, and with firepower coming from the ground, sea, and air."

Amnon and Hagai had never trained with my division, so they lacked the common language we had developed. This is why it is always preferable to have organic units who share simple, common language.

This was a permanent gap that needed to be bridged, and this was why I had always worked hard to disseminate our knowledge and developed doctrine to as many commanders and units as possible throughout the IDF.

It was now important for me to verify that Amnon understood the operational concept and his mission.

"Amnon, is the mission clear?"

"Clear."

Still, something didn't seem right.

"What's happening with Ilan's battalion," I asked, "the one that is supposed to flank from the east? Will he arrive on time from Tze'elim?"

"He will," Amnon insisted.

"Ilan," I said, turning to the Carmeli Brigade commander, "will he make it or not?"

"There's no reason he shouldn't make it," he answered.

I still was not at ease.

"Amnon, Herev are in your region, at Maroun al-Ras. They're excellent. Take them instead, and Ilan's battalion will replace them when they arrive. Isn't that better?"

"I'd rather not," he answered. "Wajdi has things to do; he's essential. He's at Maroun al-Ras and also he's been working nonstop since the beginning of the war. He's tired and needs to reorganize. I'd rather have Ilan's force, and he'll be here on time, don't worry."

"You sure?"

"Yes."

I still had doubts, but it was my impression that both brigade commanders knew what they were saying.

I continued to work on the plan, combining air, artillery, logistics, and naval forces – the control and communication plan.

"Go work on the professional orders," I requested, "and make them quick and focused. I want a division attack at midnight, and a different situation in the field by dawn."

I wanted massive presence on the way to the encirclement of Bint Jbeil, on the way to controlling Tyre, and maximum contact with various areas and Hezbollah units: a combination of the need to hold on to key areas and the need to come into fast contact with the enemy. We needed to improve the situation before a cease-fire was established, in order to allow as many civilians as possible out of bomb shelters. We had to set conditions for change, for international involvement, and awakening of the international community. And if an arrangement could not be reached, a forced arrangement would be imposed, as we had done in the past in CENTCOM after Operation Defensive Shield and the construction of the security fence. An attack deep into Lebanon at this point would create a dynamic that would bring an end to the fighting and establish a new arrangement.

But something still bothered me. There was an unsolved component in this equation.

Special Security Perimeter

"What do we want to achieve?" I asked the CGS, as we walked toward the war room. The mission in Bint Jbeil had just ended, there was much tension, and the Israeli public was widely dealing with the question of how the war was being "handled." NORTHCOM was issuing simultaneous plans and orders, using various terms such as "raids," "assault," "designing the line," and others. It was vague and foggy.

"Establish a perimeter," Halutz told me, later that day at Shomera – 300th Brigade's headquarters.

"What's a perimeter?"

"Circumference."

"I know what it means literally, but what do you want in the field?"

"Do what we have decided at NORTHCOM – establish an SSP."

"What's an SSP?" I wondered, this term being new to me.

"Special security perimeter."

I understood this to mean that we were finally going to take over territory. The idea was to minimize rocket launching, but how could we achieve this if the operation was limited in range? Hezbollah could easily fire upon the same villages from many other places in Lebanon. The concept of the Magen Ha'aretz CONPLAN was not to conquer Lebanon, only to fight short-range rockets in southern Lebanon and create pressure that would lead to a different accord or arrangement. It was clear that Hezbollah had longer range rockets, which could be fired at Israel from north of the Awali River.

During the latest war game held at NORTHCOM, we had debated this issue, and it was clear that the maneuver into Lebanon was not intended to fight all rocket launchers, but to directly target Hezbollah, exacting a heavy price and destabilizing its foundations. We wanted a better situation than the one established after the Israeli withdrawal in 2000.

We were well aware that the complex system constructed by Hezbollah under our noses for many years could not be dismantled and neutralized in a matter of days. Searching and clearing would take a long time. It was also clear that controlling the area in a way that would prevent rocket fire into Israel could only be achieved by controlling most of the area of Lebanon. We could have done it, but had no intention of doing so.

Until today, I cannot understand the naïveté and "shock" at the extent of the rockets that were fired toward Israel during the war. This was exactly what we had prepared for. The idea was to exert pressure and fundamentally change the situation *after* the war – not *during* the war.

"We should be authorized to initiate more," I had told Bogie, the previous CGS, during a private conversation we held before the war. I expressed my concern that Hezbollah was at our doorstep, "doing whatever they please."

"We need to cool, contain, restrain!" Bogie said. "Make sure it's quiet."

"But there are provocations and abduction attempts, and Hezbollah is building a massive infrastructure," I protested.

"When there's another 'battle day' you can take out your fury on them," he said, "according to the existing rules."

"There's a huge number of rockets, and a war isn't going to be easy," I insisted.

"Let them rust!" Bogie said with a hint of a smile.

"What do you mean, rust?"

"Let the rockets rust. We need to make it so there will be no reason to use them."

Bogie was echoing the policy dictated by the government, but it was clear to me what was going on. Iran was constructing a front with Israel and the West, aimed at deterring, threatening, and harassing us. This would allow them to operate an active conventional front based on Hezbollah, while continuing to build their nuclear capabilities.

My little bunker in the division headquarters was a multifunctional alcove. There was a folding bed which I hadn't had a chance to use during the war, a table, and a map board. A yellowish light was constantly on. The little room was filled with piles of packages sent to soldiers from all around the country, so it also served as a depot from which the packages were distributed to the troops out in the assembly areas.

The room also served as a dining room, a planning and briefing room, and as a meeting place where I sat with commanders and other visitors, such as generals and ministers. We were always amazed how it could fit thirty people, standing up.

"You have to get some sleep," Tal said firmly. "You only doze off here and there. That isn't good! And you've got to eat. You haven't had a hot meal in two weeks."

"OK, Tal, what can I do?"

"Find a few minutes a day to eat."

"OK, I'll try."

"Don't try, do it!" he insisted.

"I will," I smiled tiredly, as I walked out to the jeep. Tal was relating to me like a younger brother – both lovingly and tough.

I got into the armored vehicle and tried to position myself in a way that would relieve my pain. My old wounds were troubling me, and I had been feeling a sharp burning sensation throughout the right side of my body.

"This damn injury," I whispered to myself through clenched teeth. "Hold on. Shut up and move on."

Chapter 18

To Touch Them All

Briefing the Forces

Although not all my plans had been approved, I was happy that some of my initiatives were a go. We were finally setting out to a division-level attack. I just hoped that we didn't get ordered to abort at the last moment. I was receiving multiple calls on my encrypted phone, and my radio operators' hands were full. Many people were calling to offer assistance, others to find out details about our plans. I wanted to go to the units and observe the preparations firsthand.

"Maybe you should stay at the headquarters? This is a critical time," Monir pleaded.

"I have to see the preparations with my own eyes and meet as many commanders and soldiers as possible," I explained. "I have to touch them all. I'll try to make it back before H-hour."

"OK," he said, unable to hide his dissatisfaction.

"FCG – move out to the vehicles. We're off to Alexandroni Brigade."

Only in the last few hours were we overcoming extreme difficulties in concentrating the brigade. They were widely deployed all along the line, and we had a hard time pulling them back and regrouping them. It took much decisiveness and close monitoring. One of the battalions had just finished fighting in the area of Kafr Kila, and was pulled out quickly in order to prepare for the attack on HRC 1. Usually this would have taken much longer, but now we needed to do it fast.

"We must attack on time, Shlomi!" I explained to the brigade commander.

"There hasn't been enough time to prepare. They are reservists, Gal."

"Well-trained reservists. We've been working them hard for more than a year preparing for exactly this kind of mission."

"Look, they will carry out the missions, but they are spent," said Shlomi.

"This is a coordinated divisional attack," I explained, "parallel movement of a few separate efforts, and I want to create the effect of simultaneously putting pressure on the whole field – a fast takeover. This will be significant as far as the achievement. Hezbollah will find it hard to withstand an advance to contact maneuver of so many infantry soldiers – 'swarms' of infantry soldiers."

"Gal, I understand. You know I am a 'contractor' and I will carry it out. Only too bad that Philips [a battalion commander in Shlomi's brigade] isn't here. Can't you pull him out of Mount Dov?"

"When I pressured NORTHCOM about this, I got pushback," I said. "Udi Adam is worried about Mount Dov. For some reason nothing is happening there, and there is of course the objective of keeping the Syrians out of this. Bottom line – they don't want to replace forces at Mount Dov, so Philips isn't coming."

"He won't forgive you for this!"

"I know. I also want him here. It's a great battalion."

I headed out to Alexandroni's final briefings, and at the entrance of the bunker, I ran into my good old friend, Dr. Yossi "Yoli" Liran. We hugged.

"What are you doing here, Yoli?"

"That's a weird question! How long do you think I can sit around waiting for you to call me? If the mountain won't call Muhammad, then Muhammad must wear uniform and come!"

"Come with me, Yoli. I've got to run."

"But I don't have a weapon and gear."

"You'll be given a helmet and bulletproof vest. We'll see about a weapon later. I'm not even sure you're staying," I teased him.

I met the commanders of Alexandroni Brigade at Merom Galil Municipality. I was happy to see them. I highly appreciated them. They were extremely dedicated. The stress was apparent on their faces.

I briefed them shortly, emphasizing the importance of fulfilling the mission and explaining the difference between the first few weeks of fighting and what was about to take place that very night. It was a fundamental paradigm shift from defensive to offensive mode. I stressed the need to reach the targets on time and explained what other brigades were doing and how they fit into the big picture.

"You have a key role in removing threats from the western region's villages."

"Why aren't we carrying out our original plan?" someone asked. "We were supposed to attack in the area of Bint Jbeil."

"This is war," I explained, "and we must stick to the mission, not the plan. The Paratroopers Brigade is operating at Bint Jbeil and there's no point in replacing them now. The same goes for 7th Brigade, which has been fighting at Maroun al-Ras for a few days. The plan has altered, but the concept has remained the same – infiltration on foot, capture key areas, position ambushes between the nature reserves and the nearby villages, work with helicopters and some tanks, just like we did in training!"

I answered a few more questions and concluded: "It's important to complete the mission on time, and not stop during the attack. Nothing is going to stop you, clear?"

Everyone nodded.

"Good luck. We'll meet on the radio."

A few more handshakes and I headed out. I wanted to make it to the commander of 7th Brigade before the commencement of the attack.

Just then, Amnon called.

"Hi, Amnon. What's up?"

"Hi, Gal, listen, the battalion won't be able to carry out the mission. We can't do it today. We must postpone."

Hot rage enveloped me and I felt faintly dizzy.

"Amnon, do you understand what you are telling me?!"

"Yes. They can't do it tonight. That's the way it is. The battalion isn't ready."

I did not yet know at this time that Amnon had actually planned in advance to make it impossible for me to find a solution on time.

"Amnon, the attack is taking place tonight, and you are going to participate. Now, tell me how you plan to make this happen!"

"The battalion commander says that he won't be ready. They are reservists."

At this point my anger was directed at the battalion commander. I was not aware that Amnon had already spoken to the media and made it clear that he intended to bypass me and speak to my superiors about problems in implementing the attack.

My earlier concern that the battalion designated to lead the attack in the eastern region wouldn't make it on time was verified. But I did not know it would be premeditated, and it was inconceivable that crimes such as this would be committed during wartime.

"Amnon – you are attacking tonight! If the reserve battalion can't do it, take Wajdi and attack with him."

Herev was my battalion – well trained and educated. They would do great, I had no doubt.

"No chance, Gal, Herev Battalion has been fighting for three weeks, they haven't had refreshing time. Why Herev, anyway?"

"Amnon, there is a divisional attack tonight. This is a crucial time! The entire country is observing us. If there is no one setting out to the eastern maneuver from your direction, it will influence everyone – the decision makers, the enemy which will find an open flank for maneuver or retreat, and the citizens in the bomb shelters."

"There's nothing we can do," he insisted.

"Yes, there is!" I was furious. "Now talk to Wajdi and get moving because it's the afternoon already, and we don't have time. Bring Wajdi from Maroun al-Ras and have reservists replace him. He will do it, I am certain, and if necessary cut directly to the target between Aytarun and Aynata. You are to fulfill your mission!" I said angrily and decisively.

"I will talk to Wajdi, but it won't work."

"Talk to him."

"Should I update NORTHCOM?" asked Lutfi.

"No, we will make it. We must. Just update them on the change in forces. The mission itself will be fulfilled." I let my head fall back. Yoli watched me and said nothing, realizing only now the intensity of the emotional strain I was under.

Amnon was on the line again: "Forget it, Gal. Wajdi can't do it."

"I'll talk to him. Look here, Amnon, I am going to talk with your subordinate!" It was irregular, and not my style, but I had no choice. This was a time for penetrating the chain of command, making direct and personal contact, and demonstrating close-up leadership.

"How are you doing, Wajdi?"

"OK, sir, everything's OK, a little tired, sir."

I knew they were very tired. They were the only battalion that hadn't gone out for a day or two of refreshing. I had made sure that all the other units did it, as a lesson learned from previous campaigns.

"Wajdi, there's a divisional maneuver tonight: an attack. It's critical. We have a problem. A reserve battalion can't carry out the eastern outflank. I need you to do this for us."

"Sir," he hesitated, "how can we? The battalion is spent after continuous days of fighting."

"Wajdi, there's no choice," I said, and then, after another moment of thought, I added: "Wajdi, the entire divisional maneuver is on your shoulders. You're the only one who can carry it out, and I trust you."

Wajdi was silent, and so was I. It was a tense moment and my heart was pounding. It was one thing to follow orders, but doing something whole-heartedly was a completely different thing.

"Sir, we will do it."

"Thank you, Wajdi. The LMC will await you at Kibbutz Yiron. Collect your battalion and run down there. Leave all your positions in Lebanon, except one company which will join you later. Get ready fast, and by daybreak you will already be after the eastern outflank toward Bint Jbeil."

"OK, sir," he answered, doubtfully.

"Get me a map," I told Gil, a great soldier who would save my life a few days later by yanking me back after I stepped on a booby-trapped hand grenade left by Hezbollah.

Wajdi isn't going to make it to the designated spot, I thought, as I observed the map, *but at least he can create that scissors maneuver, needed from the eastern side of Bint Jbeil. Even if the encirclement isn't completed in one night, it isn't so bad.*

"Get me Amnon."

"Yes, sir."

"Amnon, Wajdi will dash down from Maroun al-Ras. The LMC will refit the battalion. Have them washed, refilled, and rearmed, and then send them quickly through Turmus route to an eastern flank. Set him a destination for tonight. Have him reach the Manhalah ridgeline."

"Got it. It's tight but this he can do."

"At least till the Manhalah, and then press on toward the 700 peaks."

"OK."

"Good luck."

"Send maximum LMC personnel to Yiron. Tell LTC Guy Gov-Ari, the divisional logistics officer, that his mission is to prepare Herev for battle tonight as a fresh force. And get me Hagai on the line."

"What's up, Gal?" said Hagai.

"You tell me."

"Proceeding as planned. Nimrod is heading out toward A-Taire as our Front

Guard, followed by the rest of the brigade. I'm leaving the 101st Battalion with Ilan for twenty-four hours. Then they will prepare for a few hours and join me."

"Very good."

I updated him for a few minutes on the situation and what was to be expected later on that night.

"Good. I got it."

"Thank you, Hagai, see you on the radio soon before H-hour."

"Bye."

"Wait a minute, Hagai, how are you feeling?" He had a cold but was continuing to function while sick.

"So-so," he said.

"I asked someone to bring me some natural medicine for you. I'll send it over. Put it under your tongue. It'll do you good."

"Thanks."

1:0 or 3:1?

"Get me Chen," I requested.

"Hi, Gal."

"What's happening, kiddo?"

"OK, I'm teaching the reservists all kinds of things they never encountered."

Chen's reserve brigade was an infantry brigade originally intended only for regional defense. Only during the year before the war had we begun preparing them for "regular" infantry missions.

"It's important that your forces clean up the south Lebanese road, agricultural areas, and the small villages."

"That's what we're preparing for."

"OK. For your information, Lebune isn't solved yet. We're still taking fire from there."

Lebune was the name of a region north of the Israeli town of Shlomi, inside Lebanese territory. It was a jagged area of dense foliage, and – as revealed during the fighting – was filled with tunnels, bunkers, and weapons. This was a nature reserve in the full sense of the term, and we experienced constant fire from there. Only when our forces physically penetrated the compound did the enemy focus more on self-defense and less on firing rockets at Israel.

I was struggling with NORTHCOM in order to allow us to enter the nature reserves. Despite our plans and training, in a blunt intervention, they prevented us from doing so, probably out of fear stemming from the first days of battle, when we lost the two soldiers at Shaked.

"Udi," I said to my commander, "they are firing from within the nature reserves. These are launch sites. We must go in there and clear them out!"

"No!" Udi was decisive in his refusal. Later on in the war, as the battle developed, I bypassed his ban and gave approval to operate inside a few nature reserves. NORTHCOM found out and ordered us to get out at once, and only besiege them and operate standoff fire. Even a heightened debate with the CGS didn't help. It drove me crazy how much we were paralyzed and limited by fear of casualties.

During the debriefing process after the war, I was amazed to hear the CGS openly explain that his decisions during the war took into consideration that the parents of 2006 were less tolerant of casualties than in the past.

"You can't conduct a war like that," I said, defiantly. "Casualties are not the leading factor in conducting a campaign! The mission comes first." I was the only one opposing the CGS, in an auditorium filled with hundreds of officers.

"You will ultimately pay a price for this," one of my subordinates told me.

Halutz's mindset relating to casualties had trickled down and influenced commanders at the tactical level.

"I made it clear to my brigade that first we evacuate casualties, and when there's a life-threatening situation, this becomes our mission," Hagai admitted. "Maybe I was wrong, but this is what I thought during the war."

In fact, Hagai admitted that he had not comprehended that it was war, not routine security.

"It's better to win 1:0 than 3:1" – that is, better to kill one terrorist and lose no soldiers than to kill three enemies and lose one of our own. This had been a common theme among senior commanders during routine security operations in J&S.

"In assessing a mission, first we compare value versus risk," Mofaz had said, setting the norm as CGS, and then again as minister of defense, relating to fighting terror. "That is, to see if the importance of the mission is worth casualties."

"Protect the lives of your soldiers," we were told when fighting terror.

An entire generation of commanders, all the way up to the CGS, was accustomed to limited conflict, fighting terror, and "routine security." They did not properly recalibrate when war broke out. This was a table-turning situation: we needed to flip from standard security mode to different procedures and priorities.

We should certainly assess the potential gain versus the risk to human life in every mission. But during wartime, when Israeli civilians are under fire in bomb shelters, the IDF must assume greater risks in order to reach a decisive victory and remove the threat looming over the civilians.

Throughout the Second Lebanon War we suffered from this inability to identify and define the situation as it really was: war.

"This isn't routine security," I reiterated and insisted daily.

"This isn't a war," was the stubborn response for many days. And even when it was clear that this *was* some sort of war, routine operational terminology kept messing things up.

The Rear Region

Another problem was troubling me in the 300th Brigade's sector.

"Everyone is passing through your AOR. You must do your best to control the chaos of thousands of soldiers and hundreds of vehicles," I told Chen.

The roads were all congested. We had already experienced this during the first days of fighting, when we had trouble timing the arrival of forces making their way through the rear region. Many times commanders do not pay attention to this factor, but here it was obvious that jammed roads were hindering our operational efforts. Dror did his best, but I needed him by my side as my operational deputy. As the problems continued, I knew I needed someone to manage our rear.

"Get me Nitzan on the line."

BG Nitzan Nuriel, who knew the region well from previous assignments, had already come to visit during the first days of battle. "Don't want to bother you," he had said. "When you need me, I'll be by your side."

I needed him now.

"Come to the division, Nitzan, I need you. You'll work under Dror, managing the rear region."

"I'm on my way."

"Thank you, Nitzan."

Assigning a brigadier general under a colonel was unorthodox, I thought, but this was war and it could work. Nitzan was someone who could put his ego aside, and Dror was practical and serious. I thought it would work, and it did.

Finkel Is Ours

Good news: "Finkel is ours!" came the report from the operations room. Steel Chariots, our armored brigade which had already been recruited, was assigned to us.

While on the move with the FCG, I gave orders: "One battalion to Ilan, two battalions and the divisional engineering battalion to Finkel. Have him take the region of Dovev–Maroun al-Ras from Amnon. Finkel should establish a new, surprising route, through the area east of Ein Abel toward Bint Jbeil. Send an armored battalion to hook up with Hagai at Bint Jbeil."

There was no point in moving tanks on the regular predictable route through Debel and Ein Abel. It became apparent that, as expected, most routes were rigged with large IEDs. It was better to use infantry, of course, but if tanks were necessary, they had to be taken through newly established, unexpected routes.

The division's forces were now interwoven. The plan was good and stable, and I felt more confident. On the way to the western region, I witnessed a sight impressive to any commander: dozens of tank transporters loaded with Merkavas were traveling along the roads leading to the division's area. On the side of the road, technical teams of reservists were treating the vehicles. Finkel's brigade had arrived. Steel Chariots was with us.

Preparations for Attacking the Coastal Region

In the western sector, Alexandroni was aligning for attack on HRC 1. My objective was to place the brigade with a tank battalion in the areas overlooking the city of Tyre from the south. There were many rockets launched from there, and I assumed that Tyre was the center of gravity (or at least one of them) of Hezbollah's rocket apparatus. But my demand to place forces at Ras el-Bayada and Shakif el-Hardun was not approved. Only after repeated pressure was I allowed to proceed to the Rajamin area – an important junction in the western region – and to the villages of Jebbain, Shihin, and the outskirts of Shama. The plan was – as in our training – "swarms" of infantry soldiers – two battalions and then a third, capture of controlling areas, and interpositioning forces between nature reserves and the villages serving as logistical centers. Later on, in the next phase which we had termed in doctrine and plans as "the presence phase," we were to systematically comb the villages and nature reserves.

It was important to me that the attack would commence simultaneously in the eastern and western sectors. I wanted all three HRCs to come under pressure at the same time, making it hard for them to focus their efforts.

Bint Jbeil drew more forces, but I did not define it as our central effort. The massive infiltration maneuver we planned that night was one whole effort, aimed at "extinguishing" the entire area, engaging with maximum areas and creating friction, while at the same time dissecting the tactical components of the system – between the various regions, and between the nature reserves and the villages. I felt that without taking over vast areas of Lebanon, we could not halt the rocket fire, but we could push it northward, farther away from the area of the border.

HRC 1 began from the coastline of the Mediterranean. A naval element joined Alexandroni's forward headquarters, in addition to the air element which had been recently added to all brigades. This naval element was to coordinate fire from Navy ships and naval commando operations, and streamline them with all Alexandroni's operations.

During the two years before the war, the Air Force had unilaterally decided to eliminate close air support (CAS) with fighter jets, and scaled back to using only attack helicopters. This led to the cancelation of tactical air controllers (TAC), which used to be embedded in the brigades. Bitter arguments did not change the Air Force's decision. This wasn't the only hastily made organizational change. The IDF canceled the corps traditionally serving as an intermediate echelon between the divisions and the regional command. Also organic divisional logistic support brigades were canceled.

But when the need arose during the war, the Air Force supported my demands with the speed of lightning. They installed new TAC teams in all brigades, and reintroduced all forms of CAS for tactical forces.

"Shlomi, what's happening?"

"Roni and Sharon [two Alexandroni battalion commanders] are already here and will be ready on time. Eran's battalion is still stuck; they aren't releasing him to me from the Steel Division's area."

"I'll take care of it," I promised, and asked my radio operator, "Get me in touch with Raviv." He was commander of 769th Regional Brigade – the most eastern under my command.

"The rest are OK," Shlomi went on. "We will set out on time; only Eran won't be able to do it in the designated time frame."

"Attack in stages, and send in Eran when he arrives. Are you lacking any components from a doctrinal-professional perspective?" In my mind, I went through the various components needed for an advance to contact maneuver: recon, observation, air, artillery, naval, tanks, engineering company. He had it all.

"I have above and beyond what I need. Don't worry. You know I'm a workhorse. Just give me missions such as this!"

He was right. Shlomi was an extremely mission-oriented officer and had already proven himself in battle. I expected him to lead well in war – and he did.

Together we went over the plan again, and it seemed good and solid.

Raviv was on the line.

"Release Eran for me. I need him for the divisional attack in a few hours."

Raviv explained that the battalion was engaged and it would take time to extract it, but I insisted.

"OK," Raviv said. "I'll transfer it to you ASAP."

I was angry at the Steel Division for not transferring the battalion on time. Eran wouldn't make it, but at least I had enough forces to begin the attack.

"An Entire Nation"

"Fifteen minutes before the attack begins, I want all commanders on the radio, following the 'Orders, over' procedure," I instructed Alex, our comms officer.

At nighttime, lacking the advantage of daytime observation capabilities, the FCG out in the field was less effective. The division HQ's elevated position, right on the front line, made it strategically advantageous for command, control, and communication, having direct line-of-sight to most of the battlefield, and convenient downlinks from various imagery assets.

These advantages outweighed the vulnerability of being exposed to direct enemy fire, so I decided to issue the orders from the war room, reassess the situation at daybreak, and consider heading out to the field with my FCG.

I wanted everyone to hear me when I issued the order to attack on the radio. It was important that they understand the big picture and how all brigades fit in to the divisional effort, and that they develop commitment to it. I wanted them to sense that they were not alone, and to fully comprehend the significance of the moment.

The headquarters was bustling feverishly. It had been three weeks of war, and we were finally attacking. I took the radio in my hand.

"Sela stations, this is Sela Actual. Orders, over."

"Orders, over," the brigade commanders acknowledged one by one.

We had conducted the orders group, they had been briefed, and I had visited them all to ensure that they understood the plans, but now it was important to follow this ceremony over the radio, as both subordinates and higher echelons listened. The measured orders would alert everyone, raise the pulse, enhance understanding, and connect everyone.

"An entire country expects us to succeed," I said.

"An entire nation!" someone corrected me. "An entire nation," I agreed, and then went on to point out directions of attack, the various missions, and a few points of emphasis.

"Move out to your missions. Over and out."

The forces launched toward their missions. Fighter jets dove toward their designated targets, ships opened fire in the western region, and the division's fires center unleashed a heavy bombardment aimed at overwhelming the enemy with massive, simultaneous strikes. We unofficially called it "red barrels," as we were to shoot at the same time until all barrels turned red.

The paratroopers moved out, infiltrating toward Bint Jbeil, in order to dominate its western flank and surround it. Herev dashed toward the eastern region, to grab the eastern flank of HRC 3. The 7th Brigade's tanks fired from Jal a-Dir and Maroun al-Ras at targets in the Bint Jbeil area. Carmeli completed its replacement of the paratroopers at Ayta. Only the 101st Battalion remained there in order to give the reservists a strong foothold and smooth transfer of the region which had been captured in two days of fighting. Alexandroni's recon battalion moved toward the Batzil Ridge in order to secure the eastern flank of the brigade and engage Hezbollah villages. The 300th Brigade began combing the villages close to the border fence.

It was all working according to plan.

But there were troubling reports from Roni's battalion in the western sector. As they breached the minefield and crossed the border, loud explosions were heard. Was it mortars? Maybe the detonation of a belly charge?

I understood that the force had stopped its movement and was evacuating a few casualties. I was very troubled. We couldn't stop the momentum. I spoke to Shlomi on the radio and expressed my concern.

"They will resume movement shortly," he said.

"Shlomi, this will stop the attack momentum. They should not deal with casualties now, but leave a few medics. Push forward!"

Roni's battalion continued its movement through a long and difficult route in a wadi filled with terraces. I knew the place very well, after having led my soldiers as a company commander to set up ambushes. I knew how hard it was.

Another delay.

"Shlomi, what's happening?"

"Roni is stuck there in the wadi. It's very difficult and he's moving slowly. The llamas are also a problem – they can't make it up the terraces."

A few months earlier, I had borrowed the llamas from a llama farm owned by an old friend from Shaldag. They proved very efficient at carrying seventy kilos (155 pounds) of equipment. They didn't flinch under fire and even provided warmth when it was cold. But now, inside the deep wadi, they couldn't make it over the high terraces.

"He must reach the junction. Look at the time!"

"It's not going to happen tonight," Shlomi said decisively, pessimistically.

"Can I talk to him directly?" I thought I could influence Roni and give him good advice.

Roni was happy to hear my voice. "How are you, sir?"

"Hi, Roni," I said in a relaxed, soft voice, although I was very stressed. I knew how intonation could affect him. He explained the situation.

"Listen," I said, going over the features of his location in my mind. "Leave all your heavy gear. It will catch up with you later. Take your battalion and proceed only with personal gear and weapons, and LMGs [light machine guns]. Climb westward, up the little ravine that is slightly ahead. Run ahead and take that junction. We must create a new situation at daybreak, Roni."

"Leave everything here?"

"Yes. Engineering will follow, break open a route for Oren's tanks, and the heavy equipment will come later with the llamas and the APCs. Don't delay, go fast and lightweight, engage the villages with fire and take over that junction. We have a mission, Roni!"

"I understand. It will be done," Roni said, encouraged. "I'm running."

"Run, Roni. You can do it!"

And he did.

Seeping and Diffusion – Or Friction and Contact

The sun rose over southern Lebanon, and I was satisfied, as the night infiltration went well. This was a form of advance to contact maneuver by which instead of engagement, our forces seeped through enemy lines, into their ranks. It was clear to me that Hezbollah couldn't defend the entire area – not even its key positions. Nightly infiltration on foot was taking away its advantages – snipers, ATMs, and mines on the roads.

Many years earlier, in my high school lab, I had learned the scientific characteristics of mixing different substances. I found similarities to those processes in advanced doctrines of force movement, allowing swift seizing of territory while avoiding contact and circumventing difficulties and barriers.

I valued this mode of operation and found it suitable and effective in many situations, depending of course on the enemy's nature and deployment. I proved its suitability during training and exercises throughout the preparation and learning period before the war. I viewed criticism and mocking of terminology such as the "cloud of wasps," the "humming effect," and the "swarms" as a lack of creativity and imagination.

I truly believed that maneuvering without distinct vector patterns in a chaotic and unpredictable manner could collapse almost any rival system. This pattern means positioning asymmetry against asymmetry, and in doing so, creating a new symmetry: "swarms" versus guerilla troops; commandos versus irregular forces; "flooding," "diffusion," and "seeping" versus close battle abundant with ATMs and IEDs.

But here there was another problem, and it related not only to the ability of our forces to comprehend the mission. The commanders in the field had understood. They had received a simple, tactical mission, and the accumulation of all the missions made it into a different, advanced systemic picture. The big picture was for senior commanders to comprehend. Not all understood it, and I didn't have time to explain it to everyone. Those who had served and trained with the division knew and understood. But those who had joined us during the war from different backgrounds thought these were fantasies.

"Your job is to fantasize, and mine is to bring you back down to earth," Hagai told me jokingly when I briefed him on Bint Jbeil.

After the war, during a personal debriefing we held, he said: "I thought you were fantasizing. You saw Bint Jbeil from the beginning and soon began talking with me about Tebnine and Haris Junction. I thought these were fantasies, but we really got there. You really meant it."

Of course I had meant it. But I had also intended to make it there in a night or two, using our "diffusion" tactics that we had developed and rehearsed. But in this war we didn't begin any form of attack maneuver until the beginning of August! It was only defense and raids. After all the planning and training – under fire – NORTHCOM refused to implement all that we had prepared, and had us doing things we had never planned or trained to do.

The accumulation of hundreds of simultaneous infiltration missions from various directions was designed to create the "humming" effect. A wise combination of kinetic strikes and psychological warfare brought about this deadly, combined, and decisive effect. This was how the successful maneuvers were conducted during the war. But where we acted in a linear, modeled fashion – as doctrinally suitable for the Syrian front – we played into the hands of Hezbollah.

And there was another problem: the expectation of quick achievements. The political and military leadership wanted to see many dead enemy fighters and documented perceptional accomplishment in fighting against guerillas.

When a mission is defined as conducting a raid and killing as many enemy fighters as possible, this requires pushing for engagement, creating friction, and bringing to bear our comparative advantages in short-range combat, especially at night and in urban terrain, following our vast experience in J&S. This form of close combat, which took place during the first days of the war, led to our forces killing many Hezbollah fighters: thirty at Maroun al-Ras, more than a hundred at Bint Jbeil, and approximately eighty at Ayta.

We had lost some thirty soldiers during these battles – the price of choosing this pattern of friction and engagement. This is what I was ordered to do up until COD 8 in the beginning of August. They wanted battlefield footage, they wanted heavy enemy casualties, they wanted to see bodies, they wanted POWs, and they wanted it fast. But in fighting guerilla warfare, one cannot expect to see images such as the toppling of Saddam Hussein's statue in

Baghdad during Operation Iraqi Freedom. A photographed achievement such as this when facing guerilla forces is extremely exceptional and rare.

When following these instructions, I chose to go to direct engagement, immediate friction, and urban battles in various forms, mainly placing ambushes. But there was an opponent, and sometimes it was he waiting for us. This was how we lost the eight Golani soldiers at Bint Jbeil and the five at Maroun al-Ras. This is war!

From the moment the SSP concept emerged, and the GS and NORTH-COM recalled the Magen Ha'aretz plan, as we had practiced and rehearsed – only then was the division requested to capture key locations, move forward, conquer areas and enemy groups, isolate zones, and comb them later. This was exactly what we had wanted all along. This was what we had trained for. And we implemented this from the first night of the attack, in COD 8, on the night of July 31, 2006.

Delays in Advancement

"Now you sleep," ordered Tal, and I obeyed immediately, asking to be woken two hours later.

It was imperative to maintain continuity and not to halt the momentum. Following the forces were engineering units, trying to breach new routes in the rear of the fighting forces, for logistics and reinforcements. The terrain was challenging and they were under constant fire, but they were brave and pushed on tirelessly.

Not far from Rosh Hanikra, MAJ (Res.) Nimrod Hilel climbed into a bulldozer, replacing the driver, and led the preparation of tank ramps, so they could supply cover for the continuation of logistics work. An ATM penetrated the vehicle and he was killed instantly. He died setting a personal example and demonstrating the creed instilled in Bahad 1: "Follow me!"

My situational assessment concluded that Hezbollah had not yet identified and understood the overall scope of our maneuver. Here and there, short battles took place between Alexandroni soldiers and Hezbollah fighters in and around the western region villages. In one instance, a force had entered a house and found a group of women seated on a couch. When the commander insisted that they rise, they revealed an antiaircraft squad of three men, fully equipped. They were apprehended and taken to interrogation.

Another force hid between Rajamin and the nearby nature reserve, assuming

Hezbollah would need to resupply. Sure enough, a group of Hezbollah fighters came up heavily from the gully, unaware of the ambush awaiting them. Well-trained Alexandroni reservists took aim, and the enemy fighters fell with a short burst of fire. The nature reserve was neutralized and its launching capability destroyed. But there were many more rockets coming from the north.

In the evening hours, engineering forces breached the way, and tanks I had assigned to Shlomi made their way toward Rajamin Junction, held by Roni's men. A bulldozer quickly prepared a protective ramp, and they positioned themselves and began firing.

I needed approval to move westward in order to complete the engagement with the area of Tyre, but it had not yet come. This wasn't good. I thought of flying a small team to the ridge overlooking the area, so it could direct fire onto the rocket launchers firing into Israel. At least they would give us visual cover until Shlomi's forces made it there. I knew it would be best if I could put my hands on an elite team from Shaldag or Maglan, but all special forces had been taken from me and put under a newly established special forces headquarters, intended for operating deep inside Lebanon and not in my AOR.

"Shlomi, I want your recon battalion to extract a team to the rear, which will prepare and deploy by helicopter to Shakif el-Hardun and remain there until you link up with it later."

"That's impossible. How can I pull them out now?"

"It's important," I insisted. "Hezbollah are firing at our towns from that area, and you haven't reached it yet!"

Shlomi insisted, and requested to join me and explain. He arrived with his operations officer, and they explained why they thought there wasn't enough time. He did not disclose the real reason, which was that the recon battalion's commander, feeling ill, had been evacuated to the rear, and his absence was having a negative impact on his battalion.

I calculated time and space and understood that it couldn't take place that night. I also got word that we might receive Maglan for the mission, and that, in general, there had been approval to push forward toward the coastline.

"Continue, Shlomi," I asked. "Tonight you push on toward the western region and complete the mission."

"OK." He got up, and obviously embarrassed, insisted to further explain: "This is not reluctance to fulfill the mission. We would like to perform the helicopter landing. It's just that it doesn't work out."

"Clear, Shlomi. Continue and don't stop. Good luck."

A few hours later I received official orders to proceed to the coastline.

During the night, Eran's battalion was supposed to make its way to Rajamin Junction, their equipment carried on APCs. One of them turned over, and all the equipment was trapped underneath.

Eran's forces reached the area of the junction, but without their gear, they had to stop and could not proceed as planned. Roni's battalion continued his "presence phase" as planned and as trained, initiated engagement, and combed the villages, taking prisoners to interrogation.

In the morning I received word that a Kornet ATM had hit one of the tanks at the junction – three soldiers were killed and one injured. A Black Hawk helicopter flew in fast and low to extract him, and the tank was towed to the rear.

Also in the eastern arena, the advancement was hardly apparent. Despite my repeated pressure on Amnon, 7th Brigade was extremely slow. What was going on out there? I went to see Amnon, and his explanations did not satisfy me.

"Go there yourself," I directed. "Personally enter that sector and open up the blockage."

In the western region, I ran over to Shlomi's FCG and asked that they push on. An argument erupted. There were problems with moving vehicles on the breached dirt road. A bulldozer that finally arrived ran out of fuel, so they improvised a makeshift fuel tank which they welded onto the blade, but it wasn't enough – there were other reasons for delay.

During the argument, MG Ben-Reuven arrived and joined the conversation. Tones escalated. I was insisting that they push on despite the logistical setbacks. The asphalt roads were not safe, but I wanted to airlift or airdrop – whatever it took to move on.

Shlomi's FCG was clearly in distress, and we both held our ground in the argument. I broke off to consult with Eyal, and together we devised a way to bridge the gaps. It was decided that forward movement would commence within a few hours. But then came another setback. A Navy commando operation was to take place, and NORTHCOM decided we could not get in their way – so the order came to dig in and hold until the following day.

I still insisted that we must land a team on the ridge overlooking Tyre. I finally got Maglan. Eliezer, Maglan's commander, had been called home to his wife, who was giving birth. He requested to stay on duty, but I demanded that he go to the hospital and leave Amos, his deputy, in charge.

I briefed Amos: "I want you to 'freeze' the area south of Tyre. Make it so no one can move or fire rockets from there. Meet me for a final briefing at Dovev, where I will be briefing Finkel's Steel Chariots before their incursion into the central sector."

Finkel Route

Dovev outpost became Finkel's forward HQ. Between the area of Maroun al-Ras and Ayta was an entire zone with operational significance. In my opinion, it was correct to use this space where not much was going on, just as a ball is sometimes kicked to a remote area of the soccer field. The idea was to stretch the enemy's efforts. I wanted to send Steel Chariots to the region between Yaroun and Ayta, while opening a new route using the division's engineering battalion. They had trained extensively for this mission.

Before entering Finkel's HQ, I approved Amos's plans.

Maglan's mission included more than thirty operators equipped with advanced technology. They were self-sustainable for a few days, and were to wait until Shlomi's force arrived. They were to direct PGMs from air, sea, and land toward launching sites; kill enemy fighters; and push the enemy north of Tyre.

"Good luck, Amos. This is a very important mission. I trust you to take Acre out of rocket range."

I had just received word that eight civilians had been killed in the Israeli town of Acre.

"Thank you, sir."

Next I listened to Finkel's brief and gave a few points of emphasis.

I wanted to have tank fire toward Bint Jbeil augment the paratroopers' effort. Together with 7th Brigade, this would mean the town would be targeted from all directions. Finkel was to breach a new, hidden, and surprising route because all the regular ones were booby-trapped.

Lutfi came over. "Gal, NORTHCOM doesn't approve Maglan's mission. They say that the Air Force objects because they won't be able to rescue them and it's too dangerous."

I was about to explode with anger. Dangerous?! For an elite commando unit? But civilians were being killed in Acre! What was going on here?

"I'm finishing up with Finkel in a moment, Lutfi. Tell NORTHCOM that I object to their objection. Tell Amos *not* to stop, and to continue as planned. Tell Dror to assume command of the region for an hour and tell NORTHCOM that I'm on my way, and they should set up an urgent meeting with the CO!"

The Israel Defense Force

"It's good that you came," I was told when I reached NORTHCOM.

"Gal, there's a dilemma here about Maglan," Udi said, straight to the point. "The Air Force has reservations. What do you say?"

"I say that we are the *Israel Defense Force!*" I raised my voice. It must have sounded strange to Udi and his staff. It felt strange to me.

"Civilians are being killed in Acre. We will set out with the best soldiers our nation has. In a day or two Alexandroni will link up with them. If there's a problem, we can extract them or resupply them from the sea. What is it? I don't get it! I insist that this mission be carried out!" I shouted.

People shrank in their seats in light of my onslaught. A representative from the History Department was recording and taking notes. The room became silent.

"OK," Udi said, after a minute of thought. "Give them approval."

"Thank you." Relieved, I ran out to the hallway, looking for Lutfi, who was waiting for me, attentive and stressed."

"They can take off!"

He said nothing, only turned on his heel and dashed out to the radios in the jeep.

Chapter 19

"As Fast as Your Heart Beats"

"God Help You if You Don't!"

"What's happening with you guys, Shlomi?" I inquired of the Alexandroni Brigade commander.

"We're fine."

"What do you mean, fine? You aren't moving."

"There are some problems."

"What problems?"

"The tanks aren't moving because there isn't a bulldozer to shave the asphalt off roads to uncover the expected IEDs. Eran is already on the outskirts of the Shama village, and the tanks – "

"Have them move forward without a bulldozer. It's a reasonable risk – this is war!"

"I know, but the tank battalion commander isn't budging."

"Do you want me to speak to him?"

"Go ahead."

I called him over the encrypted radio, and he answered me right away: "Yes, sir."

"Why aren't you moving your tanks westward? It's urgent you get there! They're shooting at Nahariya and Acre. Your tanks are very important to us on the Shakif el-Hardun ridge, and tonight special forces will be there already. You need to rendezvous with them," I emphasized.

"Sir, I understand, but I can't move without the engineers, and they aren't available, and there are going to be fuel problems because this is the Merkava Mark 3, and – "

I couldn't listen to this anymore, and the entire war room was shocked by my shouting at the battalion commander: "Get a hold of yourself and start moving, do you hear me?! Get your tanks moving forward. This is no exercise and this is no simple patrol along the fence – this is war! Put your mission in motion right away, and God help you if you don't!"

The war room was silent; they had never heard me yell before. The war had been going on for three weeks now, and I had yet to raise my voice. But during these few hours I had been shouting at everybody – even at Udi. What was happening to me?

"Wilco," replied the battalion commander.

I dropped into my chair exhausted. "Can you get me a bottle of water?" I asked.

"There are supply problems with Eran's battalion," Shlomi updated. "They want to break into a local supermarket."

"To take what?" I asked.

"Water," he answered. "And maybe a few more things," he added.

"Water is fine; let them break in and take what they need. We'll pay them back after the war through the UN," I said. "But nothing else – there can't be any looting."

"Of course," Shlomi answered. "They will only take water."

"Fine."

At the end of the war, the soldiers from the Alexandroni Brigade complained that I had accused them of looting. It was the journalist Nahum Barnea who had provided his own interpretation of the dialogue between Shlomi and me on the subject of breaking into the supermarket.

"I wrote it because that is what they told me," he said in his defense.

"You could have simply asked me!" I hurled back bitterly. He had not even taken the time to clarify the facts with me, and by not doing so he had tainted my relationship with my reserve soldiers, presenting me as insensitive and irresponsible. It was only after the war was over that he admitted in his column that he had been mistaken about me. But who paid attention to that amidst the massive media storm? The damage had already been done.

This was not the first time the Israeli media had accused and convicted me before clarifying the facts.

Despite these rough moments, from this point on, the missions went well. All were carrying out their missions. COD 8 was going according to plan and would be completed within three days, even though I had wanted and hoped that it wouldn't take more than two.

We carried out the missions, although not according to schedule, I thought to myself. But what was the significance of time here? There were no stipulations in the order issued by NORTHCOM, and the section beginning with the words "in order to" (in other words, the expressed purpose of the mission) was unclear. What was the reason for moving forward, beyond the desire to kill the enemy and to control more territory? Aside from a few general statements at the beginning of the war concerning the killing of enemy fighters, and then later about controlling key areas of territory, there had been no forward strategic planning.

I did not comprehend what achieving the objective was supposed to lead to, so without this coherence, the objective seemed meaningless, and the next expected stage was unclear. The result was that most of the time, I aggressively initiated maneuvers myself and then put them into action – sometimes after a discussion with NORTHCOM and sometimes not. I also was unable to carry out my plans in one step, as I had planned. Our forces were restrained by a sort of leash and collar, and when I tried to run, the collar pulled me back.

In the western sector, Maglan soldiers were pounding Hezbollah. The operation had been even more successful than expected – fifty-six enemy targets were destroyed in two days, the launchings from the area had ceased, and the effect was felt deep inside Israel.

"Nice going, Eliezer!"

"I always aspire to act as fast as your heart beats," Eliezer told me. It was a very special thing to say.

The concept of operation adopted by Maglan in this operation was nothing new to me, and it was easy for me to believe in it. After all, this was the way Shaldag had operated under my command back in Operation Grapes of Wrath in 1996 – dispersed warfare – "swarming" at its best.

Alexandroni forces linked up with Maglan as I had planned. In a firefight in Ras el-Bayada, one of the reserve soldiers was wounded and evacuated. The western sector was completely under our control. Now we needed to go to the "presence stage" for searches and opening routes. But intel reports showed that HRC 1 had been crushed, and I saw this for myself in the field. Enemy equipment had been collected and enemy fighters were brought in for interrogation. This was decisiveness. In a joint operation with elite units – Navy, Air Force, and Alexandroni and 300th Brigades – the western sector had been "extinguished."

Reserve forces still saw launches toward Israel, not far north – a very frustrating sight – but this was the way it would be. The more we progressed, the more the rockets retreated, and the launches would always be north of us. The current plan was limited in its scope, and there was no plan and no intention to conquer all of Lebanon.

Continuation of Combat in Ayta

Concerning HRCs 2 and 3 in the central sector, I was not satisfied at all. In the Ayta region, Carmeli continued its operations. Their mission was to secure the flank of the forces proceeding toward Bint Jbeil. The transportation route to Bint Jbeil and Jabal Amel was adjacent to Ayta and was exposed to the rear.

There were enemy casualties, but we also had sustained casualties, and it was irritating. The forces moved forward toward Koza and Bint Jbeil, but there was still fighting in the area close to the border. I had no intention of searching the entire village of Ayta, nor was I able to do so, at least not at this stage. The paratroopers had taken control of the city and had inflicted heavy casualties on Hezbollah, but then COD 8 orders were issued. I wanted the paratroopers to take Bint Jbeil and the surrounding area, so I replaced them with Carmeli, while ordering one regular service paratroopers battalion to remain, in order to enable a safe and gradual entry for Ilan and his reserve units. These paratroopers would then gradually fall back and join their brigade.

Unexplained pressure was put on me from Tel Aviv to complete the overtaking of Ayta. I did not understand the reason for this, for the village had actually already been captured. It was surrounded and neutralized, and slowly, but surely and carefully, "grinded" using bulldozers, tanks, and infantry. This did not in any way hold back the advancement of the attack, because I had intentionally isolated it with the mission of the paratroopers, and – most importantly – Carmeli continued to maintain the route to Debel open. It's not that the area was entirely clear. An occasional ATM was fired at our forces, but this was natural for such a complex area, and it was expected that completely clearing it would take time. Considering the extent of forces at my disposal, and in light of the scope of our missions, I thought it was reasonable.

I objected to the pressure to fully conquer Ayta, as searches to neutralize every threat would require many long days because the forces would have to operate carefully to reduce casualties.

I addressed Eyal and Udi on the matter and received confirmation to my understandings: "You're right. Keep it neutralized, and keep going forward."

I allocated the forces I had to Ilan – bulldozers, artillery, air support tanks, and Roni's excellent armored battalion from Finkel's brigade.

The battle at Ayta continued while I tried to achieve the surrender of enemy forces through a negotiating team, special forces, and activating observation and ATM units. Heavy fighting took place in the village – many enemy fighters were killed – and the bulldozers advanced slowly and demolished enemy positions in the casbah.

But the pressure from the outside continued. Kaplan, Halutz, and Eizenkot all called Ilan *directly* to see if "everything was all right," if he "understood his mission in Ayta," and other unnecessary expressions.

Somewhat stressed, Ilan came to my FCG. "What do they want from me, Gal?"

"Keep going, and turn up the pressure," I said, trying to calm him down. "That's all, nothing's changed. Your job is to neutralize the village, so it doesn't bother our forces advancing toward Bint Jbeil and Jabal Amel. Secure this route for me, Ilan, and finish up in the village as soon as you can."

Ilan's troops were entering houses and operating from within them. There is no better cover in an urban environment, but these houses sometimes turn into traps. A salvo of ATMs hit a house where a company was located, and one of the soldiers was killed. A subsequent fire broke out, suffocating the soldiers. This trying incident ended with a few casualties.

That same night, Ilan decided to move the battalion that was hit to the rear. It was a serious mistake, since it breached the array clamping down on Ayta. The achievements were abandoned to Hezbollah, and it would later take Ilan a long time to retake this area, with the help of his excellent deputy brigade commander, LTC Hoshea Friedman. Worse than that, the unauthorized decision was not reported to me, so I did not understand why the combat in Ayta was taking so long. I only found out about it during a postwar debriefing.

Change of Direction (COD) 9

North of the village, the paratroopers had taken control of the A-Taire area and dominated Bint Jbeil from the west. The situation concerned me, as we were in a relatively lower area compared to the Sylvester ridge. I had been requesting to capture the ridge for a long time, but was never authorized to do so. On August 4, I put in another request, ordered Hagai to commence planning, and updated Eyal Ben-Reuven. This time authorization was given. On August 5, the paratroopers moved toward Shakif al-Nimel. Herev Battalion, which was allocated to 7th Brigade, moved toward Beit Yahoun, and the ridge was taken. Now only one objective remained in order to complete the mission I had planned prior to the war – the Haris Junction and the region of Jabal Amel.

With the wisdom of hindsight, it was a mistake not to move directly toward the junction in the first stage of the offensive. I had requested this and had not received authorization, but maybe I should have fought harder than I did. In my opinion, taking the Haris Junction and engaging Tebnine in the first night of combat, just as I had planned in MHTA, could have shortened the war. I believe that a new operational term needs to be introduced into the language of senior commanders – "campaign-shortening moves." But the battles in this war were managed like routine security operations – authorizing each operation one by one (a "reverse salami," as we coined it – constructing the salami slice by slice). It's a shame, but how many times could I make a scene, and how many arguments could I conduct during combat?

Maybe I should have "turned off the radio" and run forward, disregarding orders? What impact would this have had on NORTHCOM? Could I have done the same thing I did back when I was Shaldag commander? It's one thing doing it with a handful of soldiers behind enemy lines, but an entire division is a completely different story. I decided not to break the chain of command, and to carry out orders. I certainly interpreted them broadly every now and again – I initiated and aggressively strove to engage the enemy – but I made sure to uphold the spirit and essence of the order.

A commanding officer in the field often encounters this leadership and command dilemma: how much to stick to the order, and how much to act according to its spirit and take the initiative and at times even perform contradicting actions. The decision of which course of action to take needs to be revisited over and over. It's a continuous process of personal decisions about one's own comportment, about loyalty, about responsibility for the continuity of command and the military structure, and about responsibility for the Spirit of the IDF. One must always take into account the atmosphere and level of trust between commanders and soldiers, and between military leaders amongst themselves.

For me, this is an inherent tension in generalship, and I had faced it many times. The art of bridging it is one of the skills every military leader needs to master.

In the meantime, reserve units from other divisions were being recruited, in preparation for a large-scale operation. I hoped they would finally approve the full-scale operation according to the CONPLAN.

I was trying to initiate a move where I would continue toward the Litani River or encircle Tyre, in order to achieve a substantial operational and perceptional impact, but I failed to bring NORTHCOM around to my point of view.

"Relax," I was told, "you have plenty of missions as it is."

Turn Around and Go Back

"Gal, we want you to capture Bint Jbeil," Eyal Ben-Reuven told me.

"What?!"

"Yes, you will get Golani back, and you are to capture the city."

"What's the point? We passed it already, and it's now in the rear of our forces. I am already on the Sylvester Ridge, facing Jabal Amel, Tebnine, and the Haris Junction. This should be the next step as far as I am concerned."

"I know," Eyal said, "but they want a significant achievement for public awareness: to capture the city, remain there, and raise a flag."

"Turn around and go back?" I asked again. I couldn't believe what I was hearing.

I then spoke to Kaplan and tried to make sense of what they wanted.

"You need to conquer," Kaplan told me. "Capture the governmental area and bring in columns of tanks to the center of the city so we can traverse it without being bothered."

"That requires making house-to-house searches. It will take time. There is a difference between taking control and capturing and thoroughly combing."

"That is what needs to be done, and this time make proper logistic lines. Not like the first time."

"Kaplan, the first time was defined as a raid! You don't build logistic lines for a forty-eight-hour operation. Neither do you bring in tanks if they might get stuck. You saw their antitank capabilities. Tanks need to be employed moderately and following proper planning. Now you say conquer? I will breach the routes and bring in armored columns."

"Thanks a lot," Kaplan replied sarcastically.

"You're welcome," I answered in the same tone.

At that time, there was a plan to bring the minister of defense to speak in Bint Jbeil, and also Benny Gantz had spoken to me more than once about Bint

Jbeil being a perceptional achievement, to contrast with Nasrallah's famous "spider web" speech.

"When will you be ready for the operation?" the NORTHCOM war room was pressing.

"Let me do some planning, I will let you know in a few hours."

"It needs to be right away..."

I set aside all concerns and focused on the task at hand.

My plan was to implement a powerful, simultaneous attack on the city from all directions and from all dimensions: air, ground, and perceptional. Initially there was to be infiltration and taking control of dominating key areas, then several long days of cleaning up, introducing armored vehicles, and ensuring the captured city's civil functionality by an IDF governing unit that I had under my command.

When darkness fell, I asked Joad, the commander of the FCG, to quickly prepare for entering deep into enemy territory. I wanted to observe the field again, to walk the ground myself and ensure the plan was robust.

A small group of vehicles was prepared. Not far from Avivim, we turned sharply to the north, in order to avoid detection by the enemy, and sped into Lebanese territory. Joad spoke quietly into his radio, communicating location codes with neighboring forces. My small convoy stopped near a building between Maroun al-Ras and Bint Jbeil. I linked up with the commander there and observed the area with him. I requested to organize a small team for a foot patrol.

"Is there a problem with that?" I asked.

"No problem, sir," he said, and ran to get a machine gunner, sharpshooter, radio operator, and everything that was required.

We moved out and made our way downhill, toward the outskirts of Bint Jbeil. I switched between night-vision goggles and binoculars to assess the terrain, and consulted with the team members, etching various understandings in my mind. I returned early in the morning, soaked with sweat, to the position of the FCG, to complete the plan and construct the order for an attack into the heart of HRC 3, the Aynata Ridge, Tzaf al-Haawa Junction, and the city of Bint Jbeil.

As always, there was a sense that this was to be the final maneuver of the war, because as we were continually being told, there was "no time."

I designated the four reduced brigades under my command for the attack, along with an artillery brigade, all of the division staff elements, and a special Air Force task force which worked with the fire and intel centers. As previously mentioned, these pivotal centers had been combined before the war, and they performed well together. It was anything but a simple decision, but the contribution to the war effort was clear. Information was quickly processed into targets – a critical quality in a war against time-sensitive targets (TSTs).

I planned to turn around the paratroopers, who had already passed Bint Jbeil, and have them attack their targets from an unexpected direction – from the city's rear.

I was sorry to see most of the brigade's forces leave their advantageous positions on the Sylvester ridge and Shakif al-Nimel, but there was no choice. I could not hold so much territory, certainly not when the paratroopers would be attacking in an urban environment, which would naturally swallow up forces. One house could sometimes engage an entire company.

I received Golani as planned, and I designated them to attack from east to west, along Amnon route, through the 7th Brigade, toward territory dominating the village of Aynata. They were to attack at the same time the paratroopers attacked, and right in front of them as they attacked from west to east.

This plan would ensure that all of the controlling areas on the Tzaf al-Haawa Junction would be engaged and attacked at the same time. In the past, this had been a central intersection in the city. As far as I was concerned, it was key territory, and I considered taking it to be the act by which COD 10 would be decided.

I left the 7th and Steel Chariots Brigades in their positions, which controlled the Bint Jbeil region from Yaroun–Maroun al-Ras ridges. I planned for Finkel's forces to continue forging a route for armored fighting vehicles (AFVs) toward the outskirts of Bint Jbeil, adjacent to the Shalabun Ridge, so tanks could be brought to firing positions in the area where the paratroopers were operating – an unexpected location and nonconventional route for tanks. This would enable an attack from all directions with tanks and infantry toward key areas. The fires center would coordinate artillery and aerial assets and pound Hezbollah with a massive blast of firepower, as planned prior to the war, and as had been put into action from the beginning of the divisional battles at the start of the month.

I completed my instructions to the logistics and manpower center (LMC) and determined the PIR and collection missions for the intel center. I verified the command and control method with the teleprocessing center, issued more assignments in the field of perception, and dictated the mission and operational concept to the operations center. Following a situational assessment session and choosing a course of action, we had plans. Now they needed to be turned into written orders, battle layout charts, and professional plans.

I presented the plans to Eyal.

Green light to proceed.

"Golani Is with You!"

The first battle at Bint Jbeil was defined as a "raid," and the required outcome was maximum Hezbollah operatives killed, which is why I chose an approach of high friction and direct engagement. Now I was implementing a different approach, so I decided to neutralize HRC 3 by severing it from its logistic rear – the city of Tebnine. The extent of enemy casualties was less important at this stage. This I deduced from NORTHCOM's operational order – not friction, but gaining control. We finally returned to the reasoning behind MHTA.

My goal was to correctly identify the system constructed by the enemy, or enforce upon the situation a systemic logic, codify it as a system, and then dismantle it.

I thought we could do without conquering Bint Jbeil on the way to crushing HRC 3, but since the rationale was to achieve a perceptional effect, and taking Bint Jbeil was defined as a required achievement, my plan was aimed at reaching it.

The plan was to grip the city from both sides of the main junction, cutting off the city from its rear and attacking from all directions – literally 360 degrees. While I was briefing the orders to the commanders, Tamir, the Golani Brigade commander, indicated that he wished to have a word with me. I nodded.

"We very much appreciate what you're doing," he said. "When we heard we were assigned back to the 91st Division, there were cries of joy in our brigade."

I was silent and looked at him. Much criticism was voiced about the division's conduct during the preliminary stages of the war. Some of it had reached the press directly from Tamir, and some from LTC Mordechai Kahana, Egoz commander, who was under Tamir's command. Tamir had already tried to apologize during the raid on Bint Jbeil, at the end of July. "I didn't know it was for an article," he said. "You know that reporter. I only talked to him . . . I didn't know he was going to publish it."

Yes, I knew that reporter, and I had seen him stalking Tamir's headquarters from the beginning of the war.

But now, during the last few days, I had been receiving heartwarming verbal and text messages from Golani commanders, expressing appreciation, support, and comradeship.

I looked at Tamir for a long time. He was a very good brigade commander, and we formed a good connection during the war. His words seemed honest. I was silent. I didn't know what to say. I thought it would be best to focus on the war and not internal tensions, so I chose to leave him with a good feeling.

After the war, a senior officer told me that Tamir had told NORTHCOM Commander that "If there is another war, I am only following one division commander – Gal."

"Golani is with you!" he concluded. Then we got up and embraced.

"Good luck, Tamir."

On August 7, the division began the capture of Bint Jbeil under the name COD 10. The attack was carried out by Golani, Paratroopers, 7th, Steel Chariots, and artillery brigades.

Before the advancing forces, our fires center coordinated a massive combined strike on Hezbollah strongholds, including nature reserves, in order to prepare and suppress the area before entering the urban area.

Under the cover of these preliminary attacks, Golani and the paratroopers proceeded according to the plan, from both sides of the Tzaf al-Haawa Junction.

Tanks from the 7th and Steel Chariots Brigades proceeded toward their positions and fired at targets within the city. We had learned important lessons from Hezbollah's use of deadly antitank capabilities: our battle formations included bulldozers embedded into every tank platoon. They quickly erected earth barriers, allowing Merkava turrets to emerge and spit fire for several seconds before backing down for protection.

"That's the way to do it!" the tankers said enthusiastically. "This is how you operate tanks in a battlefield!"

First Battalion Exercise under Fire

A large percentage of the regular service tankers were not skilled enough in operating their tanks. Most commanders had never experienced a company-level exercise, much less a battalion or brigade one. They had been busy carrying out routine security missions in J&S and Gaza. Now they were quickly adapting and learning the doctrine, while fighting. Interestingly, the reservists, who had extensively exercised before the war, were more professional.

Tankers were not the only ones who weren't trained. Most of the battalion commanders performed their first battalion-level maneuvers during the war. Many of the brigade commanders had participated in computer-simulated tactical training sessions, but not out in the field. I was happy that my division had comprehensively trained all brigade commanders before the war.

The role of battalion commanders is central and crucial in fighting units. It is a senior position but at the same time very "soldierly." A battalion commander is a fighting soldier himself, leading from the front, and it is his spirit that defines the spirit of the entire unit. Without him, a battallion is no more than a bunch of companies. His leadership is the binding glue and the driving force. Although our battalion commanders had not trained enough before the war, most of them performed remarkably, relying heavily on the strength of their leadership and personal example on the battlefield.

The battles in the city continued, and a new problem emerged: I was surprised to learn that the Air Force had limited the number of targets we could attack in any given hour. Additionally, attack helicopters could only attack from within "corridors" cleared from our own artillery fire. This limited our flexibility, and it took us much valuable time to figure out how to operate artillery and helicopters simultaneously, at the required operational capacity. I was also surprised to hear that the Air Force forbade helicopter pilots to fly north of a safety line defined *south* of the border, inside Israel, for fear of being hit by antiaircraft fire. In the rare occasions when pilots did cross the border – contradicting the air controller's instructions – they were effective and delivered valuable assistance to ground forces.

I operated, therefore, multi-layer fires, ranging from the high-flying fighter jets through attack helicopters in "corridors" or in alternation with artillery and, at the lowest level, tanks employing low-trajectory fires.

When the forces were all in place, I gave the attack order. Battles were taking place in short ranges within the urban area. Hezbollah, in defending the junction area, fought with what they had left, from within the buildings and the surrounding hills. Unfortunately, as is typical in multidirectional combat, we sustained casualties from "friendly fire" near a large building nicknamed "the monster." As I observed the area through binoculars, I wondered why we hadn't flattened it before the attack.

"Amnon," I asked the commander of our fires center, "can we knock it down?"

"Not anymore. It's too close to our forces now."

I had a serious dilemma with the hospital at Bint Jbeil. We knew for a fact that besides medical purposes, the place served Hezbollah fighters and their commanders. There was no doubt that it fell deep within the definitions of a legitimate military target according to international law. I debated several times whether to attack the building, and also considered sending in special forces. But I assessed that the public relations effect of targeting the hospital might resemble that of the incident at Qana. I postponed direct strikes toward the hospital, but gradually allowed attacking Hezbollah targets closer and closer to the building.

The paratroopers were now operating in close proximity to the hospital. It certainly posed a risk, but still I held back.

"Only if you are being fired at from the hospital, return precision fires," I repeated over and over, adding the words that every officer in the division knew well: "We do not relinquish the Spirit of the IDF and ROE."

It's not that I didn't have doubts, but this was my decision, and I left it at that. I did make up my mind that if we later cleared the city and established military rule, I would send in a special unit to comb the hospital.

During the raging fighting near the junction, Finkel's armored forces proceeded toward the positions I had designated for them, using new routes prepared by our engineering forces. The bulldozers worked continuously day and night in difficult terrain, while tanks protected them from surrounding threats. On the morning of August 7, their effort was detected by Hezbollah, and a barrage of ATMs was fired at the force. During the ensuing battle, a company commander and a soldier were killed.

Zaks, a reserve battalion commander, demonstrated tenacity in the mission, and with his quiet leadership, he stubbornly led his battalion to the top of the ridge, from which they opened fire at the surprised enemy. Hezbollah now understood that this flank was no more secure for them, and that the untraversable route to there had been breached by our armored forces.

"Eizenberg needs you urgently!" I was told one morning.

"Give him to me."

BG Eyal Eizenberg's Airborne Division had traversed mine, in a coordinated corridor, and at daybreak, his front forces took up positions inside houses in the outskirts of the village of Debel. But they were spotted by Hezbollah, and one house sustained a direct hit from a barrage of ATMs.

Eyal asked me to assist in rescuing the many reported casualties. I decided to lead the rescue effort and ordered the recon battalion from Carmeli Brigade, which was deployed near the village of Koza, to head toward Debel. They slid down the ridge on foot and began rescuing casualties. The area was under heavy fire, disabling the possibility of evacuation by helicopters, so the stretchers were carried by the soldiers, running all the way to the border.

"Ilan, what's happening there, report!" I asked Carmeli commander, while I was commanding the battle at Bint Jbeil.

"Gal," he said excitedly, in the midst of conducting the rescue operation, defending the logistic route, and fighting at Ayta, "listen – my recon battalion…they are heroes!"

They most certainly were.

On another day I was commanding the effort to break HRC 3. Hagai updated me on casualties, including from friendly fire.

Under heavy fire, Golani and the paratroopers performed coordinated, mutual assistance and cover. A Golani tank formation was sent by Tamir to help Hagai.

Hanoch, a daring company commander, risked his life under heavy fire to save the paratrooper casualties.

I observed the battle, received intel, and assessed that HRC 3 was soon collapsing. I issued the following update: "A little more pressure. Don't stop; push onward to the junction area."

The Paratrooper Recon Battalion, commanded by Nimrod, continued to operate from one side, 890th Battalion pressed from the controlling area on the other side, and Golani operated in the area of Aynata.

"Gal," Avi, the intel officer, yelled as he came running. "Gal, 'Three' collapsed! They're completely finished. They're fleeing!" He showed me intel material. It was true. They were retreating and searching for refuge, each man to himself.

"What's happening, Gal?" Kaplan, the deputy CGS, called to get an update.

"Listen," I said carefully, "it looks like we broke them. It took a few hours and the city crumbled. They're on the run."

"I agree with you. It certainly looks that way." He had probably read the same reports Avi had shown me moments earlier.

"I want to push forward, Kaplan. Don't want to stop."

"What do you want to do?"

"To go back to the Sylvester Ridge, to Shakif al-Nimel, to Haris and Tebnine," I asserted. "Let us utilize the success. We can't stop!"

There was no point in dealing with the city itself anymore, certainly not to comb and clear it or bring in a military governance unit. For that there would be time later on, if necessary. We needed to move on before Hezbollah set up a new line of defense.

"I agree," said Kaplan, "but there's probably going to be an orderly command-level attack. So hold your position and I'll get back to you."

Orderly attack? Stop now? I grasped my head. But then I took a deep breath and summoned my staff for a situational assessment.

Throughout the division's AOR, the fighting continued, and the forces combed and cleared the area while preparing for the next phase. In the battles north of the Israeli town of Shlomi, we lost two more reserve soldiers from the 300th Brigade. We continued the "presence" activities throughout the region and also prepared ourselves for the closing maneuvers of the war.

Stay Focused

Within a few hours, NORTHCOM's picture crystallized: We were right in assessing the fall of HRC 1 and 3; HRC 2 was still fighting for its life. The Steel Division positioned itself in the area of Taibe. I identified the situation as an opportunity to broaden the offensive to the entire region. Another fresh division, the Path of Fire Division, commanded by BG Erez Zukerman, was also being prepped to join the fight.

"It will operate in the area of Marjeyoun," said Eyal Ben-Reuven, who had joined me in my FCG, appearing upbeat. This was beginning to look like a real maneuver, as Eyal had planned long before the war.

"And what will Guy Tzur's Steel Division do?" I inquired.

"They'll take the Litani River."

"And Eizenberg?" I wanted to know what the elite Airborne Division was set to do.

"They will probably continue in the area of Yater and Kafra."

"Don't get the logic. These are my areas. I planned them, trained for them.

We have geographical continuity. I am positioned a few kilometers from these villages. What's going on here?"

"You've got enough work on your hands," Eyal said, repeating his usual mantra. He attempted to keep calm, but I could sense his frustration.

"Eyal, there's no point in having one division pass through another this way. And I can't open up a 'corridor' in the middle of my division for the Airborne Division."

"By the way," Eyal let down another blow, "prepare to transfer the paratroopers to Eizenberg."

"Where is he headed?"

"The area of Kafra, probably."

"They're a few kilometers away. They can simply walk over there."

"No, they will come back to Israel to reorganize, and they will be flown in by helicopters."

"What?" I couldn't believe it. "But Hagai is so close to his destination. Why take him out and fly him back in?"

"Transferring to another division necessitates an orderly battle procedure and preparation. It's going to take place immediately, so think who can replace him in the area he now holds."

I slumped back on my bulletproof vest.

I leaned over the map, imagining Guy Tzur's movement from east to west along the Litani River. Our division would serve as an anvil, protecting his movement from the high ground overlooking his route.

"Give me a marker."

"Here."

"Eyal, I want to reach here, and here," I pointed to the ridges of Tebnine, Jabal Beit ed Douara, and Haris Junction. "From here I'll cover Guy Tzur, and if something happens in his region, I can replace him, slide northward to the river basin, and then westward toward Tyre."

"Yes, that makes sense. Prepare it and I'll let you know what gets approved."

Eyal was constantly trying to assist Udi in shaping a maneuver that fitted his understanding of Hezbollah. The problem was that entire maneuvers that had been planned before the war were not being approved, and when they were, it was in segments lacking continuous and complete logic, as the many assignments and mission definitions proved.

"I'm driving to the NORTHCOM HQ," said Eyal. "Don't disappear into the field. They'll probably want you to be there for the orders group."

"OK."

"See you later."

"Hagai," I told the paratroopers commander over the radio, "you may be heading out on foot tonight to rejoin your original division, for another assignment."

"OK…" Hagai answered, expecting more.

"Under which division would you rather serve?" I teased him.

"That's not fair," he answered. "It's like asking me who I love more – my mother or my father."

I instructed Hagai as to the sensitivities of transferring divisions. I was always very careful when it came to assisting sister and neighboring units. Having learned the bitter lessons from the 1973 Yom Kippur War, I decided not to let murky relations develop between NORTHCOM and me, and no tensions develop between my division and others.

"We host other units here as if they were princes," I would instruct my staff and brigade commanders, when many IDF forces came through our division during the war. "I don't want to hear any slander or 'war between generals' here."

But at that time a different 'war between generals' was evolving behind my back. Officers who had been far from the fight – in staff jobs or not assigned to NORTHCOM, were intervening, inciting, and sullying.

One brigadier general was calling my subordinates and undermining my authority. He would offer "advice" and warnings, sometimes in reference to orders that had not yet been given, as he had inside information from my commander's table.

Other senior officers acted behind the scenes downward to my subordinates, and upward to the GS. They would contradict and compromise my division's plans by "alerting" senior staff on my moves.

I believe that such negative conduct laid the foundation for the irresponsible interviews given by tactical commanders during the war.

A particularly arrogant example was demonstrated by one brigadier general who sent a note to my commander, asking to replace me during the war. His reasoning: he thought he could do it better than me. It didn't end with that.

During a visit to one of our logistics depots, he briefed a group of reporters that this was "no way to run a war." He even came to the logistics center at my division HQ and told my subordinates that the war wasn't being conducted properly. A few days later, when word had reached him that I knew of his sabotaging behavior, he came to my headquarters and woke me up from a short nap to tell me, "I came to show my support."

Interestingly, this same officer had attacked me in a newspaper interview back when I was commandant of the officers' training school, for relieving one of his subordinates. He was reprimanded by the CGS and called me to apologize and "make peace." I agreed to put it behind us – until he did it to me again during the war.

All this internal undermining and backstabbing was making me extremely heavyhearted, but there was nothing I could do about it then and there.

"Stay focused, Gal," I told myself. "You are fighting a war, and thousands of soldiers are under your responsibility. After the war you can fight them all."

I shed from my back the burden of self-pity, dust, and exhaustion, and bent over my maps. It was already five weeks into the war.

"Lutfi, get my planning team together. We're convening in fifteen minutes."

I began constructing the operational concept and urged myself as to the appropriate attitude: Don't let them linger; fires ahead; engage and contact the next areas; begin preparing the following mission even if not yet approved; attack from standoff; send commandos, ships, jets, artillery; prepare forces for the next phase; collect everyone's assessments on the situation; keep in touch with all the personnel. Speak using a stable and low voice. Stay keen-sensed and sharp.

Presence

The way the campaign had developed, it came about that part of the division was still engaged in stage 2, infiltration, while others had completed this stage and moved on to stage 3, presence.

Before the war we had defined various stages: the fires stage was an early stage of suppression and achieving shock and awe, followed by the stage of infiltration and taking control of key areas. Then came the presence stage, during which we would carefully comb nature reserves and villages – each and every house, cave, and burrow – in order to dismantle the complex system Hezbollah had constructed.

We did not find a customary term for this stage, as it was not part of the attack, was not defense, not advancement, and certainly not retreat. So we coined it "presence" and carried out various activities to ensure proper implementation. We rehearsed and trained it endlessly, aiming at performing it with minimum casualties.

Transitioning to the presence stage entails many dangers. If an enemy operating with subversive and flexible guerilla tactics identifies that the forward momentum of the attacking army has halted, and that it is aligning itself for extended presence, the enemy will quickly adapt and attack the assembling forces, logistics, and the many fixed targets that a regular army provides. We had learned from similar test cases in military history, including our own experience in Lebanon during our extended presence there. Our regular activity was constantly targeted, as were US-led coalition forces in other campaigns in the Middle East, during counterinsurgency phases, coming after the initial invasion phase.

Time and time again it has been demonstrated that the old, classic concept of decisive victory is irrelevant in asymmetric warfare. Continuous learning and accumulated achievements are more relevant. An army must learn how to transform from a wall into bricks, and when necessary, to master the ability to collect all its bricks into a new wall, according to context.

This is how you build a suitable and relevant response when faced by a challenge. War entails learning and creating. It is a continuous process of creation, contradicting what has been created, reconstruction, and so on and so forth – all under harsh conditions and under great pressure.

The division commander's greatest challenge is the continuous translation from the vast accumulation of operational understandings to the techno-military realm. From idea, concept, and creation, to plans and orders, briefings and debriefings, training, and preparations for the mission. It isn't easy. Laying all the bridging network between the echelons and the components of military actions is a work of art.

I believe that this is the art of war in our time.

At the time when I was working on the attack on Haris Junction and Tebnine region, as part of the overall NORTHCOM plan, the 300th, Alexandroni, Carmeli, and segments of the 7th and Steel Chariots Brigades were already engaged in combing and clearing. In fact, the division was conducting a campaign composed of several templates and battle forms, and I wanted to divide the control over all efforts between the HQ and the FCG. Divisions usually had the chief of staff lead the planning of the next phase from the war room at the HQ, while current affairs were commanded and controlled from the FCG. But now I saw fit to conduct the attack myself, from my FCG, while the rest – combing of the villages and open areas, interrogation of POWs, collection of captured equipment, and demolition of infrastructure – would be managed from the war room. These missions were all slowly bearing productive fruit, as expected during the presence stage.

While we were conducting the presence stage, NORTHCOM repeatedly interrupted and demanded that we stop clearing the nature reserves and exit them. I was outraged at this interference, emanating from their fear of casualties, but I knew that it was important to carefully manage my time and choose my fights.

I confirmed that the presence stage was advancing well, spoke with the brigade commanders, and delved into planning the next phase, which was now called COD 11 – Command Attack.

Orders were disseminated as to the way territory was to seamlessly change hands between the paratroopers who had captured it and Golani and 7th Brigades, who were to assume control.

I had an operational concept and the plan was coming together, but I always completed the planning process with a combined planning session with the commanders. In order to save time, the staff officers received instructions to carry out assignments that could be carried out now, even before my plan had been introduced and approved by NORTHCOM. We needed to prepare ammunition packages and construct new attack plans. There was a new logistics plan to make, and we had to align the situational picture as to manpower and casualties, carefully verifying that all centers held a complete and accurate picture.

The fighting continued. The forces were moving about, initiating, combing, and searching for the enemy. Even without authorization to advance, this didn't mean we had to stay in place. It was essential to change positions, ambush retreating or resupplying enemy forces, and remain agile.

We also continued bringing down precision fires on enemy locations. Our array of observation points collected vital intel and directed fires, from land, sea, and air, onto identified targets. The intel picture was kept coherent and comprehensive by UAVs and aerial photography. Engineering units were hard at work opening new routes through minefields, demolishing suspicious buildings at Ayta, detonating bunkers, and establishing new logistic lines of communication. Pallets of equipment for airlift and airdrop were prepared for the following night. Planning teams labored over the expected missions.

Chapter 20
Command Order

The Holiday of Love

The briefing room at NORTHCOM was filling up. Four divisions attended the session where the command operational order was to be handed down. At the same time, forces were being recruited to defend the Golan Heights, should the Syrian front erupt.

I walked through the hallways of the underground facility, saying hello to friends, subordinates, and others who greeted me. Before entering the room, I asked Lutfi to keep constant contact with the division in order to verify that the paratroopers were heading out as planned, that our AOR was held as it should be, and that all orders were being fulfilled. I expected to be out of reach for at least two hours, and I hated the feeling of being detached from my forces. But I knew that it was essential to conduct this briefing, at the outset of a new phase in the war.

"So much has happened in one month," I thought, as I walked over to my seat. So many storms, so much sorrow, so much power, and yes – sadly and shamefully – also so much tension and intrigue.

Out of the corner of my eye, I saw Kaplan speaking quietly with someone. He had been recently dispatched by Halutz to NORTHCOM and positioned above Udi. There have been precedents in the IDF to this extreme act. In the Yom Kippur War (1973), former CGS LTG (Res.) Haim Bar-Lev was appointed as an "advisor" to MG Yitzhak Hofi, NORTHCOM commander. Later on in the war, the Southern Command was in fact expropriated from its commander, MG Shmuel Gonen (Gorodish), and Bar-Lev was imposed as "commander of the southern front" until the end of the war. Unlike previous cases, this time it was all over the media in real time, and presented as a dismissal of Udi. It was inappropriate, insensitive, and unjustified. If the

General Staff wanted to be involved in the campaign, they should have done so from day one, instead of managing things by remote control from Tel Aviv wearing class A dress uniforms.

This was not a limited operation, but a war, and the General Staff should have managed it closely. Why perform such an indecent move, which appeared to be led more by politics than by operational considerations? It had a negative impact on morale, especially within the ranks of the skeptical veteran reservists – but not only them.

After the first battle at Bint Jbeil, I had bluntly demanded from Halutz to demonstrate close involvement in commanding the war. I remembered how Bogie Ya'alon, as CGS, was criticized for arriving at NORTHCOM to personally oversee a command-level exercise. Senior officers complained that he should have let NORTHCOM run the show, as the exercise scenario was focused mainly on the northern front. Bogie insisted back then that there was no contradiction. On the contrary, NORTHCOM would lead the campaign, but when the theater of war was also the theater of operations, there was no reason why he should not be present and personally be involved. He was right.

The session began, and missions were given to the divisions and various command components. There wasn't much variation from what I had known and initiated. My division was to attack the Tebnine region (in fact I had already begun doing so hours earlier, when I forwarded tanks to the Beit Yahoun Ridge, ordering them to open fire while activating artillery), take over Haris Junction, and serve as an anvil for the Steel Division's fighting along the Litani River.

There was one point that seemed odd. Eyal Ben-Reuven and I had agreed that the Steel Division would cross the Saluki River at a specific location which I knew to be suitable due to a shallow basin and relatively low banks. I also discussed this with Guy Tzur, and we decided to operate shoulder to shoulder in the area of Barachit, because it was the right place from which to move through to control the Litani Basin.

To my surprise, there was an empty space on the map in between the divisions, marked as "region of attack with fires" – that is, no forces were to be there, and NORTHCOM would collect intel and attack independently. The Steel Division was set to cross the Litani under Froun and Ghandouriye, in an extremely steep and rocky segment, which was also overlooked and controlled by villages on the Nabatiyeh Ridge. I had walked in the Saluki

Wadi many times in the past, and knew how tough it was on foot. How could they do it with tanks?

"Why are we doing this?" I asked during the briefing, "and why is there such a gap between the divisions?"

There were concurring nods in the room, but nothing was changed – this was the way they had planned it.

When I came out, I received word of a problem in my division: the key area of Shakif al-Nimel had been abandoned for several hours by the paratroopers, who had withdrawn immediately instead of waiting to be replaced by a Golani force that I had sent.

"How did it happen?" I was furious.

Apparently there was a disconnect somewhere along the line. Improper. Very bad.

I quickly set the schedule ahead. A combined planning and order alert session was set to take place on Naftali Ridge, allowing observation toward the battlefield, with the brigade commanders and center commanders. I had been conjoining these sessions for years, and found that during wartime, if time allowed, it proved very efficient. If it wasn't feasible to physically convene, I would make sure to brief the situational assessment and the orders over the radio.

I spread out an orthophoto (digitally aligned aerial photograph) and pulled out a few markers, in order to outline our planned advancement in the sea, air, and land, as well as enemy compounds (to which I usually gave female names). Without specific intel, I analyzed the expected enemy presence and designated enemy compounds according to the terrain and other characteristics.

I explained the operational concept and spelled out the required conditions needed to fulfill it. The commanders asked questions and made remarks. I tried to make the plan as simple and descriptive as possible, and shared and explained accumulated lessons learned.

As the session went on, the orthophoto filled with black, blue, and red lines and arrows. Usually it was the intel officer who would plot the red (enemy) and the operations officer would mark the blue (our forces) and black (boundaries and lines of advancement), but from my experience, the commander embodies all these functions himself. I like to draw the battle layout myself, and of course I personally write the mission definition and the operational concept.

Tamir, Golani Brigade commander, requested a few changes, so we had more consultations. The 7th Brigade commander added his input. The division's center commanders explained their plans. Maglan commander addressed his missions. He seemed concerned, and I motioned him to meet me later.

I summed up the plan and explained it, pointing at the schema. Golani was to move on foot and take the Sylvester ridge. The 7th Brigade would strengthen Herev Battalion with additional tanks in the area of Beit Yahoun, and continue to engage the Tebnine region. Merkava Mark 3 tanks would be augmented to Golani (that is, added to its existing forces) and move to hold the ridge seized by the infantry.

At this point, when Sylvester Ridge was in control and with enough tanks at hand, and Tebnine and Hadatha both being engaged, Golani battalions would flank Hadatha and Haris from the south and attack Haris Junction.

At the same time, Maglan operators would be landed by helicopters on Jabal Beit ed Douara, completing the encirclement of Tebnine from all directions. Tebnine was the logistical rear for Hezbollah and also a symbol as the Shiite focal point of Jabal Amel, where the Shiite movement in Lebanon originated.

In this move to Jabal Amel, the division would be penetrating to the heart – and the soft belly – of Hezbollah, and would reach a crossroads from which it would be able to branch out to all of Lebanon, enabling the development of NORTHCOM's attack to whichever direction they chose.

I ordered to construct a diversionary attack. Alexandroni was to lead a parallel move to simulate a wide-scale attack along the coastline toward Tyre, making it look as if this were our main effort.

I instructed Amnon, 7th Brigade commander, that the next stage after capturing Haris Junction and attacking Hadatha would be to conduct a logistic-operational maneuver to open the route leading from Bint Jbeil to Haris Junction, in order to allow movement of vehicles and tanks, should we develop a westward attack toward the Litani River or Tyre. For this mission I allocated to him an engineering unit. He already had a battalion from Givati Brigade, as well as our strike force – the finest, most professional and well-trained unit at our disposal – Herev Battalion.

They had been fighting for a month with minimum casualties – creatively, undauntedly – while implementing the fighting principles we had developed before the war. They initiated and were satisfied with meager means without complaining. They always fulfilled their mission, and did it on time.

I added a set of instructions to the forces under my command from the Navy, the Air Force, and the intel collection units. Lastly, I issued points of emphasis to brigades that were not part of the attack but complemented the plan by implementing the presence phase and combing southern Lebanon.

Now that all planning was done, it was time to turn it into a written order. My staff would carefully copy all the drawing and scribbling, and feed all the data into our computerized systems. They would also produce and disseminate workable maps to be used in headquarters and command posts, up and down the chain of command. They did a great job and were getting better and better at it as the war progressed.

We exited the building. I approached Eliezer, who had shown some concern during the brief, and he expressed reservations regarding his distant and isolated mission.

"It's dangerous, Gal, and you know that we are not the type to be afraid."

We spoke a little longer. I explained, convinced, and also found a suitable solution. We made the appropriate adjustments. Eliezer was more relaxed, and so was I.

It is possible to impose orders and force subordinates to comply. I prefer looking them in the eye and convincing them.

I made my way back to the division HQ using dirt roads, as the main roads were crowded with AFVs and supply convoys. I asked my FCG to stop in the assembly area of one of the armored battalions and went over to where the staff was convened.

I was happy to meet two company commanders who had participated, as students in the Command and Staff College, in a preparation process I had conducted a few weeks before the war in collaboration with their commander, COL Pinky Zuaretz. They had spent an entire week in the division planning for war, by reviewing the operational plans, learning, and making sharp observations. It had been a positive and constructive discourse, and they reported to Pinky that they were impressed with the openness and willingness to hear them and learn from them.

This had always been my way. I believe that controlled opposition serves as a balancing and restraining element that is an important part of leadership.

I took a minute to speak to them near the tanks as they prepared to move out.

"Hey, guys, let's talk a bit."

From all over, company commanders and others came running over to hear the division commander. I explained the development of the war and described the current situation. I introduced questions to test their fluency in what was going on, including the operational concept and their understanding of the enemy.

They are excellent, I thought to myself. They were brave and learned from battle to battle. As our conversation developed, they seemed to me encouraged and instilled with battle spirit.

But now an unexpected thing happened. Their battalion commander suddenly lashed out: "We can't withstand Hezbollah's ATM capabilities – and besides, tanks are not suitable for this kind of fighting."

I was astonished at the severity of his words, at his fractured voice, his lack of faith, and mainly his insensitivity to the effect he might be having on the soldiers who heard him.

I attempted to correct the effect his words had on his people. I clarified that our main effort was with infantry, but that at this point in the fight, it was appropriate to step up our use of armored vehicles, unlike what we had done so far.

I emphasized that we had learned and improved, that Hezbollah had been delivered a heavy blow, and that its ATM capabilities had been compromised. There were still risks and threats, and we could expect more casualties, but by employing and deploying our forces and means in a calculated manner, we would be able to minimize them while fulfilling our mission.

"It's a fact," I emphasized. "Look how far we have come already."

Yes, we had sustained hits to our tanks, but fewer than in previous wars. It was being blown out of proportion in the media, partly because some time had passed since we had operated forces in this magnitude.

I could feel that my words had a mollifying effect. There were more and more smiles, and the questions were becoming relaxed and practical. But I was still worried.

"That's just the way he is," said Amnon, who joined the briefing. "Don't take it too seriously."

"Oh, but I do take it very seriously," I answered. "I don't remember when I last heard a commander speak that way. Where is his fighting spirit?"

"You're right," said Amnon. "But you said the right things. That was an excellent discussion. You really uplifted the battalion. Look at them. Can you also speak to Basiuk's 82nd Battalion?"

"Amnon, a command-level attack is about to begin, and everyone's waiting for me!"

"But they're right here," he said, pointing to a group of vehicles with tarp spread out between them.

"OK, come." I walked over and lifted a flap to enter.

"Sir!" Basiuk called out, as the officers jumped to attention.

"Hey, Gal," company commanders and staff officers called out happily, patting me on the shoulder and shaking my hand. This battalion had been with my division for a few months and was now like one of our own. It had lost one tank chasing the abductors and then two more during the battle at Maroun al-Ras, and had gone on fighting for a month. And yet – what an incredibly positive atmosphere, what seriousness, what friendship, and what exemplary leadership by Basiuk, their commander.

We bent over the maps and battle charts. The plans were clear, simple, and smart. Commanders asked me questions about the situation in other arenas and the overall picture. They had confidence in their tanks and in their ability to operate them effectively against Hezbollah. We concluded by hugging – which had become the norm by now – and talked of meeting after the war.

"See the difference, Amnon?"

"I sure did," he answered proudly. "It's a 7th Brigade battalion – what did you expect?"

"Keep an eye on that other battalion commander, will you?"

"Sure. Don't worry."

En route to the division HQ, I received notice that there was a twenty-four-hour postponement due to a political directive, and that a cease-fire was being discussed again.

"Sela stations, this is Sela Actual," I addressed my forces over the radio that evening. I delivered a situational update and various instructions, and concluded with a personal message from my heart: "It is the fifteenth of the Hebrew month of Av – the Jewish holiday of love – today, and I did not yet tell you how much I love you all. Over and out."

The Public Isn't Ready Yet

That evening, Minister of Defense Amir Peretz came to my FCG again. The last time he had come was for an entertaining TV talk show, and I had been asked to clear my command post to make room for it.

"It's very important," I was told when I expressed my objection.

I had just come back from the battlefield and couldn't believe that this was appropriate during wartime.

"No!" I had said firmly.

"But it's going to be live in prime time. How can you sabotage something like this?"

They finally found an empty space inside the bunker and did their important show.

Now here he was again, listening to my updates and insights as to what should be done next – the offensive maneuver. He listened attentively and asked questions.

"We should have done this long ago," I said.

"Well," he said after a few seconds of thought, "there was a conceptual problem. It was thought that Hezbollah's rockets would rust."

He was referring to Bogie Ya'alon's remarks on the subject. He went on to explain that we had not conducted the maneuver earlier in the war because there was a need to prepare the public, which had been locked in the "Lebanese quagmire" paradigm (a term used to describe the many years of Israeli presence in Lebanon).

It enraged me to hear this. Of course a ground maneuver into Lebanon wasn't popular, but it was unheard of to evaluate strategic, national interests according to public perception and atmosphere. If it was determined that the right step to take was a ground incursion, public opinion should have been a secondary consideration.

Leadership is to lead toward what *is* right, not only what *looks* right.

"Sir," intervened chief of education BG Ilan Harari, an honest person, who had served in fighting positions his entire career. "You have here an excellent division and a commander who has been fighting for a month under harsh conditions, achieving excellent results."

The minister nodded.

"I think that when you return to Tel Aviv, you should call Gal's wife and tell her what you have seen here."

"You took the words out of my mouth," Peretz said, smiling. "That is exactly what I plan to do."

Close to midnight, the phone rang at our home, and the minister of defense spoke to Donna briefly. I appreciated the gesture.

Sixty Hours in August

In the morning, MG Gadi Shamni, who was now the military secretary to the prime minister, arrived at the observation point at my FCG, which was positioned that morning on Mount Adir. We had known each other for years. He pushed aside the branches put in place to conceal our position, entered, and slumped down heavily beside me.

"What's up, Gal?"

"Hi, Gadi." I looked up from my charts, which I then used, with the aid of a pair of field binoculars, to give him a rundown on the sights and sounds of battle all around us.

"Wait a second," he said, pulling out an encrypted cell phone and dialing a number. He spoke quietly: "I'm with Gal now. It looks OK. Do you want to speak with him? Yes, yes, he's here, I'll put him on."

"Here," he said, shoving the device into my hand.

"Who is it?"

"The prime minister. Talk."

"Hello, sir," I said.

"Gal, how are you?" Prime Minister Ehud Olmert said, and continued without waiting for an answer: "Look, I know that you are poised and ready, and you're stretched to the limit, but there are factors holding us back because there are negotiations for a cease-fire."

I listened and then answered him quietly that I understood that there were wider considerations, and that we would fulfill any mission given to us, as I had told him just the other day. Still, I expressed my opinion that the planned move was important, could be swiftly implemented, and would improve our position tactically.

We exchanged polite words, and the conversation was over.

"Let's go outside," offered Gadi.

We stepped out of the position and leaned against one of the vehicles in a reverse slope.

"How much time will we have?" I asked Gadi.

"Sixty hours," he answered, using a phrase that would be repeated over and over in the coming months.

"It'll do."

"So, how are you doing, Gal?"

At first I said nothing, merely looking at him with inquiring eyes. Finally, I spoke, describing tersely that I had heard the rumors and stories about my performance in the war being told behind my back.

"This stuff reaches all the way up here to my FCG," I said.

"It will intensify; I hope you understand this," Gadi said, with a strange look in his eyes.

I did not understand what he meant. But before I could ask him, an urgent call had me running back to the observation point. I was focused on fighting the enemy and defending my people, not on this kind of backstabbing.

Another postponement led to another day of stressful waiting.

"The LORD Is with You, Mighty Warrior"

On Friday night, the long-awaited approval arrived, and I conveyed the orders to the waiting forces, poised out in the field. I reviewed the orders, verified that they were clear to all, and requested assurance that while the attack was underway, all other activities related to the presence phase would continue, including defending the villages and resupplying the forces in the rear.

I decided to begin the night in the war room at the division HQ, where communications were better, and then to move to the forward position where I could observe better – just as I had done during the first attack in COD 8.

I used the short time until the attack to get some rest, and immediately fell asleep with all the gear on me. But I awoke minutes later and leaped out of my field bed, drenched with sweat and heart pounding. I had dreamt a dream. Donna's late father, Shlomo, stood before me alive and well – unlike the last time I had seen him in the hospital, deteriorating from cruel metastatic cancer. How I missed him – this warm and compassionate father and grandfather.

"I do whatever I can," Shlomo said as he stood before me in my dream, donning his uniform and battle vest. His words echoed in my brain over and over. What did they mean?

I jumped up and made my way through the dark room toward the lit hallway, from which I could hear the humming voices of people praying. Dozens of soldiers stood in prayer during the Sabbath evening service, crowded in the narrow hall near the commander's room, which had been serving as a makeshift synagogue, shelter, and clinic for treating injuries.

I leaned on the lintel and listened to the fervor of the hearts filling the hallway. I was overcome with emotion in a way I find difficult to explain. Tears welled up in my eyes. Something deep-rooted and fundamental hit me. It took me back to my prayers during the High Holidays when I had gone with my grandfather to the synagogue.

Here was the power of Judaism, penetrating the heart in silent prayer. I am not what you would call in Israel "religious," certainly not Orthodox, but I have a strong connection to our traditions and feel that our very existence as a nation rests on these strong foundations. I make a point of owning key books at home and preserve traditions in fulfillment of the instruction in the Passover Haggadah from Exodus 13:8: "*V'higgadeta l'bincha*" (And thou shalt tell thy son). With us it is daughters, and we make a point of instilling in them their heritage.

When I became commandant of Bahad 1, my first request to the chief rabbi of the IDF, Rabbi Israel Weiss, was to place in my office a selection of the most fundamental Jewish texts, and to establish a Jewish library on base.

"It is a message to an entire generation of Israeli officers," I told him.

I also promoted the establishment of a spiritual center, a large synagogue, and a learning center – all valuable assets for generations to come.

Since childhood, I would walk the Holy Land, navigating with a Bible in hand. I read it, experienced it, and was deeply moved by seeing it before my eyes.

I would stand on a hill overlooking Michmash and visualize Jonathan, the son of Saul, and the man who bore his armor, as they climbed uphill and infiltrated as commandos into the Philistine camp. I stood on the roof of the Tomb of the Prophet Samuel, with subordinates or visitors from overseas, and pointed out where the biblical city of Gibeon was located – the place where Abner said to Joab: "Let the young men, I pray thee, arise and play before us" (II Samuel 2:14). I explained the battles led by Joshua and described the history of Jerusalem. At Beit El, I would tell of Jacob's ladder, and at Shiloh, the first capital of Israel, we would look at the surrounding mountains and imagine how glorious it must have been when the people of Israel gathered by the thousands during times of pilgrimage.

I was filled with awe and pride as I toured our country from Dan in the north to Eilat in the south, witnessing firsthand evidence of the story of the Jewish people. Rachel's Tomb near Bethlehem, the City of David, the Western Wall Tunnel, and many other sites are places of profound significance, connecting our past with our modern Jewish state. You need to learn, take the Bible in your hand, and start walking. When you do this with your children, you are fulfilling the mission of "thou shalt tell thy son."

To this the voices of prayer reconnected me, in the midst of all the smoke and exploding shells and shrieking mortars. I felt that I belonged to something greater than myself. I was a Jewish warrior. I stepped out into the hall to join my soldiers, and was quickly surrounded, hugged, and grasped.

"Sir," "Gal," "*Shabbat shalom*," "May thy hands be strengthened," "Good luck," "The LORD is with you, mighty warrior."

When the prayer concluded, I gathered everyone in the war room. On Friday nights during the war I made a habit of personally making the Kiddush – the traditional blessing on the wine. Then I gave a brief update and said words of encouragement and praise to the men and women who were doing such an incredible job. Many soldiers gathered in the crowded bunker to attend our little ceremony.

Suddenly I remembered something. Out of my dog tag cover, I pulled an old piece of paper which I had taken from my father-in-law Shlomo an hour after his passing. It was a prayer to be said before heading out to battle, and he had carried it with him since the Kadesh Operation in 1956 (known as the Sinai War or the Suez Crisis). Also my grandmother, Leah, carried something wherever she went. One day she asked me to come to her old age home, and with trembling hands handed over a small plastic sleeve. "This was your grandfather Marco's and it should be yours now." Inside were his Haganah and War of Independence campaign ribbons. People have possessions that they carry close to their hearts. Such was the prayer for Shlomo, and such were the campaign ribbons that my grandmother gave me before she passed away, two years before the war.

Now, in front of many of my subordinates looking at me in the dark, I read from the prayer that had meant so much to Shlomo. Then I added: "We are going to beat them," folded up the yellow piece of paper, and headed out into the night.

"Please Don't Stop"

In total darkness, my small FCG positioned itself for the divisional attack on the Jabal Amel region. Final arrangements were made by the various professionals, and my security detail raised the height of the sandbag protection wall. The position had been hit by rocket fire, and we were close enough to the battlefield to sustain direct ATMs. As usual, I carried on my chest a regular pair of binoculars, which I found more effective than night-vision equipment.

H-hour was approaching, and I whispered last instructions into the radio.

Then, all at once, the entire firepower of our division opened up in a massive, coordinated barrage, from land, sea, and air. Immediately after the first strike, 7th Brigade and Steel Chariots' tanks moved up to their assigned positions, and we could see the red streaks of their shells cutting through the air toward their targets. Tamir and I exchanged a few words of awe at the overwhelming firepower coming down on Hezbollah positions, nature reserves, and Katyusha rocket launch sites.

I verified with him that Golani forces were already running toward the village of Hadatha and encircling Haris Junction.

I watched as a Hercules C-130 performed low-altitude airdrops resupplying the fighting forces near Beit Yahoun. I had initiated these missions and believed in them, but was still moved at the spectacular view of the large aircraft diving so low over the battlefield, using the massive fire campaign as cover.

While we were fighting our divisional campaign, there were three other divisions engaged in fighting in other regions. I followed the advancement of these neighboring forces through periodic updates by my staff.

Things were going well for us. Before daybreak, Golani and Herev advanced and reached their positions, and Maglan completed their assigned mission for the night. In my AOR there was also fighting still going on in areas which, although under our control, had not yet been searched and cleared. In a large-scale battle in Ayta, multiple forces comprised of Carmeli Brigade, Air Force jets, artillery, tanks, and bulldozers launched a coordinated strike on a location used as cover for dozens of Hezbollah fighters, resulting in many losses on their side. We also lost officers and soldiers during this battle, and later another Golani soldier was killed in close-quarter combat at Hadatha.

Before dawn I watched a marvelous sight as a blanket of clouds covered the battlefield. It looked wonderful but also meant trouble for us, for with zero visibility we had lost our air support and visual intel collecting.

Then, disaster struck.

While making its way to join Golani forces, one of the tanks accidently ran over a group of soldiers. Two were killed and there were also wounded needing immediate evacuation. Helicopter pilots searched for a break in the clouds and bravely penetrated them, putting their own lives at risk to extract the wounded soldiers and bring them swiftly to a hospital.

"Continue," I ordered, "no stopping now under any circumstances."

Later that morning I reported to my commander: "I have it."

We had reached our designated targets and controlled them, but now there were many things to do in order to strengthen our positions and prepare for further developments.

Merkava Mark 3 tanks were supposed to move toward Shakif al-Nimel to reinforce Golani and shape conditions for continued fighting. They were to be later augmented by engineering forces in order to prepare the main road toward Haris Junction. There was a possibility that we would need to further take over Tebnine and maybe move toward the Litani River, but there was a problem.

I wanted to engage the Tebnine area. Basiuk's tanks, Herev Battalion, and Golani were all in position, but the tank battalion that was supposed to link up with Golani and cover their advancement had not yet arrived.

"Tamir, what's happening with the tanks?"

The tank battalion that I had allocated to join Golani was still at Aynata and wasn't moving as planned. Their commander was the one who had worried me with his demoralizing remarks before the battle.

"The battalion has not yet moved out. The commander doesn't want to move. He says he will wait until nightfall to refuel, and then they will move out and maybe link up with me."

Tamir sounded frustrated and angry.

"Is that what he said? Did you speak with him personally?"

"Twenty times! And it's always the same answers. Nothing new. The operational conditions are not being met in order to support the continued attack. I need those tanks with me on the ridge!"

He was right.

"Should I speak with him?"

"Yes, please do. I have nothing more to say to him!" Tamir said furiously.

"There you have it," I said to myself quietly. I had seen his conduct in front of his own men right before battle. I had witnessed his lack of leadership and lack of confidence in his people and his tanks. Shouldn't I have replaced him right then and there?

"Get me in touch with him," I requested.

"Sir," the battalion commander said on a secure line.

"How are you?"

"OK."

"Is there a reason why you are not proceeding with your mission?"

Sure enough, as Tamir had said, he had many reasons – fuel, daylight, ATM threats, and more. I told him that we were in a critical phase of the war, before the declaration of a cease-fire; that Golani were alone on the ridge, deep within the villages; and that they needed the assistance of his tanks.

But he persisted: "I don't have fuel."

"Do you have enough to reach your positions?" I asked, knowing that he did.

"Yes."

"Then move to your positions and refuel at night when you're already there. It's essential that you make it. We don't have anybody else!"

"But..." he broke into another set of excuses.

I wouldn't take it anymore. There simply was no time for this.

"Move out to your positions and perform your mission as ordered! Over and out!"

"Wilco," he said.

His tanks headed out and made it to their positions, assisting the neighboring division with fire. One tank sustained a hit from an ATM and four tankers were killed. But the mission was fulfilled and the ridge was taken.

Word reached me of the difficult battle that was raging in the Saluki River. That same day we lost another tank at Ayta, and its four-man reservist crew was lost.

That night, Maglan was ordered to strengthen their grip on Jabel Beit ed Douara, and our division was to continue improving our hold throughout the region, although we knew that we were hours away from a cease-fire. I urged my forces to push forward, and they did, while resupplying, rearming, and preparing for whatever might come next.

Another significant maneuver planned for that night was a massive airlift of reserve and regular forces of the Airborne Division into the region of

Kafra and Yater. At dusk, we conducted a situational assessment and issued final orders.

That was it – a few more hours to go before this would all come to a halt.

The night was as difficult as the day that had just ended. A CH-53 Yasur helicopter was shot down, killing the entire crew of five. Luckily, it happened seconds after offloading dozens of paratroopers.

The airlift operation was halted.

"Why?" I was angry and disappointed. This was war, and helicopters can be hit just like tanks and infantry. This was no reason to cancel a mission! I was notified that Eliezer's mission had also been aborted. Everything was being called off because of the downed helicopter.

"Get me Shkedi."

I had known the Air Force commander since he was A3 and I was Shaldag CO.

"Shkedi."

"Hey, youngster," he said, as he always did.

"You guys are doing excellent work out there." I thanked him for the vast array of missions the Air Force was performing, from attack to intel collecting, rescue, and special operations with Shaldag.

"I especially admire your helicopter pilots on medevac missions. They are saving lives with their bravery."

"Yes, they are awesome!" Shkedi said with satisfaction.

"Please don't stop."

I told him that I believed that the loss of a helicopter in battle should not disrupt our operational momentum. We went on to discuss the situation for a couple more minutes and ended the conversation.

"Thank you, Gal."

"Good-bye, Shkedi."

To my dismay, the airlift did not resume. I only found out after the war that it had been BG Eyal Eizenberg who decided to stop the flights, not the Air Force. We were all shaken by the loss of a helicopter, for it was more than just another platform, but a cultural symbol of power and technological dominance. Yet still, the Air Force had not requested or intended to abort its mission.

Around noontime, my good friend Amir Boker dragged me into a trench dug between some trees, where I found a mattress and a sleeping bag.

"You're going to sleep a little!" he ordered. My protests were to no avail – Amir was a stubborn man. He had been at my side for years, from when he was a soldier in May Company of the 202nd Battalion in 1986, following me from position to position as a member of my close staff. He was an experienced warrior and a talented officer, and also always close to my family, as a brother and friend.

After a while, I was shaken and called out of the ditch.

"The CGS is arriving in a few minutes."

Halutz arrived, appearing cold, alienated, distanced, and silent. He slouched down beside me in the observation point, accompanied by Dan Margalit – a renowned Israeli journalist. I presented the divisional battle scheme, pointing out the positions on the terrain before us.

Margalit asked for my binoculars, "just to see what it feels like," and peered out over the battlefield, which was now relatively quiet.

Halutz seemed preoccupied and hardly spoke. He nodded occasionally as I explained things, and then made an insignificant comment. He stood up and exited the position, but I intentionally delayed inside, raised my voice, and addressed the soldiers, who were looking extremely tired and dusty after five straight weeks of deployment: "Guys, thank you very much, you're doing a great job!"

Halutz froze, reentered, and exchanged a few words with the soldiers. Then he left us and drove off.

Cease-Fire

During the night I evaluated the division's situation and made a round of updates with my subordinate brigade commanders.

"In position," said one.

"We have it," said another.

I continued receiving updates from all our forces as to their position and status, and drew blue lines on my charts, updating our deployment picture.

I closed the tip of my blue marker feeling a sense of satisfaction. All had completed their assignments as directed. Throughout the war, the 91st Division had fulfilled all of its missions. We fought, sustained casualties, changed and adapted as necessary – but the job got done. We were now holding the positions that I had planned for and aimed for before the war, and we were implementing all the plans as directed by NORTHCOM.

At daybreak, on Monday, August 14, 2006, I received the order: "Cease-fire taking effect at 0800. No more maneuvering. Preparing for withdrawal in coordination with the UN."

United Nations Security Council Resolution 1701, approved by Lebanon, Hezbollah, and Israel, mandated cessation of hostilities and withdrawal of Israeli forces to the United Nations' "Blue Line" border definition (the internationally recognized Israel-Lebanon border, physically marked by blue barrels), and, in the long run, deployment of the LAF in southern Lebanon and disarmament of all armed groups.

We were issued a map dividing southern Lebanon into sectors, and each day we were to evacuate another sector. I was extremely satisfied with the fact that the LAF was to replace us, as this was their first deployment south of the Litani River since 1968, and a positive indication of Lebanese sovereignty. My observation outposts and forces on the ground were sending in reports of truckloads of LAF soldiers entering the villages in the south. A few days later, while personally visiting the western region, I watched as new and improved UNIFIL forces landed on the beach and moved in to replace the old and failing mechanism, support the LAF, and shape a new reality.

As far back as a year and a half before the war, I was being repeatedly asked what I thought to be the ideal situation in the Lebanese front. My answer was: LAF deployed on the border, UNIFIL – as we know it – out, and a different Hezbollah, diminished and far from the border.

It was now all materializing!

We proceeded as planned to hand over areas to UNIFIL, who in turn introduced LAF presence. During this time, my division dealt with dem-olition of Hezbollah infrastructure, including bunkers and tunnels. By the beginning of October, we were repositioned on the Blue Line, and the trilat-eral Israel-UNIFIL-LAF coordination mechanism had come into effect.

Within a few days, I constructed a new and updated defense concept for the border region, and introduced and approved it at NORTHCOM. I issued new routine security measures and verified their implementation. At the same time, my forces began regaining operational status at all headquarters and contingency depots. The process of releasing the reservists and regaining operational qualification was relatively swift, and we also began the process of thorough and intense debriefing, a task that I led personally, for dozens of hours, while leading the rehabilitation process.

I was determined to make the debriefing and lesson-learning process open and revealing, starting with transparently presenting my own mistakes. I was ordered by the GS to have MG (Res.) Yoram Yair ("Yaya") at my side for the process.

By November, the division's forces were debriefed, equipped, and redeployed along the border, in a new and suitable operational concept. I absorbed new personnel in the division's HQ and brigades and determined the main points for further preparation for the "next round," if and when we would again be called upon to defend Israel's northern border.

Chapter 21

Diamonds – The Lessons Learned

The Four Stages of the War

My subordinates throughout the years have come to know my method of debriefing, where I ask them to bring to the table not raw data, but the final product of an analytical process. I ask to see not graphite or carbon, but the polished diamonds themselves.

Here are my "diamonds" pertaining to the war (some of which repeat the essence of previously described events or insights).

In retrospect, the war can be divided into four main stages:

- **Fire campaign** – July 12–19: Beginning with the abduction, continuing with the preliminary actions and destruction of Hezbollah infrastructure along the border.
- **Raids** – July 19–31: Counterattack, raids and continuation of the fire effort while creating engagement and friction. Controlling areas were captured and a few raids were carried out, the biggest being the first battle of Bint Jbeil.
- **SSP** – August 1–14: Capturing territories in order to reduce rocket launches, kill enemy fighters, and promote better conditions for a negotiation. The offensive began, reserves were recruited, and the division carried out battles at Bint Jbeil, Sylvester Ridge, and Haris Junction. Three other divisions operated in nearby areas.
- **Presence** – August 14 until the last IDF soldier left Lebanon: Systematic dismantling of enemy infrastructure, transferal of the area to the UN, withdrawal, and realignment.

The campaign in Lebanon was characterized by several changes in direction and directive – including missions and makeup of forces – that I considered professionally unreasonable. This was due to the way the situation had been identified and defined, the ORBAT and resources allocated to and by NORTHCOM, and the public and media pressure emanating from the extensive impact on the home front.

A division is a large and diverse organization. During the war I commanded nine brigades – a much larger force than doctrinally defined for a division.

Even with a flexible division, it takes a reasonable lead time to implement mission and force-structure changes. The changes in plans and mission orders given to the 91st Division were unreasonable, to put it mildly.

Besides the issue of speed and nature of change, there were other fundamental challenges that prevented the division from fully utilizing its capabilities.

Identification and Definition of the Situation

At NORTHCOM HQ, the situation had not been perceived as a war, leading to routine-security mentality and procedures for an extended period of time. The division was required to pass a tiresome approval process for every action, contrary to the command and control doctrine typical for wartime.

This had been the main tension during the first days of the war, and the situation began to change only toward the end of July, when we were given a green light to recruit our reservists and implement the attack plan. Even then, we set out on every attack as if it were to be the last. In this state of mind – where missions were perceived as singular events, after which peace and quiet would come – timelines weren't clear and the operational orders did not even define the purpose of the mission being carried out.

Statements made by leaders, recruitment of reservists, and attack orders were all excellent ways to shape perception, "reset" situational awareness and recalibrate everyone to the new reality. But there would have been an even better way, which was to use code names and contingency plans that had been predefined before the war – and this, regretfully, was not done. The division had prepared well for this war, from the conceptualization through plans and procedures and down to the critical element of training. We had made a point of carefully simulating and rehearsing everything we would later encounter during the war – the weight carried on the soldiers' backs, the distances they were required to walk, the harsh weather, fighting for extended periods of time with ceramic protective gear, facing a multitude of enemy threats, etc.

But when we were sent out on the missions – at least initially – the connection to all this training was not made. The soldiers were denied the realization that this was it – this was the war we had prepared for!

A Cumulative Campaign

The war had a cumulative characteristic, where the understandings, the situation, the ORBAT all accumulated gradually, eventually leading to a cumulative success. This was no way to conduct a war. The "purpose" segment of operational orders, following the words "in order to..." was frequently too vague. Without continuity, the objectives could not be understood. Every battle stood alone, and there was no overall strategic picture. Moreover, this lack of continuity assisted the enemy! Our combat momentum could not be achieved, and Hezbollah was able to exploit this in order to regroup and rehabilitate.

Severe Restrictions

Draconian instructions kept coming throughout the war: no deploying reservists, no moving on roads, no fighting in nature reserves, no fighting in daylight, no use of APCs, and even no use of FCGs inside Lebanon. Under these circumstances, I had no choice but to constantly disregard instructions.

The directive from NORTHCOM to try to reduce rockets being launched into Israel came at a time when it contradicted the directive of avoiding the nature reserves – for those were the main launching sites. There seemed to be over-confidence in, and over-reliance on, the fire campaign, mainly airpower. The Air Force's successes in the Gaza Strip had shaped our operational concept in the first phase of the war, and it took too much time until there was willingness for change.

Time was also a restriction in this war. There was a constant sense of urgency for various reasons: Israeli civilians in bomb shelters, the international hourglass of legitimacy, the Qana incident, the ever looming cease-fire, and pressure by commanders. Every battle was perceived as "the last battle." There was a need to synchronize three different clocks – political, civilian, and operational.

Missions

All of our missions had been fulfilled, but not always in the time frame defined. Friction is an integral and central element in war, leading to many uncertainties. Many of our actions were conducted for the first time in battle, without training or previous experience.

Since NORTHCOM's directive as to the objectives of the campaign were unclear and inconsistent, I set my own stable focal point as the key objective – realization of the original Magen Ha'aretz plan that I knew and valued. This constant direction ultimately led to the division being positioned on the predefined lines by the end of the war.

While conducting the offensive effort, the division was constantly preoccupied with other aspects in the rear – planning and approving further moves, together with the vital effort of shaping the border region and defending the villages along the line. The constant demand for focusing attention to strong defense contradicted the need to implement a strong offensive. It is impossible to be strong and effective everywhere simultaneously. It contradicts basic principles of war. (This isn't to say that defending the villages didn't prove to be important, for there were attempts by Hezbollah to penetrate, and they were thwarted near the fence.)

We made a point of initiating, striving to engage and be ready on time, but these all required basic preconditions: a clearly defined mission, region boundaries, time and space, organic forces, and training and standard practices. Although we were lacking these necessities, the division's conduct in the war was characterized by always pushing forward, taking the initiative, and having an offensive mindset.

A regional division behaves like a living tissue, absorbing other forces, which all rely on the unique knowledge, intel, and assets that have been accumulated by the frontline division. Serving in this capacity, my division supplied sixty thousand maps, orthophotos, and additional planning materials to other units, not all of them even subordinate to me.

Reducing the Rocket Launchings

As my division advanced northward, so did the launches, for Hezbollah possessed capabilities to fire from longer ranges throughout Lebanon. Therefore, the claim that rocket launching could have been completely prevented by a direct ground maneuver was completely baseless. It could be argued that the IDF could have conquered all of Lebanon, but this was not the intention. The maneuver that was carried out was aimed at creating external, international pressure on Syria, Lebanon, and Hezbollah, leading to a different arrangement at the end of the war. We never presumed or pretended that a limited-scope operation would bring an end to rocket launching toward Israel; rather, we pledged to reduce the threat.

Operational Effectiveness

During the war, we implemented the principles of fire application that we had been constructing for many months, mainly uniting our intel and fires centers. Our objective was to be as efficient and fast as possible in closing circles when striking low-signature, time-sensitive targets. Not only narrowing the gap between sensors and shooters, but practically merging them (that is, identifying the target and shooting immediately in real time), is a leading principle in force building and technological development. Still, we experienced mistakes in the field of realizing intel. Some of it was so well protected that it never reached the forces in the battlefield. It is critical to find the balance between protecting sources and making timely use of available material.

We implemented a broad range of deception tactics, leading to substantial success in the battlefield.

We also derived many lessons on the need to improve command and control, such as maintaining full situational awareness on the position of our forces.

We never targeted civilians deliberately, making every effort to differentiate between civilians and combatants. Minimizing collateral damage and harm to uninvolved civilians was an important operational consideration, and we took extreme measures to avoid hitting sensitive locations such as UN positions. We never lost our adherence to Ruach Tzahal, the Spirit of the IDF, our official ethical code of conduct.

Another key principle, which I emphasized and implemented throughout the war, was to make sure that our forces all "interlocked" in creating a continuous and coherent presence throughout the division's AOR. This is why I was baffled to hear claims suggesting that there was no unified divisional campaign.

The claims were of course baseless. My division realized the full sense of a divisional effort, including having all augmented forces deployed in my AOR acting under one logic and directive, and fully supported by all the division's resources and centers.

These accusations were rejected by experts who reviewed and assessed my division's conduct during the war, among them former CGS LTG (Res.) Dan Shomron, who was tasked with debriefing the General Staff. After one of the sessions in Tel Aviv, he called me aside and expressed his astonishment at the claim that one of the battles did not appropriately develop into a divisional effort.

"I'm afraid that we're going backwards," he said. "Generals think of a division as if it were a company with the platoons covering each other. We experienced these problems in 1973, but I thought we had overcome them by now."

"I admire what you have done here," a senior American general told me shortly after the war, as we stood on the mountain, in the same spot where my FCG was positioned throughout the war. I was honored to share with him my experiences and insights and was happy to receive positive feedback.

"You carried out a most impressive divisional maneuver," another expert in operational art told me.

During the war, the division carried out various types of combat: raids, defense, attack, ambushes, advance to contact, and retreat and delay (during the deployment of LAF). Types of combat will always be mixed and mutually contained, as during defense there will be offensive measures, and during the offense, there will be defensive actions. In all of them, there will always be raids and ambushes.

The principle of infiltration – "swarms" of infantrymen – in order to take over controlling areas and outskirts of urban areas before sweeping and clearing them out turned out to be a good tactic. It succeeded everywhere it was implemented. It would have been a mistake to counter guerilla fighters with armored forces driving on defined routes.

Special Forces

A relatively large number of successful and important special ops were carried out in the division's AOR, in close coordination with the tactical battle. Every available SOF capability was immediately utilized and implemented.

Special forces were a resource constantly in shortage. I had established a special operations command and control mechanism at the division, and concluded that this model should be implemented in other divisions too.

Airborne missions should not come under the heading of special operations, and it's about time that we saw airlift operations for what they are – another form of transportation. During the first few weeks of the war, we found it extremely hard to acquire helicopters, and it took a long time to receive approval for airborne missions, as if they were a special capability. There seemed to be a psychological barrier when it came to air assets, although they had been successfully employed by the IDF in past campaigns.

Preparing the Area, Engineering, and Logistics

I learned once more that, as in every campaign, preparing the battle space was an essential endeavor, and that every preliminary effort eventually paid off. This included clearing minefields, preparing staging areas, loading and offloading platforms, etc. We found that the rear region and routes were a constant challenge.

As in the past, we experienced a severe shortage of engineering forces and equipment. It is not predestination that engineering must always be the bottleneck, and we must change this by proper force building.

One of the false myths that spread following the war was the "logistics failure." Certainly there were a few instances where supplies did not arrive when needed, but the stories morphed into a completely distorted description of what had taken place. The IDF had known harder times with logistics in previous wars. It was to be expected and most soldiers understood this and improvised accordingly. A small group of soldiers blew this out of proportion and shaped a distorted perception, as if our forces had been neglected, left hungry and without logistical support.

Some unique solutions for combat logistics in fighting guerilla warfare had begun to materialize before the war, but not all were ready when the war began. Those which were ready proved to be very efficient.

Logistical lines of communication were prepared during the war, but they did not reach the full capacity needed by the forces on the ground, and this was compensated by air supply. I always disliked sending in convoys and thought that delivering supplies by airdrop and landing was a vital capability even for very short distances, close to the front line. I disagree with much of the criticism that was voiced after the war and still believe that we should continue to develop the ability to supply our forces from the air as a substitute for convoys when necessary.

Organization of Forces and Maintaining Organic Units

Keeping the organic structure of forces is an important principle which saves us time and energy under stressful conditions. We had done so during Operation Defensive Shield, so I understood the importance of insisting on it this time too. The brigades received full force packages as dictated by doctrine (recon, intel collection, engineering, fire support, armor, and special forces). Divisional resources were decentralized and allocated to the units, including fire and observation from the sea, UAVs, PGMs, and intel units.

ORBAT management was a challenge in this war, however. Throughout the war, units were dispersed and allocated to different divisions in a way that compromised the organic structure and efficient use of forces and resources. In addition to frequent mission changes, there were constant force changes which required new battle procedures to incorporate newly conjoined forces. Force buildup was slow, cumulative, and disorderly. There was no decisive decision as to changes in priorities and recruitment policy.

Weaponry

Creative moves were performed beyond the confines of standard doctrine, such as using equipment in missions it wasn't intended for, employing direct fire with high-trajectory weapons, and using demining (mine detection and removal) equipment for clearing fortified streets in urban environments.

We found that there were many gaps in developing designated weaponry and fighting equipment, and after-action review (AAR) helped us to better direct these efforts for future development. Such was the case with friendly fire, which we had experienced during training and from which we suffered losses during combat.

We lacked means for neutralizing nature reserves, such as burning the brush to expose the infrastructure below, and munitions to penetrate underground facilities.

First Battle Effect

The battles at Maroun al-Ras and Bint Jbeil shaped the perception and influenced decision making of leaders throughout the war. This had ramifications on the entire war, sadly also in a negative way. For instance, the fabricated narrative which claimed that Egoz had been mistakenly sent in daylight to

Maroun al-Ras led to the leadership halting all daylight movement during part of the war, contrary to basic warfare doctrine.

The first tanks hit by ATMs led to a demonization of this threat, although the IDF had known about it from previous campaigns, and the extent of losses from antitank weapons was substantially low (a huge credit to the developers of the Merkava protection systems).

Initial challenges we had with traversing minefields led to a false perception that minefields were an acute problem.

Logistical challenges were exaggerated, leading to a perception that entire units were deprived of supplies for many days, which was not the case.

One downed helo immediately influenced the way all helicopters were deployed.

Casualties at the first nature reserve we attacked (Shaked) made every nature reserve into a "disaster area" to be avoided at all cost. One battle (since it was the first) negatively impacted the perception for the entire region, although we had extensively trained for this before the war.

The first battle reflects a transitional phase between two states. From storage warehouses and training to a heated battlefield, from routine security and holding the line to intense war with less restraint, and from short battles to continuous fighting for days and weeks, requiring much moral strength and durability.

First battles will usually be dramatic and get high publicity. It is essential to do everything possible to avoid hysteria emanating from singular events, and to refrain from making sweeping, all-encompassing decisions based on them. This requires leadership, proportionality, controlled combat-learning methodologies, and effective shaping of media and public perception.

Informal Discourse

Modern warfare enables simultaneous formal and informal circles of communication. During the Second Lebanon War, the informal circle posed a substantial threat to the quality of the formal one, leading to serious consequences. The immediate availability of the newly deployed encrypted cell phone allowed everyone to exercise the Phone-a-Friend method (a gimmick in which contestants on a TV game show could call and consult a friend), even during the heat of battle. This behavior was flawed from a moral perspective, reflected a lack of steadfastness and loyalty, breached the chain of command, and compromised the framework of the organization and the unity of the information.

Language, Concepts, and Operational Thinking

Multiple articles and books have been published around the world, and in Israel, on Revolution in Military Affairs (RMA), dealing with various aspects of the ever-evolving battlefield. I am proud of the role I played in developing this new language. Those who objected to this before the war took advantage of the bedlam typical to the aftermath of war, and these valuable assets were being ridiculed and disregarded. Only now, many years later, are the people who were tossed out in fury finding their way back –and bringing back their knowledge – to senior courses within the IDF.

It was a grave mistake to hang all the faults of managing the war on operational concepts, systemic language, and knowledge-development processes in the IDF. Those who negated operational design after the war have washed down the drain oceans of knowledge and excellent methodologies. It was a serious mistake to burn this military-intellectual achievement on the stake.

Plasma Displays

One of the most publicized criticisms following the war was the false notion that commanders led their troops from behind, sitting in backward command posts, facing computer screens. To the best of my knowledge, it was Halutz who originated this misconception, due to false information on one specific incident. By this he caused injustice to the entire chain of command.

In certain circumstances, command and control from an FCG post cannot be overruled. Still, on the whole, IDF commanders lead from the front, demonstrating the "Follow me!" creed.

The pointless and cynical media scandal over the so-called "plasma displays" may someday backfire, when a commander chooses to situate himself in a disadvantageous position just in order to avoid being perceived as a "plasma commander."

Casualties

During a battalion commander AAR held after the war, CGS Halutz explained that he took the issue of the number of casualties into consideration because he knows "the Jewish mother." This was a serious mistake. Once a mission had been ordered and was underway, it needed to be fulfilled, while trying to minimize casualties of course, but without hesitation because of their possible occurrence. Posing a precondition of zero casualties is unheard of, and means in fact giving up on the feasibility of carrying out the mission. Every human being is a universe, and IDF commanders are exceptionally devoted to each one of their soldiers, but war is not a cakewalk.

Advantage over Hezbollah

Soldiers with previous combat experience from Gaza and J&S contributed to a substantial advantage over Hezbollah, in their level of fighting, equipment, and TTPs. There was not one battle during the war where Hezbollah succeeded fully, and in the few instances when they attempted to carry out a counterattack, they exposed themselves and suffered many casualties.

The understanding that Hezbollah is a guerilla army and not merely a bunch of terrorists in uniform was an important development of our conceptualization of the northern arena. Surprisingly, Hezbollah rarely operated at night, except for extracting casualties, so we enjoyed total advantage and dominance in non-daylight hours.

AAR

In my opinion, the debriefing process conducted in the 91st Division after the war was deep and serious, unlike the one at the General Staff. With all the criticism and negative fallout after the war, I found it difficult to focus and define measurable indexes by which to evaluate our performance. It was challenging to disconnect the operational AAR from the raging external criticism, influenced by the media and politicians – both civilian and uniformed.

Values

Values define the results! And it was our values that led to our tactical accomplishments and victories in the battlefield. Sadly, it was also values at the core of what I perceive as the main failure of the war: the failure of value-based leadership.

I believe that Halutz, and even the political level above him, were wronged by those who attributed to them everything that went wrong – or was perceived as having gone wrong – during the war.

As someone who has studied warfare from a young age, I know that many wars and campaigns in history have seen similar challenges and developments as those we experienced in the war of 2006, including the making of fundamental mistakes. But I have no doubt that all were made without negligence or malice.

Halutz was the first pilot to serve as the CGS, and some claim that after the war of 2006, he will also be the last. I believe this is nonsense, and in a way reflects the immaturity of the IDF in fully grasping the essence of jointness.

The only serious failure I find in Halutz's performance relates to his leadership – the fact that he did not demonstrate loyalty and give full backing to his subordinates. This was a breakdown of codes and values. He did not assume full responsibility and deflected criticism about the war by throwing lower echelons under the bus. This kind of behavior may be expected of politicians – but not commanders.

LTG Dan Halutz devoted his life, and risked his life, for the State of Israel, and should be credited for being a great warrior and devoted officer and commander. But at the moment of truth, leading the IDF in war and its aftermath, I believe that he failed bitterly, mainly from a values perspective.

Part 3

Love Story

Chapter 22

What Was This War All About?

A Negative Narrative

The war was over. How strange it suddenly felt.

A soldier, a warrior, waits eagerly for war. It is the essence of his being and the culmination of his training.

When war breaks out, you don't always see it coming, and even when you're fighting it, it takes time to comprehend that this is really war. As I experienced, it sometimes takes time and effort for this understanding to sink in and make its way up the chain of command.

During combat, you must learn fast if you wish to win the next battle.

The first battle takes its toll, as friction and changing states force you to learn on your feet. The faster you adapt and learn, the lower the price you pay.

During the war, you discover amazing things about yourself, about your comrades, and about comradeship. War tests the system – and tests you within the system – under the harshest conditions.

If your soldiers are united around you, and you are appreciated as a person and loved, it's not that it will be easy – there will always be difficulties and setbacks – but it will certainly work.

This is true from you downward. From you upward, it depends on the leadership, values, and integrity of higher commanding levels. It has much to do both with organizational culture and the individuals involved, and there's not much you can do to influence it.

During war you cannot fight backwards and homewards, or else you lose your focus and violate your responsibility.

The war had ended. But there was no way of knowing how long the fragile cease-fire would hold. Still, within days, arrangements for the new situation could be seen on the ground.

LAF forces deployed as our forces retreated – mostly by night in order to avoid exposure to ATM and sniper threats. I did not trust Hezbollah or the arrangement with it. My mission was to bring my forces back home safely.

No more firing. A strange quiet fell over the entire region. But the work was not over.

I led various forums with staff officers and commanders, including out at my FCG, where we observed the area. I heard updates, gave out instructions, and made sure the division maintained continuity, order, and discipline. The division was functioning well. Even after a month of intensive fighting, the strain had not eroded its strength.

I met and spoke with regular units and reservists who were being released back to their normal lives. Some conversations were constructive, but others surprised me with criticism and even rage – about insufficient equipment, unclear missions, and even general confusion such as "what was this war all about, anyway?"

I discovered that some tactical units had lacked an understanding of their place and role in the big picture, and this had led to frustration. I acknowledged this as an important lesson learned, and emphasized it during the first brigade commander AAR after the war.

"Brigade commanders must constantly explain the broader context to the units under them," I stressed, "in order to give the soldiers a sense of purpose, avoid frustration, and allow them to improvise while keeping the big picture in mind."

Among soldiers, a twisted and distorted perception had been instilled by the overall public atmosphere of criticism. These false messages had been planted in people's minds by the media throughout the war and after it. Contributing to shaping this negative narrative were irresponsible leaders and politicians, different interest groups, and senior IDF commanders who fed the media in order to make headlines and generate spin.

A few years after the war, I discovered that instilling the perception of failure among the Israeli public by inciting the reservists had been a premeditated plan by politicians seeking to topple Prime Minister Ehud Olmert's government and seek an advantage in succeeding him.

The war was irresponsibly made into a story of failure, with the blame attributed to the fighting echelons – the easiest prey and scapegoat. This cynical political maneuver of manipulating the public's perception caused serious damage that will take many years to correct.

Reservists make up the backbone of the IDF. Those who serve, leaving behind families and careers, risking their lives to join the fight for freedom, are worthy of every expression of gratitude this nation can give.

They are our national team.

My division was comprised mainly of reservists. Their contribution was valuable, and I respect and love them. But after crossing the border during the war, there were those who crossed the line when they came home, by waging a brutal and malicious campaign against me, blaming me for shortcomings in training, equipment, and the conduct of the war.

I see the actions of this minority as a threat to the unique construct of the IDF. Criticism must remain constructive and focused on professional improvement, not on creating a rift between commanders and those who might someday be called up to serve under them in battle.

The negative perception of the war also took an immense emotional toll on bereaved families, as they faced harsh narratives of failure instead of glorious sacrifice and contribution, as they deserved.

A nation must honor its fallen, whatever the circumstances. *Those who have made the ultimate sacrifice for their country have not fallen in vain!*

As for me personally, I felt a looming cloud over my head, as well as a heavy heart. I realized that my situation was serious. As I followed the media, I was exposed to the horrible slander being smeared daily. There were invented stories of my supposed suspension and reassignment during the war, the claim that I had failed to carry out an order to bring back bodies of Hezbollah operatives, and various quotes of different alleged statements supposedly made by me. There was talk of failure, disconnection from the field, and as usual, my "ambiguous" and "vague" language.

The fire was being deliberately and maliciously directed toward me. Someone understood that the war was not managed as it should have been, or not perceived publicly as successful, and decided to blame me for it. Of course there were those who took advantage of the situation to improve their own positions in promotion boards.

It did not hit me only at the end of the war, but was apparent from the beginning, with rumors and publications reaching me during battle. Aside from my close friends and subordinates, I felt completely alone, unwanted, attacked, and a scapegoat for every perceived failure.

I felt completely abandoned by my superiors. With the unwavering backing and loyalty I demonstrated throughout the war, I could not comprehend how they could have done this to me.

I do not subscribe to the idea that a person must "take responsibility." I do not need to *take* responsibility, for I have never given it away. The responsibility had always been mine – for my mission, my AOR, my subordinates, and for the civilians whom I fought to protect.

Conversations on the phone with my family were extremely difficult. There was shock, insult, anger, and pain. Donna, the girls, and the entire family, who had carried the burden of my sacrifice all these years, and knew my passion and commitment to my service, could not comprehend how it was possible to transition instantaneously from a hero to a failure in the eyes of so many. They were appalled by the expressions of denunciation being fed to the media.

Unlike past challenges, in which I had felt an overwhelming support from the public, now it was only a close circle of relatives and friends who supported me. Wider circles of the community expressed alienation and abandonment.

I was exhausted physically and mentally from a difficult year of preparing for war, five weeks of fighting, the pains from my old wounds which had worsened during the war, the pain of losing fifty-eight soldiers from my division, and the torment of having been unable to prevent the abduction in the first place.

After so many years of success, now came the stunning feeling of failure, betrayal, and loneliness.

But still, I needed to hide my feelings from my soldiers and continue to lead them – especially now.

The media was full of negative references to my conduct during the war. I was depicted in one cartoon as standing before a firing squad, and in another I was seen tied to a gallows.

Professional public relations advisors worked overtime in service of their senior clients. My character was ridiculed, torn, and trampled upon, in the press and online, promoting feelings of loathing, rejection, and even hate.

"Is it true what they say?" a reporter asked my deputy.

"What do they say?" asked Dror.

"That he didn't care that soldiers were dying?"

This is how bad and how low it got.

Halutz forbade me to speak to the media, supposedly for professional reasons, but I suspect for personal reasons too. Preventing me from defending myself served the overall campaign of deflecting all criticism from those who were responsible – the CGS, the minister of defense, and the prime minister himself.

"How foolish of you!" a senior journalist said to me bluntly. "You're the only one following the order not to give interviews. Don't you see that they're shutting you up on purpose?"

"I'm here for you," said IDF spokesperson BG Miri Regev. But she failed to follow through and did not defend me or enable me to defend myself.

"You manage PR for the CGS, not for me," I told her.

She didn't like it, but it was the truth.

The Image of the War

The image of the outcome of the war has been distorted and twisted. Instead of focusing on specific mistakes and areas requiring improvement, an overall image of failure has been deliberately shaped and promoted.

The IDF should not have been portrayed as being so clumsy. I see this as a grave mistake in public diplomacy, and a failure in representing the IDF and representing the truth.

Official Israel failed to portray reality, shape the public's perception, and perform the appropriate expectation management. The result was a complete disconnect between what had taken place on the ground in Lebanon and what was taking place in the media and in people's minds. Soldiers returned from the war, where they had witnessed firsthand great accomplishments and decisive victories in every battle, only to find a nation with a negatively distorted picture of failure.

The media serves not national goals, but their own need for boosting circulation and ratings. Sadly, the majority of reports were characterized by shallowness and hysteria, and served various agendas, including those of personal individuals.

Reporters had been too freely embedded and allowed direct and intimate access to commanders and headquarters. Some officers had conducted operations with wireless mics pinned on their uniforms, enabling intimate analysis and exposure of internal debates. There was no restraint and no control.

I acknowledge that we missed some of the opportunities during the campaign. I am aware of the professional failures that occurred. But I refuse to accept the hysterical and reckless talk of "losing" the war. I even don't appreciate the formulation that we "haven't won."

The real results are known: hundreds of dead Hezbollah fighters, the Dahieh Quarter of Beirut in rubble, Nasrallah hiding in a bunker, international intervention in Lebanon, LAF on the border, long-range rocket capabilities destroyed, and horrible damage wherever we operated.

Only people lacking historic perspective, ignorant in matters of war, or those who benefited by instilling a perception of failure can dare describe this war as a failure!

As I write these words, ten years after the war, residents of the Galilee still cannot remember such a quiet period. Although I believe another war will come and Hezbollah remains a substantial threat, it is deterred for the time being. The achievements of the war are still apparent and even seen in a different light compared to other campaigns fought since then (such as in Gaza).

I see the inability to differentiate between the achievements on the ground and the fact that Israel was under a constant barrage of rockets as a serious failure of leadership.

It should have been made clear to the Israeli public, which is capable of withstanding extreme pressure. Someone should have shaped and constructed realistic expectations, but failed to do so.

The Information Was There!

After one of the AAR sessions with my staff, Avi – our intel officer – asked to speak with me in private. He had seemed pale and troubled throughout the meeting, and I was anxious to hear what was on his mind.

"There was information," he said, clearly distraught.

"What information?"

"There were several specific intel items. IDI had it and it never reached us."

"This cannot be."

"It's true."

"Did NORTHCOM get it?"

"No. It was stuck at IDI."

"What was the intel?"

Avi showed me the material. It consisted of various segments of information, each of which would have led to action and changed the outcome, if we had been exposed to it. There was no doubt that if I had seen even a fraction of what existed at IDI, I would not have canceled the high alert and would not have opened the roads. *The abduction would certainly have been prevented.*

I felt dizzy for a moment.

I demanded that a full inquiry be conducted, but the report that finally reached me was shallow and evasive. The bottom line according to the report was that IDI's conduct was flawless. I read it and could not believe my eyes.

I later learned from the media that an intel officer in a sensitive position had been transferred, and his inexperienced successor had misunderstood the importance of the material in front of him. This was never mentioned in the official report that I received.

Fifteen Years and Five Weeks

"How are you feeling, Gal?"

Halutz had summoned me to his office, for the first time since the war. Tel Aviv was like a different planet.

"I…" I opened my mouth to speak, but hesitated for a moment, as if the words were stuck in my throat.

"I admired you for fifteen years, and I've been furious at you for five weeks."

"I can understand that," answered Halutz quietly, as he jotted down something in his notebook.

"Why are you doing this to me?" I shot out. "My blood is being shed in public! You see what is being done to me!"

"I know that you performed well in the war. Commanders and subordinates all attest to this."

I was astounded. "So say it," I demanded. "Tell the public!"

"I cannot, and it will do you no good."

"Sir, I have been demonized in the eyes of the average Israeli. Do you understand how people react when they hear my name?" I asked in pain.

"I don't care about the average Israeli," he said, sitting up straight.

"Well, I do. Everything I do is for the average Israeli."

"Do you know what they're doing to me?!" Halutz cried out. I knew that he, too, was under attack. Public criticism of him had begun ever since it became known that, on the first day of the war, he had spoken with his broker and given instructions to sell stocks.

"You are the chief of the General Staff," I said, looking him straight in the eye. "You have reached the very top. And from your position, you should strengthen me and give me backing."

Halutz did not respond, only made a few more notes.

"I have been seriously wronged, and suffered great damage – to my name, my family, and my kids!" I insisted.

But the discussion was over.

Heartbroken and at Peace

Sixty soldiers were killed and dozens were wounded in my division. While leading the rehabilitation and reorganization efforts, I went to visit the wounded in hospitals and began visiting the bereaved families.

The emotional strain was immense. It is always extremely hard to face the grief of those who have lost their loved ones, but this was much more than that – I was their commander. They were entrusted to me, and I failed to return them safely to their families. And with the negative public slander portraying me as responsible for all that went wrong, some families saw me as personally responsible for their loss.

Sadly, families were fed false information both on specific circumstances and the overall context of the war. What a terrible thing it was to see parents who were led to believe that their sons had died in vain, or because of "one big fiasco."

I spent many hours explaining what had happened on the ground and how it all fit into the big picture. Many times I could see the positive impact to bereaved parents of understanding the right context, with both facial and verbal expressions such as "Why weren't we told this before?"

There were those who chose not to meet me. I did not blame them or attempt to impose my presence. Many opened their homes and hearts to me, and amazed me with their honorable and noble conduct, combining piercing questions and strong support.

I traveled by night throughout Israel and entered the homes of families whose worlds had fallen apart. I came out physically and mentally exhausted, and felt simultaneously heartbroken and at peace. Each morning I would return directly to another intense day at my division.

I objected to the actions of some bereaved parents who took it upon themselves to campaign against certain officials – both military and civilian – seeking their dismissal. In some cases, bereaved families insisted on conducting their own investigations on the conduct of the war, and I believe this was inappropriate.

"All Because of Your Father!"

The school year began two weeks after the war ended. Like many Israeli fathers that year, I had been away the entire summer, so my family had not really experienced a "summer vacation."

The girls debated whether to go to school, fearing the reaction of other children after their father had been portrayed in such a negative way for weeks. During one of the first days at school, Ofri was approached by a few children.

"Your father failed!"

"What?" Ofri was stunned.

"Everyone says that your father is a failure."

"Who told you that?"

"It says so in the papers, and my parents told me that it's all because of your father."

Similar incidents occurred many times to other members of my family.

Ofri was even approached on Yom Hazikaron, the Day of Remembrance for the Fallen Soldiers of Israel, and told: "The soldiers died because of your father!" Ofri told Donna what had happened, adding, "Don't tell Dad. He is suffering enough."

The pain of betrayal took its toll on all of us. It was during this difficult time that our parents' health began to deteriorate, and I attribute this to the collapse in all of our emotional states.

Donna and the girls came to be with me on the High Holiday of Rosh Hashanah – the Jewish New Year. It was the first time I had allowed them to join me since the war. Normally my phone would be exploding with endless holiday greetings, but this year it was very quiet.

"Your shares are dropping," one of my family members said. "Why should anybody want to call you?"

It was just another symptom of the isolation and alienation I had been experiencing.

Farewell from the Wall

One evening, a debriefing session was convened in the office of the CGS, attended by division commanders and a few members of the GS.

"I ask that we conduct an open discussion," said Halutz, requesting that every division commander present his division's battles and share insights and lessons learned.

There was much tension in the room.

We began briefing as requested, but were brutally interrupted with critical comments by Kaplan. To my surprise, MG Gadi Eizenkot attacked me and accused me of lacking self-criticism and other ostensible failings.

I had had enough and lashed out.

"I want to make it perfectly clear," I announced, "what Gadi just said is completely false, and I have no idea where he got this information from."

Gadi recoiled and said nothing. The opportunity was now seized by others to critique my actions, including one division commander who conceitedly explained how *he* would have done it better. Not only had he not participated in the war, but I had heard of his disruptive actions behind the scenes.

"Why did you go on like that, with all those rockets being fired on the north?" asked another swellheaded and hypocritical division commander. He would later go around with his laptop giving briefings on how he would have prevented the abduction and done it all better.

But besides the "ambush" by the group which had become known as the "junta," there were a few division commanders who supported me and spoke on my behalf.

"You have said things about Gal on record," one of them addressed Halutz. "If you have something to say about him, say it here and clarify. If you didn't mean what was published, say that too."

Another reserve division commander reiterated other expressions of support and added, "You should back up Gal!"

To most of these comments, Halutz did not respond, or mumbled something and made notes.

As I exited the room, I realized that this was it. The last shred of optimism I had held on to was gone. The harsh things that were said in that meeting – and even more importantly, the things that were not said – made me realize that I was the one who was going to pay the price.

In the hallway, I stopped and looked at the wall where all former IDF CGSs were portrayed. When waiting in this hall for meetings, it had once been common for colleagues to point at the empty space following the last photograph and say, "You're going to be up on this wall, Gal. Just about here."

I would smile and wave off the praise, but in my heart I dreamed of this exalted position, as a culmination of the aspirations of a military officer who has devoted his life to the service.

I now looked up at the wall and with great pain, but acceptance, bid it farewell.

This Is Harder to Fix

The Spirit of the IDF, an ethical code that hangs on the wall in every unit, reflects the core elements of our resilience and strength. This code of conduct serves as a beacon of values to the entire Israeli society.

Cracks in comradeship and loyalty and breaches of fundamental ethics within the senior ranks are a source of great concern and cannot be taken lightly.

In his retirement ceremony following his resignation, MG Udi Adam spoke of this and said that the main failures in the war were breaches of collegial loyalty – which makes them ever so much more difficult to fix.

Of course this does not reflect the majority of IDF officers who are decent and worthy. The problem is that those who do not live up to that description are creative and manipulative, and their devious ways make them influential and dangerous.

The catch is that those who carry the real burden of Israel's defense, the doers, are all too often targeted by those standing on the sidelines, the talkers. When it came time to relate to what had happened in the war, however, the talkers suddenly became mute in order to keep themselves out of trouble. This would have been the time for support and camaraderie, but they were silent.

When the IDF left Lebanon in May 2000, the commanders were highly criticized for the way the retreat was conducted. Footage of Hezbollah taking over the Fatima Gate border crossing, near Metula, created a heavy sense of humiliation. Gabi Ashkenazi was NORTHCOM CO, Kaplan was 91st Division CO, and Benny Gantz commanded the Liaison Unit.

I had made a point of expressing support and complimenting commanders, both in closed forums and publicly. The same was my conduct after the abduction in October of that year. I felt it was the right thing to do, especially in opposition to those who criticized. I knew that this was part of fighting terror, guerilla warfare, and insurgency. It was impossible to always succeed.

Word reached me that one of my battalion commanders had been spreading disinformation and slander about my conduct and decision making during the war. It seemed as if, by blaming me, he was trying to deflect the mistakes that he himself had made. At a certain point he approached me and begged for forgiveness. I put it behind me and sent him back to his battalion for continued debriefing. But soon after, I heard that he was continuing his campaign and had even given a lecture in another defense agency, where he personally criticized me. I confronted him and told him that he should be ashamed of himself. This was no way for an officer to behave.

After the war, I began receiving apologies from people who had made my life miserable during the war. An evil spirit struck the IDF at that time, and officers – mainly senior – acted behind the scenes in subversive and manipulative ways. "Me" came before "we," and I was stunned by the extent of this phenomenon. Apologies couldn't fix the damage already done.

The war was over, but the internal battles raged on.

It was one thing to see my peers doing this, but the conduct of retired major generals came as a bad surprise. They sat in TV studios and filled the air with their learned remarks and analyses, targeting me. Some even called for my dismissal. I couldn't help but suspect that this was part of the same orchestrated campaign to make me the scapegoat, which was very convenient for them, since I was denied the opportunity to defend myself against this babbling, and they were free to shape my public image.

The hypocrisy was so obvious, it was ridiculous. One minute a general was smooth talking me with words of support, and an hour later he would appear in the media and resume his campaign of spreading rumors and gossip about me.

I can only guess what purpose this served – from settling old scores to wanting to return to the spotlight and promote political aspirations. These generals who were once a source of admiration were now wreaking havoc on morale and sabotaging unity among the ranks.

To my relief and joy, there were also generals who were honest and truthful.

They showed up at my HQ during and after the war, offering a kind word of advice and a pat on the shoulder. We also have people like this, and we should be proud of them.

The CGS was also under heavy fire from these former generals. His tactic was no less than genius. He called up two of the leading critics – Generals Doron Almog and Yoram ("Yaya") Yair, recruited them to the IDF as reservists, and sent them on an inquiry mission. He directed them my way.

Almog was assigned to investigate the abduction, and Yaya was asked to "assist in learning the lessons from the war." Yaya was a highly decorated and appreciated commander and warrior, but I was concerned because he was speaking out on every media platform, his main themes being praising the deeds of the past and criticizing the actions of the present.

I met with him and promised to integrate him in our debriefing process, but I also told him that I did not accept his constant media presence.

"I heard you on the radio a little while ago," I told him sharply. "I am not going to work with you this way."

"From now on, I'm out of the press," he promised.

Chapter 23

"Unprecedented" Debriefings

Scapegoated

I personally led a rigorous debriefing process, in which we systematically analyzed the development of the war. It was obvious that each person experienced the war differently, according to rank, position, and specific location in battle. Only through detailed combined analyses were we able to comprehend the big picture. The process took place while we were still leading security initiatives on the northern border.

Yaya would join us, wearing uniform and a red beret, accompanied by an entourage of assistants. He contributed from his vast tactical experience, but I found that his understanding of operational art and modern warfare at the divisional level lacked perspective, and some of his ideas and insights were far from relevant to contemporary warfare.

On October 16, I was to be the first division commander to present his debriefing to the GS. A day before, I was notified that the main findings would be presented to the media. I strongly objected and spoke to the IDF spokesperson, BG Miri Regev, but she only quoted the orders from above, and I felt as if I were listening to a recorded message. I understood the need to feed the media with tangible facts about what (and who) went wrong, but I doubted that the public would get a comprehensive picture in a few minutes about a war that had lasted five weeks.

I presented a detailed and structured briefing in front of the entire General Staff and senior commanders. Many of them were seeing for the first time what the war looked like from my division's perspective, with the frequent changes in directive throughout the war. I was constantly heckled, and occasionally loud arguments broke out with bitter accusations. It was stressful and emotional for everyone involved.

I was asked to make it short and focused, but then harassed by Kaplan for "lack of information" or "shallowness." When I explained details, I was urged to "move on," as this was "not a divisional-level session."

Jerry, CO of the Home Front Command, took to the podium and asked if there was anyone in the GS who had ever commanded a battle of such magnitude before, or if anyone had ever commanded a division at war. The room fell silent. Jerry knew the answer was negative.

"This is just to teach us," said Jerry, "that you should not judge your friend until you have been in his shoes."

Following questions on the matter, General Klifi spoke and negated the claims that the orders I had issued were not clear enough, and stated that he had reviewed the protocols and found my orders to have been by the book.

During the meeting, I received word that the media had been fed information by generals in the room, probably using text messages. Reports on a "harsh debriefing" and "failure" were out before I even began my presentation.

As soon as the session was over, Yaya broke his promise and shocked me by presenting the division's findings on TV. Other commanders hurried off to their own reporters to get their message out.

As I had expected, the result was catastrophic. The headlines did not reflect the complex briefing I had given and just bombarded the public with melodramatic accusations: "91st Division Failed to Understand That This Was War," "The Division Commander Who Failed," and so on.

I told Yaya how furious I was with his hasty and shallow coverage, but he said that it wasn't his call.

"The CGS ordered it."

"You should have disagreed. You could have backed me up. There are regulations making our findings privileged. Halutz and his spokesperson have made a grave mistake!" I said angrily.

"I protected you," he claimed. "The problems in the war were not with you but higher up."

"Right," I said bitterly, "but who is receiving all the heat?"

The following morning Halutz understood the mistake of going public with the findings and ordered that from now on divisional debriefings would not be published. It was the right decision, but too late for me, and now the average Israeli was fixated on the falsehoods plastered all over the papers.

One of the popular conclusions was that the new terminology of operational art was at fault. I was blamed, as before, for using an exalted language which, it was claimed, was not fit for the IDF. There were those who had waited for this chance to attack the field they had always despised and get rid of OTRI methodologies.

I continue to insist that in a modern army there must always be the combination of *"safra v'sayfa"* – book and sword. High language, learning, research, and writing are virtues, not faults.

Another committee to investigate the abduction was appointed during the war by NORTHCOM CO. It was led by BG Avi Ashkenazi (Gabi Ashkenazi's brother), CO of a reserve division whom I knew back from when we were cadets together in Nachshon Company. Even our families were close and kept in touch. But he didn't support me and occasionally confronted me.

Incredibly, the time was coming for his committee to present its findings, but they had only spoken to me briefly during the war and had not interviewed key officers, such as Dror, my deputy; Monir, my chief of operations; or any of my battalion commanders.

My attempts to reach out to them and read the initial report were met with various evasive maneuvers. Only one day before presenting his final conclusions, Avi summoned me and let me have a look at the "facts" chapter, but not the "recommendations," which he only outlined orally.

To my amazement, the issue of early warning from the undisclosed intel was omitted. I knew that he knew of the information that had never reached me, so there was no way of explaining this other than that it was another planned ambush, aimed at targeting me. Avi made my "language," and "over-conceptualization" into the focal point of his report, supported by incorrect details and a general lack of understanding of what had taken place.

I was overwhelmed by the tendentiousness and shallowness, and even identified wording that seemed dictated (I had no doubt by whom).

I drove to see Donna at her workplace and waited outside the gate for her to come out to me.

"They're closing in on me, Donna. Ashkenazi's report is part of the overall campaign. There's no fact finding. It's all biased and populistic. Not much I can do about it."

"What do you mean, there's nothing to do?" Donna was upset. "What's going to happen now?"

"This is probably the end, Donna. With this orchestrated agenda, it will take a long time for the full, truthful picture to emerge. But in the meantime they will have achieved their target, making me the scapegoat."

"So what's next?"

"I think it will end with a forced resignation or a dismissal."

I hurried back to the north. With everything going on and everything on my mind, my main concern was still the force under my command, and the continued responsibility of defending the north.

When Avi presented his "findings" to NORTHCOM and the GS, I confronted both his methodology and recommendations, and pointed to the deliberate course of action being taken against me.

To my surprise and relief, the report was completely rejected by the CGS and my response was commended. Halutz later informed me that he planned to appoint another committee to investigate the abduction, and I regained a touch of trust in the system.

The Almog Committee of Inquiry

One evening, Tal, my assistant, updated me that MG Doron Almog had been assigned to lead a special investigative commission to review the abduction.

"Oy," I flinched.

"What is it?" Tal asked, worried.

"This isn't good. Doron has . . . well . . . a very specific character," I said, keeping it vague.

"What do you mean? He was a paratrooper and your commander, wasn't he?"

"Yes, he's an intelligent and experienced commander."

"So?"

"He's also very opinionated, extreme, and target-oriented."

"Is that a problem?"

"Not yet, but it will be." If Almog was locked on an agenda, he would promote it all the way. I knew that he had already been criticizing the way the war had been led.

I had known Almog for many years, and our relationship had had its ups and downs. As my commander, he influenced me and encouraged me to read and write, but we also clashed regularly, such as over his choices of units for operations.

I had not told Tal about the latest dispute I had had with Almog, when I refused to appoint his former aide-de-camp to a position for which he was not qualified. My considerations were totally professional, but Almog had taken it personally and was very angry with me.

I assessed that Almog's appointment was deliberately made by Halutz in order to deflect all the negative attention onto me and prevent criticism from reaching the CGS and the government.

Almog had a unique image in the Israeli defense establishment and the entire Israeli society, not only due to his career accomplishments, but his exemplary conduct and personal example in struggling with personal family tragedies. A reflection of his unique public image can be seen in the fact that Yair Lapid once wrote that Almog was a "holy man."

I knew that Almog's conclusions and recommendations would be taken as irrevocable, and feared that his grudge against me would influence his findings. I wanted to believe that Almog would know how to separate personal and professional issues, but I had lost my naïveté under the circumstances. The IDF was not devoid of personal considerations and calculations.

The makeup of the committee was a sham and a scam, having Almog surrounded mostly by senior intel officers, who seemed to have been carefully selected by IDI. This made it clear from the onset that the committee would disregard the intel screwup that had led to the abduction. In fact, it was not a committee, but a one-man-show, with a fictitious supporting team put in place to defend the IDI.

It took many days before the committee came to speak with me at the division HQ, and when they did, the interview was conducted in a hurried, shallow, and superficial manner. I had prepared a detailed presentation, but they spent only three hours with me (including a tour and lunch), and it was the last time we met!

Almog did not seem attentive to my briefing, and the responses from him and his team were odd and evasive, especially when I spoke of the intel withheld from us that would have changed the entire outcome.

I would later hear of the many forces at play, including external intervention and interference with the committee's work. One of its members, overwhelmed with regret and pangs of conscience, revealed to me a year later that Halutz had told Almog that I should have been "taken care of" long ago, back when I was Shaldag CO. I was the target, and the others were not to be touched, and the division level would be the only echelon to be blamed.

It had been discussed before the war that I was slated to become the head of the Strategic Division at the Planning Directorate (J5) of the GS. Halutz told me that he considered this an important position, close to him in the General Staff, and a "springboard" for promotion to major general.

But I now requested to stay on for another year as 91st Division commander in order to implement the lessons learned from the war. This was leaked to the press, which turned it into a scandal. "How dare the commander who failed request to continue in his position?"

I received a phone call from Halutz notifying me that I had been officially selected to the post at J5, as originally planned.

"I think it suits you. I ask you not to make any 'gut decisions.'"

When the appointment was made public, the media turned that also into a scandal, and Minister of Defense Amir Peretz responded by announcing that my appointment was suspended. He did not even show me the courtesy of speaking with me before this cowardly and careless expression of no-confidence. He probably wanted to boost his image while deflecting criticism of his own failures in the war. In doing so, he simply sacrificed me as a pawn, just like any other lowly politician.

I am still amazed and disappointed at how people in sensitive leadership positions could put their own benefit before public interests. A minister of defense is a political appointee, but the national importance of this position demands the conduct and integrity expected of senior leaders and commanders.

A Fateful Week

It was Sunday evening, November 5, 2006. I was at my HQ preparing for a briefing when Doron Almog called me on my cell.

"Hi, Doron."

"Hi, Gal, how are you?"

"OK. Working. What's up?"

"The situation is critical," he said, referring to his son Eran, who had severe autism and mental retardation. "He's in intensive care."

"Oh, no." My heart went out to him. "What is his condition?"

"Bad. We almost lost our boy."

"Be strong," I said.

"It's tough. Very tough," he said, and then almost without a pause, he added: "There's no choice, you're going to have to end your service in the IDF."

"What?!"

"Yes. We have a serious incident here. A failure. No one looked after that patrol."

"Have you found that I was negligent in any way?"

"Of course not! You would never be negligent, Gal. Not you."

"So?"

"The IDF needs a wake-up call."

"I cannot accept this. Why should I be held accountable for the mistakes of higher echelons?"

"Don't worry, Gal. You're young and talented. You'll have a second career."

"Doron!" In a few seconds dramatic and outrageous things were being hurled at me. I couldn't believe it.

"I refuse to accept this!" I said forcefully.

But the conversation was over.

I conducted the briefing I had been preparing before the call as planned, and at 1 AM headed home to speak to Donna, leaving my new deputy, Avi, in charge.

I asked Dror, my driver, to stop on the side of the road, then stepped outside and called the office of the CGS. A few minutes later Halutz was on the line, sounding alert. I updated him about what Almog had said, and it was obvious that this did not surprise him.

"Are you going to back me up?" I asked directly.

"Back you up on what?" he said.

I was shocked at this response. "Halutz, he wants to dismiss me from the IDF!"

"We'll see. I don't know... I'll think about it and get back to you."

I got back in the car and called Donna to let her know I was on my way home, then I called Benny Gantz, Ground Forces CO, and updated him on what was going on.

He was stunned.

"This means war!" Benny said angrily. "I'll call you later."

I reached home and had a long and painful talk with Donna. At 4:30 AM

I said good-bye, kissed the girls in their sleep, hugged Shoko, our Labrador, and set out back to the northern border.

In the morning, I was busy as usual with matters in the division and received no call from Halutz. Someone brought me the morning paper, with headlines already revealing Almog's intention of having me dismissed.

"Incredible! They have this planned like clockwork."

I updated everyone, during a staff meeting, on the latest developments.

On Wednesday, I received a message from Halutz that he now allowed me to speak openly in the press and give my version. I thought about this and came to the conclusion that this was a bad sign, as it had been three months since the war and this came in connection with Almog's warning of an imminent dismissal.

I was also notified that the committee was to present its findings to the GS the following Sunday, November 12.

That evening, after a few background discussions with members of the media, I spoke to Gadi Eizenkot.

"Halutz is in a tight spot," he said. "Doron has maneuvered him into a corner."

He explained that there were a few possible scenarios, such as dismissal or disqualification for command positions.

"Gadi, I refuse compromises and deals. I want full backup, just as Aviv Kochavi received after Gilad Schalit's abduction in Gaza. No negligence was found in my conduct. On the contrary!"

"I understand. I will pass on this message."

"And I want to see the report," I added. "They're going before the GS, and I haven't even seen it yet. They keep saying that it isn't written. How am I supposed to defend myself?"

"Understood. And you are right."

"Gadi," I stressed again, "I expect full backing!"

Friday and Saturday went by with the media campaigning and building up for Sunday's session. I did not receive the report.

Again I called Ronnie, Halutz's PA. I told him firmly that I had not yet received the report and without it I would not attend the meeting.

"I'll send it to you with a courier," Ronnie promised.

I spoke on the phone with Tzur Keren, the committee's secretary, who explained, "As it is written and presented, you will not be able to remain in the service." It was clear now: they were going for decapitation. I was to be their scapegoat.

I asked my friend from Shaldag – now my lawyer – Dror Brotfeld to join me at my home, and together we reviewed the final report.

"There are no findings – only conclusions," he determined, after reviewing the material. "This looks like a premeditated conspiracy."

The objective was to get rid of me. A compromise was devised whereby I would be disqualified for command positions and sent to a staff job. Such a decision would be for me tantamount to dismissal. Expulsion from commanding troops was a harsh move suitable as a punishment for moral turpitude, and I had never been charged with such an offense.

They were leaving me no choice. Commanding soldiers had been my main driving force my entire career. They were pushing me to a resignation, which I intended to submit under protest. I could see no option of remaining inside a system that did not back me up, and furthermore I thought there was no way I could go on defending myself this way, having been the target of an orchestrated political and military campaign.

I spent a long night writing my resignation letter. I spoke of my responsibility for my division and my AOR, and expressed, as I had done many times, that I did not need to take responsibility, for I had never given it away. I laid out my serious reservations relating to the way my division had been made a scapegoat, and protested the lack of backing from senior leadership. I explained that Almog's committee was biased and that the final conclusions were comparable to drawing a target around an arrow after it had hit the board. I begged that no actions be taken against my subordinates, as they had performed superbly. I concluded with emphasizing the importance of values, as a compass and beacon for our national resilience and defense.

Before sunrise, I wrote a personal letter to Donna, bringing me to tears. I donned my class A uniform and felt as if the insignia on my chest was burning through the cloth and into my heart.

I woke Donna and kissed her, and kissed the sleeping girls.

"So this is it?" Donna asked.

"This is it," I said, and pointed to the letter I had left her on the table.

Or, my trusty driver, whisked me to the IDF HQ in Tel Aviv, in time to hand in my resignation before the scheduled presentation by Doron Almog.

"Good morning, sir!" said the sentry at the gate, and saluted.

"Good morning," I said, returning his salute, and made my way into the building and upstairs to the CGS's office. My heart was pounding, and I was adrenalized as if this were a mission deep in enemy territory and I was now storming the target. I felt I must push forward and engage, but it was as if waves were hurling me back. There was a side of me that wanted to retrace my steps and retreat. How in the world had it all come to this?

Halutz was stunned. He probably thought that I would remain in the IDF at all costs, but he was wrong. At that moment he realized that his attempt to hide behind my back had failed, and that he too was doomed.

Even after all these years, I still will not describe what took place in his office during those few minutes on Sunday morning, November 12, 2006.

The entire IDF GS convened for the final reports on the war.

Not only was Almog's report biased and shallow, but he launched an aggressive personal attack, waving his papers and pointing at me repeatedly, and asking open-ended questions while gesturing to his audience.

"You're not the victim here, Gal!" he lashed out at me. "The only victims are the soldiers who died!"

He even stooped so low as to play a recording of a reserve platoon commander from the unit of the abducted soldiers, screaming in pain and frustration.

It was a despicable and shameful display, and even Halutz had to restrain him: "Enough, Doron, carry on."

After Almog's disgraceful show came the intel committee's review. Within minutes, the room was filled with angry voices, as the team had completely ignored the information that had been withheld from us. Chezi, NORTH-COM J2, jumped up and protested what he called the "intel cover-up." Yadlin defensively expressed disappointment in his own team's conclusions. His deputy, BG Yossi Baidatz, asserted that there was no doubt that the information would have influenced our situational assessment and decision making.

Kaplan demanded that Halutz reject the intel report, and he did so, ordering a secondary review (which never took place).

The IDF spokesperson was coming in and out with notes for Halutz, as my resignation was already making headlines.

I requested permission to speak and updated the forum of my resignation under protest. I did not bother relating to the report. It was not worth my attention.

The room broke into an uproar. SOUTHCOM CO MG Yoav Galant immediately demanded that Halutz ask me to withdraw my resignation letter. Kaplan hypocritically chimed in and asked the same.

Benny Gantz attacked Almog for his "one-man" committee and its inherent "intel bias."

Halutz issued his closing remarks. He halfheartedly noted that he'd heard the requests to ask me to cancel my resignation. Using verbal jugglery, he rejected Almog's findings relating to himself and his staff, leaving all responsibility solely on my division.

I left the room followed by Benny Gantz, who asked me to come with him to his office. I sat down and asked for a glass of water. I felt as if I were on fire. We sat in silence for a few moments, then Benny asked me to explain my actions, and I did. Finally he stood up and so did I. At the door, he shook my hand and said, "What has happened to the IDF with Gal Hirsch is extremely severe."

On the way up north, I was told that Halutz wanted to meet me. I refused at first, but was answered that Halutz insisted on seeing me right away. I was still a soldier, so I obeyed and doubled back to Tel Aviv.

"Are you determined?" Halutz asked, as we met.

I hesitated before answering. What could have changed since the previous meeting? I knew that Almog was supposed to speak to Halutz right after the meeting, to talk about my "punishment," but with my resignation this seemed irrelevant.

I knew that Almog was planning a press conference that evening. My strong objections had been answered with reassuring promises that he was only to read a statement by the CGS. But I chuckled at this absurd promise, for I knew the people involved only too well. Doron was not going to give up his chance for a spectacle. My lawyer suggested that we issue a legal restraining order, but there was no way I was going to fight my IDF legally. At least that's how I felt at the time.

"What if I decide to stay?" I asked Halutz.

"Then you will no longer command soldiers."

So my assessment was right, and they had spoken about it even after I resigned.

"What justification is there to prohibit me from commanding?" I asked.

Halutz shrugged and said, "There was a committee and – "

"Thank you, but there's nothing more to say," I said as I stood up and turned to leave.

"Do you plan to leave immediately? What about your division? You should at least stay until we appoint a replacement."

"Wait a minute," I turned and faced him. "Didn't you just say that I cannot command? Aren't you afraid that I might act irresponsibly in the coming days?"

"Yes, I know what this looks like," Halutz answered, embarrassed.

"I don't need you to tell me to go back to my division! I command those people and will be there as long as it takes."

"Thank you, Gal, I appreciate it."

I saluted and left the room. Many journalists were waiting for me outside the HQ, and some followed my car on motorcycles. I heard that the same was happening at home, and it broke my heart that Donna and the girls were being followed and harassed.

Friends and colleagues appeared on all media channels, defending and explaining as best they could. Eyal Ben-Reuven prominently went from one studio to the next and backed me up by telling the story of the war more accurately and in more depth than anybody had done so far.

During all the mayhem, I received a fax offering me a tempting job overseas. It was one of the first indications that I was soon to be a civilian.

War from Within

That evening, on live television, Doron Almog conducted his grotesque show. Waving his papers, he criticized and ridiculed not only me, but the soldiers from the ambushed patrol, irresponsibly claiming that they had set out as if on a hike.

It was a one-man-show, with no one to balance or control him. What a sad spectacle it was, especially knowing that no one would stand up and contradict his slander of the IDF, its soldiers, and its commanders.

Many people, including former chiefs of the General Staff, have since expressed their objection and disappointment at the fiasco of Almog's "commission" and the public circus that he insisted on staging. During those days he had been coping with his son's illness, and a few months later the young man passed away. I believe that under those circumstances, it was a serious mistake to have entrusted him with such a sensitive inquiry.

Almog was my commander. Until this day I cannot fully comprehend his conduct, and still feel the stinging disappointment. This was not the heritage of the Paratroopers Brigade.

That evening, I received a call from the minister of defense. Amir Peretz dramatically notified me that he had decided to accept my resignation.

"Minister of Defense," I said calmly, "I am the commander of your largest division. Don't you think that it might be appropriate to meet me and hear my side of the story before accepting my resignation?"

There was an awkward pause.

"That is exactly what I was going to say!" Peretz declared. "We shall have a very important discussion. I had already asked that such a meeting be scheduled."

I am still waiting for this important discussion.

At the division there was a heavy atmosphere. I convened my staff and explained my considerations. I told them about my career and stressed that values had led my life and should guide all of us. At the end of the day, it is values that define the results of our actions. As I spoke to my beloved soldiers and officers, my voice broke. Avi, my deputy, noticed this and called everyone to attention. Everyone stood as I exited and slipped away to my room, where I leaned on the wall and covered my face with both my hands.

I couldn't believe this was happening to me. After all these years of fighting and war, of sacrifice and service, my downfall came from within.

Shock Wave

Four days later, I presented to Halutz a detailed legal opinion showing that Almog's report was flawed and illegal. I firmly demanded a correctional move within the IDF. I wanted a real investigation, or I would appeal to the Supreme Court.

Halutz pressed a button on the intercom and the judge advocate general was on the line.

"Avi, Gal is here. He has a legal opinion."

"I know," answered the chief military advocate general (MAG, Israel's equivalent to the JAG). "His lawyer came to see me."

"Does he have a point? Did I break the law?"

"Apparently yes."

"Can you stand up to it before the Supreme Court?"

"I'm not sure."

We spoke for a few minutes, and I explained that I did not intend to back down and was determined to clear my name. I also made it clear that I was not only doing it for myself, but so that he would not be able to do to other commanders what he had done to me.

The following day, I received a message from the office of the CGS as follows: "Your demand has been accepted by the CGS. You are to present your case at a hearing."

We had very few days before the hearing, and I divided my time between commanding my division and preparing for this new, strange battle that was forced upon me. A close team of friends worked day and night and carried out a series of initiatives and countermeasures.

On my team I had Dr. Yossi (Yoli) Liran; Benny and Modi Keret; architect Eli Armon; media specialist Danny Kiper; my PA, Tal Miller; my former PA, Guy Raveh; excellent field operator Amir Boker; Eitan Drori, who consulted from overseas; my lawyer, Dror Brotfeld; and as always, businessman Yaniv Adam – no longer my deputy, but always at my side.

They achieved impressive coordination and accomplishments. In fact, they did what the authorities should have done in the first place – they backed me up.

On the media front, my clash with Halutz and continued confrontation with Almog were widely covered. Public opinion was shifting in my direction. On the Friday before the hearing, a large profile covering the case appeared in the country's main newspaper, *Yedioth Ahronoth*, under the title "Gal Hedef" ("Shock Wave" – *gal* means "wave" in Hebrew). Its readers were exposed to a different story (and different person) from the biased agenda that had been pushed.

The Hearing

The room was packed with generals. It was apparent that an agreement that the MAG had made with me on limiting the participants had been breached, as there were additional people present, but I disregarded this.

I presented my case and dismantled Almog's claims one by one. I also said that it had been inappropriate to appoint him in the first place, after he called for the dismissal of the CGS.

"That's a lie!" screamed Almog, "I never said that!"

"It was all over the papers."

"So what if it was in the papers!" he went on yelling.

I faced him directly. "Look me in the eye, Doron. You were my commander. How can you behave like this? How could you appear on live TV, wave the CONPLANs in front of everybody, and shame me like that?"

He hunched up in his chair and scribbled something on a piece of paper.

"Doron, when I was commandant of Bahad 1, we took all the mishaps and incidents that happened under your command in SOUTHCOM and used them constructively to extract lessons learned – not what you are doing now."

I continued to shatter Almog's loosely constructed thesis and showed that there was no connection between facts and his conclusions.

"This report is tendentious, inappropriate, unfounded, and biased," I concluded.

At a certain point in the discussion, MG Gadi Eizenkot lashed out at Almog: "There's no correlation in this report between facts, conclusions, and recommendations!"

I repeated arguments that I had presented many times before: Routine security terminology was irrelevant to this situation. Fighting Hezbollah was a war against guerilla forces. The paradigm that had been adopted now, as if it were possible to always succeed in countering the enemy's plans, was a utopia, and therefore delusional.

"A mission cannot be fulfilled under every set of constraints," I emphasized, "and we had many extreme and complex constraints."

At one point I expressed my frustration to Halutz. "What do you think happened to me and my people?" I hurled at him. "That all of a sudden our brains switched off? Have you all forgotten everything that took place along the border before the war? How many times did I alert, request, demand, and beg? Where were you then? And how come you all have this twisted hindsight now?"

I took out a newspaper clipping and showed everyone. It read: "Gal Hirsch killed soldiers, and among them my son."

"It came to this because you have deserted me," I said quietly.

A few generals asked to see the paper.

I presented to Halutz a multitude of files showing the meticulous preparations we had performed before the war, and I even handed over my personal schedule for the whole year prior to the war.

"Look at my schedule and tell me what you would have done to prepare better," I said.

I pointed out bitterly that toward the end of the war I had asked a few generals for assistance, and some did not lift a finger. There was discomfort in the room. Some generals got up and stood by the wall. People were looking down, finding it hard to make eye contact. It was an extremely difficult situation for all of us.

I called in my witnesses who described what had taken place in the division before and during the war. They completely negated Almog's findings and described a thorough preparation process and a close alignment to what then took place during the fighting. They specifically contradicted Almog's claim that Kartago was only theoretical, and described it as a continuous pattern and a "way of living" in the division.

Avi, my G2, came in and made it clear that the missing piece of intel would certainly have changed the outcome. But the intelligence authorities did not budge. They still haven't, to this day.

The hearing was over, and I stepped out of the room, leaving the generals to their deliberations. My pulse was racing so fast that I was seriously concerned that I might have a heart attack. A kind soldier brought me a glass of water.

I looked down at Tel Aviv from the fourteenth floor and tried to calm down. Then I ran down the stairs, out to my jeep, and headed north, to continue all the work that needed to be completed as I prepared for transitioning command.

"What next?" I thought. "Retirement, or maybe a miracle will happen and there will be a shift in our leadership's fixation and an awakening will come – to me, to all of us – from this bad dream?"

I stopped by to see my mother. I was still very upset and could not relax. We sat together in silence for a while.

"This can't be happening," I told her. "It's like everything went crazy."

Chapter 24
Change of Command

Farewell

On December 5, 2006, a change of command ceremony was held at the division. BG Yossi Bachar was appointed as a temporary replacement until a new division commander would be appointed.

I asked to open the day at the Ghetto Fighters' House Museum, in Kibbutz Lohamei HaGeta'ot, which was founded by Holocaust survivors. I wanted my last day of service in the division to be dedicated to a seminar on values, in this place that was so significant to me.

I had been debating what to say during the ceremony planned for that evening. I spoke to Gadi Eizenkot in the morning. He expressed his concern that I might try to "settle the score" with those who had wronged me.

"Wait and see," I said, leaving him in suspense. But I chose to make this day national, not personal, and left settling scores to another time.

Gadi had been extremely supportive after the war. Since he'd assumed command of NORTHCOM, we had been in close contact, and he had expressed his appreciation for me in various forums.

He assessed the situation along the border as a strategic change, having Hezbollah far from the fence and the LAF deployed in the south. He told the media that he now saw things in a totally different light than previously observed from Tel Aviv, and that the significant change along the border should be attributed to my actions during the war. He also was deeply impressed to see the love and appreciation expressed toward me by my subordinates.

Gadi acknowledged the operational achievements my division had accomplished and pointed out that we had, in fact, fulfilled the mission as planned before the war and depicted in our CONPLANs. Gadi still occasionally points out that I was the one who successfully carried the main operational ground effort in the war of 2006.

It was reassuring to know that not all had lost their professional and moral judgment.

A huge crowd came to bid me farewell, including not only commanders and subordinates, but bereaved families, residents of the north, heads of municipalities, and of course my own family. Even CWO Taito came all the way from Bahad 1.

Before sunset, with the Galilee Hills behind me and facing all the people whom I cared for so much, I spoke words I had written the night before. From time to time my voice faltered, but I raised my voice and spoke out strongly.

FAREWELL SPEECH FROM THE 91ST DIVISION – GALILEE

Our IDF – my IDF – my division.

An officer of the IDF is one who has been imprinted with a commitment to the State of Israel, the Israeli society, and the Jewish people.

He is a person, a fighter, a thinker, a learner, a reader, and a writer. "*Safra v'sayfa*" – the book and the sword.

A fighter, a superb professional – but first and foremost, a person, instilled with values. Being an officer and commanding soldiers is like a fire in his bones.

My IDF is my team: the company, the battalion, the unit, the department, the brigade, the training base, and the division.

It is the sunrises and sunsets, total darkness, a heavy load, the phosphorus glow of my compass, and a tightening grip.

It is operating on the edge of the envelope, walking a tightrope, climbing steep inclines, far from home.

It is the beating of the heart, great suspense, excruciating pain, a big smile, the comradeship of fighters as a tempest rages all around us.

My IDF is the surgeon's scalpel, the sound of sirens, and clods of earth placed into fresh graves. Volley salute shots, a sense of grief, a lump in my throat.

It is Amnon, and Amir, and Tzion, and Eitan, and Samuel, and Amit, and Yoav, and Yuval, and Yiftach, and Nimrod, and many more, my brothers-in-arms – names and more names. Each a world in himself; in the air, sea, land, and in the shadows; they are all mine; they are all with me, forever.

The pain of the wounded and anguish of the maimed, I can understand more than many.

With great yearning I seek the safe return of Gilad, Eldad, and Ehud back to their country and back to their homes.

My IDF is one of a kind. It is *our* IDF. It is different in that it serves as a beacon of light unto our nation. Therefore values lead its way: tenacity of purpose in carrying out the mission and the drive to victory, purity of arms, human dignity, responsibility, and more.

It also stands for other values – friendship, comradeship, and loyalty, learning and criticism as well as high standards.

People are like flowers – they wither when they are not cared for. They are precious treasures, and fragile, despite being strong. It is important that the IDF protect both the land and the people.

In the book of Isaiah (6:8), God asks: "Whom shall I send, and who will go in our name?" And Isaiah responds: "'Here am I; send me."

Saying "Here am I; send me" guarantees the continued willingness to participate in the long journey of establishing the State of Israel, reinforcing it and defending it.

It has been my privilege to lay stones in constructing this country, with its human landscape, and with the people who dwell in its landscape.

What a privilege it has been to "plant carob trees" (a Jewish symbol of investing in future generations) – to teach, to command, and to lead.

This is Zionism in my eyes, and it is a privilege to be a Zionist: protecting the country, serving in the IDF, and striving for a meaningful service.

It is investing in education and human infrastructure, lifting up the weak, caring for them, and bringing them closer to the core of society.

I grew up in the south, in the Negev, and served there, and today we stand here, in the north, in the mountains of the Galilee.

From north to south and from east to west, Israel is our "start-up." I have always looked upon it as such.

It is a place to build and be built, and we should invest every minute in doing so.

It is a personal, exciting, and special project, which has risen from earth and ashes, forged in fire, and we shall safeguard it as the apple of our eye.

There is no substitute for the initiative that is the State of Israel, nor is there any for the IDF, its commanders, and its soldiers.

We must remember, embrace, and cherish.

"Shall the sword devour forever?" (II Samuel 2:26). I do not know, but for the foreseeable future – indeed yes. And we should educate our children and our youth to traverse the paths of this land and to love and defend it.

My IDF is my division.

Sela stations, this is Sela Actual – words cannot describe all that is in my heart.

In the trails of the Galilee and the mountains of Lebanon we have striven together for the defense of Israel.

The war brought much devastation. But it also forged us in fire.

I found in you – the division's regular and reserve fighters and commanders – my IDF, our IDF, which I love with all my heart.

The sacrifice and the valor, the will and devotion, the professionalism and the comradeship, the responsibility and the Zionism – all these I found in you.

There is a great gap between what actually happened during the war and what is now perceived, and it will be many days until the story of the war becomes properly balanced.

We have not succeeded in all our endeavors. There is much we must learn and teach, but we fulfilled our missions and served a mighty blow to our enemies. They are no longer on our borders, and we may build tourist resorts on fertile land instead of on a tinder box.

To the people of the division: I love you all with great affection and feel much appreciation for all the work and effort you have done. I wish to convey to you and to the people of the Galilee my sincere gratitude for your support and embrace before, during, and after the war.

Sela stations, this is Sela Actual – moving on.

My replacement, BG Yossi Bachar, is an experienced and professional commander, a brother-in-arms who is deeply familiar with the Galilee and Lebanon. He will no doubt lead the division to new heights. Yossi – good luck.

To NORTHCOM commander MG Eizenkot, I wish you all the best and success in protecting this region.

I have only many words of love and affection for my family and friends who were like a fortified protective wall during days of hardship. A wonderful group of comrades and lifelong friends.

To Donna – my wife, my friend, my love – a true woman of valor: together with Meori, Ofri, and Nir, we have built a warm household and taken a firm position for the defense of Israel. Not all will be said here, except that together we are a whole and our hearts beat as one.

Commanders, soldiers, friends, family, bereaved families, people of the Galilee, and all members of the security forces, thank you for coming here today.

I, Brigadier General Gal Hirsch, commander of the Galilee Division, wish to salute the flag and salute you.

I descended from the podium and approached my staff, who stood in formation. But the formal military protocol was disrupted, as each officer not only saluted but embraced me. Some shed tears. I passed through them all, saluting and hugging, until I reached Avi Peled, the new deputy CO, who replaced Dror Peltin.

The ceremony was over, and I was engulfed by friends, comrades, and bereaved families. The love and support I received was overwhelming. I was embraced, kissed, thanked, and congratulated.

Little Nir came up to me and I hugged her, burying my face in her hair, and we stayed like that in a long embrace, as I disconnected from the commotion around me.

Later that evening, at Maalot, a farewell event took place, in which people spoke of friendship, comradeship, gratitude, and sacrifice.

Wajdi said, "The Almog commission has spoken, but in our commission – comprised of commanders and soldiers who fought with you – you won."

Dror Peltin spoke of the unique teamwork our division shared throughout the war.

Mayor of Maalot and chairman of the Borderline Villages Forum Shlomo Bohbot said, "Those who didn't want to see you promoted to major general will see you become minister of defense" (a paraphrase of words said by Uri Dan about Ariel Sharon).

The division's education officer, Hadar, had assembled a series of letters that I had written to Donna before, during, and after the war, and had given them to Pablo Rosenberg, a famous Israeli singer. He had taken extracts from them and composed a beautiful and moving song, which he sang for us that evening.

Throughout the farewell events, I made a point of not reflecting negativity and resentment, but many people who spoke did express the disparity between what had really taken place and the newly constructed narrative. I was overwhelmed by the support I received.

Late that night, after a long, eventful, and emotional day, feeling sad, we drove home together – Donna, the girls and me – alone.

Exoneration and Cover-up

It wasn't easy to transition into this new mode after all these years, especially with my family traumatized and hurt. We took time for ourselves and invested in rehabilitation, reflection, and closure.

Wherever we went, people recognized me right away, and I was constantly approached for a handshake, a smile, and words of encouragement. It was heartening to know that people knew the truth and felt that I had been wrongly cast out to shield those in power from confronting their own errors.

Sometimes the attention was overwhelming, and my close friends assisted in shielding us from paparazzi photographers.

I was receiving messages from influential people who were in touch with Dan Halutz and Gadi Eizenkot. Apparently there was a plan to ask me to withdraw my resignation. They were considering revoking all the conclusions of Almog's committee, including the provision of barring me from commanding soldiers.

I hoped with all my heart that sanity would take over and push out the madness, and I conveyed my wish to continue to serve, if the bogus ban from command positions was overturned. I lived in great uncertainly and awaited an official decision. Herzl Bodinger and Gadi continued to toil on my behalf, and I was receiving more hints and messages that things were progressing positively.

One Friday morning, I heard on the radio that Halutz had called Almog to discuss the outcome of his committee. Saturday came, and then Sunday, and there was no word as to the outcome of the meeting.

This didn't look good. I had no doubt that there could be only one explanation to this silence: Almog must have been satisfied with whatever Halutz told him – for if not, he would have made a commotion about it and stormed the media, in his usual manner.

At last I received a call from Maya, Halutz's secretary, inviting me to meet him the following night at 10 PM.

The next night, as I was on the way up to the fourteenth floor for the meeting, IDF radio called and asked for my reaction to the decision.

"That's it," I thought. "They're burying me, and as usual, are doing it in the most unprofessional and immoral way."

I entered the office of the CGS, where Halutz sat wearing his class A uniform. His PA, Ronnie, was in the room with us.

Halutz read from a paper in front of him, mainly the conclusions from the hearing. As he read, it became apparent that the outcome was in my favor, but to my amazement, it ended with: "Since the officer has decided to resign, this is no longer relevant."

I asked for clarification: "I understand that you do not want me as a commander in the IDF."

"You're the one who resigned!" Halutz said angrily, leaning forward.

"You know very well what brought me to this. I did not resign willingly, but was forced out."

Halutz returned to reading from the document and did not continue the discussion.

I asked him for the document, and he promised to have it delivered to me.

I saluted and turned sharply toward the door, and Halutz awkwardly tried to escort me.

It took two weeks for the summary of the hearing to reach my lawyer.

"We won!" Dror exclaimed cheerfully over the phone.

"What do you mean?" I asked, puzzled.

"Our arguments were accepted one by one and you weren't even disqualified from command positions. This is a landslide victory. I just spoke to the MAG, who confirmed this and said that you did not have to resign."

I was overwhelmed with what seemed like a complete turning of the tables.

The document, signed by Halutz, decisively canceled Almog's conclusions. Kartago had stood the test three times, foiling abductions, and Halutz commended my initiatives and commitment in striving to find optimal solutions to complex challenges.

It was stated that I had acted above and beyond what would be expected of a division commander, and that I performed appropriate staff work in joining all forces to the combined mission.

Halutz also acknowledged the efforts, reports, and demands I had made before the war, in trying to replace the reserve battalion.

Most importantly, it was clearly asserted that there was no flaw in my conduct from the perspective of values.

Halutz also wrote, however, that I had failed "repeatedly" in leading a battalion to operational status and that I should have better analyzed the region and located the weak points. He had to have something negative, so he added this and a few more things that I supposedly should have done and didn't do – all nonsense.

"This isn't what was released to the public," I said.

"Exactly. The public was deliberately deceived by the IDF spokesperson's press release."

"Can't we publish this document and clarify everything?" I asked.

"Here's the catch. Halutz deliberately had it classified as 'Secret,' so we can't make it public." Of course there was nothing secret about it.

"What do you mean, we can't? Take care of it."

"I already did. The MAG said I was right about this and he will talk to Halutz about changing the classification."

Halutz never approved it, and the document never saw the light of day, despite endless petitions on the matter to the IDF's MAG.

"How Can You Live This Way?"

Two days later, I began preparing for the "Commission of inquiry into the events of the military campaign in Lebanon," chaired by retired Supreme Court judge Eliyahu Winograd. BG (Res.) Shmuel Tzuker, a former commander of the 91st Division, was appointed to review the operational aspects, and he debriefed me for more than thirty hours.

Unlike any other previous "debriefer," Tzuker delved into the material, reviewing documents, charts, maps, and schedules.

He asked informative and even critical questions, but one evening he seemed very upset, and asked to say a few words: "You did a lot. I didn't do half of what you did in order to prevent an abduction. You did a lot," he said again, for emphasis.

Another evening he said with great pain: "I feel for you. I don't even understand how you can live this way."

I spoke to the committee member who was appointed to review the intel aspects, but discovered that the cover-up plot was still functional, and again there was no intention to contravene the picture that had already been constructed. It was no use.

I sent the committee a detailed document, backed up with boxes full of cataloged documents. It took an enormous emotional toll, as did writing this book.

I appeared before the committee in Tel Aviv. Committee members asked me questions relating to a wide array of issues – from basic and informative to inquiries requiring a deep understanding of doctrine and situational analysis. Sometimes the answers were straightforward, but there were also questions stemming from misunderstanding and even disinformation. One such case involved the distinction between a commander's intent and operational orders, and I did my best to clarify this, using IDF doctrine books to show how perfectly aligned we had been.

It was a long and difficult day, and I was mentally exhausted. But the committee was beginning to realize that the picture that had been publicly portrayed was far from the truth.

Professor Ruth Gavison asked, "With your extensive fighting career, you could have now been appointed to a senior position. Why did you resign?"

I thanked her for her question, and explained that there was no reason to deny me from commanding soldiers, for I had not committed a crime or acted neglectfully. Commanding was the essence of my life, and I would not serve if immorally barred from leadership.

Judge Winograd listened for a long time in silence, and then said, "I wish to ask BG Hirsch a question. If asked to do so, would you be willing to return to serve in the IDF?"

"As a commander?" I asked.

"Yes, yes. As a commander, of course."

My entire life, dreams, and aspirations flashed in my head.

"Without hesitation!" I said. "This resignation was forced upon me."

Everyone stood, and all the committee members approached me and shook my hand warmly.

MG (Res.) Menachem Einan took me aside and whispered, "You know how it is with commanders. Like a wheel – sometimes you're up and sometimes you're down. Do not give up."

The room emptied, and the committee's secretary said, "What the judge has just asked you says it all!"

I met Donna, who was waiting for me outside, and updated her on the proceedings.

Then Or took me down to the beach. I left my telephone in the car and walked on the beach for hours.

Despite Judge Winograd's empathetic words, I understood that the committee was not going to do anything. The plot had succeeded. My entire life's journey had been severed with an axe. This was a moment of truth.

Darkness fell and I still wandered aimlessly on the beach. The wind howled in my ears and inside me there was a storm raging. Was it all ending now? Maybe tomorrow would bring something new? What was it?

So many thoughts and considerations were tumbling in my mind. An unsolvable riddle. What was to become of me?

Defensive Shield

I realized that even if the Winograd Commission were to pave the way to return me to the IDF as a commander, this would only happen when they had concluded their work – a matter of at least a year.

I decided to begin constructing an alternative route as a civilian, while also seeking medical treatment for my old wounds, which were causing me great pain.

I was officially on leave from the IDF, which could lead to my retirement or – if things worked out – back to service. I received approval for pursuing an alternative civilian career.

My friends did not leave me alone for a moment, and I found myself approached and interviewed by senior executives in leading companies. But I also noticed that despite all the compliments I was receiving, there was always alienation. No one really wanted to hire a "hot potato" like myself, who would possibly draw attention.

I made up my mind that, even if I ever did return to serve my country, I would never find myself defenseless and without means, and that I must secure my family's financial stability. I decided to establish a new company and called it Defensive Shield. The reference to Operation Defensive Shield was not coincidental.

Starting out with some old comrades from the paratroopers and other teammates, we built a vibrant new business model.

We started out integrating knowledge and technology and moved on to a variety of projects related to R&D, developing and integrating knowledge, strategic consulting, and retail management.

We signed contract after contract, and our growth rate was phenomenal. After only one year of operations, I looked back and could not believe we had come so far.

Raising the Flag

Israel's Independence Day had always been a special day of celebration and expression of our endless love to our homeland – our "start-up," especially with our personal commitment to its defense, serving as a link in the historic chain of realizing the Zionistic dream.

But this year was different. I was immersed in terrible feelings of abandonment and betrayal. My days and night were bitter. My country – my beloved country – where was it?

I saw Donna outside our house, holding the Israeli flag which we always hung over the entrance to our house as Independence Day drew near. She stood there in agonizing hesitation and then hoisted it up and flew it proudly above the entrance.

"I couldn't hang the flag," she said, as if apologizing.

"And...?"

"I couldn't *not* hang the flag."

On Independence Day, the first one after the war, we also celebrated Ofri's bat mitzvah.

I was disappointed by the interim report of the Winograd Commission, which was not sufficient to allow me to realize my dream of returning to the IDF, and I awaited the final report, which I expected to positively address the issue of returning to serve in a command position. My life was already accelerating on a new civilian track, but deep down I needed closure.

But the politicians – both military and civilian – who were out to get me found a clever way to keep me down. They appealed to the Supreme Court of

Justice, leading to a restraining order on the Winograd Commission, depriving them of the authority to reach personal conclusions. Usually this would mean limiting the committee's ability to cause negative consequences for people who had been interrogated, but in my case it was the other way around – the committee could not deal with the positive aspects of reversing Almog's recommendation to remove me from command positions.

I wrote to the committee and requested that my personal matter be addressed. Judge Winograd replied that due to the Supreme Court's ruling, they could not fulfill my request. It was becoming clear that if a correction of the injustice done to me were ever to be reached, it would have to be by different means.

Halutz resigned and LTG Gabi Ashkenazi was appointed in his place. I requested a meeting with him, hoping he could review the situation and lead to a breakthrough, but my letter to him went unanswered for months.

I appealed to Minister of Defense Ehud Barak, who had known me for many years. Barak proved no different than Peretz in this regard, and I never received an answer.

"Start-up"

We stood on a hilltop in a faraway land, overlooking the construction of a new project my company was developing, enjoying the spectacular landscape of yellow fields waving harmoniously.

As my team gathered for a briefing, I whispered to Amir and Adam, "What are we doing here? How did we get from the Galilee hills to here?"

I was flooded with emotions. The scenery, the people – everything was so beautiful. But it wasn't mine.

April 29, 2008. We were gathered for a ceremony in the southern town of Sderot – a symbol of withstanding the hardships of living near a challenging border. For years they had been suffering a constant bombardment of rockets fired by the Hamas terror organization. This was why we had chosen it as home for a new Zionistic endeavor – the Israel Leadership Institute (ILI), dedicated to educating and nurturing generations of value-based leaders. Together with Eyal Ben-Reuven and others, I served on the board of directors, and I was tingling with excitement at this new creation.

"There is hope," the founder and executive director, Eeki Elner, said passionately. "If people like Eyal and Gal, who experienced fighting in the Second Lebanon War, have come here to teach and create, then there is hope."

Israel is a "start-up" country – a work-in-progress – and we are building, investing in, and establishing it every day.

I believe in a free, strong, and vibrant Israel, which creates long-term infrastructure enabling creativity and initiative.

Still, I object to privatization of fundamental national services, such as welfare, education, and healthcare. Despite the importance of a free market, not all areas should be subject to clashes between the market forces, and we must ensure a life of dignity for all citizens.

So while investing in the tip of the spear – in technology, military, finance, and academia – we must also identify and care for those in the rear.

This requires value-based leadership, emanating from core conviction and dedication to the sustainment of the Jewish people as a nation, in its historic homeland, as well as promoting a prosperous and free democracy for all its citizens.

Here's to the Heroes

During my business endeavors, my family and I continued to suffer from overimaginative and frenetic journalists.

My activity has always been strictly coordinated with the Israeli authorities, and I have never engaged in anything even remotely removed from strict ethical codes of conduct. But this hasn't deterred members of the press from creating an image of the retired Israeli general involved in supplying weapons and even in influencing decision making in areas of conflict around the world.

I was accused of investing my special operations and commando experience in faraway lands instead of in Israel. Complete nonsense. Perfectly legitimate endeavors, such as in Georgia, were maliciously twisted in order to damage my business and tarnish my name. Some fictitious reports placed me in countries I had never visited and even told of a courageous rescue mission that I had supposedly led personally in the jungles of South America.

I value the importance of journalism in a democracy, but believe that much of what we see today lacks patriotism and dangerously deviates from the ethics and professionalism that should be core values of those who sometimes deal with issues of life and death.

I sadly conclude that irresponsible, unrestrained, and self-serving media outlets bear responsibility for a wrongly perceived outcome of the 2006

Second Lebanon War, forever engraving a biased image on the Israeli national consciousness.

During a family trip to the United States, we visited Sea World in Orlando, Florida. I was surprised to see a special line for servicemen and women, under a banner that read "Here's to the heroes." Before the show began, a touching video was shown, demonstrating the various military services and honoring those who serve. Then the trainer asked that all attending service members, veterans, and members of allied forces rise, and the audience honored them with a long ovation. We joined and applauded with tears in our eyes.

The stark contrast to what my family and I had experienced in Israel was overwhelming. This was how to honor heroes. And we had to travel to the United States to see it.

Although I had set out on a new successful business career, the war had left distinct emotional traces in us all. Bitter disappointment, a sense of betrayal, and the huge contrast after many years of sacrifice and contribution – these all severely hurt me and my family.

I could see how the frustration, anger, and disappointment negatively affected my entire family in various aspects – mentally, emotionally, and financially. A dark cloud was hanging over us. My family could not understand why I had been so severely punished, and neither could I. They all did their utmost to show me that everything was OK, especially to enable me to move on with my life, but I knew that the pain was gnawing away at them and to my dismay also influencing their health.

During a business trip with my father, Yitzhak, in 2011, he asked that we take a walk along a seashore pier. There he told me that he had been feeling very ill and that he thought it must be something serious. I acted quickly, and the test results soon revealed that he had not withstood the heartbreak, his body had weakened, and he had terminal cancer. Within eight months of suffering and struggle, he passed away and was buried not far from Amnon. Parting with my father was extremely painful, especially under those circumstances, and I miss him every day.

The War Is Now Over

It was too late for me, but the final report completely cleared my name and reversed all the baseless allegations.

My preparations for war were commended, stressing the emphasis I had given on preventing abductions, pointing out the thoroughness of the newly written operational plan, and praising the new doctrine and derived training process.

It was acknowledged that the shortage in resources as well as the operational restraints we were working under made the abduction inevitable. The committee concluded that systemic faults should have been addressed, and one point of failure at the operational level (the abduction) should not have been singled out.

It was asserted that there was no reason to have maintained a high level of alert, as there was no information indicating a need for it. Keeping a constant level of heightened alert would have meant redefining a new unrealistic and unsustainable norm for routine activity.

I was resoundingly exonerated.

One of Israel's leading journalists said that evening, "In light of this report, Gal Hirsch should be returned to the ranks of the IDF." Other media reports, including a *Haaretz* editorial, echoed similar sentiments.

Two years after the war, in July 2008, the bodies of our two soldiers, whose abduction had triggered the war, were returned to Israel, in exchange for the terrorist Samir Kuntar – who had been held in Israel – and the bodies of 199 Hezbollah operatives.

The exchange deal with Hezbollah was yet another demonstration of its ruthless and heartless nature, since up until the last minute they would not disclose to the families whether their loved ones were alive or dead. We had assessed from the beginning that they had been killed, or at least mortally wounded, during the incident, but there was no certainty.

I supported the deal, despite the obvious considerations and ramifications. I still believe we must do whatever it takes to bring our soldiers back, alive or dead. I think that our enemies can see in this not weakness, but a testimony to the balance of power and casualties ratio, as well as our values and the price an advanced and free society is willing to pay even for its dead.

I couldn't sleep the night before the funerals, and listened to the hourly newscasts. My daughter Meori, who was serving in the IDF radio station, reported on the upcoming funerals and spoke the names of the fallen.

I attended both funerals and visited the families during the seven days of mourning.

"The war is now over," read the newspaper headlines. It was then that I decided that now that the war was really over and my soldiers were all home, I could complete my own battle, reflect on my story, and tell the truth of what had happened.

Crossroads

The bitterness relating to the way the termination of my service in the IDF had been brought about reverberated within me for years, but it was never an option to wallow in self-pity.

As was my way, I strove to take the initiative, focusing on planning for the future and engaging in constant creativity. I carved out a new life track, and the company that I had founded – Defensive Shield – became the main axis for my financial activity, in Israel and overseas.

Despite the injustice inflicted on me, I did not change my attitude toward the State of Israel, and my connection with the defense establishment continued along various avenues. As a civilian, I immediately became an instructor in various command courses in the IDF. I thought it very important to share my operational experience with as many commanders as possible, at both the tactical and operational levels.

My positive experiences in the business world could fill a separate book, but here I will only point out that this financial success enabled me to divide my time between work and service as a reservist in the IDF. At the same time, I contributed socially as a board member and lecturer at the Israel Leadership Institute.

In 2007, Bogie Ya'alon turned to a political career, and I was asked to replace him as chairman of the Noam Association, founded in memory of my subordinate Major Eitan Belhassen, commander of the Paratroopers' Sayeret, who was killed in Lebanon in 1999. The association commemorates him through educational programs which strive to instill leadership and values.

I met Bogie at his home, and we discussed the war and what followed. Bogie believed that the injustice done to me could be corrected only by the intervention of a former CGS or a Supreme Court justice.

That evening, I relayed this discussion with Bogie to Guy Raveh (my former PA in the division) and asked for his opinion.

"Yes, you need a judge. But not just any judge. You need someone like Cheshin."

Judge Mishael Cheshin, vice president of the supreme court of Israel, was a prominent figure, known for being proactive, stormy, and strong-minded. His verdicts were famous for their creative imagery and colorful language. His style was far from typical, and his personality was charismatic and inspirational.

I thought about Guy's idea and agreed. I did need someone like Cheshin.

The iron gate squeaked outside the house built from Jerusalem stone, and I was greeted by the cheerful barking of Keren and Tito, Judge Cheshin's dogs.

We conducted many meetings and long discussions, and became fast friends, I called him Misha; he called me Galgal.

Misha told me that he had identified the injustice done to me back when the Winograd Commission held their sessions, and had even addressed the members and asked that corrective action be taken. He had not known me personally, but the story touched him. From the moment we met, he fought indefatigably for my vindication. Even after losing his son, Shneor, in a tragic accident, he did not cease his efforts.

Misha tried to facilitate my return to full service in the IDF during LTG Gabi Ashkenazi's tenure as CGS. Gabi met with me several times, and I understood that he intended to have me return when he anticipated that, after the elections, Bogie would become the next minister of defense and would instruct him to bring me back.

When, instead, Ehud Barak was appointed as minister of defense, my reinstatement was no longer on the agenda.

My return to service was discussed with three candidates for CGS: Benny Gantz, Gadi Eizenkot, and Yoav Galant. All three admitted that I had been wronged and that it would be appropriate to utilize my capabilities in the IDF, especially in my field of expertise – special forces and special ops. When Benny Gantz was appointed as CGS (after a scandalous twist of events nullifying the nomination of Galant), discussions intensified, a few alternatives were discussed, and I agreed to them all.

At this point in my business career, I had much to lose by returning to the ranks of the IDF, but I was prepared to transition from Lexus to APC in a heartbeat. Serving my country had always been my top priority.

Toward the end of 2011, Gantz and Barak approached me with the need to establish a new strategic command focused on remote operations deep in enemy territory, with better usage of special forces. Ehud Barak summoned me for a meeting on the matter that lasted far into the night.

I liked the idea very much. As a longtime commando operator, I believed that the IDF would benefit from a General Staff-level organization to oversee special forces, rather than having them separately activated by the services.

In January 2012, I joined MG Shai Avital, who was called back from retirement. I was appointed his deputy, in reserve status, and together we worked to establish the new Depth Command. Benny had connected this appointment with the possibility of my returning to the force, saying, "Making your way back to the main axis through the reserves is the right track."

I was very happy for the opportunity to take part in such an important, groundbreaking endeavor, and I enjoyed the creative work.

The establishment of the Depth Command was accompanied by the usual clashes inherent to reorganizing and shifting responsibilities, ranging from conflicting opinions on doctrine to issues of power and ego. But after decades of off-and-on deliberation on the matter, the decision was finally made and a new organization for third-tier operations was established, aimed at a comprehensive approach to challenges in the strategic depth, beyond the traditional AORs of the regional commands.

Due to the clandestine nature of this field, I will limit my description here to broad themes, as already published in various Israeli media outlets.

The enemy has long since realized that Israel cannot be subdued using head-on conventional force, so vast efforts have been made to build standoff capabilities, using local proxy elements that are strategically equipped and operated.

While there is talk of options that are "on the table," much is being done "under the table" in order to thwart emerging threats and prevent substantial capabilities from reaching the wrong hands and tipping the balance of power in the region. The Depth Command combines various elements of national power in fulfilling this important mission.

Much has been written about the fact that since the end of World War II, we have been witnessing a reduction in the scope of "classic" warfare: low intensity conflicts, operations other than war (OOTW), asymmetric warfare, and a host of other terms have evolved in an attempt to characterize the nature of the new conflicts. Apparently, the abundance of terms mainly reflects confusion and gaps in understanding, interpretation, and the development of ways to cope with the problem. Ahead of us is a generations-long journey along the way to "classicizing" the phenomenon of war as it seems today.

The opponent has changed. He has become sophisticated, agile, and diversified, and has a faint intelligence signature. He utilizes the state-of-the-art infrastructure developed by the free, enlightened world – the world that aspires to prosperity and progress. He uses the legitimate organs and restrictions of the state as a mechanism for attacking the state and its citizens. He "innocently" infiltrates through the state's official passages, converts civilian resources (passenger aircraft or agricultural fertilizers, for example) into lethal weapons, maintains a close linkage to criminal activities and criminal organizations, and makes it extremely difficult for the security organizations of the state to keep abreast of his ever-evolving processes. State security organizations are based on procedures, on legislation, and on hierarchical management and administration, and are inherently "heavy" – this is particularly characteristic of state military organizations, whose primary mission is to defend the national borders against threats imposed by other countries.

From coping with an enemy that has an address and whose signature is clear and solid, the world has switched to a conflict against cells, organizations, and organizational fragments – an opponent that has numerous addresses, most of which are "straw addresses." This opponent has a blurred signature and a complex identity, and it operates in multidimensional realms under the cover of the civilian population. Additionally, for a while now, even opponent states have begun using such methods, and by employing organized state-sponsored terrorism by proxy, they strive for asymmetry and prefer a toolbox that contains nonstandard, unconventional, and not purely military capabilities.

The Next Revolution in Military Affairs

The security challenges facing states should be properly categorized and divided into security challenges, homeland security (HLS) challenges, and military defense challenges. Each one of these categories is further divided into tactical, operational, and strategic aspects. Accordingly, we have assembled a matrix of nine different realms, with each realm possessing its own unique characteristics and presenting its own specific requirements.

Security is provided to the citizens of the state by civilian security elements and law enforcement agencies (e.g., police). HLS requires multiple organizations and integration between security services and other state authorities. Military defense requires that the military organizations cope with an invader or some other threat that compels the military to maneuver within a given space using the various modes of battle.

The need to cope with the various challenges outlined above necessitates a supreme leadership, high-standard management/command, close linkage, coordination, conceptual-doctrinal practice, and consolidation between security and law enforcement agencies, government ministries, military organizations, secret services, and other elements. Any state wishing to build an effective parapet against terrorism and subversion must advance from a collection of bricks to a defensive wall, and this necessitates leadership, advanced integration, and interagency capabilities. The state should set up a mechanism into which each government ministry and each security, law enforcement, and emergency organization or service can "plug and play," immediately becoming smoothly integrated into the situation at hand.

The fact that the opponent is unique and different constitutes a trend that turns out to be stable and ongoing in various confrontation focal points. To counter this phenomenon, states should develop a dedicated, specialized solution encompassing all of the categories: security, HLS, and defending against an external threat (military defense). This dedicated solution should be so special as to be revolutionary! The Revolution in Military Affairs (RMA) has been regarded mainly as a technological process in the last few decades. This is not enough, however. We do not have a choice anymore – at the moment, we are facing the next RMA.

To handle the challenges presented by the kind of opponent described above, a national conceptual-organizational revolution, combined with technology, is required. The all-too-familiar formula C4ISR (command, control, communications, computers, intelligence, surveillance, and reconnaissance) is currently lacking one key element.

In their books, futurists Alvin and Heidi Toffler divided the evolution of warfare into waves: the first wave was associated with agricultural tools, the second wave was associated with the industrial revolution, and the third wave was influenced by computing and information warfare. In the 1980s, technology and the needs of the hour facilitated the Revolution in Military Affairs (RMA), whose categories and characteristics evolved into the C4ISR formula. Recently, many have accepted the fact that the fifth c in the formula stands for cyber, but facing the security challenges I have outlined in the fields of security, HLS, and defense, I believe that this is not enough.

In order to harness all of the technological opportunities currently available into an effective response to the present-day opponent, we must bring about the next Revolution in Military Affairs, regard it primarily as a conceptual-organizational revolution, and develop military-security organizations to match the unique challenge we are facing. We do not require organizational changes such as "adjustments" and "capability development," but rather the shifting of the center of gravity of the force build-up effort and a structural-organizational-technological revision of state security organizations.

Systems always strive for symmetry, and in the face of asymmetrical threats we develop capabilities that offset the difference (refer, for example, to the Iron Dome system developed to cope with the steep trajectory threat). In his book *The Pursuit of WOW!*, Tom Peters argues that "Crazy times call for crazy organizations," and we must, indeed, adapt ourselves promptly and rebuild symmetry opposite the asymmetry facing us. We should develop unique, irregular organizations and regard them as our main force for these times – formations based primarily on a proper balance between technology and three different types of forces: commando, special forces, and secret services. These forces complement one another and ensure the optimal utilization of the concept of an interorganizational force. As we have grown accustomed to using the letter c, we shall continue to use it in order to represent this pattern as a whole. Accordingly, the sixth c to be added to the standard formula stands for commando.

Democratic law-abiding states cannot employ terrorism and subversion. States that do so as a matter of policy are regarded as members of the "axis of evil." In coming to fight back, the state should employ a solution that will offset this asymmetry and even gain an advantage.

The official state-military capabilities opposite terrorism and subversion (as far as flexibility and effectiveness are concerned) are provided by special forces, commando units, and secret services (the "sixth c" formations). These elements rely primarily on state of mind, a different approach, agility, and on being prepared for and capable of taking calculated risks responsibly.

These forces may operate under their own legislation and procedures. They are educated to improvise, to develop relevant knowledge, to initiate, and to evolve constantly. They possess the ability to develop – in the relevant context – methods, advanced weapons systems, and creative operational ideas, while conducting their instruction and training activities under the most realistic conditions possible. These forces must have a stringent screening process, the best personnel, and the highest standards of command, control, and leadership, because these sixth c formations are the only ones capable of coping effectively with the opponent's nature and rate of learning and evolution, as outlined above.

In the past mainly air forces, intel, naval and armored forces enjoyed the benefits of RMA, but state-of-the-art technologies (miniaturization, for example) and demands from the field will make it possible to provide the sixth c formations with new, innovative capabilities. Over the years, commando and special forces have been employed as "spices" sprinkled over the primary maneuvering plan. The bulk of the task is based on a dominant ground maneuver, on intelligence, or on firepower from the air, sea, or land. Military history has shown that the special force is normally committed to battle in order to support the ground maneuver, bridge over or fill gaps, and sometimes for strategic missions. I believe that we are ready to move on to the next phase.

The next Revolution in Military Affairs can bring into the arena a new concept that offers new operational patterns, in the context of which special maneuvers will be executed, complete operational moves will be based primarily on commando forces and tactics, and the operational manifestations of the modes of battle, combat doctrines, and combat techniques will undergo a significant change.

In the past the base of the pyramid consisted of the standard forces, and "commando spices" were added to its tip, but currently available technology and the way the opponent conducts himself could even compel us to invert the pyramid so it stands on its head. The special force can constitute the basis for the maneuver and bring into the campaign, in its backpacks, the full capabilities of the standard military and even more.

So, the little entity (the sixth c formations) becomes very big, and the big entity (the standard military), when dealing with a challenging opponent, becomes very small. The established concepts of operational-organizational elements – company, battalion, brigade, division, and so forth – may also attain a different meaning if we transform them into C6ISR formations and fuse them with the special forces concept and with the latest technology and everything it has to offer.

The C6ISR formation can bring into the battlefield the strength of a division, and even more, but its force makeup will be completely different. Such a special formation will deliver, through a very small ORBAT of fighters, substantial capabilities and strengths, including everything required of a ground force with regard to the aspect of capturing and maintaining territory, using a smaller but more effective ORBAT. These versatile formations will be adapted to the type of conflict and to the battlefield, be it a large-scale war, a limited-scale war, or an attack on the bases of a criminal/terrorist/subversive/guerrilla organization.

Parts of the concept outlined above are not new; we have been discussing decentralized/diffused warfare and the potential strength of small, lethal forces for years (we in the Israeli military community are all aware, for example, of the approach formulated by MG [Res.] Yedidya Ya'ari and Haim Assa in their book *Diffused Warfare: War in the Twenty-First Century*). But the opponent is growing increasingly more sophisticated, technology is advancing, and now is the time to decide! There is a constant struggle relating to balance. Our innovative actions to counter the asymmetry imposed by the enemy create, in a way, new symmetry. The enemy is the one who keeps disrupting this balance, and we try to rebalance it. The idea here is to change the rules of the game. Our objective should be to initiate and innovate, precede the enemy and break the symmetry ourselves, forcing the enemy to struggle and keep up.

In order to change the rules of the game, we need new players and new game boards. Accordingly, we need a different force buildup effort – new force patterns, different maneuvering modes and – definitely – new research, development, and technology trends.

A conceptual-organizational change on such a scale is a matter for the highest leadership and necessitates a farsighted command. Directing the buildup of the concept and the R&D activity requires that abstract concepts and ideas be connected to practice and that dramatic organizational changes, in inter-arm and interorganizational terms, be put to the test. Primarily, we need the courage to enter new battlegrounds, step into dark new realms, and venture into a conceptual no-man's-land.

A true leader will also retain the different, nonconformist (even eccentric) individuals in his organization – there are many of those within the ranks of the special forces, and they could constitute an important asset in the staging of a breakthrough. Breakthroughs are normally the outcome of hardship! Provided that one is aware of the conceptual fixation and restrictive paradigms, these nonconformist individuals can be the ones to embrace hardships as opportunities for leading to breakthroughs.

Instead of responding to the harsh results of conceptual fixation, we should prefer to design, revise, and develop an alternative paradigmatic format that is relevant to the context, through the establishment of the C6ISR formations, even if we have to challenge phenomena regarded as force majeure in the realms of war. Here are a few examples:

- Friction, which von Clausewitz defines as a primary phenomenon of war – the one that generates uncertainty and randomness – will not disappear, but it may be countered and much can be done in order to ensure that the force undertakes its missions under low friction, just like a knife cutting through butter. Friction is important and necessary in order to study the opponent and the battlefield, but friction that leads to delays can be minimized by the C6ISR formations.
- The fact that the asymmetrical opponent is agile and has a faint intelligence signature has imposed on us the predicament known as "short target life-cycle," along with the difficulty of connecting the sensor with the shooter within a relevant time interval. The short target lifecycle phenomenon is regarded as a force majeure, and this must be challenged – we should strive for immediate closure of the kill chain, and I do believe that the C6ISR formations will be able to adapt and kill faster.
- The phenomenon of frontier areas, no-man's-lands allegedly under state sovereignty, except that this sovereignty is not being enforced (for example, in the Sinai and on the Syrian Golan Heights) – necessitates an operational solution that would enable us to operate within those areas highly effectively and without generating a signature. The C6ISR formations will be able to effectively deal with this challenge.
- We would like to reduce to an absolute minimum the probability of disastrous surprises in the context of operational missions generally and routine security missions in particular (for example, kidnapping of personnel). The C6ISR formations will take the initiative, be the first to act and disrupt the opponent's ability to initiate such surprises.

There are numerous challenges and the response to date has been only partial. Relevance and a revision of the response formula are required. We no longer need a military that adapts itself, but a complete system developed to deal with the missions of the new era – an organization of organizations that are just as crazy as the times. For the examples I have presented and for other challenges, I suggest the C6ISR formula.

In order to advance this revised formula to the point of operational implementation, a significant, concentrated effort must be made with regard to R&D and the characterization of resources for the commando/special forces/secret service element, so that it will be able to come into its own on the battlefield. I would expect the special force to carry in its backpacks the very best of the technological potential currently available in every arena: fires, C3, mobility, lethality, logistics, intelligence, and more. This will enable it to change, improvise, adapt, develop a prompt response in a concrete context, and, using a metaphor from Bill Gates's book – to execute operations at the speed of thought.

Even today, the elite units of the world's military organizations are the leaders in technology and in a creative approach. This is true, but not sufficient. The specialist units currently constitute a "boutique capability," and are not the main element of the national response potential. The sixth c formations should bring a critical mass into the battlefield and decide the outcome of campaigns on their own.

The classic ground maneuver, organized in columns and rows, is intended for a symmetrical collision between simple, mass-based geometrical shapes, on a clearly defined battleground. This primarily bidimensional maneuver reflects the peak of the second wave – the industrial wave. The emergence of the third wave has brought RMA into play – command, control, computing, communication, intelligence, surveillance, and reconnaissance capabilities (C4ISR). All of these elements created the conditions for the development of a campaign encounter between complex, network-interconnected geometrical shapes, based on the development and control of the battlegrounds. So, maneuvering has become tridimensional, and the opponent should cope with a combined presence – ground, sea, air, space, and cyberspace.

While standard military forces operate according to structured patterns, using standard weapon systems and through combat doctrines and procedures "strictly along the lines," the C6ISR formations will operate between the lines, away from the highway, not in line with what can be expected from a military force and not even within the same framework. In fact, the special maneuver and the special organization expand the battleground, and conceptually, it operates in a different realm and in a different dimension that are not familiar to the opponent. We must use new and updated legal tools. The rules of the game are surprising and dictated by the sixth c, and the asymmetry is revoked.

The advanced capabilities of C4ISR will, in fact, be augmented by two capabilities that add depth to the fighting potential – cybernetic depth and the conceptual depth of operating outside the concept/box and according to new rules.

In his book *The Black Swan: The Impact of the Highly Improbable*, Nassim Nicholas Taleb analyzes the phenomenon of the unexpected surprise primarily with regard to economic activities, and calls this surprise the "black swan" (as it was once the prevailing belief that only white swans existed, until black swans were discovered in Australia…).

In an analogy to the world of security – if in the past terrorist and subversive organizations presented us with black swans and shocking, devastating surprises (refer, for example, to the major terrorist attacks in Manhattan, Madrid, London, Bali, Beslan, Nairobi, and the list goes on and on), the state may now present them with a lethal black swan of its own: the C6ISR formations. The idea is to work in the "fourth dimension" – that is, in the dimension of unpredictable, irregular chaos – turning the terrorists' own tools and methods on them. This calls for "four-dimensional" maneuvers – unique and creative, employing uncertainty, illegality, and disorder, far away from the expected and from the accepted conceptual pattern.

Terror is a global threat. Israel is always the front guard, but the free world has learned that fundamentalism, radicalism, and jihadi extremism are not only an Israeli problem. The world needs its defensive shield, and it starts with state of mind and an appropriate force buildup. The right solution is the C6ISR – the operationally relevant answer to terrorists, the world's current enemy.

Who Can Make That Straight

The Israeli media covered my appointment to the Depth Command widely. It seemed that I was receiving broad support, and many saw this position as the corrective measure I deserved. I did not.

I was happy to be appointed to this pivotal commanding position, contrary to the wrongful and spineless decision made by Halutz and Peretz.

I perceived this reserve position as a bridge to full service in the IDF

General Staff. I worked extremely hard, literally around the clock, putting in intense and almost daily service in the Depth Command, while at the same time I still had to lead Defensive Shield, supply services to our customers, pay the salaries of our employees, and sustain the reputation of the company.

It was important for me to ensure that my business endeavors would neither contradict nor even appear to contradict my military service, so I signed a detailed conflict of interest agreement with the IDF, and fully exposed my business affiliations.

My friends, including Misha, were all happy with these developments, but I was not at rest. I knew how the internal operational politics worked within the IDF, and wondered who would try to trip me up and prevent my return to full service. When I began to sense that Benny was mumbling instead of clearly defining a track for return, I realized that these forces were already at play. Misha sprang into action and spoke with Benny at length, laying out both legal and moral considerations. He later also spoke with Bogie, now minister of defense, and sensed that he was preaching to the converted.

There was no doubt that the leadership had great appreciation for me, as well as an understanding that correction of what had been done to me was due, but the question was whether they would demonstrate the appropriate decisiveness.

The pressure to reinstall me was mounting from different directions, including senior reservists in the Depth Command, and Shai Avital himself, who wrote Benny and spoke with him several times, insisting that this was the right thing to do.

In January 2014, Judge Winograd requested to meet CGS Gantz and asked him to correct the injustice he felt had been done to me. Pangs of conscience led him to use sincere and scathing words. He felt that when the efforts to oust me had first begun, his committee should have acted to reinstall me to full service immediately, but they had been banned from interfering, and he now asked – almost demanded – that the CGS do the right thing.

When Misha told me about this dramatic development, I asked to meet with Judge Winograd. It was the first time I had seen him since the stormy days of the inquiry after the war, and I was very excited. Winograd described his discussion with Benny and the positive way in which Benny related to me.

I was amazed at the clarity and honesty of his words. I thanked him from the bottom of my heart, and explained to him the profound significance this reflected, for me and my family. I also told him that a lack of written documentation of the current proceedings would diminish the historic significance of the corrective action being made.

Winograd asked to think it over, but a day later, I received an e-mail from him, notifying me that an official letter had been delivered to the CGS. He attached a copy of the letter and said that I could make it public.

The letter was sharp and piercing. I could not have dreamed of a stronger exoneration:

To: Chief of the General Staff, Lieutenant General Benny Gantz

Sir,

I would like to thank you once more for our meeting on the 15th of this month in the matter of BG Gal Hirsch.

I requested this meeting because ever since the submission of the Winograd Commission report pertaining to the events during the Second Lebanon War, my conscience has tormented me, as we could not, as we had meant, include a warm recommendation that the IDF offer Gal Hirsch to return to full service in its ranks. We had thought that this was the right thing to do, and I am still of the opinion that it is unfortunate that this has not been done until now.

You know Gal Hirsch better than I do, and during our conversation you expressed your utmost appreciation of him, as an excellent military professional, as well as a devoted person who is valued by all of his subordinates.

I was happy to realize that you, too, believe that Gal Hirsch's place is in the IDF, and that you have made, and will continue to make, every effort, despite the hardships, to realize the aspirations of this individual, who yearns to continue and serve his country within the ranks of the IDF.

I truly hope that soon I will hear of Gal's return. It would be an expression of respect and appreciation to the man and his deeds in the IDF in many years of service, after the difficult years he underwent and is still suffering, since his forced retirement.

Very respectfully,

Dr. Eliyahu Winograd

After this dramatic move, a momentum was created. Bogie invited me to a personal meeting to discuss the possibility of nominating me to a senior position in the GS. The written summary of the discussion was decisive, and in another personal discussion with Benny, I was under the impression that things were moving in the right direction. Also Gadi Eizenkot joined in support of this move.

As it was obvious that I was soon to be called back to service, I found myself torn in three directions: business, defense, and public service.

Time passed, and despite more innuendos and comments by Benny and Bogie, no decision was made. Gadi replaced Benny in February 2015, and he too, despite countless previous discussions and strong support, made no decision pertaining to me.

In May 2015, Misha invited me to his home in Herzliya. We sat on the porch and talked, as usual. I knew Misha had been suffering from cancer, but he now shared with me that his situation was deteriorating and that he felt his end was near. Rather than talk of his own suffering, Misha expressed his disappointment that he would not be able to complete the mission he took upon himself: facilitating my return to the IDF.

He led me to his study, where he entrusted me with two copies of a statement he had written pertaining to my case. I was touched and shaken by his profound words. We hugged.

The statement was titled "For who can make that straight, which He hath made crooked" (a quote from Ecclesiastes 7:13). In powerful, elevated language, Judge Cheshin wrote that I had been gravely wronged, and that the process leading to my forced departure from the IDF had been deeply flawed, both on a moral and legal basis.

He described the events that had led to my resignation and clearly defined the results of the hearing conducted by CGS Halutz as a total exoneration and negation of Almog's report and recommendation.

He wrote that he felt it was his duty to share with the public the injustice inflicted on me, in order to lift a heavy burden off his chest. He also described his tireless efforts and appeals, and his disappointment when nothing was done.

In July 2015, the Movement for Quality Government in Israel (MQG), of which Judge Cheshin was a member, made a public announcement, revealing Judge Winograd's letter to Gantz, as well as the statement written by Judge Cheshin. The public was also exposed to a segment of a documentary that was being produced by Yair Elazar, the son of former IDF CGS David "Dado" Elazar, in which Judge Winograd spoke.

Judge Cheshin was too sick to be interviewed. I visited him periodically, as his situation deteriorated and he was in and out of hospitals. It was heartbreaking for me to see him this way.

The impact of this public announcement was overwhelming, and I received waves of love and support. Finally, after nine years of injustice, two former Supreme Court Judges helped set the record straight and granted me a decisive exoneration.

A month later, I concluded my three-and-a-half-year tenure as deputy commander of the Depth Command, and was replaced by BG Nitzan from the Air Force. I felt extremely satisfied with what we had accomplished, introducing a new and valuable pillar to Israel's defense.

CGS Gadi Eizenkot made a surprise appearance at the change of command ceremony and asked to address the audience. "All who know you," he said, "don't need learned judges' opinions in order to know and admire what you have done." He praised my abilities and conduct during the Second Lebanon War and said that after the dust had settled and the public hysteria diminished, a professional examination proved that the division under my command had performed superbly during the war, and that the citizens of the north owed me these many years of tranquility. He also thanked me for my willingness to return to serve and my achievements in the Depth Command.

"You are exemplary," he concluded, "and an Israeli patriot."

Although this was said in a closed military forum, the IDF spokesperson released the video of Eizenkot's speech, generating a wave of public discussion and support, lasting for several days.

Returning to the IDF was no longer practical, but my goal had been achieved: the Israeli public now knew that I had served them with all my heart and with all my might.

With the dramatic public statements by Justices Winograd and Cheshin, and this sweeping official exoneration by the IDF CGS, I felt that the Second Lebanon War was finally over.

My daughters continued the family tradition. Meori served in the IDF in the rank of captain, and continues to serve as a reservist. Ofri has recently completed her officer training and currently serves in an operational capacity as an officer in the Israeli Air Force. Nir is a diligent student and a member of the Israeli Scouts.

These days, as I conclude the English version of my book, I see my goals and course of action as follows: I will continue to serve and contribute to Israel's defense, relying on my operational experience. But most importantly, I choose to continue and lead, doing the best I can for the State of Israel and the people of Israel. This is my way and my path, and by no means the end of the story.

Afterword

I have a few last points that I wish to convey to you, my reader.

This is my story, and I wrote it with all my heart.

I know that people can experience the same events differently, and this is especially true when dealing with wars. I have given you my own point of view. I promise that I have spoken only the truth and told it just as it happened to me.

My life journey was cut short after the war of 2006, in the wake of a great crisis and breakdown of values. It should not have happened. This is not how soldiers and commanders expect to be treated by their leadership. This is not what their families or their nation expect.

I invested in much soul-searching before writing this book, as a great question arose whether we as a society and as a fighting family still possess the values, heritage, leadership, and loyalty that we all cherish.

I searched and found that they are still there – within fighting units. But sadly, parts of the senior leadership have conducted themselves as if blinded by a moral eclipse.

Fundamental ethical flaws caused us to be struck by "friendly fire." Only worse – because it has been deliberate, malicious, and devoid of restraint, friendship, or compassion.

Still I believe that although we have been diverted off track, we can and will resume a steady and clear course. This is not our way, and should be seen as a dark and anomalous chapter of our history – or at least I hope so.

I have suffered severely from the acts of politicians – both civilian and military – who have used me as a human shield and made me a scapegoat. They failed to demonstrate loyalty toward and backing for commanders during wartime. Abandoning commanders is shirking fundamental leadership values.

I was naive and focused only on fighting the enemy, even as I was being stabbed in the back. Still, I recommend that fighting commanders direct their efforts forward, to the enemies of the nation, and refrain from fighting the political wars from within.

A leader must always act according to core morals, preserve his integrity, and be willing to pay the price. It is essential to view each and every position as if it were the last, disregarding career considerations.

For this reason, whenever I speak to young leaders, I ask them, "Will you keep your integrity and will you be willing to pay the price?"

My great wish is that this book will serve to help people prevent such things from ever happening again. It is a lesson on how to avoid a descent leading to the abandonment of values and of brothers, and a betrayal more painful than any physical wound.

Throughout the writing process, I have also had in mind, as my mission, to pass on lessons and insights that may serve to shape and develop future warriors, commanders, and leaders. I hope that you may learn from my experiences, from my successes, and mostly from my failures.

After witnessing everything that my family and I have gone through, there were those who predicted that I would give up and wallow in bitter loneliness in some faraway land.

No chance. I am here and pushing onward.

The battles of my life come in tidal waves. I will continue to serve and contribute to Israel's defense, relying on my operational experience.

I choose to continue and lead, doing the best I can for the State of Israel and the people of Israel.

I love my country and have dedicated my life to its defense and the realization of the Zionistic vision. For this is the story of my life – a war story and a love story.

Appendices

Appendix A
The Israel Defense Force (IDF)

Structure of the IDF

The IDF has been a conscript army since its inception in 1948, for both men and women. Termed "the people's army," it is one of Israel's most valued and respected institutions, serving as a melting pot for all segments of society, forging strong friendships and comradeship for life. For new immigrants to Israel, serving in the IDF is, no doubt, the best way toward cultural assimilation and integration.

The IDF is seen as a national organization entrusted not only with defending the country, but also serving as a beacon for values, and immersed in national challenges such as education and integration of minorities and people with disabilities.

The backbone of the IDF is the reserve component, constructed from discharged soldiers and officers who maintain their operational status for many years. The regular army is seen as entrusted with routine security, and maintaining plans and means for quick activation and recruitment of the larger reserve force during wartime.

The IDF is a modern military, equipped with the world's most advanced weaponry and technology (much of which is made in Israel), and on the cutting edge of innovation and development of operational art in an-ever changing world.

The IDF follows a proud heritage of valor and sacrifice, and stresses not only leading in intelligence, technology, and doctrine, but in serving national goals while following the highest moral values, code of conduct, and rules of engagement (ROE). Ruach Tzahal, the Spirit of the IDF, serves as an ethical directive for all IDF personnel, explicitly defining the core values, based on universal moral values as well as Jewish tradition.

The IDF organizational culture has been forged through many years of combat and emanates from both the Israeli mentality and the harsh environment of existential threats. As the name of the IDF implies, the core mission is the defense of the State of Israel.

IDF doctrine is based on the unique geographical and strategic challenges in the Middle East, and the basic understanding that Israel cannot afford to lose a single war. A huge effort is invested in preventing escalation and war, through deterrence and early warning. Once engaged, the aim is to swiftly transition to counterattack and deliver a fast and decisive victory, in order to return to extended stability.

The IDF chain of command is hierarchical under the chief of the General Staff (CGS), who commands the entire force (unlike the US military). He answers to the government, and is subordinate directly to the minister of defense.

The General Staff includes typical directorates. Although the IDF does not use the following terminology internally, a system of numbered and lettered categories corresponding to international military nomenclature may be used to refer to these directorates. For example, using the letter J for "joint" (i.e., General Staff), one may refer to manpower (J1), intelligence (J2), operations (J3), logistics (J4), planning (J5) and C4 (J6). The same responsibilities in the services may be coded as A (Air Force), N (Navy) and G (Ground – positions in regional commands). So for example the Air Force chief of operations is the A3, the Navy logistics chief is the N4 and NORTHCOM's intel officer is the G2.

Under the General Staff (GS), operations are conducted by three regional combatant commands: **Northern Command** (NORTHCOM), **Southern Command** (SOUTHCOM), and **Central Command** (CENTCOM).

The **Home Front Command** (HFC) is a regional command responsible for civil defense. During wartime, HFC assumes overall authority for protecting Israeli civilians, streamlining military and civilian efforts.

Unlike many other military forces, the IDF also conducts operations directly by the **Air Force** (IAF), **Navy** (INF), and **Israel Defense Intelligence** (IDI), who serve a dual role of service (force building) and operational command (force activation). In some other armies, the service branch builds the forces but they are employed operationally only by combatant commands; in the IDF, these services (IAF, INF, and IDI) do both force building and force activation.

The **Ground Forces Command** (GFC) is a headquarters (HQ) unifying all field forces: infantry, artillery, armor, engineering, and field intelligence. But unlike the other services, the GFC only leads force building, acquisition, and training. Forces are commanded and operationally employed only by the regional or strategic commands.

The IDF does not have a stand-alone special operations command. Each service maintains its own elite special unit, which mostly promotes the unique missions of the service, but also participates in national, General Staff–directed operations, such as hostage rescue.

The **Depth Command** is a strategic command entrusted with remote operations, deep in enemy territory, and serves as a General Staff–level HQ for activation of special operations.

As reported in Israeli media, in December 2015, the IDF established a new commando brigade under the airborne division, unifying elite units such as Maglan, Duvdevan, and Egoz, previously associated with separate infantry brigades.

During wartime, the IDF differentiates between the "theater of war" – which refers to the entire geographical area where the IDF is engaged, and the "theater of operations" – specific areas of responsibility (AOR) under regional combatant commands. The General Staff's focus and responsibility is for the theater of war, and each combatant commander is responsible for his own theater of operations.

The term *army* is used to describe the entire IDF, not one service. Therefore, a navy officer may say he "joined the army."

All IDF personnel begin as regular-service, conscript soldiers. Following a selection process, some soldiers attend the officers' training school, Bahad 1 (Bahad is the acronym for *basis hadrachah*, "training base" in Hebrew), after which they receive an officer rank. There are no direct commissioning programs in the IDF. Only selected special units have internal officer courses, such as the Air Force Academy.

IDF insignia is equivalent to that of most armies in the world. The highest rank is lieutenant general (three-star general) and is held only by the CGS. Only the Navy and Air Force have separate uniforms (blue and white). Rank names and insignia are equal throughout the force (including the Navy). From the rank of LTC and up, ranks are typically directly attached to position, so promotion comes only with assignment to a higher-ranking billet. Therefore there are no separate promotion boards, but "manning panels." Assigning a brigade commander (whose rank is COL) as a division commander, for instance, implies also the promotion to BG.

IDF Planning Cycle

A **contingency plan** (CONPLAN) is a modular package of tools that serves as a basis for real-time implementation. Following situational assessment, the plan may be adapted, in full or modularly, to answer the operational objective.

Situational assessment is a pivotal component of the decision cycle. It is an iterative commander-centric process, carried out during routine or contingency, enabling the commander, assisted by his operational staff, to review all available data and accumulated knowledge, comprehend the changing circumstances, and issue new or updated orders. Maintaining **situational awareness/understanding** is a challenging, ongoing process.

A key component in the operational process is the **commander's intent**, which serves as a directional guide driving all efforts toward a clearly defined end state. The commander's intent helps focus commanders and staff even when events unfold differently than planned.

The IDF **operational planning cycle** begins with a **warning order** by higher authorities, laying out the overall objectives and end-states, to be reached by applying military might, in coordination with all national efforts. A **battle procedure** is the methodological process leading from the initial warning order to **execution**.

The commander convenes an **orders group (OG1)**, in which he defines the situational picture, missions and objectives, and **planning guidance**.

The product of OG1 is a written **operational order** issued to all subordinate units, summarizing the objectives and triggering detailed planning and preparations in the units.

Planning takes place simultaneously in all staff departments. This phase ends with a **final commander's briefing**, called **orders group 2 (OG2)**, in which the plans are collaboratively introduced and coordinated between all units and stakeholders.

Following the OG2, the operational order is refined.

Throughout the planning phase, commander and staff coordinate and supervise final preparations, including clarifying and tweaking the operational order.

All staff components and various centers engage in activities aimed at setting the stage and bringing about optimal conditions for execution, from **intelligence collection** and **logistics** to conducting **preliminary operations** in the field, such as **recon** and **special operations.**

Toward execution, units conduct **planning approval** sessions, beginning bottom up. Depending on time constraints, various preparation activities may take place, such as **war games**, **mission rehearsals**, and designated discussions and planning sessions, such as **"what-if scenario analysis."**

The commander must verify that his intent had been understood and implemented in the plans, and that the operational maneuvers are expected to bring about the required situation or effect.

All units conduct **final briefing**s, and commanders may choose to personally attend and address subordinate units at this last point of intervention, especially in order to personally touch and inspire soldiers.

Following execution, **debriefing** sessions take place at all levels, aimed at extracting tangible and applicable **lessons learned.** By Israeli law, operational debriefings are immune from external ramifications, allowing openness and an in-depth, profound, and uncompromising process.

Appendix B
Abbreviations

IDF Ranks

Conscripts
private (PVT), corporal (CPL), sergeant (SGT), staff sergeant (S SGT)

Warrant Officers/Noncommissioned Officers (NCO)
sergeant first class (SFC), master sergeant (MSG), sergeant major (SGM), warrant officer (WO), master warrant officer (MWO), chief warrant officer (CWO)

Academic Officers
professional academic officer, senior academic officer

Officers

ABBR.	RANK	COMMENTS
2LT	second lieutenant	First officer rank, pinned on upon graduation from officer training.
1LT	first lieutenant	Promotion one year after 2LT.
CAP	captain	Promotion three years after 1LT.
MAJ	major	
LTC	lieutenant colonel	Upon selection to an LTC billet, such as battalion or squadron commander.
COL	colonel	Upon selection to a COL billet, such as brigade commander.

ABBR.	RANK	COMMENTS
BG	brigadier general (equivalent to a one-star general)	Rank of division commanders and branch COs, such as the chief of armor in the GFC.
MG	major general (equivalent to a two-star general)	Rank of service chiefs and regional command COs.
LTG	lieutenant general (equivalent to a three-star general)	Highest rank in the IDF. CGS is the only active duty officer in this rank.

Military Acronyms

ABBR.	ENGLISH	COMMENTS
Actual	commanding officer of a particular unit	Used on the radio in combination with the unit's call sign to identify the commanding officer.
AAR	after-action review	Debriefing after an operation in order to extract lessons learned.
ADS	active defense systems	Systems such as the Iron Dome, David's Sling, and the Arrow that protect against ballistic missiles.
ATM	antitank missile	Designed to penetrate and destroy heavily armed vehicles. Modern missiles such as the Russian-made Kornet pose a serious threat in the battlefield and lead to the development of advanced countermeasures and tactics.
AOR	area of responsibility	The geographical area assigned to a unit or command. AOR refers to the area in which operations are carried out, whereas area of interest (AOI) refers to a wider area that can influence the AOR.
AFV	armored fighting vehicle	A heavily protected combat vehicle. May be wheeled or tracked. The IDF employs the Namer (based on the Merkava tank) and the Nagmashot (see Nagmashot).

ABBR.	ENGLISH	COMMENTS
AHT	armored hunting team	Forces for destroying antitank teams.
APC	armored personnel carrier	A protected vehicle designed to transport infantry and equipped mainly for self-defense, not direct combat. The IDF uses the Israeli-made Achzarit, based on the T-55 tank.
BCCP	battalion casualty collection point	A medical platoon which serves as an integral part of every combat battalion. Equipped to treat trauma injuries and transfer them to a hospital in the rear, via helicopters or vehicles.
CENT-COM	Central Command	Combatant command responsible for forces in the central region of Israel, including the Jerusalem area and J&S.
CGS	chief of the General Staff	IDF commander.
CAS	close air support	Aerial assistance to ground units by jets or helicopters.
C4I	command, control, communications, computers, and intelligence	
C4ISR	command, control, communications, computers, intelligence, surveillance, and reconnaissance	
CO	commanding officer	
comms	communications	
CON-PLAN	contingency plan	Operational plan that serves as a basis for real-time adaptation and implementation.
DCO	district coordination office	Coordination office between the IDF and Palestinians, established following the Oslo Accords.
EOD	explosive ordnance disposal	Bomb dismantling.

ABBR.	ENGLISH	COMMENTS
FCG	forward command group	People, vehicles, and equipment that comprise a mobile command station.
GFC	Ground Forces Command	A multi-corps command headquarters for all ground components. Serves as a third arm of the IDF, alongside the Air Force and Navy, but unlike them, deals only with force building, not operating, which is done by the regional commands.
H-hour	exact time when a mission is set to start	
Helo	helicopter	
HLS	homeland security	Organization of governmental and military agencies to protect the civilian population from mass threats ranging from terrorism to natural disasters.
HQ	headquarters	Command center.
HRC	Hezbollah Regional Command	Hezbollah's operational deployment in southern Lebanon was according to regional commands or brigades.
IED	improvised explosive device	Improvised bombs, often laid as mines.
Intel	intelligence	Collection of secret information about enemy activities and positions.
IDF	Israel Defense Forces	Armed forces of the State of Israel.
IDI	Israel Defense Intelligence	Known as Aman in Hebrew, it is the overall intelligence body of the IDF.
ISA	Israel Security Agency	Responsible for internal defense challenges. Subordinate to the prime minister.
J&S	Judea and Samaria	Areas of Israel to the north, east, and south of Jerusalem, generally referred to as the West Bank.
KIA	killed in action	Soldier killed during active combat.
LZ	landing zone	Touchdown site for aerial dropoff or pickup of troops.

ABBR.	ENGLISH	COMMENTS
LAF	Lebanese Armed Forces	Armed forces of the Lebanese Republic.
LIC	low-intensity conflict	Conflicts with small groups such as terrorists and guerilla groups who don't fit the profile of a full army. Relevant contemporary terms: operations other than war (OOTW), asymmetric warfare.
LMG	light machine gun	Compact, portable machine gun for individual use.
LMC	logistics and manpower center	Center for each division that arranges logistics and manages recruitment.
MAG	chief military advocate general	Chief legal officer responsible for exercising the rule of law in the IDF.
medevac	medical evacuation of casualties from a battlefield	Usually refers to evacuation by helicopter.
MIA	missing in action	Soldier who goes missing during active combat.
MOD	ministry of defense	Political head of the IDF as well as of research and development programs such as Israel Military Industries and Israel Aerospace Industries.
Mossad	Hamossad l'Modi'in u'l'Tafkidim Miyuchadim	Institute for Intelligence and Special Operations, responsible for external defense challenges. Subordinate to the prime minister.
MP	military police	Enforces the rule of law within the IDF.
Nagma-shot	combination of the words *nagmash* (APC) and *Shot* (the Centurion's Hebrew name)	Armored personnel carrier (APC), based on the hull of the Centurion tank.
NORTH-COM	Northern Command	Combatant command responsible for forces in the northern region of Israel, including Lebanon and Syria.

ABBR.	ENGLISH	COMMENTS
OG	orders group	OG1 is a commander's briefing in which he defines the situational picture, missions and objectives, and planning guidance; OG2 is a final commander's briefing in which plans are collaboratively introduced and coordinated between all units.
Ops	operations	
OPSEC	operations security	Protection of information against exploitation by the enemy.
ORBAT	order of battle	The structure, construct, and size of a military force.
OTRI	Operational Theory Research Institute (Hebrew acronym MALTAM)	The IDF's school of operational art, founded in 1995 and disbanded in 2005.
PA	Palestinian Authority	The self-government body of the Palestinians, established in the Oslo Accords.
PA	personal assistant	
PGM	precision-guided munition	Intended for hitting a specific target and minimizing collateral damage.
PM	prime minister	
PIR	priority intelligence requirements	Definition of valuable intelligence needed for planning and decision making. Used to prioritize collection assets and efforts.
recon	reconnaissance	On-site information collection about enemy territories and plans.
Res.	Reserves	Indicates an officer or soldier on reserve duty.
Ret.	Retired	Indicates a retired officer or soldier.
RMA	Revolution in Military Affairs	A concept relating to the study of the evolution of warfare and the application of advanced and innovative technologies and doctrine.
ROE	rules of engagement	Directives for the precise circumstances in which military force can be operated.
RPG	rocket-propelled grenade	Shoulder-mounted antitank weapon.

ABBR.	ENGLISH	COMMENTS
SOF	special operations forces	Highly trained, specialized combat units for recon and commando operations.
SOI	signal operating instructions	A detailed order including frequencies, codes, and call signs, for enabling streamlined communications.
SOUTH-COM	Southern Command	Combatant command responsible for forces in the southern region of Israel, including the borders with Jordan, Egypt, and the Gaza Strip.
SSP	special security perimeter	Strip of enemy territory taken over to protect domestic borders.
TAC	tactical air controllers	Personnel embedded in ground units, who coordinate air assets.
TST	time-sensitive target	Target that is only valid for a limited amount of time due to enemy movements, light or weather conditions, etc.
TTPs	tactics, techniques, and procedures	
UAV	unmanned aerial vehicle	Popularly called "drones."
UNIFIL	the United Nations Interim Force in Lebanon	Originally deployed in 1978 following the withdrawal of Israeli forces. Following the 2006 war, under Security Council Resolution 1701, UNIFIL expanded its size and mission.
Wilco	Will carry out	Subordinate acknowledges over the radio that the orders are clear and will be carried out.

Appendix C

Milestones in Israel's Defense

WAR/ OPERA- TION	YEAR		ISRAELI SOLDIERS KILLED*
War of Independence	1948	A day after David Ben-Gurion declared Israel's independence, a coalition of Arab states attacked the outnumbered Jewish force. After 10 months of fighting, Israel managed to repel the attacks and conquer large areas originally intended for the Arab state in the partition plan, which was rejected by the Arabs. The war ended with the signing of the 1949 Armistice Agreements. The armistice line became known as "the green line."	6000
Sinai War	1956	Originally called the Kadesh Operation, but designated as a war many years later. Known internationally as the Suez Crisis. An attack on Egypt by Britain, France, and Israel in order to allow free access through the Straits of Tiran and the Suez Canal.	231
The Six-Day War	1967	A war between Israel and all surrounding Arab countries, resulting in a decisive victory and a significant expansion of Israeli-held territories, including the West Bank (from Jordan), Sinai (from Egypt), and the Golan Heights (from Syria). The cease-fire lines were termed "the purple line."	776

* Military death figures are from various sources and may be approximate in some cases.

WAR/ OPERA-TION	YEAR		ISRAELI SOLDIERS KILLED
The War of Attrition	1967– 1973	Prolonged hostilities initiated by Egypt but involving also Jordan and Syria, aimed at eroding Israel's success from the Six-Day War. Ended with a signed cease-fire, and without territorial changes.	1,424
The Yom Kippur War	1973	A surprise attack on Israel by a coalition of Arab countries, led by Syria and Egypt. Despite the successful joint attack, and penetration of Syria into the Golan Heights and Egypt into the Sinai, the war ended with a decisive Israeli victory, and Israel conquered territory inside Syria. Disengagement negotiations led to an Israeli retreat to the purple line and the establishment of the UNDOF demilitarized zone.	2,688
Operation Litani	1978	Also known as the South Lebanon conflict. An Israeli incursion into southern Lebanon up to the Litani River, aimed at targeting Palestinian terrorist organizations.	20
The First Lebanon War	1982– 1985	Initially called Peace for Galilee Operation. Developed into a prolonged campaign and 18 years of Israeli presence in southern Lebanon.	1,216
First Intifada	1987– 1993	Large-scale violent uprising by Palestinians against Israel, mainly in the West Bank and the Gaza Strip. Mostly spontaneous, although the PLO later attempted to assume responsibility for its orchestration.	34
Operation Law and Order	1988	IDF raid on a Hezbollah stronghold in the city of Maydun.	3
Operation Account-ability	1993	A week-long attack against Hezbollah following a deterioration in the security in northern Israel and escalation of attacks against IDF forces in Lebanon. Ended with UN-brokered cease-fire and "understandings" with Hezbollah.	1

WAR/ OPERA- TION	YEAR		ISRAELI SOLDIERS KILLED
Operation Grapes of Wrath	1996	Campaign against Hezbollah, aiming to end rocket fire toward Israeli villages. Ended after 16 days in cease-fire and new "understandings."	3
IDF with-drawal	2000	IDF forces withdrew from Lebanon after 18 years of presence.	n/a
Abduction at Mount Dov	2000	A cross-border raid by Hezbollah resulting in the abduction of the bodies of three IDF sol-diers. They were returned in 2003 in a prisoner exchange.	3
Second Intifada	2000– 2005	Second Palestinian uprising, characterized by severe terror attacks and suicide bombings targeting Israeli civilians. The IDF coined the operational actions in this period Ebb and Flow. The Second Intifada marked the crum-bling of the Oslo Accords.	332
Operation Defensive Shield	2002	The largest IDF campaign in the West Bank since the Six-Day War. The IDF conducted a strategic operation aimed at clamping down on Palestinian terrorist activity and dramatically reducing the threat to Israeli civilians. The effects of the operation can be seen as proof that terror can be fought and even defeated. The security situation in the West Bank still reflects the results of the operation, and the understanding that only constant operational presence leads to stability.	30
Operation Deter-mined Path	2002	Following Operation Defensive Shield, the IDF continued operation in the West Bank countering Palestinian terror. Unlike the focused effort of Defensive Shield, Operation Determined Path entailed continuous small-scale raids, aimed at constant pressure and deteriorating terror capabilities.	0
Abduction of Gilad Schalit	2006	Abducted by Hamas during a cross-border attack near the Gaza Strip. Released in 2011 in exchange for over 1,000 terrorists.	2

WAR/ OPERA- TION	YEAR		ISRAELI SOLDIERS KILLED
Second Lebanon War	2006	A 34-day conflict in southern Lebanon, also known as the 2006 Israel-Hezbollah War. Hezbollah triggered the war in a wide-scale attack and abduction of IDF soldiers. The war ended in a cease-fire and adoption of UN Security Council Resolution 1701, which enabled LAF deployment in southern Lebanon and establishment of a new and improved UNIFIL.	121
Operation Cast Lead	2009	Also known as the Gaza War. A three-week clash between Israel and Hamas, following escalation and repeated rocket launches into Israel.	10
Operation Pillar of Defense	2012	An eight-day campaign in Gaza, following deterioration in the security situation in southern Israel.	1
Operation Protective Edge	2014	A 50-day offensive on Hamas-controlled Gaza Strip, following a massive barrage of rockets launched toward Israel. Another Hamas-led escalation, serving their internal and international goals. Hostilities ended with a brokered cease-fire, but no significant mechanism to prevent another round of violence.	67

Appendix D

Awards and Honors Received by Gal Hirsch

1982 – Outstanding military academy graduate

1984 – Outstanding infantry officer course graduate

1991 – BA, cum laude in Middle Eastern studies from Tel Aviv University

1992 – Paratroopers Brigade commander award for multidisciplinary excellence to 202nd Battalion

1994 – Chief of the General Staff quality and safety award to Shaldag

1994 – Chief of the General Staff award to Shaldag

1996 – Air Force Commander Citation for Operation Grapes of Wrath to Shaldag

1997 – MBA Tel Aviv University

2000 – Chief of the General Staff award for operational units to Benjamin Brigade

2001 – Chief of the General Staff award for operational units to Benjamin Brigade

2003 – Chief of the General Staff award for educational units to Bahad 1 officer training school

2004 – Chief of the General Staff award for educational units to Bahad 1 officer training school

2006 – Second Lebanon War campaign ribbon

2014 – Protective Edge campaign ribbon

Index